THE AGGRESSIVE
CONSERVATIVE
INVESTOR

INTRODUCING WILEY INVESTMENT CLASSICS

There are certain books that have redefined the way we see the worlds of finance and investing—books that deserve a place on every investor's shelf. *Wiley Investment Classics* will introduce you to these memorable books, which are just as relevant and vital today as when they were first published. Open a *Wiley Investment Classic* and rediscover the proven strategies, market philosophies, and definitive techniques that continue to stand the test of time.

MARTIN J. WHITMAN
MARTIN SHUBIK

THE AGGRESSIVE CONSERVATIVE INVESTOR

WILEY

John Wiley & Sons, Inc.

Published by John Wiley & Sons, Inc., Hoboken, New Jersey.
Published simultaneously in Canada.
Originally published in 1979 by Random House.

Limit of Liability/Disclaimer of Warranty: While the publisher and author have used their best efforts in preparing this book, they make no representations or warranties with respect to the accuracy or completeness of the contents of this book and specifically disclaim any implied warranties of merchantability or fitness for a particular purpose. No warranty may be created or extended by sales representatives or written sales materials. The advice and strategies contained herein may not be suitable for your situation. You should consult with a professional where appropriate. Neither the publisher nor author shall be liable for any loss of profit or any other commercial damages, including but not limited to special, incidental, consequential, or other damages.

For general information on our other products and services or for technical support, please contact our Customer Care Department within the United States at (800) 762-2974, outside the United States at (317) 572-3993 or fax (317) 572-4002.

Wiley also publishes its books in a variety of electronic formats. Some content that appears in print may not be available in electronic books. For more information about Wiley products, visit our web site at www.wiley.com.

Library of Congress Cataloging-in-Publication Data

Whitman, Martin J.
  The aggressive conservative investor / Martin J. Whitman, Martin Shubik.
    p. cm.
  Originally published: New York: Random House, c1979.
  Includes bibliographical references and index.
ISBN-13: 978-0-471-76805-0 (pbk.)

    1. Investments.   I. Shubik, Martin, joint author.   II. Title.

HG4521.W474 2006
332.67'8—dc22

                        2005051067

To Lois, Jim, Barbara and Tom Whitman,
and to Julie and Claire Shubik

ACKNOWLEDGMENTS

This book had a lengthy gestation period, during which we were helped by numerous people who read the manuscript, or portions of the manuscript, and made many invaluable suggestions. The names are too numerous to mention but our thanks go to them all—family members, friends, students, Wall Street practitioners, accountants, tax lawyers, securities lawyers and academic colleagues at Yale and other universities.

Two people worked especially diligently in bringing this book to fruition—Albert Erskine, our editor, and Marilyn Hainesworth, administrative vice-president of M. J. Whitman and Co. Inc., who oversaw the many housekeeping chores involved in preparing the manuscript.

Errors and shortcomings, of course, belong to us alone.

The difficulty lies, not in the new ideas, but in escaping from the old ones, which ramify, for those who have been brought up, as most of us have been, into every corner of our minds.

J. M. KEYNES

CONTENTS

FOREWORD

I first met Marty Whitman and Martin Shubik while we were students at Princeton Graduate School. We played poker together on a regular basis, often well into the night. I doubt if any real money ever changed hands, probably because we had none to wager, but when we reminisce about that time we each remember being the big winner. While we may have been gamblers at the time, Marty and Martin have taken few gambles since, either with their own money or with the money entrusted to them by investors. I didn't recognize it then, but they were starting to exhibit the tendencies that would make them successful investors. They knew when to take the calculated risk, when the payoff merited exposure, when to cut their losses, and when to raise the ante. I guess it proves the old adage "If a dog is going to bite, he's going to do it as a pup."

Obviously I have known the authors for a long time, Marty Whitman in particular. I know he is smart, honest, and successful, three characteristics I admire not only in business associates but also in friends. That he is successful should come as no surprise and would be a given for anyone who proposes to write a book on investing. After all, who would buy a book from someone with a history of breaking even? But Marty has taken success to levels most portfolio managers are hard-pressed to imagine. For example, since 1984 he has been the principal at Equities Strategies Fund and Third Avenue Value Fund, while Martin served the same two firms as an independent director. During that time, directed by the investment strategies outlined in this book, these funds on average vastly outperformed any relevant market index on a long-term basis, and for a majority of the time.

I can also speak from personal experience. Marty has served on the boards of both public companies of which I have been chief executive officer and today is the lead director on the Nabors Industries board. He is a man of extraordinary wisdom and insight, and I can honestly say I never make a major move without his input. He is the king of due diligence, spending an enormous amount of time collecting and analyzing information before pulling the trigger on any transaction. I have heard it said that he has been extremely fortunate in some of his investment decisions, but I have observed that the harder he works the luckier he gets.

His counsel has served me well on many occasions and in a broad range of situations. For instance, he advised me on a passive investment in a Japanese company called Tokio Marine, which netted the first serious money I ever made. I subsequently sought his counsel on my very first acquisition. I had let my ego usurp my good sense, agreeing to personally guarantee a note we had issued to the seller. Marty told me to get out of the guarantee or get out of the deal, and that if I didn't take his advice I should never ask for it again. I did, and I still look back on that as representative of the kind of no-nonsense, pragmatic perspective that has characterized his investment history.

More recently Marty's financial acumen and market savvy were invaluable in the issuance of a $700 million convertible debenture with zero coupon and zero accrued interest. He recommended that Nabors take advantage of this low-cost capital even though we didn't need the money at the time. We followed his advice, and it gave us much greater financial flexibility.

So what makes this book unique? It certainly goes against conventional wisdom. For instance, the philosophy of safe and cheap investing ignores price fluctuations for securities and other market risks, guarding only against investment risk, something going wrong with the company, or with the interpretation of securities covenants. Likewise, relying on the "Nifty Fifty" or the top 100 common stocks of large, well-organized companies as the only source of high-quality investments has been abandoned. Discarded also is the notion that a concept of general risk is useful for analysis. Macro data, such as predictions about general stock market averages, interest rates, GDP, and consumer spending, have been abandoned as irrelevant as long as such investments are undertaken in countries marked by political stability and an absence of violence in the streets.

But this book is not about what the authors don't believe. The nuggets in this book are what they do believe, like the principle of "good enough," which encourages investors to content themselves when a good return has been realized, even if it is not perfect. Adhering to a long-term philosophy is also bedrock investment advice, which the authors personally subscribe to and encourage, regardless of the age of the investor. Another key principle involves taking advantage of the era of expanded corporate disclosure, closely scrutinizing a company's public communications to direct or influence investment decisions. Of course, the principle of buying stocks that are safe and cheap is at the heart of this book and is a philosophy every serious investor should embrace.

Who should read this book? The obvious answer would be anyone looking to develop a sound investment strategy, or anyone striving to incorporate into a portfolio some useful ideas that bring value long-term. However, it is equally valuable for anyone who runs a business, or aspires to run one. Many of the principles that direct the Nabors operating philosophy, and that are responsible for the success we have achieved in spite of the cyclical nature of our markets, are direct parallels to personal strategies espoused by the authors. There are many examples. Like the authors, we downplay the macro, refusing to overly concern ourselves with the price of commodities. When prices are up the company has impressive earnings, but when they are down we use our liquidity to make acquisitions, or grow organically if conditions are favorable. We also understand that access to capital is critical for companies in a growth mode, following the authors' recommendation to gain that access before we need it. Simply stated, the time to borrow is different from the time to spend.

The Aggressive Conservative Investor is a must-read for any investor looking to develop a sound, long-term growth strategy and should be a fixture in every business library. The authors have the ability to take complex financial concepts and articulate them in terms that virtually anyone can understand. They describe this as the bridge between Wall Street and Main Street. I think you will find it a bridge worth crossing.

Eugene M. Isenberg
Chairman of the Board
Nabors Industries
July 2005

INTRODUCTION

Dramatic changes have occurred since *The Aggressive Conservative Investor* was published in 1979. The basic thesis of the book—emphasizing financial integrity—remains at least as valid today as it was then, and because of subsequent developments, may be even more valid now. Moreover, changes since 1979 in the disclosure area, it seems to us, have made it easier for a diligent person to become a successful aggressive conservative investor than was possible in the late 1970s.

The Aggressive Conservative Investor includes six major areas that warrant review today:

- Changes in terminology
- Performance data
- The disclosure explosion
- Our changed, or modified, beliefs
- The changed environment
- Troublesome regulatory problems

CHANGES IN TERMINOLOGY

When we initially wrote *The Aggressive Conservative Investor,* we named our strategy "the financial-integrity approach." We now like to think of it as "the safe and cheap approach" (which sounds less pompous and is more direct).

For a common stock to be an attractive investment, *The Aggressive Conservative Investor* outlined four essential characteristics:

- The company ought to have a strong financial position that is measured not so much by the presence of assets as by the absence of significant encumbrances, whether a part of a balance sheet, disclosed in financial statement footnotes, or an element that is not disclosed at all in any part of financial statements.

- The company ought to be run by reasonably honest management and control groups, especially in terms of how cognizant the insiders are of the interests of outside security holders.
- There ought to be available to the investor a reasonable amount of relevant information that is akin to full disclosure, though this will always be something that falls somewhat short of the mark.
- The price at which the equity security can be bought ought to be below the investor's reasonable estimate of net asset value.

These four characteristics describe common stock investment under both a financial-integrity approach and a safe and cheap approach. Especially since there have been quantum improvements in the quantity and quality of information available, these four concepts hold as firm today as in 1979.

The other terminology change is the use of the acronym OPMI (outside passive minority investor) to describe outside investors and passivists as well as non-control and unaffiliated security holders. OPMIs run the gamut from day traders to most institutional investors to safe and cheap investors who do not seek elements of control over the companies in which they hold securities positions. The reason for using the term *OPMI* rather than *investor* is that the word *investor* is one of the most misused and misunderstood words on Wall Street. Most of the time it seems as if those using the term *Investor* really mean short-run speculator—either individual or institutional—so we've mostly discontinued use of the word *investor* in favor of *OPMI*.

PERFORMANCE DATA

Since 1984, the authors have been either the principal, or an independent director or trustee of two mutual funds—Equities Strategies Fund and Third Avenue Value Fund—whose modus operandi has been to follow the safe and cheap approach in investing in securities.

How have the two funds fared from 1984 through mid-2005? They have vastly outperformed any relevant market index on a long-term basis, on average, and for a majority of the time. Efficient market theorists will carp that the funds have not outperformed relevant indexes consistently. *Consistently* is really a dirty word meaning all the time. In investing, *consistently* should have relevance only for day traders, not long-term buy-and-hold investors.

A comparison of the Equity Strategies Fund's performance with that of the Standard & Poor's 500 Index is contained in Table I.1. We took over management of Equity Strategies in April 1984. Prior to that, the fund was invested in options. In 1994, Equities Strategies Fund was merged into Nabors Industries on a basis where each one share of Equity Strategies received 5.84 shares of Nabors Industries common. An investor investing $10,000 in Equity Strategies in April 1984 would own Nabors common stock with a market value of over $286,000, in April 2005. This equals a compound annual return for the 21 years of 17.2%.

Before the Nabors merger, Equity Strategies was a unique mutual fund in that it always was fully taxed as a subchapter C corporation, and never qualified, like all other mutual funds, as a subchapter M corporation. M corporations do not pay federal income tax as long as they distribute all their income and net capital gains to shareholders. Despite being required to accrue a liability for deferred capital gains taxes on unrealized appreciation, a $10,000 investment in Equity Strategies had a market value of $38,643 as of April 30, 1994. A comparable $10,000 investment in the S&P 500 Index had a market value of $23,163 as of April 30, 1994. If Equity Strategies had reported its net asset value the same way M corporations reported theirs, the Equity Strategies market value would have been approximately $52,000 in April 1994 after adding back to net asset value the liability for deferred capital gains taxes on unrealized appreciation. At that point in 1994, the compound annual returns on the Equity Strategies investment was approximately 16.2% before deducting the reserves for capital gains taxes on unrealized appreciation.

Third Avenue Value Fund came into existence on November 1,

TABLE 1.1 EQUITY STRATEGIES FUND v. S&P 500

		Equity Strategies Fund			S&P 500 Index		
		Return	Investment	Value of Investment	Return	Investment	Value of Investment
1 YEAR	4/30/84		$10,000.00	$10,000.00		$10,000.00	$10,000.00
1 YEAR	4/30/85	5.08%	$10,000.00	$10,508.00	−0.094%	$10,000.00	$9,990.60
1 YEAR	4/30/86	24.69%	$10,000.00	$13,102.43	−1.126%	$10,000.00	$9,878.11
1 YEAR	4/30/87	18.87%	$10,000.00	$15,574.85	22.435%	$10,000.00	$12,094.26
1 YEAR	4/30/88	3.02%	$10,000.00	$16,045.21	−8.439%	$10,000.00	$11,073.62
1 YEAR	4/30/89	17.28%	$10,000.00	$18,817.83	22.689%	$10,000.00	$13,586.12
1 YEAR	4/30/90	29.64%	$10,000.00	$24,395.43	10.658%	$10,000.00	$15,034.13
1 YEAR	4/30/91	21.12%	$10,000.00	$29,547.74	17.541%	$10,000.00	$17,671.26
1 YEAR	4/30/92	−2.61%	$10,000.00	$28,776.55	13.980%	$10,000.00	$20,141.71
1 YEAR	4/30/93	41.25%	$10,000.00	$40,646.87	9.193%	$10,000.00	$21,993.33
1 YEAR*	4/05/94	−4.93%	$10,000.00	$38,642.98	5.320%	$10,000.00	$23,163.38

*S&P 500 Index is as of April 30, 1994.

1990. Since then its performance has tracked that of Equity Strategies with a compound annual return since inception of 16.8%. The annual performance of Third Avenue Value Fund compared with the S&P 500 Index is shown in Table I.2.

Besides Equity Strategies and Third Avenue Value Fund, other investment vehicles following a safe and cheap approach also have outperformed relevant indexes. Three of these funds are sister funds to Third Avenue Value: Third Avenue Small Cap, Third Avenue Real Estate, and Third Avenue International Value. Professor Louis Lowenstein of Columbia University Law School in an October 11, 2004, article in *Barron's,* reviewed the performance of 10 well-regarded value funds from 1999 through 2003. All 10 outperformed the S&P 500 for the period. The other funds compared were FPA Capital, First Eagle Global, Legg Mason Value, Longleaf Partners, Mutual Beacon, Oak Value, Oakmark Select, Source Capital, and Tweedy Brown American. In short, very good performance results have been obtained a majority of the time by those funds that have followed a safe and cheap approach or a reasonable facsimile thereof.

Consequently, during the last 26 years, the efficient market hypothesis (EMH) and efficient portfolio theory (EPT) have been increasingly discredited insofar as EMH and EPT purport to describe a generalized stock market behavior. EMH and EPT just do not describe value investing—never have, never will. Rather, EMH and EPT describe a very narrow special case. EMH and EPT describe financial markets populated solely by day traders vitally affected by immediate price movements in securities. These market participants are strictly top-down speculators devoid of virtually any bottom-up knowledge about a company or the securities it issues. This just isn't most markets and it probably isn't most investors. Not only do EMH and EPT fail to describe the safe and cheap investor, the theories also are utterly devoid of any realistic explanations about the operations and techniques of control investors, a group that heavily influences the dynamics of most financial markets.

TABLE I.2 THIRD AVENUE VALUE FUND V. S&P 500

	Third Avenue Value Fund			S&P 500		
	Return	Investment	Value of Investment	Return	Investment	Value of Investment
1990	8.60%	$10,000.00	$10,860.00	9.43%	$10,000.00	$10,943.00
1991	34.41%	$10,000.00	$14,596.93	30.46%	$10,000.00	$14,276.24
1992	21.29%	$10,000.00	$17,704.61	7.62%	$10,000.00	$15,364.09
1993	23.66%	$10,000.00	$21,893.52	10.08%	$10,000.00	$16,912.79
1994	−1.46%	$10,000.00	$21,573.88	1.32%	$10,000.00	$17,136.04
1995	31.73%	$10,000.00	$28,419.27	37.58%	$10,000.00	$23,575.76
1996	21.92%	$10,000.00	$34,648.77	22.96%	$10,000.00	$28,988.75
1997	23.87%	$10,000.00	$42,919.43	33.36%	$10,000.00	$38,659.40
1998	3.92%	$10,000.00	$44,601.88	28.58%	$10,000.00	$49,708.26
1999	12.82%	$10,000.00	$50,319.84	21.04%	$10,000.00	$60,166.87
2000	20.76%	$10,000.00	$60,766.23	−9.11%	$10,000.00	$54,685.67
2001	2.82%	$10,000.00	$62,479.84	−11.88%	$10,000.00	$48,189.01
2002	−15.19%	$10,000.00	$52,989.15	−22.10%	$10,000.00	$37,539.24
2003	37.08%	$10,000.00	$72,637.53	28.69%	$10,000.00	$48,309.25
2004	26.60%	$10,000.00	$91,959.12	10.88%	$10,000.00	$53,565.30

THE DISCLOSURE EXPLOSION

The improvements in the disclosure scene since 1979 have been dramatic and far-reaching. This has happened in two areas—substantive disclosures and improved delivery systems. As a consequence, there is a vast improvement in the amount and quality of disclosures, especially documentary disclosures, available to those using the safe and cheap approach. *The Aggressive Conservative Investor* seems to have understated the degree of knowledge one can obtain about a company and the securities it issues by relying solely on the public record. The book, however accurate for the disclosure environment in 1979, inadequately describes the quantity and quality of disclosures available in 2005.

The role of disclosure ought to be to provide outside investors the same level of disclosure that is provided to an investor with clout (e.g., commercial bank lenders) who are able to undertake due diligence. The Securities and Exchange Commission (SEC) and the Financial Accounting Standards Board (FASB) seem to have done a pretty good job from the point of view of the safe and cheap investor.

For the vast majority of issuers—excluding Enron and Worldcom—disclosure documents seem to be prepared on the basis that companies, their officers, and their directors do not want to be sued, and especially not sued successfully. Thus, there is a tendency in public documents to disclose all admissions against interest, however remote. Such laundry lists give safe and cheap investors an unweighted for probabilities inventory of what could conceivably go wrong. Almost the first question any safe and cheap investor asks is what could go wrong. Having a carefully prepared list of risk factors helps answer that question. This laundry list of risk factors is contained for U.S. issuers in Form 10-K, Form 10-Q, Form 8-K, prospectuses for the cash sale of securities, merger proxy statements, exchange of securities documents, and cash tender offers. They are also contained in the footnotes to financial statements that comply with GAAP.

Chief executive officer letters and other communications to stockholders seem to have become more comprehensive, more complete, and, in many ways, more honest in terms of what management thinks about long-term promises and problems. Admittedly, most management communications do seem to focus on the immediate earnings outlook, something not of much interest to the safe and cheap investor. Nonetheless, communication seems to have vastly improved since 1979. Top management communications are contained in annual reports to stockholders, quarterly reports to stockholders, teleconferences, investor conferences, and one-on-one meetings.

Principal new disclosures since 1979 that have been a boon to safe and cheap investors both as put forward by the SEC and FASB include the following:

- Integrated disclosure between the Securities Act of 1933 and the Securities and Exchange Act of 1934.
- Disclosure of earnings forecasts under rules that provide forecasters a safe harbor from liabilities for forecasts, which while honestly made, turn out to be wrong.
- Expanded proxy statement disclosures that include (1) existence and functions of various committees; (2) attendance record of directors and committee members; (3) expanded transactions detailing relationships between the company and its insiders; (4) resignations of directors and top officers.
- Environmental disclosures.
- Reserve recognition accounting (RRA) for exploration and production oil and gas issuers.
- Management discussion and analysis of financial condition and results of operations (MDA) implemented and eventually expanded. This is a quarterly filing.
- Expedited use of Form 20-F for foreign issuers (equivalent of a Form 10-K for a U.S. domiciled issuer).
- Summary sections in prospectuses and merger proxy statements.
- Shelf registrations.
- Disclosure of rating agency ratings.
- New real estate guidelines.
- Edgar and other electronic communications—a virtual revolution in delivery systems mightily benefiting safe and cheap investors.

In 1979, obtaining documents filed with the SEC but not mailed to securities holders (Forms 10-K, 10-Q, 8-K) tended to be cumbersome or relatively expensive.

- Electric and gas utility guide.
- Financial reporting requirements for banks and bank holding companies.
- Consolidating financial statements distinguishing between guarantor subsidiaries and nonguarantor subsidiaries.
- Increased disclosure of management backgrounds.
- Sales and income by industries sector disclosures.
- Sales and income by geography disclosures.
- Basis for accounting estimates disclosures.
- Cash flow reporting.
- Expanded Form 8-K reporting.
- Reporting comprehensive income.
- Disclosure of information about capital structure.
- Accounting for income taxes.
- Accounting for leases.

Increasingly there has been disclosure of non-GAAP financial measures regulated by the SEC under Regulation G. Non-GAAP financial measures include periodic cash flow data and various appraisal values. Hopefully, disclosures of non-GAAP financial measures, used as a supplement to GAAP, rather than as a substitute for GAAP, will continue to grow. In any event, what has been done so far in disclosing non-GAAP financial measures has been a boon for safe and cheap investors.

Some new regulations are not particularly relevant for safe and cheap investors. In the safe and cheap approach, little or no use is made of esoteric derivatives. The safe and cheap investor cares little about the timing of disclosures. Regulation FD is designed to assure that material information is distributed to all of the Street simultaneously. A characteristic of safe and cheap is that such investors are usually the last to know. The secret to success in safe and cheap investing is not to obtain superior (or earlier) information, but rather to use the available information in a superior manner.

OUR CHANGED, OR MODIFIED, BELIEFS

We no longer believe all, or even most, markets tend toward an instantaneous efficiency. We now believe no financial market can approach instantaneous efficiency unless there is strict and appropriate regulation imposed by governments, quasi-governments, and various private sectors.

We now believe that a strong financial position consists of a combination of one or more of three elements. The first attribute of a strong financial position is a relative absence of liabilities, whether disclosed on the balance sheet in the financial statement footnotes, or existing outside of any financial disclosures. The second attribute of a strong financial position is the existence of high quality assets, i.e., either cash or assets convertible into cash. Such assets are not measured by the accounting classification of an asset as a current asset, but rather the definition of a high quality asset depends on the economic characteristic of the asset. For example, we would tend to think a well-maintained Class A office building rented on long term leases to AAA tenants is a high quality asset. For accounting classification purposes, this asset would be called a fixed asset rather than a current asset, even though it probably is readily salable for cash. The third attribute of a strong financial position exists where a company has free cash flows from operations available for its common shareholders. These free cash flows, however, are a relative rarity since most companies, as going concerns, seem to have earnings rather than free cash flows. Earnings are defined for corporations as creating wealth while consuming cash. Wealth creation while consuming cash seems to be what most prosperous operating companies do.

While it is true that governments are often the problem, not the solution, it is also true that much of the private sector is often the problem, not the solution. Management entrenchment, for example, over a broad range of companies, probably detracts significantly from national productivity. It certainly detracts from corporate values and common stock values. Increasingly, securities law and regulation have the purpose of entrenching management in control rather than providing investor protection.

Macro data such as predictions about general stock market averages, interest rates, the economy, consumer spending, and so on are unimportant for safe and cheap investors as long as the environment is characterized by relative political stability and an absence of violence in the streets.

The concept of risk is meaningless unless it is preceded by a modifying adjective. There exist market risk, investment risk, credit risk, failure-to-match-maturities risk, commodity risk, terrorism risk, and many more types of risk. The idea of general risk is not helpful in a safe and cheap analysis. When financial academics and sell-side analysts refer to risk they almost always mean only market risk and usually very short-run market risk.

We now believe that we ought to guard against investment risk—that is, something going wrong with the company or securities covenants. Market risk (i.e., price fluctuations of securities) is of little concern in this type of investing.

Unlike Graham and Dodd, we would no longer define *blue chips* as those picked from the top 100 companies. Disclosure has now become so good that there is no reason for OPMIs to rely on the top 100. In addition, many of the common stocks of companies that were in the top 100 proved to be unsound speculations, including Enron, General Motors, Eastman Kodak, Xerox, and U.S. Steel. Companies whose common stocks we define as blue chips in 2005 include Brascan, Forest City Enterprises, MBIA Inc., Toyota Industries, Millea Holdings, Cheung Kong Holdings, Investor AB—companies most OPMIs probably have never heard of.

We now believe investors seeking cash return should look for such cash return from being creditors (e.g., bondholders) rather than common stockholders.

We now believe that a principal advantage to buy-and-hold investors in being holders of common stocks of companies with strong financial positions is that such strong financial positions permit reasonably competent managements with five-year or so time horizons to be opportunistic (i.e., the managements are able to take advantage of markets that are inefficient inherently from a five-year point of view). For example, sometime during the five-year period there is likely to be a buoyant equity market into which to sell common stock issues at extremely attractive prices (for the company and the insiders) or interest rates in credit markets are likely to become extremely low.

We now believe that the most attractive value investments are in the common stocks of extremely well financed companies, which sell at material discounts from readily ascertainable net asset values. Such bargains in 2005 seem to be centered on financial institutions and companies owning income-producing real estate, much of which is located offshore from the United States. This is true even though U.S. taxpayers in acquiring offshore securities are disadvantaged because many of these issuers are passive foreign investment companies (PFICs) for U.S. tax purposes. Holders of PFIC common stocks are usually taxed annually at ordinary income tax rates on unrealized appreciation for the year.

Diversification is only a surrogate, and usually a damn poor surrogate, for knowledge, control, and price consciousness.

Generally accepted accounting principles (GAAP) are most useful when the following conditions exist:

- Financial statements should be directed, first and foremost, to meeting the needs of long-term creditors, not stock market speculators.
- The company is a stand-alone, separate and apart from its shareholders and its management.
- The accounting statements are governed by the modifying convention of conservatism.
- Principles are more important than rules. Principles are things like the modifying convention of conservatism. Rules are things like FASB 133, Accounting for Derivative Instruments and Hedging Activities.
- GAAP financial statements are useful because they give the trained user the only objective benchmarks available, not the truth. An approximation of truth might sometimes be contained in non-GAAP financial measures, a supplement to, not a substitute for, GAAP.

- GAAP financial statements are most useful when they are consistent and reconcilable.

In the United States there are various types of accounting systems promulgated for the purpose of meeting the needs of specific constituencies. In the insurance industry, statutory accounting is directed toward policyholder protection; in regulatory accounting for broker/dealers, the goal is to meet the needs of customers for financial protection; and in income tax accounting, the goal is to determine what a taxpayer's tax bill ought to be.

It is a fool's errand to think that GAAP ought to be designed to meet the perceived needs of stock market speculators. A stock market speculator is defined as anyone or any institution that believes, for whatever reason, that its income and fortunes are vitally affected by day-to-day securities price fluctuations. The exception to this definition is the risk arbitrageur. A risk arbitrageur is someone who invests based on the probabilities that there will occur a relatively determinate workout event in a relatively determinate period of time. A good example of a risk arbitrage situation is when there has been a public announcement of a merger between two companies. Risk arbitrage does not exist when one invests in the common stock of a going concern with perpetual life where the investment is based on a view that near-term earnings per share will increase. GAAP can't protect short-run stock market speculators effectively simply because GAAP can't tell them the truth. Rather the goal of GAAP ought to be to meet the needs of long-term creditors who look to get their obligations from the company repaid with interest either from the internal resources of the company itself or from the company remaining creditworthy enough to refinance. To achieve this, long-term creditors rely on getting a lot more information from GAAP than just periodic earnings per share as reported.

As a matter of law, stock market speculators do, of course, deserve disclosure protection, the same as all OPMIs involved in the financial community. To protect them, however, it makes much more sense to us to have them rely on non-GAAP financial measures. These non-GAAP financial measures do not need the objectivity and relatively strict rules and principles of GAAP. Rather, non-GAAP financial measures can make use of, say, subjective management judgments whose scope would be limited to statements given a safe harbor under an expanded Regulation G. The current value accounting of the early 1980s is one example of a productive use of non-GAAP financial measures.

All GAAP figures are important in a safe and cheap analysis. There is no primacy of the income account. Primacy of the income account means that corporate wealth is created only by flows (i.e., having positive earnings or cash flows for a period). In addition, we believe that corporate wealth is also created by resource conversion activities (e.g., mergers and acquisitions) as well as access to capital markets on a superattractive basis. While income statement and balance sheets are integrally related in safe and cheap investing, there usually is no basis for assuming that income account data are more important than balance sheet data.

We learned a great lesson from the current value accounting supplements of the early 1980s. Here inflation accounting was supposed to help the analyst appreciate that because of inflation many corporate depreciation charges were woefully insufficient to provide a reserve for replacing aging and obsolescing equipment. The current value supplement, however, could in no way account for the benefits to a company because inflation might make it prohibitively expensive for new entrants to come into the industry to compete with the company that had very modest sunk costs. Deciding what the net effect of rampant inflation might be on a company is a decision best left to a trained analyst, not a preparer of GAAP financial statements, albeit the non-GAAP disclosure of current value was helpful to the safe and cheap analyst trying to make investment judgments.

We now believe that corporate finance requires different and more sophisticated tools of analysis than does project finance. The differences can be great. In project finance, for each project to make sense it must generate a positive net cash flow over its life; for example, it has to have a net present value (NPV) greater than 1. Most prosperous corporations, though, have earnings (i.e., the businesses consume cash while creating wealth). Creating wealth is their primary objective. For these cash-consuming corporations to remain prosperous they generally have to remain creditworthy. Creditworthiness for a company is a matter of corporate finance, not project finance.

We now believe that for the vast majority of companies and investors, wealth creation takes precedence over any concept of primacy of the income account, albeit that for many companies they have little choice but to create wealth through either cash flows or earnings, both derived from income accounts.

While we recognized the conflicts of interest and communities of interest inherent in relationships between managements and OPMIs, we overemphasized the conflicts in 1979 as it relates to the vast majority of companies in which Third Avenue Value Fund was invested in 2005. As a group these companies seem excellently managed by people quite cognizant of OPMI interests. This positive selection process for choosing managements seems part and parcel of the safe and cheap approach. Before an equity investment is made, Third Avenue Value Fund reviews comprehensively all SEC disclosures about management compensation, entrenchment, and stock ownership, as well as the choices managements make in choosing how to account (e.g., whether to expense stock options). Our ability to choose reasonably good managements most of the time seems to be due in large measure to the improved disclosure environment that has been created in the last 26 years.

We believe that the new academic discipline, behavioral finance, has very limited applicability to safe and cheap investing. Behaviorists are people who believe that more than economic rationality drives market forces. Market participants are also influenced by emotions—fear, greed, political correctness, style, and fashion. Behaviorists, though, seem to ignore the basic point that even if investors were reasonably rational, it is context rationality that counts. Different market participants have different rationalities. What is rational for safe and cheap investors (e.g., ignore near-term market swings) would be utterly irrational for heavily margined day traders who know little or nothing about the securities they buy and sell, and vice versa.

Academic and research department concepts that are part and parcel of safe and cheap investing revolve around net present value (NPV) and present value (PV). NPV is pervasive in value analysis and is used much more broadly than merely measuring discounted cash flows (DCF). In safe and cheap, one tends to PV everything—asset values, liabilities, earnings, EBITDA, expenses—often converting fixed expenses into liabilities and assured earnings and cash flows into asset values. For example, see Table I.3 concerning Equus II Incorporated, a business development company registered as a closed-end investment company under the Investment Company Act of 1940 as amended. An above normal expense ratio (3.6% rather than 1.5%) for Equus II is capitalized as a liability and the present value of the excess is deducted from Equus II Incorporated NAV so that for value purposes Equus II common stock is deemed to be selling at only 2.8% discount from NAV, even though based strictly on generally accepted accounting principles (GAAP), it appears to be selling at a 25.5% discount from NAV.

TABLE I.3   EQUUS II INCORPORATED

Equus II Incorporated

NAV per share 7/8/05	$11.14
Annual operating expenses—2004	$2,489,425
Expense ratio based on average net assets of $70,000,000 for 2004	3.6% *
Market price of common 7/8/05	$8.30
Market price as discount from GAAP NAV	25.5%
Adjust NAV to exclude from NAV the present value of expenses in excess of 1.5% capitalized at 10%	$14,439,425
Adjusted NAV	$55,560,575
Adjusted NAV—discount from market price	2.8%

*Third Avenue Value Fund expense ratio was 1.12% for fiscal 2004.

We now think that the underlying assumptions of safe and cheap investing can, in a simplified (or oversimplified) manner, be summarized by citing a number of factors organized under five categories.

- Efficient market hypothesis (EMH)
- Efficient portfolio theory (EPT)
- Disclosure and GAAP
- Economics and markets
- Security analysis

Efficient Market Hypothesis (EMH)

The general theory of market efficiency states that some markets will tend toward instantaneous efficiency; some markets will tend toward long-term efficiency but rarely achieve it; and some markets are inefficient inherently. Which market exists is a function of four variables:

- Who the market participant is
- How complex the security, or the situation, being analyzed
- The time horizons of the participants
- The strength of external forces imposing oversight on a market (i.e., government external forces and private sector external forces)

In markets where instantaneous efficiencies exist, participants do not earn excess returns. These are the markets described by academics who believe in EMH and EPT. In other markets, earning excess returns is to be expected. Third Avenue Value Fund is, as are most who follow a safe and cheap approach, a buy-and-hold cash investor. In safe and cheap, one tends to invest in complex securities where the workout horizon is five years or more. As such, safe and cheap investors are rarely involved in markets that approach instantaneous efficiency from a safe and cheap point of view.

A good example of an inherently inefficient market is one in which a well-financed manager, venture capitalist, real estate investment builder, or LBO promoter can afford to have a five-year time horizon regarding when or how the business will access capital markets. The manager, venture capitalist, real estate activist, or LBO promoter will know that sometimes in equity markets there will be initial public offering (IPO) booms, and sometimes in credit markets interest rates will be extraordinarily low. Taking advantage of this knowledge makes a market inefficient inherently from the point of view of a sophisticated manager dealing with relatively complex securities or situations, where the manager has a long time horizon, and where the manager controls the timing of when to access capital markets.

It is a myth from a safe and cheap point of view that most markets are efficient or tend toward instantaneous efficiency because an army of trained analysts causes it to be so. First, the army probably has been trained by financial academics who are strictly top-down analysts. Second, the army is mostly analyzing the wrong things. They primarily believe in:

- Primacy of the income account
- Short-run outlooks
- Technical considerations (e.g., predictions about the near-term outlook for the general market, or a possible overhang of specific securities being readied for sale)
- What the numbers *are* rather than what the numbers *mean*

Financial markets almost never approach instantaneous efficiency unless they are strictly regulated.

A market is defined as any financial or commercial arena where participants reach agreements about price and other terms, which each participant believes is the most reasonable terms achievable under the circumstances.

Efficient Portfolio Theory (EPT)

Diversification is a surrogate, and usually a damn poor surrogate, for knowledge, control, and price consciousness. Third Avenue Value

Fund owns 103 common stock positions and the top 12 issues held account for over 52% of the fund's securities portfolio. Most mutual funds of similar size seem to hold 300 to 400 positions, and will rarely have as much as 3% of their securities position invested in any one common stock. 4% to 6% of positions are frequent occurrences for the fund.

The safe and cheap investor has much less need for diversification than most OPMI's and can afford profitably to concentrate a portfolio into relatively few issues. The safe and cheap investor is dealing in variables that are more accurately measurable than seems to be the case for OPMI's involved with conventional security analysis. The safe and cheap investor tries to buy into the existing situation, "What Is," at a discount from readily ascertainable estimates of net asset value provided that the company is comfortably financed. In certain areas, e.g. income producing real estate companies and most financial institutions, net asset values are something that can reasonably be estimated. In contrast, in conventional security analysis, the primary efforts revolve around predictions of the future— either earnings or discounted cash flows, or both. It seems as if most predictions of the future turn out to be wrong most of the time. Diversification does provide some protection for portfolios against being wrong in the analysis of individual securities. The analyst using conventional tools needs this diversification protection more so than the safe and cheap investor.

Portfolio analysis differs from individual securities analysis. For portfolios, there is no such thing as a value trap. If a portfolio performs poorly over time, blame it on poor analysis, not on value traps where cheap common stocks stay cheap forever.

Disclosure and GAAP

GAAP provide objective benchmarks, net truth, except in several special cases. Toyota Industries (Industries) provides a good example of GAAP disclosures being helpful but incomplete. Over half of Toyota Industries assets at market prices are in a portfolio of marketable securities, principally Toyota Motor Common. For GAAP purposes, Toyota Industries reports only dividends and interest received from portfolio companies since in no instance does Toyota Industries own as much as 20% of the common stock of a portfolio company, and in no instance does Toyota Industries exercise control over a portfolio company. On a GAAP basis, Toyota Industries common is selling at around 22 times earnings as of mid-2005. If Toyota Industries income account is adjusted to include the company's equity in the undistributed earnings of portfolio companies (a non-GAAP financial measure), Toyota Industries common is selling at less than eight times earnings. GAAP for the company is a good first approximation of periodic cash flow. Picking up the equity in undistributed earnings of portfolio companies is a good first approximation of the periodic wealth being created for Toyota Industries and its common stock. What actual cash flows were and what actual wealth creation took place in a period is something for the safe and cheap analyst to decide, using the objective data provided in financial statements as a starting point.

Every GAAP number is derived from, modified by, and a function of, other GAAP numbers.

Documentary disclosures to creditors and investors have never been better or more complete than they are now, at least in the United States. Some of the credit for this goes to the plaintiffs' bar.

In safe and cheap investing and control investing what the numbers *mean* tend to be much more important than what the numbers *are*. This is a point that cannot be overstated for economic analysis in general. The Toyota Industries example shows the difference between what the numbers *are* and what the numbers *mean*. Reported earnings for GAAP purposes are what the numbers are. Attributing some weight to the unreported equity in the undistributed earning of companies held in the company's investment portfolio indicates that the analyst should weight heavily what the numbers *mean*.

Economics and Markets

Because instantaneous efficiency is usually not present, measuring investment risk and market risk involves three factors:

- Quality of the issuer
- Terms of the issue
- Price of the issue

Assuming price equilibrium, there is no need to factor in price of issue. Again, this comports with the environment envisioned by EMH and EPT. If one factors in price, the lower the price, the less the risk of loss and the more the potential for gain. When factoring in price, no risk–reward trade-off exists. Safe and cheap investors are first safety conscious and then price conscious.

The basic interest of most market participants is wealth creation, an asset value concept, not discounted cash flow (DCF). DCF is just one method of creating wealth, and a method that frequently carries tax disadvantages. Over 80% of Third Avenue Value Fund's common stock portfolio consists of securities that were acquired at prices well below estimates of readily ascertainable net asset values. Current and immediately prospective price earnings ratios are either downplayed in most safe and cheap analyses or ignored.

Debts—whether incurred in the private sector or by governments—are usually never repaid. Rather, they are refinanced by those wealth-creating entities that are able to remain creditworthy. A safe and cheap investor sells common stocks immediately when the businesses no longer appear to be creditworthy. This spells a permanent impairment.

There is a long-term arbitrage between business value and common stock prices: if common stock prices are high relative to business value, go public; if common stock prices are low relative to business value, go private, or semiprivate.

Assets can have an in-use value separate and apart from any market value. The furniture and fixtures in an investment adviser's office are examples of assets with an in-use value, which is totally separate from the market value of the assets.

Fairness in financial dealings is obtained in the price and other terms that would be arrived at in a transaction between a willing buyer and a willing seller, both with knowledge of the relevant facts; and neither under any compulsion to act. In a going private situation, one is faced with a willing-buyer (who frequently is also a fiduciary), coerced-seller situation. An OPMI becomes a coerced seller when forced to sell because buyers obtaining the requisite vote, say 50% of those voting, force all stockholders to sell. The requisite vote is obtained using corporate proxy machinery. Sometimes an OPMI becomes a forced seller because of almost certain prospects that there will no longer be a market for the security held after a transaction is consummated. In a coerced-seller situation, fairness opinions need to be used and should be based on simulating the prices and other terms that would have existed were there actually a willing-buyer–willing-seller situation.

One can't understand corporate finance if all one does is look at corporations and securities wholly, or mostly, from the point of view of common stockholders who are OPMIs. This is what most financial academics do, and this seems to be what most sell-side analysts do. To understand corporate finance you have to be cognizant of the interests and beliefs of other important constituencies—managements, creditors, promoters, underwriters, and governments.

Assuming relative political stability and an absence of violence in the streets, macro factors tend to be unimportant for value investing. Third Avenues' satisfactory investment experience after 1997 in Japanese non–life insurance common stocks is a good example of this. At the time these investments were made in 1997, Fund management had no idea that the Japanese business depression would turn out to be as deep and protracted as it was, and that interest rates would stay so low for so long. We certainly had no idea when making these investments in 1997 that the Nikkei stock average would decline from 20,000 to 10,000. Yet, the Fund's compound annual return through early 2005 was close to 10% on these investments. The investments were made at prices that represented a discount of at least 50% from net asset value before deducting reserves for taxes on unrealized appreciation.

In terms of avoiding investments in areas likely to be characterized by political instability and violence in the streets, the safe and cheap, passive investor always will eschew investments in those countries where population is rapidly increasing and family size is large, say five or more live births per adult woman. These countries will likely continue to fail to enjoy economic prosperity and be inclined to have a young average age of death, be a spawning ground for terrorism and tribal genocide, have corrupt, dictatorial governments, and have a population prone to become infected with AIDS and/or tropical diseases. Such countries include most of the Middle East, most of Africa, and some of Latin America and South America. The post World War II economic miracles occurred in Germany, Japan, the Asian Tigers, China, and India—all countries in which population growth was controlled and family size limited.

Any and all resource conversion activities (e.g., mergers and acquisitions, IPOs, restructuring troubled companies, refinancings) involve huge costs payable to investment bankers, commercial bankers, brokers, lawyers, accountants, lenders, and promoters. This expense problem seems exacerbated for small cap companies.

There exist strong Wall Street pressures to have periodic IPO booms. These pressures arise out of huge gross spreads, exclusive product, and an easy sale—all of which encourage securities salespeople to push IPOs.

Passive investment products tend to be sold by salespeople rather than bought by investors. For proof look at the relative popularity of load funds compared with no-load funds in the mutual fund industry. A load is a commission paid by an OPMI, a portion of which goes to securities salespersons.

The markets for top management compensation tend to be inefficient given top management entrenchment. Therefore, top managements, as a group and individually, earn excess returns relatively consistently.

All financial relationships combine communities of interest and conflicts of interest. Agency costs are a nonstarter insofar as there is any sort of assumption that managements of public companies, by and large, work in the best interests of passive investors. Managements, good or bad, represent various constituencies, and with each of these they will have communities of interest and conflicts of interest.

In the financial world, it tends to be misleading to state "There is no free lunch." Rather the more meaningful comment is "Somebody has to pay for lunch."

Security Analysis

Substantive consolidation of the interests of the company itself and its OPMI stockholders is a relatively rare special case. The company is the company. The company is not the management. The company is not its stockholders. Virtually all safe and cheap analyses treat the company as a stand-alone. For example, it should be recognized that stock options are a stockholder problem and only rarely a company problem. If one analyzes a company as if the person were a long-term creditor, there usually is a world of difference between paying management members with cash or equity interests. Cash payments could detract from creditworthiness while equity payments probably don't.

The worth of any security is the present value of the future cash bailouts to be received by security holders. Cash bailouts come from three sources:

- Cash distributions by issuers in the forms of interest, principal, premiums, paid to creditors; dividends, and securities repurchases, paid to stockholders
- Sales to a market
- Control

Passive securities, for most economic purposes, are a different commodity from control securities, albeit they are identical in legal form. From a safe and cheap point of view, if a passive security of a reasonably financed company is to become a control security, the holder is entitled to a premium price.

Outside of a court proceeding, usually Chapter 11, no one in the United States can take away a creditor's right to a money payment for interest, principal, or premium unless that individual creditor so consents. A creditor has only contract rights, not residual rights. The rules of the game are substantially different in many other countries.

Equities represent ownership and only very rarely require cash service. Equity owners have residual rights vis-à-vis the company and its management; management has a duty to deal fairly with stockholders.

In all transactions, a safe and cheap analyst considers the use of proceeds. Corporations can only use cash proceeds in one of four ways: to cover expenses; to expand the asset base; to service or repay liabilities; and to distribute to the equity via dividends and buybacks.

Distributions to equity holders are almost always a residual use of corporate cash. The principal exception is when the payment of dividends gives capital-hungry companies better access to capital markets than they otherwise would have (most safe and cheap investors tend not to invest in the common stocks of such companies). Excluding this consideration, buying in common stock is almost always a preferable method of distributing cash to shareholders from both a company point of view and a safe and cheap point of view compared with paying cash dividends. This tends not to be the case from the point of view of short-run oriented OPMIs.

In passive investing, decisions should be based more on a reasonable worst-case basis than on a base-case basis.

Management appraisals involve looking at managements not only as operators but also as investors and financiers.

Weighted average cost of capital (WACC) is a nonstarter for two reasons. First, from a creditor's point of view (and without getting into the issue of effective differences in cost between, say, short-term senior secured issues and long-term subordinates), the cost of creating corporate creditworthiness is very different in the case where the company issues debt securities that have a required cash cost on the one hand, and where the company issues equity securities that don't require cash payments on the other hand.

Second, the vast majority of equity financing takes place via having the company retain earnings rather than having the company market new issues of common stock. The PE ratio, or cap rate, at which a common stock sells in an OPMI market, has no particular meaning for a company increasing its equity base through retaining earnings. Here return on equity (ROE) gives a better estimate of the cost of equity capital to the company than does a cap rate measured in part by OPMI market prices, albeit many cash conscious managements and companies will view retaining earnings as a cost-free method of increasing equity capital.

The liability side of the balance sheet is a lot more than obligations and net worth. Rather, it is a layer cake consisting of at least the following:

- Secured obligations
- Unsecured obligations
- Subordinated obligations
- Liability reserves, which analytically have an equity component
- Preferred stocks
- Common stocks
- Common stock derivatives

Whether an issue is debt or equity depends on where you sit. To senior lenders, subordinated debt is a form of equity. To common stockholders, subordinated debt is debt.

Many disciplines can be helpful in contributing toward making one a successful safe and cheap investor. There are three areas, though, where it is essential that the participant needs to be well informed (i.e., needs to be knowledgeable enough so that at the minimum, the analyst can be an informed client). These three disciplines are:

- GAAP
- Securities laws and regulation
- Income tax

THE CHANGED ENVIRONMENT

In the first edition of *The Aggressive Conservative Investor* much was made of the potential value of tax loss carryforwards available in companies that could be described as clean shells. Chapter 16, "Losses and Loss Companies," covered this topic. The Tax Reform Act of 1986, particularly Section 382, changed things dramatically. Tax loss carryforwards no longer have great value mostly because their use has become so seriously proscribed under Section 382 if there has been a change of ownership. The values in net operating losses (NOL) for safe and cheap investors is no longer a matter of much importance.

There has been tremendous growth in new forms of securities such as derivatives and complex liability structures for flow through entities such as REMICs. It is something we don't understand much about and neither we, nor the companies in which we invest, seem deeply involved with these esoteric instruments. Third Avenue Value Fund, however, in 1994 earned a very satisfactory return by buying into inverse floaters, which were mortgage-backed securities with implied U.S. government guarantees. The theory of the investment was that on a reasonable worst-case basis the investment would return a minimum 8% yield to maturity no matter what happened to interest rates. Third Avenue would never have made the investment if it had to predict what might happen to interest rates in the future. It was our view at the time that on a reasonable worst-case basis a minimum cash return of 8% was good enough. Rightly or wrongly we focused in this investment only on cash returns, ignoring market risk as the price of the inverse floaters fluctuated. In investing in long-term credit instruments without credit risk, we focus strictly on cash return (i.e., current yield and yield to maturity) and eschew making judgments about what market price fluctuations might occur.

In 1979, most broker/dealers and investment banking firms employed all their capital in their own operations: trading, underwriting, generating commissions. Little or no investment was made in equities of other businesses, or in real estate, which were to be held on a permanent, or semipermanent basis. By the late 1980s and early 1990s that had changed. Almost all had become merchant bankers, investing as principals in leveraged buyouts, management buyouts, venture capital, and real estate. For many of the better broker/dealer-investment banks, merchant banking has now become their principal and major source of profitability. This seems all to the good for safe and cheap investors. A new source has come into the market to provide bailouts for holders of many publicly traded safe and cheap common stocks.

In 1979, if you were insiders in a start-up tech venture seeking to go public, the company might have been able to raise, say, $10 to $15 million by having a new offering underwritten by a firm such as D.H. Blair or Oscar Gruss. The underwriters would be compensated with a 10% gross spread, a large expense allowance, and board representation as well as five-year warrants to buy 10% of the amount to be issued at 115% of the issue price. In 1999, the same start-up high-tech venture seeking to go public would have raised, say, $150 to $200 million in an IPO underwritten by a bulge bracket banking house such as Morgan Stanley, Goldman Sachs, or First Boston whose gross spread on the deal would be 7%. Safe and cheap investors remain little involved in the new issue market, mostly not involved at all.

In 1979, commercial banks were taking huge risks in providing senior financing for leveraged buyouts, for loans to less-developed countries, for oil and gas ventures, and for real estate. The commercial banks no longer seem to take the same risks. A market for mezzanine financing has blossomed and in this market lenders such as high-yield mutual funds now take the risks that were once taken by commercial banks. For this the banks ought to say "Thank you, Michael Milken." Michael Milken pioneered the development of new credit markets where mezzanine financial institutions and individual investors now take the credit risks in corporate and real estate lending that in 1979 were taken by commercial banks. There is probably much validity to the view that U.S. commercial banks have never been sounder. Corporate, industrial, commercial, and real estate loans (excluding residential housing) seem more conservative than ever. Because of syndication, loan portfolios probably are more diversified than ever. And banks seem to have awakened to the view that fee income, an increasing percentage of bank operating income, tends to be higher quality income than spread income (i.e., the difference between interest received and interest paid). Under safe and cheap, Third Avenue Value Fund has never invested in a bank common stock unless the company was extremely well financed and the common stock was available at a substantial discount from book value. The only place Third Avenue is finding such common stocks in 2005 is in Hong Kong.

In 1979, safe and cheap investing was pretty much confined to the United States and Canada. Today much of such investing is overseas. It is however restricted to countries that are industrialized and seem politically stable. As for the companies in whose common stock we as a safe and cheap investor are interested, each is audited by the Big 4, or equivalent, and each publishes comprehensive disclosures in English. There are special risks for OPMIs investing outside U.S. borders in companies that will not subject themselves to American jurisdiction. And now that Sarbanes-Oxley is law, no foreign issuer is going to subject itself, and its executives, to U.S. jurisdiction unless it absolutely needs access to U.S. capital markets. In safe and cheap investing, hopefully, the lack of safety inherent in being denied the protection of United States law and regulation is overcome by even cheaper prices for common stock issues (i.e., foreign investing seems less safe, more cheap).

TROUBLESOME REGULATORY PROBLEMS

In 1979, we wrote in *The Aggressive Conservative Investor,* "This book suggests that the role of generally accepted accounting principles (GAAP) in disclosure should be limited to giving security holders objective benchmarks, and that it is silly to attempt to equate accounting with Truth or Value." We also suggested that there was no need to make GAAP as complex as the Internal Revenue Code.

Boy did we lose that battle and that war, and while one would like to rail against the system, it is hard to gripe in the sense that disclosures are now so good that safe and cheap investors can operate more comfortably than ever before. But accounting could be so much more useful and less onerous for issuers and regulators if the system were based on the following standards:

- Primarily GAAP has to fill the needs of long-term creditors, not stock market speculators.
- The company is a stand-alone; it is not substantively consolidated with its stockholders.

- There has to be a modifying convention of conservatism.
- Financial statements should be prepared on the assumption that the user is reasonably intelligent and trained in their use.
- There is no primacy of the income account.
- Where possible, principles rather than rules ought to govern.
- Provide consistency and reconcilability.
- Recognize that GAAP has to be objective and, thus, follow a relatively rigid set of principles or rules, such as depreciation of plant and equipment is based on original cost. As such, GAAP can almost never be equated to truth or economic reality. If one seeks truth, it has to be found in non-GAAP financial measures, such as asset appraisals. Non-GAAP financial measures can never be a substitute for GAAP. Rather non-GAAP financial measures can be a valuable supplement to GAAP.

In the area of disclosure, it is our view that the best investor protection is to give investors the facts—all the facts with a conservative bias—and then let the investor decide what is truth and what weight to give specific facts. GAAP can provide no more than objective benchmarks. This is going back to old days. It is impossible to spoon-feed investors items that purport to be truth and accuracy. In the end, the investor has to decide what is truth and accuracy.

It is our view that Sarbanes-Oxley (SOX) is grossly counterproductive. SOX regulates as if all issuers were Enron and Worldcom. This is not realistic. SOX is inordinately expensive. Some believe that it costs most companies anywhere from $2 to $7 million per annum just to comply with Section 404 in 2005. Section 404 deals with internal controls or managerial accounting. We have been relatively successful investors sticking to our style for over 50 years, relying for our accounting information only on GAAP and, of late, various non-GAAP financial measures. Before 404, managerial accounting was never on our radar screen, and if it were we doubt it would have prevented the one or two accounting frauds in which we were victimized—out of the thousands of investments we have made.

As we have already covered, SOX detracts from the appeal of U.S. capital markets for foreign issuers. This seems a sad and unnecessary loss. We have and do support many aspects of regulation but not at the cost of total lack of common sense and a political inability to make basic economic distinctions at a great cost to the productivity of our system.

CONCLUSION

We hope that you will find our 1979 work edifying in the twenty-first century. Safe and cheap seems to us to be but one route to successful investing. It certainly is not the only route. However, safe and cheap seems attractive. What we describe as safe and cheap isn't rocket science. Diligent individuals can train themselves to do it. It is the least stressful form of investing that we know. At least, for some of us it is fun! Many, if not most, practitioners seem to do reasonably well and some even wind up very rich doing what they enjoy.

Martin J. Whitman
Martin Shubik
July 2005

SECTION ONE

THE APPROACH

Chapter 1

An Overview

THIS BOOK IS DIRECTED toward investors and creditors who hold, purchase or sell all types of securities and evidences of indebtedness, and who are aggressive because within their own contexts they expect a well-above-average return over the long term. For these investors, this book presents conservative methods of investment, especially equity investment, that the authors believe minimize risk for securities holders. It is our thesis that minimizing risk does not reduce profit potentials for investors in common stocks; rather, minimizing the downside tends to enhance the realistic upside potential, especially for noncontrol investors in common stocks.

Since many of the investors and creditors to whom this book is directed are financial institutions—for example, commercial banks, insurance companies and investment companies—it ought to be useful to those interested in what U.S. financial institutions as asset managers do and why they do what they do.

Some participants in these investment processes are outside, passive investors; others are activists. Outside investors are members of the public and are distinguishable from others in three respects. First, individually they have no control or influence over the businesses whose securities they hold or contemplate holding. Second, they do not have access to information other than that which is generally available to the public. Third, they are those whom the U.S. securities laws and regulations have been designed to protect.*

Throughout the book, we refer to them as outside investors and passivists, as well as noncontrol and unaffiliated security holders. The key is that they are inactive in management and not connected with the company issuing securities in any way other than as security holders.

Noncontrol investors are also supposed to be the beneficiaries of various state laws and regulations, including blue sky statutes governing terms and conditions under which new issues may be offered;† anti-takeover statutes; statutes aimed at controlling going-private transactions; more generalized common-law and state statutory requirements covering the fiduciary obligations of those in control of corporations to unaffiliated common stockholders; and statutes defining appraisal remedies when stockholders dissent from force-out mergers or similar force-out transactions. Outside investors are additionally protected by rules promulgated by quasi-public bodies, particularly the New York Stock Exchange, among other exchanges, and the National Association of Securities Dealers.

---

*The relevant laws and regulations are the federal securities laws administered by the Securities and Exchange Commission: the Federal Securities Act of 1933 as amended, the Securities Exchange Act of 1934 as amended, the Investment Company Act of 1940 as amended, the Investment Advisers Act of 1940 as amended, the Public Utility Holding Company Act of 1935, the Trust Indenture Act of 1939 and the Securities Investors Protection Act of 1970.

†"Blue sky statutes" refers to state statutes governing the terms and conditions on which offerings to sell securities to the public or to buy them from the public can be made in that jurisdiction. There is a further discussion in Appendix I of blue sky laws as they impact on the underwriting of new issues. The origin of the term "blue sky" is derived from the promises of promoters who foisted upon unsuspecting outside investors investments that had no substance, only blue sky.

We regard as activists those participants in U.S. financial processes who have elements of control or influence over the businesses in which they invest, who have or can obtain nonpublic information and whom federal securities regulation is intended to control rather than to protect. We believe the materials in this book are of interest to both activists and outside, passive investors.

We differ from most others writing about fundamental security analysis and corporate finance. It is our view that other fundamentalists have a tendency to apply to all companies tools of analysis that in fact are applicable only to that small minority of companies which are large, stable and seasoned enterprises engaged in continuous operations. Such businesses are strict going concerns—that is, they are engaged in a particular type of operation to be financed in the future in about the same way they have been in the past. It is our view that an analysis that is useful for evaluating stable going concerns is of limited help when applied to businesses involved, even partially, in what we call asset-conversion activities—that is, mergers, acquisitions, or the purchase, sale or distribution of assets in bulk; major financial restructurings or recapitalizations; sales of control or contests for control; or the creation of tax shelter. And most businesses seem to be engaged, at least to some extent, in asset conversion. We believe it is necessary to distinguish between asset-conversion analysis and going-concern analysis.

Our underlying thesis is that in both fundamental security analysis and corporate finance a key element to be emphasized is financial position, measured by a concern's ability to have and to create liquidity (either from surplus cash or from other assets readily convertible into cash, such as a portfolio of blue-chip corporate stocks and bonds whose resale is not restricted); by an ability to generate surplus cash from operations; by an ability to borrow; or by an ability to market new issues of equity securities.

In contrast to our emphasis on financial position, conventional fundamental analysis rests on a primacy-of-earnings theory—that is, reported earnings are a principal determinant of common-stock prices. To us, the primacy-of-earnings approach is valid in special cases—that is, it is more applicable than a financial-position approach for those common-stock traders whose one consuming interest is day-to-day stock market fluctuations. It seems reasonable to suppose that most of the time, accounting earnings as reported will have a more significant impact on immediate stock prices than will perceived changes in financial position. Yet, we view financial position as normally the more fundamental factor because it is a better aid in understanding a business than are reported earnings, especially since most enterprises are not strict going concerns. In addition, most securities holders, including creditors, are not stock traders. Primacy-of-earnings concepts therefore appear to be more limited in applicability than is popularly supposed.

We are concerned with fundamental analysis rather than technical analysis. Fundamental analysis involves the study of a business and the factors that the analyst believes will affect that business. Using his study of the enterprise and the terms of its outstanding securities, the fundamentalist arrives at judgments about those securities in the context of the prices at which they are selling. Technical analysts, on the other hand, are concerned solely with the behavior of securities prices; some technicians believe past securities price behavior has predictive value for future prices. Others—random walkers and efficient-market theorists, whose practices are examined in Chapter 4—are technicians who believe that past securities prices have no predictive value.

What is a "security," at least as that term is used in this book? The key feature of a security is that it is an investment vehicle in which the holder can benefit from an inactive creditor or ownership role. The owner of a security does not, because of his holding, have to perform any managerial or other economic function, but he can anticipate benefits through someone else's efforts. Where efforts by the holder are a necessary part of ownership, no security originates, either by our definition or by most legal definitions. Examples of securities under our definition include conventional instruments, such as common stocks, preferred stocks, bonds, leasehold interests and limited partnership participations, and instruments not normally thought of as securities, such as savings-bank deposits and commercial paper. One example of a nonsecurity is ownership of a

McDonald's fast-food franchise in which, as part of the transaction under which the investment is made, the franchisee is expected or required to manage the facility.

As far as technical analysis is concerned, the material in this book notes in Chapter 4 those aspects of modern capital theory that are involved with efficient-market and efficient-portfolio hypotheses. However, we place these theories in perspective. Even granting that efficient-market and efficient-portfolio assumptions may be valid, they are not particularly relevant to the main themes presented here. Indeed, we think that efficiency assumptions are, at best, of marginal relevance to real-world financial and corporate analyses of equities.

Our tools of analysis are applied to broad spectra of investors and securities. There are two reasons for this. First, while the standards of analysis tend to be different for different sorts of securities, the analytic concepts used and techniques involved are similar, whether the security to be evaluated is a $500 million term loan from a commercial bank or 100 shares of Amterre Development common selling at around $1 per share. For the $500 million term loan, we think that understanding the business from an asset-conversion basis or a going-concern basis is essential; for the purchase of 100 Amterre Development common, such understanding is merely desirable. Understanding the business becomes increasingly important as larger amounts of funds or proportions of a person's or institution's resources are invested in a security. Understanding the business is also increasingly important as the quality of that security is diminished because of its lack of senior position as underlying or secured debt, and the lack of financial resources within the business issuing the security.

The second reason why this book covers a broad range of institutions and securities is that any type of security holder, including the outside, individual investor, is helped in his investment program if he has some understanding of why other types of investors, such as life insurance companies or deal promoters, do what they do. For example, the knowledge in 1976 and 1977 that life insurance companies were willing to lend funds to deal promoters to buy out companies such as Big Bear Stores and A. J. Industries at substantial premiums above stock market prices would have been helpful to any investor making buy, hold or sell decisions about such securities.

Note that by "understanding the business," we mean specifically understanding the finances and operations of a company, its problems and its potentials. Thus, we focus on the analysis of internal factors, especially financial position, that we believe affect the value of business. By "understanding the business," we do not mean understanding stock-price movements, interest-rate fluctuations or even prognostications about the overall economy. This is not because we feel that predictions of general economic activity are unimportant, but rather because we believe that everyone, ourselves included, has limited abilities in macroeconomic forecasting. On the other hand, we believe that the "nitty-gritty" fundamentals we stress compensate for many errors that are bound to be made by all general economic crystal-ball gazers. In this sense, this book has a different emphasis from the other fundamentalist-school investment books of which we are aware.

In the language of modern capital theory, our focus is on unsystematic risk, factors that are peculiar to specific enterprises. In stark contrast to modern capital theorists, we believe that an outside investor can obtain excess returns if he is willing to apply himself so that he can benefit from the knowledge available in public documents and thus guard against unsystematic risk. Put simply, modern capital theorists believe it is practically impossible to guard against unsystematic risk because common-stock prices are almost always in equilibrium, neither too high nor too low. We are convinced that most common-stock prices are almost always in disequilibrium, certainly for activists and also for those outsiders willing to work and think like activists.

The views of modern capital theory about systematic risk— factors concerning general market and economic conditions—are similar to those held by us, namely, that such elements as overall stock market levels and interest rates are largely unpredictable. Modern capital theorists guard against systematic risk by diversifying into efficient portfolios—that is, portfolios whose risk is minimized for a given anticipated rate of return. Efficient portfolios assume equilibrium prices. We believe there are elements of validity to such efficient-portfolio hypotheses for outside investors in limited situations where analysts are not prepared to investigate individual companies thoroughly and where portfolios are of a fixed size, without prospects for the investment of new funds in future years. Insofar as new funds for investment are created periodically, it becomes less and less important to diversify initially in order to achieve efficient portfolios.

Again, we are concerned with investing for the long term. We do not say that some may not have a legitimate interest in trying to predict short-term—even day-to-day, week-to-week or month-to-month—changes in the general level of stock prices and interest rates. Indeed, people or institutions who have borrowed heavily to carry securities or who engage in arbitrage activities almost always have to be vitally interested in market fluctuations. And, of course, anyone who does not understand the business in which he holds securities will have to be highly interested in market fluctuations if he owns any securities other than the highest-quality senior obligations. But that is not what this book is about. For us, markets are taken as given, something investors take advantage of because they understand a business.

If there is one thing that differentiates our approach from that of others writing on investments, it is our underlying conviction that the value of a business has no necessary relationship to the price of its common stock. Of course, business values are related to stock market prices: in some instances—for example, the going-concern analysis of electric utilities—virtually the same standards that seem to result in a price for the stock are used to value the business it represents. And it is also true that over time there probably is a tendency for stock prices to be equated with business values, though frankly it would be hard to demonstrate just how strong or how weak this tendency is. In a dynamic economy, moreover, disequilibrium, not equilibrium, is the rule.

Unlike many others, we believe that if there is any one factor that is crucial in determining most business value, it is the financial condition of a company—that is, the quality and quantity of its resources. According to our view, if a business has considerable financial strength and if this flexibility is used reasonably, it should be able to create future wealth that will be manifested in tomorrow's reported earnings and common-stock prices. On the other hand, we believe that for the analysis of most businesses most of the time, the differences between business value and stock market prices are more important and more significant than their similarities. The analysis of a business entails understanding its key attributes and weighing its probable future operating and investment results as well as its ability to meet its debts and to pay dividends to its stockholders. Only in the case of a few stable businesses (such as utilities) will those things thought of as highly important to stock prices—current earnings as reported and current dividends—be sufficient to help any investor understand a business.

This book seems to us to be distinguishable from most other investment books of which we are aware, whether fundamental or technical, in that it offers no arithmetical formulas to noncontrol investors. Our "magic formula" for investment success—the understanding of a business—has to grow out of experience, insight and maturity of judgment. Nonetheless, we are hopeful that what we have to say ought to help investors in gaining these requisites.

We attempt to do this by covering three general topics. First, we try to educate the outside investor to think about investment questions the way insiders and deal promoters tend to. Second, we start the outsider onto the road to obtaining familiarity with the uses and limitations of the required disclosures, including accounting disclosures, of the Securities and Exchange Commission. Third, we attempt to impart understanding about who the various role players in the financial community are and how they each participate in the investment process.

There are many ways to invest in securities, some of which (such as short selling, option writing and arbitrage) are relatively esoteric. This book, insofar as it is directed to the non-insider, is directed toward unhedged investments in relatively conventional securities—say, commercial paper, corporate bonds, certain leases, preferred stock, limited partnership interests and common stocks, among others.

Although these types of investments are frequently hybrids—that is, securities purchased in order to achieve a varied bag of investor objectives—we divide them into four types:

1. Trading investments
2. Investments in the securities of emerging companies or industries
3. Workout and special-situation investments
4. Cash-return investments

This book will be of little or no use to those whose raison d'être is to try to benefit from short-run market swings—that is, to trade. Indeed, there is a considerable dispute as to whether any outside investor using publicly available information can predict short-run movements for markets and particular stocks with sufficient consistency to make such activities profitable. Although we briefly discuss the random-walk theory in Chapter 4, we really do not have much to contribute to discussions of trading, either pro or con. It might be noted, though, that many who have trading accounts also have investment accounts, and much of the material of this book may be useful to those traders who also manage long-term money.

Since this book is about "how to" invest (and in a sense, "how to" promote), its emphasis is strictly financial; it becomes less useful as nonfinancial variables become more important. Nonfinancial variables tend to be of greatest importance in emerging security situations—that is, in enterprises based on new technologies, new inventions or ideas, and untried, untested managements. For example, a hypothetical bootstrap operation is described in Chapter 9. This was undertaken by Joe Promoter, who acquired control of a widget manufacturer. We think familiarity with these types of transactions is important for all kinds of investors as well as for promoters. However, a *sine qua non* for the transaction to be attractive to an investor—and to the legitimate promoter—is that the business be viable. And such viability probably would have to be determined not only by the availability of funds to finance the business, but also by whether the widgets are any good and can be manufactured and marketed profitably. These questions about widgets or similar nonfinancial variables are beyond the scope of this book except for us to emphasize their importance in some, but far from all, investment situations.

Additionally, there are many industries where financial considerations are not of primary importance. For example, in the drug and chemical industry, the quality of a company's research and development activities will probably be a much more important determinant of future prosperity than will the firm's present balance sheet. That, however, does not mean that the balance sheet is unimportant; rather, it gives an investor clues as to whether the company can afford to do what it proposes to do. If this book can impart to a person who is knowledgeable about the economics of drug research an understanding of financial limitations and techniques, then we will have contributed to making that person a superior investor in the securities of companies in that industry.

The themes of this book seem most appropriate for the analysis of workouts and special situations as well as for cash-return investing. Investing in workout or other special situations involves buying securities in entities that have, first and foremost, financial strength, and that are available at prices the investor believes to be well below a conservative estimate of a realistic value. As we see it, the key to this kind of investing is a combination of strong financial position and price consciousness. Here, price of the issue assumes increasing importance, and the quality of the issuer (especially insofar as quality entails general recognition by others) is relatively less important than in other types of investing. The difference between emphasizing price of the issue and quality of the issuer is discussed in Chapter 5, "Risk and Uncertainty." The factors involved in an investment program based upon consideration of price and financial position are discussed in part in Chapter 2, "The Financial-Integrity Approach to Equity Investing."

Workout investing is a subgroup of special-situation investing. A workout investment is one in which a financially strong security is priced below a conservative estimate of a realistic value, and the investor has reason to believe that an asset-conversion event might take place within a given time span. The asset-conversion event could be a merger or an acquisition, the sale of assets, a liquidation, a reorganization, a contest for control or a share-repurchase program.

The high interest rates of the 1970's made cash-return investing, in terms of percentage yield in fixed U.S. dollars, more attractive than it had been for a hundred years. In effect, cash equivalents such as savings deposits, commercial paper and treasury notes became securities affording not only flexibility and constant-dollar safety but also high return. But cash equivalents, like all other securities, have their problems: interest payments on most cash-equivalent securities are taxable as ordinary income, and in many contexts cash investing does not provide a satisfactory inflation hedge. Also, in investing for cash return there are many difficult questions: Should an investor purchase short, medium or long-term obligations? Should he purchase equity securities paying high dividends relative to price in order to obtain not only a high cash return but also a possible inflation hedge? Or should he purchase cash-return securities that also provide tax shelter? While many specific investment problems are beyond the purview of this book, the concepts discussed in it should help cash-return investors in dealing with these questions.

For many outside investors who are common stockholders, whether individuals, mutual funds or bank trust departments, the advice of Graham and Dodd in *Security Analysis* tends to be sound.[1] Their advice is that, with exceptions, such common-stock investments be restricted to choices from a basic portfolio list of one hundred primary common stocks, and that these be analyzed by emphasizing a going-concern approach. These issues should be generally recognized *by others* and *by the noncontrol investor* as high quality, based on sound capitalizations, long records of profitability and demonstrated dividend-paying ability.

Like Graham and Dodd, we recommend that outside investors in common stocks emphasize earnings and dividends of very large,

---

[1]Benjamin Graham, David L. Dodd and Sidney Cottle, with Charles Tatham, *Security Analysis: Principles and Techniques,* 4th ed. (New York: McGraw-Hill, 1962).

seasoned, well-recognized issuers in a going-concern analysis where the investor lacks "know-how" (an ability or willingness to investigate in depth) or "know-who" (acquaintanceship with knowledgeable, helpful people). Here, earnings become more significant because the investor believes that no changes in the way resources are to be used by a company are likely, and that even if they were, he could exert no influence in making changes. Dividends, too, become crucially important. For one thing, they are tangible evidence that a business's results are satisfactory, since a cash payment does not have the gimmickry potential of an earnings report. Moreover, for the unaffiliated security holder without much know-how, dividends are a hedge against the possibility of being wrong about either the market or the business; at least one can look forward to receiving a cash return. There are pitfalls to the Graham and Dodd approach to common-stock investment, and fortunes have been lost in recent years by investors who have restricted their holdings to generally recognized blue chips. But this does not invalidate the general rule that holding widely recognized blue-chip stocks is probably the least unsatisfactory form of equity investment for the outside investor who lacks know-how and know-who.

We depart from Graham and Dodd in two respects. First, we think public disclosures have become increasingly better in the years following the passage of securities acts amendments of 1964, and are now so good that diligent investors can, in increasing numbers of instances, analyze well enough to obtain reasonable results when they do not restrict their equity investments to securities that are generally recognized as high quality *by others*.

We also believe that satisfactory performance does not mean merely "beating the market" on a continual or relatively continual basis. Indeed, the only investor who attempts to outperform the market continually is the total-return investor, for whom results are measured both by income from dividends and interest and by the per-share or per-bond price of securities owned at any given moment. In our view, there are very few total-return, outside investors, nor should there be many, because they are unlikely to be successful at it for reasons discussed in Chapter 4.

We also differ from Graham and Dodd in that their advice seems directed to the outside investor who reacts to an environment where such things as general market levels and earnings per share are all-important. Our approach is geared toward activists and outside investors who want to think like activists. We believe that except for those who strive for total return, all intelligent investors willing to work hard can safely downgrade those principles that Graham and Dodd seem to believe are the lifeblood of successful investing—earnings, assessments of general market levels, and determination of the quality of the issuer by referring to opinions of others. In our view, all these elements are secondary to the financial approach discussed in the next chapter.

This book may be helpful not only for noncontrol investors, but also for promoters and would-be promoters. Almost all the outstandingly successful investors we have known have been long-term securities holders whose judgments have been based on the concepts expounded in this book. These concepts should be useful for all types of security analysts (including bank and insurance lenders), whether passive or activist, if for no other reason than that they serve as a reasonably accurate description of why such analysts do what they do. We suspect that for many, this book can provide at least a few useful new perspectives.

Other activists in the financial community—from investment bankers, arbitrageurs and venture capitalists, through company managements and control shareholders—should also find this book helpful as a description of an environment that some will recognize part of, but that others may not know at all.

Finally, we hope we have something to say to the two groups that have been crucial in making the investment environment in the United States the best that has ever existed anywhere for unaffiliated security holders: the accounting profession and the Securities and Exchange Commission. In our view, neither group seems to realize how well it has performed to date. As a consequence, there appear to be real dangers that the accountants and the SEC may change so much that they will kill the goose that is laying all those golden eggs for diligent investors. To the accountant, this book suggests that the role of Generally Accepted Accounting Principles (or GAAP) in disclosure should be limited to giving security holders objective bench marks, and that it is silly to attempt to equate accounting with Truth or Value. To the Securities and Exchange Commission, we suggest that the disclosure scheme built up, especially since 1964, is now extraordinarily good and extraordinarily valuable to all sorts of security holders. The SEC has no need to backtrack, and certainly is ill-advised if it believes that efficient-market economists who are neither practicing analysts nor investment bankers have much, if anything, to contribute to the implementation of a meaningful disclosure system.

Most of all, we think that this book, as a description of reality, ought to be useful to the many types of investors who make up the financial community by giving insights into what many of the professionals think and do.

Chapter 2

The Financial-Integrity Approach to Equity Investment

Fool me once, shame on you,
Fool me twice, shame on me.

IT HAS BEEN our observation that the most successful activists have had much the same approach to investing that the most sophisticated creditors have had toward lending. Essentially, these people approach a transaction with two attitudes, the first having to do with their order of priorities. In looking at a transaction, the single most important question seems to be, What have I got to lose? Only when it seems that risks can be controlled or minimized does the second question come up: How much can I make?

The second attitude has to do with a basic feeling that risk—how much one can lose—is essentially measured internally, not externally. The possibilities of unsatisfactory results from an investment or loan are to be found internally in the performance of the underlying business and the resources in the business, not externally in the market prices at which a company's securities might trade. Successful activists and creditors, while not unmindful of the "value messages" that are delivered by markets, tend not to be overly influenced by such messages. Their attitude is, As far as my objectives are concerned, I know much more about the situations in which I invest or in which I lend than the stock market does.

THE FINANCIAL-INTEGRITY APPROACH

A basic premise of this book is that many noncontrol investors ought to adopt the same standards of valuation that are used by successful activists, creditors, insiders and owners of nonpublic businesses. First and foremost, they must gauge the investment risk. Key variables for doing this are the financial position of the business being analyzed and/or the financial position of the securities holder. Businesses with strong financial positions are those that have access to enough liquid funds so that they can pay for whatever reasonable requirements they might have and still have access to a comfortable amount of surplus liquidity. Earnings, even accounting earnings, are, of course, frequently an important element in determining financial strength, but this is a far cry from the position usually expounded—that for unaffiliated securities holders, earnings are the primary factor, and in fact determine value.

Companies with strong financial positions tend to be less risky than those not as well situated. Furthermore, they tend to be more expandable because of their greater ability to obtain new funds. These companies also are the most attractive candidates for asset-conversion activities, such as mergers and acquisitions, liquidations, share repurchases, takeovers and other changes in control.

Our views as developed in this book are that attractive equity investments for outside investors ought to have the following four essential characteristics:

1. The company ought to have a strong financial position, something that is measured not so much by the presence of assets as by the absence of significant encumbrances, whether a part of a balance sheet, disclosed in financial statement footnotes, or

an element that is not disclosed at all in any part of financial statements.

2. The company ought to be run by reasonably honest management and control groups, especially in terms of how cognizant the insiders are of the interests of creditors and other security holders.

3. There ought to be available to the investor a reasonable amount of relevant information, although in every instance this will be something that is far short of "full disclosure"—the impossible dream for any investigator, whether activist, creditor, insider or outside investor.

4. The price at which the equity security can be bought ought to to be below the investor's reasonable estimate of net asset value.

These four elements are the *sine qua non* for an investment commitment using the financial-integrity approach, because their presence results in a minimization of investment risk. But they are not simply by their presence sufficient reasons for an investment commitment. The absence, however, of any one of them is reason enough to forgo any passive investment, regardless of how attractive it might appear based on other standards.

The environment within which an investor can search meaningfully for these four characteristics is a good one. The required disclosures under the securities laws give investors good insights into the first three characteristics. Audited financial statements, including footnotes, are particularly useful in describing and enumerating many of a concern's encumbrances, albeit some potential encumbrances, such as necessary or desirable capital expenditures, may not be disclosed. Proxy-statement disclosures about management compensation and "certain transactions" with insiders, as well as narrative Form 10-K* and financial-statement footnote disclosures about litigation, aid in

---

*The Form 10-K is an annual report filed with the Securities and Exchange Commission by most companies whose securities are publicly held. Descriptions of the 10-K and other forms filed with the SEC are contained in Chapter 6 and in Appendix III.

determining the degree of consideration insiders are likely to have for the interests of security holders. Business descriptions in annual reports, merger proxy statements, prospectuses and 10-K's have never been better in enabling investors to understand an enterprise.

In addition to the four essential characteristics, supplementary factors that can make an equity security attractive can be so varied as to defy anyone's imagination. In fact, most of these factors in most analyses will exist in various combinations. To give the reader some insight into what these can consist of, we merely enumerate possible factors under three subheadings—primarily going-concern factors, primarily stock market factors and primarily asset-conversion factors. Any one or combination of these factors could serve as a "trigger to buy" securities that the investor has already determined are attractive, based on financial-integrity standards.

Primarily going-concern factors are those that relate to the operations of a business. They encompass things ranging from investor beliefs that profitability in the immediate future will increase dramatically (the dynamic-disequilibrium principle discussed in Chapter 13, "Earnings") to tenets about dividend increases; from views that current high dividends are safe to beliefs in the potential of new developments or new research; from optimism about an industry outlook to faith in management abilities.

Primarily stock market factors encompass variables ranging from beliefs that a common stock based on existing price–earnings ratios is priced below comparable issues (the static-equilibrium concept discussed in Chapter 13), to views that the common stock looks good technically, and to ideas that the company or industry may obtain Wall Street sponsorship. Under primarily stock market factors, we would also include the myriad macrovariables that encompass investor perceptions about the economy, about interest-rate levels and about predicted movements in the general stock market or major segments of it.

Primarily asset-conversion factors that can serve as a trigger to buy can be more precisely enumerated than can factors that relate primarily to the going concern or to the stock market. Such asset-conversion factors encompass possibilities or probabilities of major refinancings, mergers and acquisitions, liquidations, certain common-stock repurchases or other large-scale distributions to common stock-holders, changes in control, reorganizations and recapitalizations.

THE BENEFITS AND USES OF THE FINANCIAL-INTEGRITY APPROACH TO THE NONCONTROL INVESTOR

Outside investors using this approach buy and hold securities because issues appear at the time of purchase, and continue to appear while held, to be risk-resistant, based on the four essential elements. In contrast to other investment approaches, little or no attention is paid to stock market price fluctuations or to predictions about the immediate outlook for equity prices.

When purchasing equity securities, an outside investor using our approach will not acquire a position for his portfolio unless he believes that the value represented by the particular security is good enough, based on the four essential elements. He does not consciously try to outperform the market over the short run. Thus, investigation in areas other than financial integrity will tend to be emphasized less than it would be if the investor was striving for more immediate performance. First, little or no time is spent attempting to gauge the general market outlook, examining technical positions or making business-cycle predictions. Put simply, there is no attempt to hold off buying until the investor believes stock prices are near bottom. Rather, the primary motivation for purchases is that values are good enough. Second, comparative analysis, though always a useful tool, tends to be less important than in other forms of fundamental analysis. The reason, of course, is that the investment goal for outside investors is to concentrate on acquiring reasonable values rather than on getting the best possible values.

Such investors tend to have a degree of confidence in their commitments that just cannot exist for those who are significantly affected by day-to-day or even month-to-month stock market fluctuations, or who believe that values are determined by elements based on "soft," or always shifting, factors, such as earnings estimates, price–earnings ratios and technical market conditions. This confidence factor can afford significant rewards in the usual (though far from universal) investment instance where there has been no fundamental deterioration in the position of companies with strong finances whose common stocks are part of the investor's portfolio. First, only an investor confident in the fundamental merits of a security finds it relatively easy to hold or average down at times when prices are depressed because there is a bear market, because earnings have declined or for whatever reason. Second, if there is confidence in fundamental merits, it becomes relatively easy to establish positions in common stocks at attractive prices when markets are depressed because of events such as panics or tight money, or because of beliefs that near-term outlooks are poor.

It is our observation that in bear markets, equity securities that are attractive by our standards may decline in price as much as, if not more than, many general market securities and market indexes. Also, in certain types of frothy markets (such as the new-issue boom of 1967 and 1968) price performance for securities attractive by financial-integrity standards tends to be much less favorable than is the case for many market indexes. Yet, we have no doubt that over time and over all types of markets, the average diligent unaffiliated investor emphasizing this approach will obtain much more satisfactory results, and a higher total return, than could be obtained using any other method of investment available to him. That is why the approach generates confidence and comfort, and why almost all deal men, creditors, major investment bankers, insiders and owners of private businesses with whom we have dealt emphasize it in committing their own funds.

In using the approach, we frequently base investment decisions solely on publicly available information. For example, from 1972 to early 1977 we recommended to outside investors that they accumulate positions in Indian Head convertible debentures as well as in the common stocks of American Manufacturing Corporation, CNA Financial Corporation, First National State Bancorporation,

Mountain States Telephone, National Presto Corporation, Orion Capital Corporation, Barber Oil, Source Capital, Baker Fentress and Christiana Securities, all in reliance on publicly available documents. In other instances, we accumulated positions only after complementing our study of public documents with interviews of managements and others. These other investments included Amterre Development, NN Corporation, Reserve Oil and Gas, and Vindale Corporation.

Obviously, most passive investments will be better investigated if publicly available documents can be supplemented with other information derived from talking to people known to the investigator (know-who) and from using the investigator's special knowledge about particular companies and industries. Nonetheless, in a wide number of instances the public record alone can be quite sufficient.*

It may be instructive in understanding the financial-integrity approach to examine briefly the reasons for our recommendations from 1972 through early 1977, which were based solely on publicly available documents.

In the cases of Indian Head convertible debentures and CNA Financial Corporation common stock, the element triggering these acquisitions was that they were the type of postarbitrage situations discussed in Chapter 17. Postarbitrage is the period after the conclusion of an acquisition in which securities are still left in public hands. Both Indian Head and CNA, when recommended by us, were selling well below the prices at which cash tender offers had taken place and in which new groups gained control of companies. CNA itself was in a weak financial condition, but it was our view that its new and strong parent, Loew's Corporation, would provide whatever financing CNA might need.

American Manufacturing's principal asset was its holdings of a

---

*In the area of contested takeovers, raiders frequently have nothing but the public record to rely upon. It appears that most successful raiders who based their pretakeover analysis on the public record were not faced with unpleasant surprises after they obtained control of companies. The surprises seem mostly to have been pleasant ones. We think this is additional evidence that the public record in many instances is quite good enough to enable investors to analyze satisfactorily.

28 percent interest in Eltra Corporation, a well-financed diversified manufacturing corporation.* The possibility that the company's financial position would be adversely impacted if the results of litigation were adverse seemed remote. American Manufacturing common was selling at a substantial discount from Eltra common. We hoped that someday Eltra might acquire American Manufacturing in much the same way that Getty Oil, in late 1976, proposed to acquire Skelly Oil. But without any real basis in fact that there might be an American Manufacturing–Eltra combination, we viewed American Manufacturing common stock as a special situation; with a realistic basis in fact, we would call the common stock a workout situation.

Mountain States Telephone, 88 percent owned by American Telephone, was somewhat similar. Although it was available on a more attractive statistical basis than American Telephone, there were logical reasons why American Telephone would be benefited if it owned 100 percent of all its operating subsidiaries. Meanwhile, the positive cash-carry feature of Mountain States was attractive, especially in light of the company's record of periodically raising its dividend rate.† (However, it ought to be noted that noncontrol investors holding common stocks or long-term bonds that are margined are, in terms of economic reality, lending or investing long and borrowing short. Changes in short-run interest rates, such as occurred in 1974, can result in changing a positive cash-carry to a dramatically negative one.)

First National State Bancorporation, available at a historically large discount from book value, also afforded an exceptionally high dividend return. And when National Presto was acquired by us, it was selling at a huge discount from a book value consisting largely of surplus cash; despite a clouded operating outlook, it had appeared

---

*American Manufacturing's public disclosures are used as a basis for the discussion in Appendix IV, "Examples of Variables Using the Financial-Integrity Approach."

†"Cash-carry" refers to the relationship of cash income to be received from holding an investment with the cost of money tied up in the investment. "Positive cash-carry" means that dividend or interest income exceeds the cost of borrowing to carry the security.

to be a reasonable candidate for takeover and merger, based on stock-holdings of certain outside groups.

Orion Capital Corporation was created out of the ashes of Equity Funding. Companies are reorganized under Chapter X* of the bankruptcy statutes only after carefully scrutinized plans, which are part of the public record, are circulated and commented upon by trustees, the Securities and Exchange Commission and other interested parties. In addition to this scrutiny, a plan had to be approved by a court as fair, equitable and feasible. "Feasible," in large measure, means that the business's financial position is at least adequate. It was determined in the various studies submitted to the bankruptcy court that Orion's reorganization value was in excess of $11 per share. Orion also, upon emergence from bankruptcy, appeared to be a prime takeover candidate. Orion common stock at the start of trading (when we recommended it) was priced at less than half its reorganization value as determined by the court, the trustees and the Securities and Exchange Commission.

Source Capital, Baker Fentress, Christiana Securities and Barber Oil were all closed-end investment companies whose stocks were available at large discounts from asset value. Source Capital and Barber Oil were takeover candidates. Christiana Securities was a candidate for merger with its affiliated company, E. I. duPont de Nemours.

THE SHORTCOMINGS OF THE FINANCIAL-INTEGRITY APPROACH

For activists and certain aggressive noncontrol investors using this approach, finding securities that are attractively priced based on the standards we have discussed is not as difficult as finding "do-able

---

*In late 1978, a new federal bankruptcy law was enacted. Chapters X and XI of the old bankruptcy law, which were concerned with corporate reorganizations, are now superceded by a new Chapter 11. Also, the old Chapter XII, which was used essentially for the reorganization of real estate partnerships, is now covered by the new Chapter 11.

deals," situations where asset conversions can be made to take place, or where there seem to be probabilities that asset conversions will take place, in the context of cash tenders for control, mergers and acquisitions, going private and liquidations. Thus, for activists in particular, the emphasis may be on spotting attractively priced do-able deals where an asset-conversion event may be made to occur. For these people, financial integrity may be only a secondary consideration; they are more willing to balance the risk–reward equation. In that sense, they differ from us in that they do not necessarily make potential risk a more important measurement than potential reward. Do-ability, which most often entails obtaining control of a business, may become the most important consideration.

The financial-integrity approach to investing is but one approach. It is not a magic formula suitable for all outside investors or even all activists. There are trade-offs and the approach has disadvantages, especially for outside investors. It requires huge amounts of work, especially reading and understanding documents. Know-who—personal relationships with those who are the shakers and movers—is also helpful, and in certain situations essential.

Using know-who does not connote using inside information. Those who use inside information for the purpose of buying and selling securities are violating both specific securities laws and more generalized antifraud provisions of law. Inside information embodies factors that are not generally known but that, if known, would be likely to have a material effect on immediate market prices. This type of information might include forthcoming earnings reports, disclosures of natural resource discoveries or a pending takeover at a price well above current markets. The use of know-who in a financial-integrity approach permits an investor who is personally acquainted with insiders to make intelligent judgments about, say, the character and ability of management, corporate long-range plans or reasons why a business would or would not be vulnerable to competitive inroads.

Timing of any individual investment where the investor lacks any element of control cannot be measured.

Frequently the most attractive securities one uncovers under the financial-integrity approach are traded in inactive markets. This tends to be especially true in postarbitrage periods.

The standards used to minimize investment risk limit the selection of attractive securities. Adherence to the approach results in missing many investment opportunities where securities are attractively priced by standards other than those used by risk-averse investors. In following the approach, an investor, whether activist or outsider, will forgo many equity investments regardless of price if they do not meet all four essential conditions. For example, an emphasis on financial position could prevent one from investing in airline equities (with the possible exceptions of Delta Air Lines and Northwest Airlines), because of a belief that the industry is dangerously financed (an example of on-balance-sheet liabilities) and would be even if reequipment programs were modified; in integrated steel and aluminum companies; in many electric utilities, because they may be encumbered with inordinately large capital expenditures requirements (an example of encumbrances that are not disclosed in accounting statements); and in labor-intensive companies with large pension-plan obligations (an example of off-balance-sheet liabilities that are disclosed in financial-statement footnotes). This does not mean that at certain prices such securities are not very attractive investments for many. They just do not happen to be attractive for adherents to our approach.

Under the financial-integrity approach, securities of issuers controlled by those believed to be predators should be avoided, regardless of price, by both activists and outsiders. The securities avoided are both equities and debt instruments. Significant clues as to who the predators might be are publicly available from documents filed with the SEC. These clues are discussed in Chapter 6, "Following the Paper Trail." Especially pertinent in these documents are disclosures about management remuneration, insider borrowings from the company and transactions between the company and insiders. These disclosures are contained either in the annual-meeting proxy statement or in Part II of the 10-K Annual Report. Disclosures about "litigation" in Part I of the 10-K Annual Report, Part II of the 10-Q Quarterly Report and in footnotes to audited financial statements can also give valuable clues to the caliber of management and control groups. Disclosure of grievances by creditors or securities holders that culminate in lawsuits brought against companies and insiders should serve as warnings that a particular company may not be a satisfactory investment using a risk-minimization approach.

Those using the approach restrict investments to situations where considerable knowledge about companies can be obtained. This is true for both control and noncontrol investors. While reliance on public information only is sufficient—or even more than sufficient for certain types of investments, such as investment companies registered under the Investment Act of 1940 and public utilities—in other areas required public information frequently provides insufficient data for making intelligent decisions, as is usually the case when a company is engaged primarily in mineral exploration activities.

There is a close correlation between the usefulness of financial accounting and the usefulness of public disclosures as tools for making investment decisions. As accounting becomes more reliable, so do required public disclosures.

Most important, since the control and noncontrol groups value using the same standards, there tend to be clear conflicts of interest between insiders and outsiders. Insiders sometimes will create additional values for themselves by forcing out outsiders via the corporation's proxy machinery that they control, by short-form mergers* or by the use of coercive tender offers. Force-outs sometimes can be at extremely low prices, because the insiders, by their actions (or lack of actions), have contributed to the depression of stock prices.

This conflict of interest presents a realistic threat that limits the appeal of a number of equity securities that would otherwise seem attractive using our approach. It is our observation that attempted force-outs at prices we would consider unconscionably low—as in the cases of Schenley Industries in 1971, Transocean Oil in 1974, Kirby Lumber in 1974, Bourns Corporation in 1976 and Valhi Corporation in 1977—are relatively infrequent.

---

*In a short-form merger, stockholders can be forced out of a company in a merger or similar transaction, and have no right to vote on the transaction.

Basically, we think most control groups in most situations attempt to treat their stockholders fairly or are forced to do so by circumstances. Examples of treatment of outside stockholders where prices offered were fair or even generous abound. These include those paid for minority interests in Indian Head, Hudson Pharmaceutical Corporation, Elgin National Industries, Utah International, Otis Elevator Company, Marcor, Veeder Industries and many others.

Nonetheless, outside stockholders are sometimes treated unfairly, and legal recourses available to stockholders are frequently inadequate. First, those who overreach at the expense of stockholders have the independent-appraisal weapon in their arsenal. Major or second-tier investment-banking houses can be retained either to recommend a force-out price or to approve one chosen by boards of directors. Many independent appraisals seem to be based on a theory that if stockholders are given more than they could realize by sale of the shares on the open market, then the deal is per se fair. No real reference is ever made to any standards other than stock-price standards.

Stockholder claims of violations of federal securities law may be only of limited help, since in most instances such suits are controlled by attorneys for stockholders who frequently have to be primarily interested in promoting settlements rather than obtaining full dollar value for stockholders. Federal securities laws are basically concerned with disclosures and with fulfilling fiduciary obligations, not fairness. A recent Supreme Court decision in *Ernst & Ernst* v. *Hochfelder,* however, raises some question as to what can be brought to bear by the private bar against professionals such as auditors who fail to fulfill professional obligations insofar as federal antifraud securities laws are concerned. In *Hochfelder,* the Court said that an auditor is not responsible under antifraud statutes for his own "inexcusable negligence" when conducting an audit, but, rather, he may or may not be responsible where there is "reckless disregard for the truth," and that the auditor is clearly liable under the antifraud statutes only if he is "an intentional participant in a scheme."[2]

Resort to appraisal rights under state law where available is of

[2]74 S. Ct. 1042 (1976).

only limited usefulness because in leading states (a) considerable weight in arriving at value is usually given to market prices, and (b) costs of litigation for dissenting stockholders can be enormous.*

State law can be helpful in affording some protection to outside stockholders in force-out situations. This has become true especially since the supreme court of the leading corporate state, Delaware, ruled in 1977 that force-out transactions ought to have "business purposes," and that stockholders are entitled to "entire fairness."[3] Also, a few states, notably New York, Wisconsin and California, have laws specifically designed to protect stockholders from being unfairly forced out in going-private transactions.† Nonetheless, overall protection for stockholders seems to be limited.

Despite the less than strong legal posture of outside, passive stockholders, we think that in general the threat of forcing out stockholders by predatory managements and control groups is not a realistic deterrent to an investment program based on the financial-integrity approach.

We think that a crucial reason why our approach has been largely ignored in accounting and economic literature is that those writing on the subject tend to attribute the perceived information and analytic needs of traders seeking to maximize total return to all investors.[4] Along with others, we believe that it is futile for outside investors to strive for the maximization of total return. It is our thesis that by not trading and by concentrating on a risk-minimizing approach, outside

---

*Unlike class-action suits in federal court, in appraisal procedures in states such as Delaware and New York dissenting stockholders may be liable not only for their own court costs, including attorneys' and experts' fees, but also for similar costs incurred by the company, in the discretion of the court.

[3]See *Singer* v. *Magnavox Co.*, 380 A. 2d 969, 980 (1977), and *Tanzer* v. *International General Industries, Inc.*, 392 A. 2d 1121 (1977).

†Contrast these statutes in these three states with state-law protections for companies and incumbent managements in corporate contests for control. At this writing, thirty-two states have enacted anti-takeover statutes to protect companies and incumbent managements from raids.

[4]For example, see *Tentative Conclusions on Objectives of Financial Statements of Business Enterprises,* published by the Financial Accounting Standards Board (Stamford, Conn., December 2, 1976).

investors can achieve good-enough results, probably "beating the market" from time to time and on an overall basis, but never continuously. For the vast majority of noncontrol investors, the best way to wealth is not to try for continuous short-term maximization, but to aim for a performance that is good enough over a long horizon. This viewpoint is explored in some depth in the next chapter, "The Significance of Market Performance."

Our approach has, as a practical matter, little to contribute to or learn from efficient-market and efficient-portfolio hypotheses. Such theories are probably valid in describing past records and prognoses for total-return, outside, passive traders. However, these theories are largely irrelevant to any financial-integrity approach.

In order to use our approach well, both activists and passive investors should have practical perspectives about risk and uncertainty. Investors using the approach need patience and fortitude if their investment programs are to succeed. After all, the underlying thesis for the investor is that, given the elements that determine value for him, he knows much more about the particular security he is interested in than the stock market does.

The conventional view of risk in equity securities involves only quality-of-the-issuer considerations.* Our approach is different. For us, risk in equity securities has three distinct elements: quality of the issuer, price of the issue and financial position of the holder.

Section Three, "Disclosures and Information," consists of one non-accounting chapter, "Following the Paper Trail," and two accounting chapters, "Financial Accounting" and "Generally Accepted Accounting Principles." This section describes the types of disclosures available publicly, and discusses their uses and limitations within the context of the financial-integrity approach. Possibly the most important lesson in this section is that once the limitations on public disclosures are understood, the types of disclosures available are not only

---

*The underlying assumption of beta-coefficient theories is that at any moment, a security price is in equilibrium, that is, correctly assesses the trade-off between risk and reward. The beta states that lower-quality securities can appreciate more and decline more than higher-quality securities.

highly relevant to a great deal of analysis, but also extremely reliable
for those following our approach.

Understanding the various factors that make businesses and
financial institutions tick is helpful for those using our approach.
There are four acronyms that serve as a slang shorthand in helping
investors understand businesses, insiders and financial institutions:
TS, OPM, AFF and SOTT. TS stands for *Tax Shelter*, OPM (pro-
nounced "opium") for *Other People's Money*, AFF for *Accounting
Fudge Factor* (something especially relevant for public companies)
and SOTT for *Something Off The Top*. The normal academic assumption is that, as a good first approximation, managements work
in the best interests of stockholders. We believe that relationships
between managements and stockholders, between managements and
companies, between companies and stockholders and between stockholder groups are best viewed as combinations of conflicts of interests and communities of interests.

The normal security-analysis assumption is that certain financial
factors, such as large returns on investment, are good per se, and such
others as intense competition are bad per se; we demur. Appropriate
judgments about most analytical factors, including high profit margins or rapid expansion, depend upon context.

In minimizing investment risk, it is important to distinguish
among variables, depending upon the types of companies being evaluated. Oil companies are not analyzed in the same way electric utilities are, nor are primarily asset-conversion businesses analyzed as
going concerns are. As we stated before, much of conventional
analysis, such as that of Graham and Dodd and *Accounting Principles*,[5] seems to be implicitly based on taking tools especially applicable to a relatively narrow, special case—the equity securities of
public-utility going concerns for example—and then trying to fit
those standards to the analysis of almost every type of business and
security. Such an approach allows earnings to become a common

[5]American Institute of Certified Public Accountants, *Current Text*, Vol. 1, &
Original Pronouncements, Vol. 2, *Accounting Principles* (Chicago: Commerce Clearing House, 1975).

denominator and point of departure. We, in contrast, consider financial integrity to be the more appropriate common denominator and point of departure for most investors.

Financial statements provide the basis for the determination of financial integrity. In determining financial position, it must be noted that the several financial statements are integrally related to each other: there are necessary relationships between book asset values and accounting earnings as well as between estimated asset values and estimated earning power.

As stated previously, we discount the importance of the concept of primacy of earnings for anyone other than total-return traders and possibly also investors in companies that are special cases, such as public utilities. It is our view that those emphasizing reported earnings are, for a number of reasons, out of step with almost everybody in the United States aiming at wealth creation. First, when primacy-of-earnings advocates refer to earnings, they tend to mean earnings as reported for accounting purposes, with a view to giving such a number a high degree of precision, precisely reflective of operating results for a past period; investment results, for example, are normally excluded by these people from earnings. Second, these reported earnings tend to be stressed for two purposes: they are thought to be the single best indicator of what future reported earnings are likely to be (here again we do not agree), and earnings as actually reported are deemed to be at any given moment the single most important contributor in determining the market price of a common stock. We also tend to believe that earnings as reported at any time will impact stock prices. We, however, conclude that in general any such impact lacks significant relevance in a risk-minimizing approach to investments.

Corporate cash and the uses to which it can be put, including distributions to shareholders, are, of course, important to investors. There is an inherent conflict between stockholder needs and benefits from cash distributions, and the needs of companies to retain cash.

There are various methods of distributing cash and property to shareholders, including dividends, share repurchases, liquidation distributions and stock dividends. Stockholders are far from constituting a monolithic group, and among them there are varied and sometimes conflicting interests concerning cash distributions.

In the management of securities portfolios, a positive cash-carry is frequently important—that is, the cash return from holding securities ought to be greater than the cash cost of owning the securities. This sometimes can also be important under our approach because both patience and the use of other people's money are easier to come by if the cash return from investments exceeds the cash cost of owning them.

A basic point about loss companies is that while such companies are sources of tax benefits, for them to have value they have to be "clean shells"—companies in which benefits to be derived from the absence of liabilities for income taxes outweigh the encumbrances to be assumed, either already existing or likely to be created by future activities. This caveat, of course, is part and parcel of our approach, and it gives essentially the same advice to activists buying loss businesses as is given to outside, passive investors buying common stocks.

We think that any person involved with finance can function better if he understands the activities and motivations of other participants in finance. We attempt to impart understanding about the financial world by examining two transactions in some depth in Appendixes I and II. These appendixes are entitled "The Use of Creative Finance to Benefit Controlling Stockholders" and "Creative Finance Applied to a Corporate Takeover."

In the first appendix, the complexities involved in taking Schaefer Brewing public in 1968 are examined. In the Schaefer case, the apparent object of the various transactions was to extract as much cash as possible from the business for the control group and still retain control of the business for that group. Although none of the securities issued to noninsiders in that transaction were suitable for financial-integrity investors, the case is still useful. First, it demonstrates that profits can be obtained in many ways by investors, as, for example, the profits garnered by those members of the public fortunate enough to obtain Schaefer Corporation common stock on the initial underwriting who then sold their stock within the ensuing eighteen months. Second, because the transaction was so complex, much is demonstrated about what motivates various purchasers of securities, from life insurance companies to total-return traders, and about various classes of securities that can be issued. Thus, the appendix is instructive because it demonstrates how insiders used the financial strength inherent in a profitable, almost debt-free business as a basis of extracting maximum cash for themselves, with the result that the successor business became heavily encumbered. The Schaefer case also briefly touches on matters that have to be the concern of any promoter or would-be promoter, including blue sky laws, the National Association of Securities Dealers (NASD) Rules of Fair Practice, Rule 144 and Registration Rights.

In the second appendix, we examine the methods by which Leasco Data Processing Company financed the purchase for cash of the blocks of shares of Reliance Insurance Company, which Leasco believed it needed to acquire if it was to obtain control of Reliance. The appendix is of interest in part because of the extremely attractive consideration that was given to providers of cash so that they obtained (a) a safe, above-average return on a tax-privileged basis as well as (b) an opportunity to participate in potential market appreciation. This was the epitome of an investment that could be deemed to be attractive using the financial-integrity approach. Yet, the transaction was also highly attractive for others, especially Leasco, because it enabled Leasco to tie up key blocks of common stock without risking cash, unless it was to obtain control of Reliance, and also to use "pooling of interests accounting" treatment in the future, with consequent beneficial effects on Leasco's reported earnings to its stockholders.

THE USES AND LIMITATIONS OF FUNDAMENTAL ANALYSIS AND TECHNICAL ANALYSIS

Chapter 3

The Significance of Market Performance

◈

A bargain that stays a bargain is not a bargain.

THE TRADERS' CREDO

THE "IDEALISTIC" VIEW

THERE IS A COMMON BELIEF among many stockholders and lawyers and much of the judiciary that stock market prices are the one realistic measure of value, and that the only way to tell how an investor is doing is by valuing his securities portfolio from time to time, even daily, based on stock market prices.[6] Common sense tells

---

[6]For a good example of how beliefs that stock market prices are the common denominator of value are used, see "Fair Shares in Corporate Mergers and Takeovers" by Victor Brudney and Marvin A. Chirelstein, which appeared in the *Harvard Law Review,* vol. 88, December 1974. The gravamen of the article is that an underlying value is established by stock market prices, but that certain gains over and above market price may be generated by a combination of two companies, and such gains, if any, should be shared with minority stockholders. (Contrast this with our view that there is no necessary relationship at any given time, nor should there be general expectations that there should be any relationship, between the market price of a common stock and the value of a business.)

us that this approach heavily distorts the facts of life because market prices are considerably less important to some securities holders than they are to others.

For stock traders, there are realistic reasons for making stock market prices the only consideration. For investors interested only in secure income, "weight to market" should be zero or on occasion even negative, because even though an investor has an ownership (long) position in a stock, it is conceivable that he would obtain more benefits from short-term declining prices than from steady or rising stock market prices. In gauging investment results for the vast majority of people and institutions, market performance at any moment should be given a weight of considerably more than zero and something quite a bit less than 100 percent. The precise weight, assuming that any precision is desirable or necessary, should be determined by the individual investor.

The concept of weight to different elements of value apparently originated, or at least is most common today, in Delaware appraisal proceedings, where stockholders dissent from a merger or similar proceeding. In these proceedings, it is usual that three elements of value—market value, earnings or investment value, and asset value—are determined. Separate weights are assigned to each of the three elements of value, with weight for all three elements totaling 100 percent. Through the determination of the three elements of value, each separately weighted, an ultimate value is determined. For example, assuming that market value is determined to be 10, with a weight of 25 percent, that earnings value is determined to be 15, with a weight of 55 percent, and that asset value is determined to be 25, with a weight of 20 percent, the ultimate value is obtained in the following manner:

Element of Value	Value	Weight	Net Value
Market	$10	25%	$2.50
Earnings (or investment)	15	55	8.25
Assets	25	20	5.00
Ultimate value		100%	$15.75

Market performance as a gauge of how an investor is doing deserves 100 percent weight when the particular investor does not know anything about the company in which he is investing other than the most superficial stock market statistics, such as market price history, recent earnings, dividend rate, stock-ticker symbol, alleged sponsors and the latest popular "story." It also deserves 100 percent weight when the investor's financial and/or personal position is such that he is vitally affected, or he believes he is vitally affected, by short-term market fluctuations. Such people need instant performance. Items that they perceive to be critical are inside information about corporate events that they believe will have market impact; technical systems that they believe will assist in forecasting general market trends and individual stock-price movements; and trading information that they can either react to or use.

Perhaps the most traumatic and significant event for this group is to see stocks go down, or even in some instances to see stocks fail to go up. Thus, there is a good rationale for their credos, Don't let your losses run,[7] and Get out of stocks that are not moving.

To us, it seems foolish to accept the needs of this group as the norm for purposes of promulgating various securities regulations and accounting rules, yet some of these rules and regulations seem directed strictly toward the desires and needs of those who think day-to-day market prices are all-important.

Many investors, of course, do not weight stock market price as being of 100 percent importance or even anything close to it. Examples of investment groups that are either indifferent to market price fluctuations or hopeful that they will go down on occasion include individual stockholders who would benefit from low market valuations for, say, estate tax or personal-property tax purposes; investors who are primarily interested in maximizing their cash returns and/or continually creating cash for new investment from noninvestment

---

[7]For example, see G. M. Loeb, *The Battle for Investment Survival* (New York: Simon and Schuster, 1965), p. 57:

"Losses must always be 'cut.' They must be cut quickly long before they become of any financial consequence . . . Cutting losses is the one and only *rule* of the markets that can be taught with the assurance that it is always the correct thing to do."

sources; and investors desiring to accumulate large positions, either to exercise control or to influence control shareholders.

It is our view that very few outside investors ought to endow short-run market performance with an all-consuming importance. First, for many, performance has to take a back seat to other considerations in terms of realizing such objectives as the creation of a reasonably well assured regular cash income from interest and dividend payments. Second, for those following the financial-integrity approach, rarely if ever is emphasis given to short-run considerations. Frequently, timing as to when something will happen is indeterminate when securities appear attractive under that approach: its four basic elements give no clues whatsoever to what near-term market performance might be like. Finally, the studies that are part of modern capital theory indicate that those who attempt to beat the market continuously do not usually do so when beating the market is defined as having a total return on a risk-adjusted basis in excess of stock market averages.* We agree with the modern capital theorists that it is a losing exercise for almost all outside investors to try to beat the market by forecasting price movements over any particular length of time, say within the next year. To us, it is true in a perverse way that one cannot beat the market by trying to beat the market. Rather, superior long-term performance comes about by indirection—for example, by buying good values as determined under the financial-integrity approach, and sticking with those holdings in the absence of clear-cut evidence that a significant mistake has been made. Evidence of such mistakes will be found in the results achieved by the business rather than in the price of the business's securities, which at any moment may or may not reflect business reality.

The importance of market performance depends in part on the character of a portfolio, and other things being equal, market performance will be more important when a portfolio is of a fixed size or subject to net withdrawals of cash, as compared with a portfolio that is the continual recipient of new cash to invest. This latter portfolio is in the nature of a dollar averager, and provided that it consists of

---

*Modern capital theory is discussed in Chapter 4.

sound securities, market performance need not be an overriding consideration. Here, poor past performance means, at least in great part, that present purchases are being made on more attractive terms than in the past, whereas good past performances spell less attractive current purchases.

It should be noted, too, that dollar averaging diminishes the need to beat inflation, because changes in the value of money probably will, in the long run, be offset by changes in the returns on securities. This has been particularly true during the fifteen years preceding 1978, when inflation was accompanied by rising interest rates. Cash that could have been invested in commercial paper to return 4 percent in 1964 could be invested the same way to return over 10 percent in 1974 and again in 1978. Cash returns available to such investors increased considerably more than did the cost of living. Among the beneficiaries from such inflation-cum-interest-rate developments were permanent investors in high-grade debt securities, provided new funds were being made available regularly for investment. Such investors included many young people with rising salaries and savings, as well as various types of insurance companies and pension plans.

The typical well-run fire and casualty insurance company is, in part, an example of a dollar-averaging investor. Its performance is measured essentially by its net investment income—income from dividends and interest after all investment expenses except taxes. The insurance company's investment departments normally receive continuous new injections of cash from the underwriting departments, growing out of increases in premium volume and, it is hoped, from underwriting profits. For such companies, as long as interest is not defaulted and dividend rates on securities held in portfolios are not reduced or eliminated, the lower the market value of the portfolio, the higher the returns that will be earned on the new funds being invested. And the higher the returns, the faster net investment income will increase. Fire and casualty investment departments do have some interest in upward market performance on individual securities, since managements prefer the securities they own to rise in price and the new money to be invested in debt or equities that are available at attractive prices. But as long as the business is adequately capitalized, such considerations are distinctly secondary to the primary purposes of the portfolios—the protection of the policyholder. That tends to restrict investments to generally recognized high-quality securities that are marketable, and to the creation of net investment income.

As a matter of fact, it was the continuing declines in the market value of portfolios of the bonds and mortgages that made up the bulk of life insurance portfolios (since interest rates were on a generally rising trend) that contributed importantly toward making life insurance stocks, in general, one of the outstanding growth investments in the twenty years after World War II. Had the market value of their portfolios not been declining, the increases in investment income would have been much slower than was actually the case.

It is true that some insurance companies tend to be harmed in bear markets because their capital adequacy is measured by regulatory authorities on a basis that values common stocks at market. Huge increases in net investment income arising out of new money being employed for high cash return cannot, in these cases, compensate for capital inadequacy. Nonetheless, the normal economic desires of such investors are that weight to market will be considerably less than 100 percent almost all the time.

OUTSIDERS, INSIDERS AND MARKET PRICE

Indeed, for most investors, market performance as an element in measuring true investment results should have a weight of less than 100 percent. An outside investor holding a completely marketable security should give weight of close to zero to market performance whenever he knows or has reason to believe that the security's real worth is *not* closely related to current market prices, and when he knows that he will neither need to liquidate in the near future nor to use the security owned as collateral for borrowings.

There is a school of thought that seems to hold that outside investors with that degree of certainty about investments in companies over which they have no control are bound to be unsuccessful— that the real world just never justifies so much confidence in a security. We disagree. It appears that many of the most successful outside investments have resulted from having such confidence, whether it was by buying and holding General Motors common through the 1933 decline, or by acquiring Japanese insurance stocks at the depth of that country's extremely sharp business recession and stock market crash of 1965, or even by buying such Japanese securities in 1970 after they had doubled, or Xerox and Holiday Inn when they were emerging securities, or Chicago Northwest Railway and Berkshire Hathaway when they were workout situations, or deep-discount, high-yield, medium-grade bonds in 1974.

For insiders and quasi-insiders, as their security holdings become less marketable because of restrictions on sale or otherwise, and as they attain positions in which they can exercise control over a corporation's affairs, market price tends to become less important than the fundamentals of the business. The purchasers of F. & M. Schaefer Corporation "restricted" common in 1968 at $1 per share (see Appendix I) did have an interest in the market price of Schaefer common stock after the company went public, and many obviously had to be pleased when the market price climbed to 59 in 1970. Yet, what was happening to the business was far more important to them. For them, the key factor in 1970 was not the outstanding market performance of the common stock, but evidence of sluggish corporate performance because of competition from national beer brands. The high price of Schaefer stock would have been useful to these bargain purchasers in a nonpsychological sense only if they could realize something based on those prices by selling their stock, even at a discount from market (they did not and most could not), or if Schaefer Corporation used the high price to issue more equity securities, either to get cash into the company or to acquire earnings properties.

MARKET PERFORMANCE AND OVERALL PORTFOLIOS

Market performance is a much more important gauge of investment results for a whole portfolio of marketable securities than it is for an individual security. For example, consider an investment program in unsponsored, special situations where the portfolio companies have high financial integrity and where securities are selling at prices substantially (say, 50 percent or more) below what the companies would be worth as private corporations. At any one time there might be three to five such securities in a portfolio. The precise timing as to when any one of these securities might enjoy substantial price appreciation is indeterminate. However, if over a period of, say, six months to a year none of these securities appreciates even in a generally declining market, it is fair to conclude that investment results are poor. But the poor results would be attributable more to poor analysis (that is, the securities were not really attractively priced in the first place) than to other factors that explain poor performance for general market securities portfolios, such as weak general market conditions or an uncertain economic outlook.

The one time when market performance of portfolios that are attractive by financial-integrity standards seems bound to be poor compared with the general market, no matter how good the analysis of the securities, is during periods of raging bull markets in speculative-grade growth stocks, such as occurred from 1961 to 1962 and in 1968. Even in this situation, though, workout portfolios still should show at least fair returns—say, not less than 10 percent—on the market values of the funds invested.

It is important to note that one of the reasons outside investors using our approach cannot give large weight to near-term market performance is that the factors that frequently will have greatest near-term market impact are not what the investor believes alters the fundamental outlook for the company in which he has invested. These factors, which he may not deem particularly important but which are likely to have a strong, immediate market impact, include the following:

- Changes in general stock market levels
- Changes in interest rates
- Cyclical changes in the economy
- Quarterly earnings reports
- Dividend changes

In considering the weight that should be given to stock market prices, it is important to remember that a stock market price is not business or corporate value, but a realization value based on the price at which a common stock could be sold. Therefore, market value as a realization figure is a very realistic figure for a shareholder who owns, say, 1,000 shares of Chase Manhattan Corporation common selling at 35. However, it does not follow that 35 represents a realistic value for all the Chase Manhattan common shares outstanding. There is no way other than in a merger or acquisition that all the Chase Manhattan shares can be sold on the market for 35 a share or any other price. Thus, statements about an individual's present worth, obtained by multiplying his holdings by the quoted market value of his stock, have limited operational meaning in many contexts. Market mathematicians may multiply numbers together, but frequently there is a difference between what the numbers are and what they mean.

MEASURING MARKET PERFORMANCE

Comparative measures of portfolio performance are imprecise. Different investment objectives, restrictions and financing make comparisons of market performance difficult. Thus, to say that Standard and Poor's 425 Industrials outperformed the XYZ Fund (or that the XYZ Fund outperformed Standard and Poor's 425 Industrials) by 10.2 percent or 11.5 percent during the past year is of limited usefulness.

Another comparative measure of limited usefulness entails adjusting investment results for inflation indexes, such as the U.S. Department of Labor Consumer Price Index. A comparison tends to be most meaningful when it can be related to specifics rather than to general indexes. For example, assume a cash-return investor—say, a manufacturing corporation with surplus liquidity—earned 7.2 percent after taxes on its investment portfolio during a period when the Consumer Price Index was up 10.1 percent but the corporation's specific costs were up 2.2 percent. Did the corporation fare well? In some very meaningful contexts, the answer is probably yes.

PROFESSIONAL MONEY MANAGERS AND
BEATING THE MARKET

Certain economists believe strongly that the goal of professional money managers is to beat the market.[8] If professional money managers fail to beat the market either individually or en masse, this is taken as evidence that they are useless. Indeed, it is stated that the outside investor does best by investing only in Index Funds—that is, unmanaged companies whose portfolios equal the Dow Jones Industrial Average or Standard and Poor's 500 Stock Index.

The kindest word we have for this point of view is that it is amateurish. First, it ought to be obvious that the vast majority of professional money managers have fiduciary obligations that require them to do much more than beat the market. Among those duties are maintenance of cash income and cash principal. Is it important that a strongly capitalized insurance company outperform the market even though its net investment income is increasing at a compound rate of 10 percent a year and even though in no instance had interest payments been passed or dividends cut or omitted on any security in the company's portfolio? We think not. The prime goal of the insurance company's professional money manager is, of course, cash income, not market performance.

Many economists also go one step further and say that there is no need for Securities and Exchange Commission disclosures and other investor protections. This viewpoint fails to observe the obvious. By and large, securities markets in the United States have been healthier during the past forty years that the SEC has been in existence than ever before. Also, financial analysis has become more important. Furthermore, the quality of securities has gone up, at least as measured by the ability of issuers to provide securities holders with cash returns, that is, payments of interest and dividends. Would this be the

[8]Myron Scholes, "Professional Measurement—Past, Present and Future," *Evaluation and Management of Investment Performance* (Charlottesville, Va.: The Financial Analysts Research Foundation, 1977).

case if there were no professional money managers and no SEC? Who knows? Perhaps if the environment were what these economists recommend, the Dow Jones Industrials in mid-1978 would be closer to 300 than to 800. But if it were 300, the average portfolio of marketable securities would have a market performance about average—the same as now.

In summary, it is important to note that the importance to be given to market performance or total return varies from situation to situation. Sometimes total return is all-important to an outside investor; in other instances, it is hardly of any moment. Unfortunately, many scholars and jurists tend to give market performance the same weight for all investments that it deserves in trading situations—100 percent. This unthinking emphasis is particularly unfortunate, partly because it gives stock market prices an emphasis that almost no one operating a business agrees with, and partly because it seems to foster attempts to beat the market on a relatively continuous basis—something most outside investors will never be able to do.

PERSPECTIVE ON BAILOUTS AND THE SIGNIFICANCE OF MARKET PERFORMANCE

In a meaningful sense, everyone who invests in a security seeks a return, or bailout, on that investment. Most of the time, "bailout" refers to the realization of cash benefits, but this is not so in one case—when ownership of a security results in obtaining various benefits associated with control of companies. Bailouts take many forms, only one of which is an ability to sell, or marketability. Insofar as other forms of bailout are unavailable, marketability and therefore market performance become increasingly important. And insofar as alternative bailouts are available, the significance of market performance diminishes. These other forms of bailout, more fully discussed in Chapter 14, encompass cash payments to securities holders by the issuer itself.

Holders of debt instruments have a contractual right to receive periodic interest income and eventual return of principal; therefore, cash bailouts tend to be far more assured for them than for holders of common stocks. Accordingly, marketability tends to be significantly less important for a bond than for a common stock. Indeed, most long-term debt instruments, such as many of the tax-free obligations of municipalities, private placements held by life insurance companies and most mortgage loans held by various types of institutional investors, are probably not marketable at all. This difference in the significance of marketability between debt and equity is even recognized in certain regulatory areas: insurance regulations require that debt holdings usually be carried on the company's books for statutory purposes at amortized cost, whereas common stocks are usually carried at market.

Insofar as common-stock ownership represents control, the importance of market performance and marketability tends to be diminished significantly. Control usually allows for two types of bailouts: first, cash bailouts through the ability to control dividend policy and to obtain salaries and fees; and second, nonmonetary bailouts through the ability of controllers to create for themselves one or more benefits that can be described as part of the three P's—power, prestige and perquisites.

In addition, there are many stockholders who buy dividend-paying stocks and whose primary objective is income. As a matter of fact, many hold utility common stocks on the theory that present dividend rates are safe and indeed are likely to be increased periodically. To these holders, market bailouts are not important, and they view their holdings in much the same way as do holders of debt instruments, with the essential difference that such common stockholders perceive themselves as holding a "bond" on which "interest" payments are to be increased periodically. To such holders, market performance tends to be a minor consideration.

In contrast, there are security holders for whom market price tends to assume paramount importance, because market is where such holders are seeking their bailouts. These types of security holders fall into three categories. The first is the common stockholder holding minority interests in which dividend income is either insignificant or not part of the holder's investment objectives. The second type is the control stockholder and company seeking to sell securities or to issue them in merger and acquisition transactions. And third is the holder who does not have a strong financial position, especially the outside investor or trader who has borrowed or intends to borrow heavily to finance his portfolio.

Chapter 4

Modern Capital Theory

"What do you want to run for this year, Joe?"
"Treasurer."
"But you cannot even add!"
"I didn't say I wanted to run for assistant treasurer."

MODERN CAPITAL THEORY encompasses efficient-market theories and efficient-portfolio theories.

The efficient-market theory is based on the assumption that most of the markets for common stocks can be regarded as having a sufficiently high volume of trade and sufficient flexibility so that no individual trader has a perceptible effect on price and special information will be discounted by the market almost immediately. It indicates that the small outside trader can neither influence nor beat the market by himself.

The basic idea behind an efficient portfolio is as follows. Suppose that an individual knows how he reacts to risk and that he must choose a portfolio from a collection of different financial instruments, such as bonds, stocks or cash. Furthermore, suppose that he must evaluate each instrument accurately in terms of risk and expected return, and that he is required to evaluate how the risk on one instrument is related to another. (He must know, for example, how changes in price of the stocks of two companies in the same industry are related; that, say, tobacco stocks or chemical stocks generally show a tendency to move as a group.) Given all of this information and the presumption that it is accurate, an efficient portfolio is one that contains a mixture of holdings such that it provides the largest expected return for a given level of risk.

It is our view that there is nothing in this book to indicate that the theories noted above are anything but valid and useful when viewed narrowly from the perspective of outside investors who strive primarily for total return. That is, efficient portfolios and efficient markets seem to describe well the environment faced by the stock trader who does not happen to be someone who also obtains something off the top in the form of fees, commissions or other trading advantages.

Total return at any given moment is a maximum valuation as measured by the sum of the present market price of securities held, and by the cash income derived from interest and dividends during the period securities are held. But many investors cannot be characterized as the kind of total-return, outside investors or traders to whom modern capital theories are applicable. In any event, this book is not directed toward nonactivists who attempt to beat the market continuously.

For all others engaged in the purchase, sale and holding of equity securities, modern capital theory as embodied in efficient-market and efficient-portfolio hypotheses is irrelevant.* It is to them that this book is directed. Specifically, technical theories lack relevance to those outside investors who are primarily interested in income, to dollar averagers, to special-situation investors who ignore timing considerations and to all activists.†

---

*Even when viewed as abstract theory, the efficient-market writings appear to us to be unsatisfactory. The theorizing fails to account for thin markets, price-formation mechanisms, nonsymmetric information and general equilibrium considerations. These items can be and have been treated by methods of noncooperative game theory.

†Although in terms of strict econometric analysis there is no hard statistical evidence that these groups have outperformed the efficient-market advocates, there is also no clear evidence that they have not. Furthermore, many of these investors may hardly be conscious, if conscious at all, of whether or not they are outperforming the market.

Efficient-portfolio theory assumes implicitly that at any given moment, the price of any stock is in equilibrium, balancing the perceived prospects of reward against the perceived risk of loss. As this book points out, however, even though stock prices may appear to be equilibrium prices to total-return, outside investors, there is no reason why that should be true for anyone else. Indeed, considering the premiums paid to acquire control of companies, it is rather obvious that the equilibrium price that an acquirer is willing to pay for control of a business is different from the equilibrium price that outside investors pay to purchase shares of stock in the open market. These two equilibrium prices are, at most, only loosely related to each other. And, of course, the two prices should not be expected to be close, because the variables the control buyer considers to be important in making his investment decisions are usually different from the variables most outside investors believe are crucial to their determinations of value.

We believe that there are many efficient markets or close-to-efficient markets, such as markets for money, many commodities and high-grade corporate bonds. From the perspective of the total-return, outside investor—that is, the securities trader seeking a maximum short-run return—even markets for common stocks may be efficient. However, such efficiencies seem less than appropriate considerations for common-stock investors who have goals other than short-run profit maximization. For one thing, specific items of information mean absolutely different things to different common-stock investors. For example, a large supply of stock overhanging the market would logically be a reason for encouraging the total-return, outside investor to sell. Equally logically, such information would be a reason for encouraging a potential control buyer to start a long-term stock accumulation program.

For another thing, efficient-market theories assume that outside investors and their advisers are highly capable and are able on the average to interpret information properly. As far as we can tell, there is no empirical evidence to support such a view. Indeed, we suspect that many stock researchers and security analysts are relatively incompetent in either analyzing or understanding businesses. Incompetence of analysts, incidentally, is just as logical an explanation of why equity markets seem efficient as the view that information is competently absorbed and immediately reflected in market prices. Unquestionably, there are many, many extremely competent practitioners within the financial community. Relatively few of them, however, seem to make a career out of servicing the perceived needs of total-return, outside investors. Rather, the best and finest brains on Wall Street seem to gravitate to fields such as arbitrage, corporate finance, private placements, mergers and acquisitions, and becoming control principals in companies.

THE COMPUTER AND MATHEMATICAL ANALYSIS

To date, the contributions of computers and mathematical analysis to security analysis, corporate finance and portfolio analysis appear to be limited to technical rather than fundamental approaches. These methods simply are not useful much of the time in most investment situations. This is so because most of the time in the complex world of finance, the sneaky little nonquantifiable variable or the ugly little fact lurking in some financial legal document that has been left out of the model happens to be a key factor in an analysis.

Does this mean that the mathematical model builders who study financial problems and who grind out large computer runs are useless both in practice and in the creation of a body of knowledge that may eventually be useful? No, it does not. What it does mean is that they, like cost accountants, lawyers, bookkeepers, and other technicians and consultants, have a limited applied value to actual investing. They can help to work out details and to structure the banks of information they are given. They can tell you what the real yield will be from a debenture with an 8 percent coupon, selling at 84¾, prepayable at the issuer's option at 105 after five years and maturing in 1990. But there is nothing to indicate that in general there is anything in mathematical finance that makes it a very good tool for picking the key controlling variables and factors in an equity-investment situation that involves more than a straightforward problem in actuarial science or a comparison of relative costs of money.

This will become clearer as we look at the three major topics that fall under the broad category of mathematical systems applied to finance. They are (1) systems for playing the market, (2) arbitrage and (3) the design and balancing of portfolios.

ON SYSTEMS FOR PLAYING THE MARKET

> *I've a system that's devilishly clever*
> *that I have learned from a croupier friend,*
> *and should go on winning forever,*
> *but I do seem to lose in the end.*

CANDIDE

The dreams of the roulette player, the horseplayer and the technical-market analyst are all variants of the same belief: that just by studying the previous spin of the wheel, the form sheet or the action of the market, a magic mathematical formula will enable the market player to use a "scientific system" to beat the game.

Granger and Morgenstern[9] and several others have shown that for the individual devotee who confines himself to following the movements of the market, tomorrow's prices are linked to today's by a random walk. In other words, there is *no* system that can remove the uncertainty of period-to-period fluctuations.

In particular, Granger and Morgenstern cast considerable doubt on a series of old wives' tales. Are there significant *seasonal variations* in stock prices? They find no evidence. Do certain stock-price movements lead others? The answer is no! Can stock prices be predicted from the "technical analysis" of price charts? The answer is no.

There are two groups of individuals who limit their interests to prices and trading volume, without concern for detailed study of the

[9]C. W. Granger and O. Morgenstern, *Predictability of Stock Market Prices* (Lexington, Mass.: D. C. Heath, 1970).

firms behind the stocks and the economy behind the firms. These are (1) chartists, or technical-market analysts, and (2) random-walk theorists.

The chartists believe that by studying the charts alone they can divine market psychology and the dynamics of price movements. A true chartist, who drinks in his numbers "straight," may even avoid reading company reports because they would dilute his thinking.

The best-known chartist theory is the Dow theory, and a devotee of this and the many other chartist techniques soon learns his own language and looks for "triangles," "heads and shoulders," "significant reversals" and so forth.

The first question we might ask about the chartist approach is, Is it necessarily nonsense or illogical or irrational? The answer is no. One could agree that the movements of the market reflect aggregate behavior. Perhaps in the future, some behavioral scientist will be able to find a chartist method that works. Up until now, however, the track record of the chartists taken as a whole seems poor.

Opposed to the chartists are the random-walk theorists. They are frequently completely misunderstood by most of those who have heard of them. All that the random-walk theorists claim is the reverse of what the chartists claim. The random-walk proponents argue that at any instant, price changes follow no predictable pattern. In the language of the statisticians, they act like a set of random numbers.

It is important to understand that the random-walk theorists are playing the same game as the chartists. They are allowing themselves as information only prices and volumes of trade. They are *not* concerned with prediction based upon any type of basic economic analysis or inside information.

The evidence supports the random-walk theorists. Using the relatively advanced statistical techniques of spectral analysis, Granger and Morgenstern[10] as well as others such as Mandelbrot[11] have obtained clear negative results. Given the trading information alone, there is no evidence that short-term price changes can be predicted.

[10]Granger and Morgenstern, *op. cit.*

[11]B. Mandelbrot, "The Variations of Certain Speculative Prices," *Journal of Business,* XXXVI (1963), pp. 392–417.

We agree basically with the conclusions of the random-walk theorists. Using only trading information, we think there is no predictability of short-term price movements in the markets.

The results of the random-walk theorists should tell the intelligent investor something that some of us strongly suspected—that is, that outside investors could spend their time more wisely than by trying fancy calculations or even simple rules on the numbers that do not have the story. The random-walk results imply that the various systems—filter rules, formula-timing theory and so on—will not work.[12]

The general idea behind a filter rule is as follows: using a 2 percent filter, if the daily closing price of a security goes up at least 2 percent, buy it and hold it until the price moves down at least 2 percent from a high. At that time, sell and go short until another significant reversal, at which point you cover and go long again.

The formula-timing plans provide simple investment rules. Graham and Dodd attribute the original plans to the administrators of the Yale University and Vassar College endowments. There was a flurry of interest in these plans in the late 1940's, as can be seen from the writings of Ketchum,[13] Weston[14] and others. The simplest plan is dollar averaging, which has the investor purchase equal dollar amounts of securities at equal intervals of time.

Possibly the best thing that can be said about the blind application of mechanical rules is that they should prevent the investor from being suckered into go-go markets or into the mass-psychology flights of fancy that sweep across the exchanges on occasion.

ON ARBITRAGE

Arbitrage is an occupation for the professional. It is a special topic, and it calls for a detailed understanding, plenty of calculation, a

[12]S. S. Alexander, "The Movements in Speculative Markets: Trends or Random Walks," *Industrial Management Review,* II (1961), pp. 7–26.

[13]M. D. Ketchum, "Investment Management Through Formula Timing Plans," *Journal of Business,* XX (1947), pp. 157–58.

[14]J. F. Weston, "Some Theoretical Aspects of Formula Timing Plans," *Journal of Business,* XXII (1949), pp. 249–70.

minimization of trading costs (a common-stock arbitrager probably should be a member of a New York Stock Exchange firm) and a meticulous attention to detail. Thorpe and Kassouf have a good professional book on the subject, which describes what arbitragers do and leaves the reader with a clear impression that a professional arbitrager of this variety earns his extra returns from the market by work.[15] Since these authors are what they claim to be, they can afford to publish their system because they know that few readers will be dedicated and skilled enough to follow their advice in detail. The disadvantages of the possible increase in competition is more than offset by the publicity and professional recognition resulting from publishing their book. Furthermore, much of Thorpe's competitive edge is protected by his own computer programs. Professional arbitrage, especially risk arbitrage, is discussed briefly in Chapter 17.

PORTFOLIO BALANCING

An important development in the application of relatively mathematical methods to the stock market came about with the work on portfolio selection, originally developed by Harry Markowitz.[16] On Wall Street today, fat books of calculations on security-risk evaluation and the beta coefficient are churned out monthly by such firms as Merrill Lynch Pierce Fenner and Smith. "Beta" is the estimated market sensitivity of a stock, measured in terms of an expected incremental percentage return associated with a one percent change in return of the Standard and Poor's 500 Index or a comparable index.

What are the assumptions behind the portfolio-selection work? What does it mean? For whom is it useful and what are its limitations? These are the fundamental questions we must answer in order to put this work into perspective.

Markowitz assumes that an analysis of a group of stocks has

[15]E. O. Thorpe and S. T. Kassouf, *Beat the Market—A Scientific Market System* (New York: Random House, 1967).

[16]H. M. Markowitz, *Portfolio Selection* (New Haven, Conn.: Yale University Press, 1959).

been performed. Furthermore, the portfolio manager not only can form a picture of the individual riskiness of any stock in particular, he also can calculate the correlation among the returns from given stocks. For example, industries as a whole may encounter good or bad times; thus there may be a more direct relationship between the behavior of the stock of General Motors and Ford than, say, General Motors and AT&T.

A problem which faces a mutual-fund manager or any other individual who has to run many millions of dollars is that in his selection of a portfolio he may have to consider trading expected returns for safety. If there were the choice of portfolios A and B, both of which had the same expected returns but one of which, say B, had greater uncertainty, clearly A would be superior. The whole of the Markowitz analysis is aimed at finding efficient portfolios, or portfolios such that any improvement in expected returns could be obtained only at the cost of increasing risk. Suppose we had three portfolios, A with 7 percent expected return and 10 percent risk, B with 6 percent expected return and 10 percent risk, and C with 8 percent expected return and 11 percent risk. Portfolio B would be called inefficient because A offers more with no added risk. C, however, has a bigger risk than A, but a higher expectation. Thus, the choice between A and C is a matter for the portfolio manager to decide— trading risk versus expected return.

The basic approach of the Markowitz method is to select a list of stocks, measure the historical average return from each over some selected time range, determine a measure of the variability in the returns from each stock by calculating a statistic known as the standard deviation, and then calculate the level of correlation in the stock movements—that is, the degree that various stocks appear to move together in a market. These calculations serve as the basic data from which to examine the expected returns and risk associated with a portfolio consisting of any mixture of holdings of the basic stocks.

Markowitz stresses that a portfolio analysis begins where security analyses leave off. The security analyst need not use historical data to judge the expected return and variability of a stock; he may have many other methods to do so. Furthermore, consideration must be given to taxes, assets other than stocks, trading costs and many other detailed variables that a realistic model must take into account.

We stress security analysis of the most fundamental sort, corporate finance and self-analysis. We emphasize how to evaluate individual stocks, and how the merits of these stocks fit in with individual goals and financial plans. We believe that in the case of the individual investor who is reasonably sophisticated, problems occur far more with security analysis than with portfolio selection. All of the computer runs in the world will not help the investor if he is selecting from a menu of a dozen poorly analyzed issues. If, on the other hand, by following a financial-integrity approach and seeing angles that others have not seen he has four or five potentially superior stocks, he scarcely needs portfolio analysis to calculate what to do.

If you are managing the Dreyfus Fund and the daily pressures of several hundred million are on you, our advice is to obtain computer runs which suggest changes in the composition of your portfolio. You may not like what they suggest and will probably end up by doing what you intended to do in the first place. Or you may modify both your portfolio and the one suggested by the computer. Nevertheless, as the runs are now relatively cheap and the basic idea behind the portfolio-selection method is sound, it is a useful exercise when the sums and the need for diversification are large enough.

FUNDAMENTAL SECURITY ANALYSIS AND CORPORATE FINANCE

In spite of the frequent assumptions of many economists about the perfection and efficiency of markets, it has been our observation that where control of businesses is not involved, there are fewer individuals capable of analyzing equity securities in depth than there are opportunities to analyze.

The fashion in thought among many of those who teach the more mathematical brands of financial analysis is indicated in this quote on fundamental security analysis.

There are thousands of professional fundamental security analysts at work in the United States . . . As a result of the efforts of this army of professional fundamental analysts, the price of any publicly listed and traded security represents the best estimate available at that moment of the intrinsic value of that security. In fact, the fundamental analysts do such a good job, there is no reason for anyone who is not a full time professional to bother with fundamental analysis.[17]

As far as we can tell, the above statement could not be more wrong. Good fundamental security analysis involves perception, training, understanding and a high degree of abstraction in implicit or explicit model building—that is, in picking the right variables and causal relations. There are not too many skilled practitioners, especially among that vast army more interested in predicting stock market actions than in following fundamental approaches.

An interesting book on the simulation of trust investments was devoted to building a computer simulation of the behavior of a bank trust officer in selecting portfolios for customers.[18] The book showed how this could be done with considerable success. It has an important lesson to teach us: the legal and institutional constraints on the average trust officer are so large that it does not require an extremely sophisticated program to be able to perform roughly as well as the officer.

In our opinion, it will be a long, long time before anyone builds a computer program of a first-class security analyst that can perform in anywhere near the manner he performs.

CALCULATION OR EVALUATION

We have suggested that computers may not be the great new conquerors of Wall Street, insofar as the analysis of equity securities is

---

[17]J. R. Francis and S. H. Archer, *Portfolio Analysis* (Englewood Cliffs, N.J.: Prentice Hall, 1971), p. 187.

[18]C. P. E. Clarkson, *Portfolio Selection: A Simulation of Trust Investment* (Englewood Cliffs, N.J.: Prentice Hall, 1962).

concerned. However, it is important not to underestimate the considerable and valuable contribution that computers have made and will continue to make in other financial areas, such as the automated quotation system, back-office record keeping and the analysis of money-market instruments.

There is little doubt that a number of talented analysts have prospered using complicated computer calculations, especially in areas such as options and commodity trading. There will be more complicated methods that will replace them or improve upon them. But these individuals, like other superior analysts or deal makers, earn their livings by being professionals and by being able to judge the limits as well as the power of their type of analyses. Markowitz and Thorpe may well have been able to use their skills to do better than average; but it seems as though Ben Graham and some of his non-computer colleagues have also prospered.

Much of the work of economic theorists has been based on such assumptions as the existence of perfect capital markets, firms run by managements with the single purpose of looking after their stockholders, a world with perfect accounting and clearly understood information. In such a world, the advanced economic theorist is willing and able to make allowances for uncertainty in the form of probability distributions over various events. But in the world that we live in, statistical uncertainty is one of our least worries. Of course we want to be able to get figures and statistics. The problem that faces any serious analyst, however, is more what the figures mean, and not so much what the figures happen to be. It may not be significant to know only that Company X's real estate holdings are carried on its books at \$1.5 million or \$1.3 million; but those numbers, coupled with the information that they represent 100,000 acres of California coastal land carried at the 1880 purchase price, are significant.

We believe that economic thinking is invaluable to good financial analysis. A full understanding that investment in one project implies investment forgone in another is a lesson that many individuals find hard to learn. Yet, at the same time as we endorse economic thinking, we feel that the relevance of such economic theory to public or personal economic problems is minimal, not because we are opposed to abstract thinking, but because we are opposed to poor models of economic reality, a misemphasis on the controlling variables in our economy and a blind belief that by leaving out the institutional facts of life, somehow a mathematical financial analyst is going to produce a great general abstract theory of value.

A textbook on portfolio analysis begins with the following statement:

Changes are occurring rapidly in the teaching of investments. Investigation of the legal intricacies of the various securities, the tax status of different sources of income, how a stock exchange operates, the needs of the various investing institutions, and other descriptive and institutional matters are giving way to deeper analysis. The newer courses treat problems on a more abstract and general level.[19]

We believe that such a statement really means that some of the business schools in the United States have faculty who prefer the comfort of teaching mathematical techniques in the hope that it will better train students to learn about the real world later, rather than teaching them about the real world now. Perhaps they are right. We disagree. It is not that we think that abstractions are unimportant. It is just that, we think, the more that people who are engaged in investments understood about the real world, the better off they will be.

One further example should help to illustrate our point. In the perfectly liquid, friction-free, tax-free world of much of microeconomic theory, the statement that on December 18, 1974, Company X had a net worth of $475,000 has a specific meaning. In the world that we live in, virtually any individual who by any measure is worth around half a million is not in a position to calculate his wealth at any point of time with much accuracy unless the purpose for evaluation and conditions for liquidation are all specified. It will be one value for estate planning, another for income taxes and yet another in obtaining a loan.

Economic thinking is critically important in interpreting and understanding tendencies in economic systems. But tendencies should

[19]Francis and Archer, *op. cit.,* p. 3.

not be confused with actualities. It is likely that there is some tendency toward efficiency, even for equity markets. Among other things, rules and regulations of the Securities and Exchange Commission have resulted in increased informational efficiency of U.S. securities markets. However, when we look at the history of the New York Stock Exchange over the last sixty years, it can scarcely be described as a mad rush toward economic efficiency, even though there probably has been some tendency in that direction.

Chapter 5

Risk and Uncertainty

Is this a game of chance? Not the way I play it.

W. C. FIELDS

EVERY INVESTMENT situation involves an element of risk. Something can always go wrong. The investor can, of course, work to understand and minimize the risks inherent in his financial activities, but he cannot hope to eliminate them.

The omnipresence of risk may seem all too obvious to the reader. Many outsiders, though, seem to believe that some investors—specifically insiders—can wholly avoid uncertainty and risk. Even the insider who obtains outstanding bargains cannot do so without a degree of uncertainty. (Consider the F. & M. Schaefer Corporation discount purchase, detailed in Appendix I.) To say, then, that insiders get a "free ride" is far from the truth. They usually assume risks when they invest in securities. It is true, however, that the outside investor faces greater risks and uncertainties than the insider, for a number of reasons.

For one thing, the outsider cannot acquire complete knowledge of a company, no matter how many documents he studies or how intimate he is with management. Even in the case of investment trusts registered under the Investment Company Act of 1940, which are subject to the most complete public disclosure requirements in existence, the outside investor sees only quarterly portfolio transactions. He cannot find out about day-to-day investment changes. In fact, if by some chance he did find out about them and chose to act on the basis of his knowledge, he would assume the risk of possibly violating the antimanipulative provisions of the securities laws.

Aside from the handicap of incomplete knowledge, the outsider (and the insider as well) is always faced with the possibility that his analysis is wrong. This may be due to out-and-out error, such as a failure to account for some crucial factor in an evaluation of a company. For example, in 1972 one of the authors recommended Okonite subordinated bonds, which were the principal debt of Okonite Corporation. The debentures were selling around 42, to yield about 13 percent. Okonite appeared to be a financially capable and strong issuer. What the author failed to take into account, though, was that Okonite's parent, Omega Alpha, a weak, bootstrapped company, could merge Okonite into itself without obtaining bondholders' consent. The merger did occur. The debentures may or may not eventually have a workout value exceeding 42, depending on the outcome of Omega Alpha's Chapter X bankruptcy proceedings.

Analysis may also fail because of a misappraisal of management. Such appraisals are crucial in many areas of financial analysis and especially in the field of emerging securities. We do not know, however, of any reasonably objective standards by which to judge whether a management is "good," except for the standard of honesty. American Telephone's management may be fairly good for running Telephone; it would be horrible for Vindale, a sectional-home manufacturer.

Even if the outside investor avoids errors in his analysis or appraisal of management, he may still turn out to be wrong, simply because the future is unpredictable. The cash-return investor who buys a broad range of long-term, high-grade, income-producing securities may find that high interest rates caused by a tight money market substantially depress the market value of his investment, as was the case from 1966 to 1975. Or an investor using the financial-integrity approach may find that the company whose common stock he has chosen has dissipated its assets. An example is the experience of Pacific Coast Properties in the mid-1960's. That company had a highly sophisticated and very well regarded control group with a long record of success, and it enjoyed a huge cash position. The company loaned the bulk of its surplus cash to VTR, a marginal company. When VTR defaulted, Pacific Coast Properties common stock plummeted from $10 to about $1, and the company, now heavily burdened with debt, has asset holdings (primarily California real estate and a large tax-loss carry-forward) which may have little or no net value.

Finally, even if the outsider is correct in his analysis that a security has large intrinsic values that are not dissipated, there is no certainty that he will ever be able to realize these values. For one thing, the values may not be reflected in the stock market for an indefinite period of time. For example, U.S. banks and utilities have enjoyed steadily rising earnings and dividends (as well as revenues and net asset values) over the past decade. Yet in 1974, Standard and Poor's 60 Utility-Stock Average ranged between 40 and 24, as compared with a range of between 60 and 51 in 1961. Price–earnings ratios had shrunk during the interim, and sixty Utilities that had sold at from nineteen to twenty-five times earnings in 1960 sold at only six to nine times in 1974. It sometimes happens too, as we have pointed out before, that sound investments fail to prove attractive because active financial operators preempt the intrinsic values for themselves by effecting force-out mergers or similar corporate events at a time when a stock's price is depressed or underpriced because of relatively recent developments within the business.

The uncertainty that results from the outside investor's incomplete knowledge—and from the possibilities of erroneous analysis, adverse future developments and the preemption of intrinsic value by others—can never be eliminated. Rather, the goal is to tip the risk–profit equation as far in favor of profit as possible, and we believe that intelligent use of our approach achieves this result. In tipping the scale toward profit, it is useful to have an understanding of the separate elements that go to make up investment risk.

ASSESSING THE INVESTMENT ODDS: RISK AND REWARD

Conventional wisdom tells us that the key to investment risk is the quality of the issuer. A high-quality, or primary, issuer is most commonly defined as a large, well-known company, popularly recognized by others as a high-quality company, with a long record of dividend payments on its common stock. Because popular recognition is crucial—indeed, probably the single most important element in the definition—the value of the issuer is, of course, likely to be reflected in the market price of its securities. It follows, then, from this conventional wisdom that the securities of lesser-known issuers, so-called riskier investments, will have greater capital appreciation potential. Thus the cliché, You have to take chances if you want to make money.

It is our view that though the quality of the issuer is important in assessing investment risk, it frequently is not crucial; still, it happens to be the key for investors who are neither knowledgeable nor diligent nor likely ever to be in a control position. But for the investor with a modicum of know-how, perceived quality of the issuer is only part of the story. Other factors that figure into calculating the risk–reward ratio are the price of the issue and the financial position of the security holder.

QUALITY OF THE ISSUER

The tendency in the financial community is to stress quality of the issuer in assessing risk, and to ignore price of the issue. Thus, the view is that there is less risk in purchasing, say, American Telephone and Telegraph common than there is in purchasing little-known stocks, such as Federated Development Corporation or Standard

Shares. Perhaps the best-known advocates of this approach are Graham and Dodd, who in *Security Analysis* state

The basic portfolio list should consist of a substantial number—say, not more than 100—of primary common stocks. (These companies are large, prosperous, soundly capitalized and *well known to investors*) [our emphasis added]. The actual portfolio would be constructed from between twenty and thirty of those issues which, at the time of selection, showed the most favorable relation between market price and the analyst's appraised value. Some limitation as to the amount committed in any one industry would be imposed to assure adequate diversification. If this process takes place at a high level of the market, the issues selected may actually be selling above their valuations; that would be the necessary penalty for making commitments at what appears to be a basically unfavorable time. (No doubt those who are convinced that the 1962 levels are *not* excessive will in their individual valuations apply multipliers high enough to make many issues appear absolutely as well as relatively attractive. Typically, they will conclude that certain promising issues are selling at thirty or more times earnings).

Our problem would allow for the substitution of secondary issues in place of primary ones—but only if the value conservatively found for a secondary issue shows it to be *substantially* cheaper than the *most attractive* primary issue it would replace in the list. By "substantially cheaper" we imply a required differential of at least 25 percent.[20]

This approach is based on an implicit assumption that the market knows more about the value of a given investment than the individual investor does. Within a context that concentrates on accounting earnings as the basis for valuing a going concern, this undoubtedly has some validity. Outside investors who are not well informed about the companies they are investing in, and who are not conscious of the quality and quantity of net assets in a business, tend to find it difficult to assess the reasonableness of the price of an issue in any meaningful way. Thus, it seems prudent to weight quality-of-the-issuer

---

[20]*loc. cit.* p. 448.

considerations more heavily. For these investors who lack independent knowledge of securities and companies, it is important, too, to diversify an equity portfolio to provide a modicum of additional insurance against the possibility that the market, which is assumed to be well informed about any particular security, is in fact not.

Still, emphasizing issuers of high quality in an investment strategy does have its own special difficulties. As noted above, popular recognition is probably the single most important element of high quality. This means that a company can become high quality simply because influential people say it is. The hard facts are that many issuers that have been selected by the recognized arbiters of the financial-quality fashion parade have turned out to be quite the opposite.

For example, in the era before the 1920's, the foremost blue chips were railroads and traction companies. Included among these high-quality issuers was the Pennsylvania Railroad, which until its 1968 merger to form Penn Central Company had a dividend record dating back to 1848. In the 1920's, investment trusts and utility holding companies were regarded as high-quality issuers. In recent years, common stocks such as the Great Atlantic and Pacific Tea Company have been wrongly acclaimed as high quality. The damage done to investors who purchased stock based on the high-quality reputation of these issuers tended to take the form of double stock-price depreciation: first the shares went down because earnings declined; then the shares went down even more when the issuers lost their high-quality image and the high price–earnings ratios evaporated.

Notwithstanding these pitfalls, there is sufficient validity in an investment strategy based on a diversified selection of high-grade issues that an outside investor who is willing to trade infrequently and to realize only a modest return on investment will probably do moderately well most of the time. Even this investor must be careful to follow two basic rules, however. First, do *not* buy what is popular when it is being highly touted; this is usually when it is most overpriced. Second, if your investment matters to you, obtain at least a rudimentary knowledge of the company before you invest in it.

PRICE OF THE ISSUE

We agree that quality of the issuer may be the most important factor in evaluating risk for the outsider who is short on know-how. It is also the most important factor in risk evaluation for the cash-return investor. But for the outside investor who is reasonably well informed about the company in which he is investing and who understands the whole array of factors, including financial ones, that figure in the valuation process, quality-of-the-issuer considerations cover only part of investment risk. Because we believe economic and financial information is so good in the United States that an intelligent investor can become relatively knowledgeable, and in fact more knowledgeable than the market, we tend to emphasize price of the issue in evaluating most securities.

Smart investors, whether active or passive, tend to worry more about how much they can lose than how much they can make. In this sense, investors are truly "risk averse." In this context, then, the higher the price of a security, the greater the risk; the lower the price, the less the risk, and so the greater the potential reward. Price-of-the-issue considerations tell us, then, that in a given situation, there is less money to lose and more money to make if you invest $5,000 in American Telephone common stock at 50 rather than at 60, or if you invest the same $5,000 in Orion Capital common stock at 5 rather than at 10. It also tells us that there may be considerably less risk in investing $5,000 in a lower-grade security, such as Orion Capital common stock, at 5 than investing in the common stock of a high-quality issuer, such as American Telephone, at 60 or even at 50.

This poses a dilemma, then. Quality-of-the-issuer considerations tell us that if you want to make money, you have to take risks. Price-of-the-issue considerations, on the other hand, tell us the opposite—that the less risk you take, the more money you can make.

We recognize that this view runs counter to an economic theory which assumes that at any moment market price reflects a rational price equilibrium between risk and reward. Where a security entails greater risk, it is assumed that it will be assigned a lower price by market forces. In contrast, the investor who analyzes risk in terms of price of the issue assumes implicitly that stock market prices are virtually always in disequilibrium.

This assumption also runs counter to the views of many in the financial community. Broker-dealers, investment companies and commercial lenders tend to steer clear of securities that have a low per-share price. Common rules tell us that low-priced common stocks (under, say, $10 per share), whether undervalued or not, are per se speculative.* Thus, many brokerage firms will not permit their salesmen to solicit orders for stocks selling below a certain price. At Merrill, Lynch, the minimum is $5. Banks as well as brokers normally will not accept low-priced stocks as collateral for margin loans.

This institutional approach of damning low-priced stocks assumes implicitly that the investor, the broker and the lending bank are uninformed or badly informed about the situation, or that the market knows more than they do. A low price is seen as strong evidence or even proof that the issue is a dangerous speculation. We do not accept the proposition that this must necessarily be, or even usually is, the case.

This is not to say that we advocate the indiscriminate buying of low-priced stock by the unwary. The conventional wisdom that warns against low-priced stock does have some objective basis in fact. For one, it is true that common stocks of formerly prosperous businesses that encounter financial problems so dire that they threaten the company's solvency will almost invariably sell at low per-share prices, no matter how small the number of shares in the outstanding common-stock capitalization. For another, a promoter of a blatantly speculative venture, such as a uranium discovery, will deliberately price the issue at a low price, usually below $5. Finally, the trading costs involved in buying and selling low-priced stocks tend to be higher, and so detract from the investment merits of the

---

*In price-of-the-issue considerations, a security is deemed to be low-priced or high-priced only in relation to the analyst's perception of the underlying values behind that security. The actual price per se is immaterial. Under this approach, a common stock selling at 2 can be high (overpriced) and a common stock selling at 200 can be low, or underpriced.

security. These three points are obviously things the investor should bear in mind. But to take the position that one should stay away from low-priced stocks in general because they are speculative is to make the wrong deduction; for long-term investors, buying and selling costs are unlikely to be material considerations.

In practice, of course, there are shadings of judgment that investors must make about both quality and price. For example, in 1972, using the financial-integrity approach, we believed that Federated Development at 7 was attractive, combining substantial appreciation possibilities with minimum risk. Federated had an unencumbered asset value—in either cash or assets readily convertible into cash within a two- or three-year span—of not less than 17, and a management and control group that we thought were honest, capable and motivated toward converting Federated's asset value into earning power that would be reflected in a market price that would be at a premium over a growing net asset value. Even though we favored it, we did not recommend Federated for widows or orphans who need highest-quality stocks, and would not have recommended it to them even if Federated had paid dividends. The fact that Federated did not have a continuing, recurring, profitable operation—a consideration that goes to quality of the issuer—cautioned against it as an investment for such holders. For them, the fact that Federated was attractive under the financial-integrity approach was not a sufficient condition to recommend the stock.

Parenthetically, in October 1973, an outside group obtained control of Federated by purchasing 51 percent of the stock outstanding (57 percent of the stock tendered) at $12.25 per share. Our remaining shares—that is, 43 percent of our original holdings—were sold in early 1977 at 11. Considering that no distributions were ever made on Federated shares, these investment results probably are best described as no better than reasonable.

While shadings of judgment are useful in resolving the inherent contradictions between quality and price considerations, there are insights that tip an investor's scales toward quality and away from price, or vice versa. Insofar as an outside investor lacks knowledge, or the time or ability to obtain knowledge, quality considerations should dominate. Conversely, insofar as an investor is or can become knowledgeable, and is or can become an activist in terms of influencing corporate affairs, price considerations assume greater and greater importance.

FINANCIAL POSITION OF THE HOLDER

The third element in the risk–profit equation is the financial position of the holder. The investor who buys a stock of even the best quality at a fraction of its underlying value is engaging in an extremely dangerous speculation if he cannot afford to make the purchase.

An inappropriate financial position can arise out of borrowing too heavily to own the securities. For example, U.S. government bonds are generally regarded as a high-quality issue. For the financially weak holder who has borrowed 95 percent of the purchase price, however, all it takes is a small fluctuation to give rise to a Las Vegas–style gamble. It is not healthy for a small speculator to get caught in the cross fire between the Treasury and the Federal Reserve when his protection is a 5 percent margin and an empty bank account.

An inappropriate financial position can also arise because an investor does not have enough funds to live on. There are many examples of investors who suffer large losses in an apparently undervalued security because they do not have the financial position (or temperament) to tough it out. Many of the most successful long-term investments of the last ten years, which appreciated from five to ten times cost, were in issues which paid small or no dividends and on which the holders realized no profits or paper losses for two, three or even four years. Examples are Tokio Marine and Fire Insurance, Fargo Oils, H. J. Heinz and Northwest Bancorporation.

The wherewithal to weather a temporary setback is particularly important for the investor who believes, as we do, that he can know more about an issue than the market does. It is an important condition for investors following the financial-integrity approach. It is suicidal to ignore the general market unless you have the resources and inclination to sit tight, or can actively influence the business. Any approach that minimizes market factors can give only a margin of safety in terms of investment risk. We do not know how an outside investor can guard against stock-price fluctuations unless he has the resources to ignore them.

PORTFOLIO DIVERSIFICATION VERSUS SECURITIES CONCENTRATION

As pointed out above, it is logical where measures of risk are based on quality of the issuer that portfolios of such securities be diversified, providing added protection to compensate for lack of knowledge about individual securities. In contrast, the investor who, because of know-how or control, has confidence in an equity investment based on price of the issue, and who has a financial position that will allow him to survive the short term, does not need the extra protection that comes from diversification. Such protection comes from a lack of encumbrances upon the investor. He stands to gain most from concentrating his investment in the area where his knowledge (and perhaps control) tips the risk–reward ratio for the particular security very strongly in his favor.

CONSIDERING THE CONSEQUENCES

Astute financial people do not measure potentials simply by reference to the risk–reward ratio. It is not sufficient to calculate that, say, there is five times as much chance that the investment will appreciate from one to twenty points as there is that it will depreciate from one to twenty points. Such a calculation reflects only odds.

The astute person examines consequences as well as odds. For example, consider the situation where the odds are five to one that an investment will appreciate, but that if it fails to do so, the investor will become insolvent. He might well conclude that the consequences of disappointment are so dire that the particular investment is unattractive, notwithstanding the favorable odds.

This "consequences" view of risk is another way of looking at some essential, practical limitations in finance. Most companies, institutions and individuals tend to (and should) be limited to things that are affordable.

RISK AND INVESTMENT OBJECTIVES

Don't go out with chorus girls or buy second mortgages.
ADVICE OF DYING FATHER TO HIS ONLY SON

Investment objectives figure into the risk-measurement process in two ways. First, the cash-return investor will base his investment decision on different factors in evaluating risk than will the workout special-situation investor, even where both of them use the same factors (say, the four elements that make up the financial-integrity approach) for part of their analysis. Second, the risk–reward ratio will provide the investor with a guide to use in defining his investment objectives.

The investor who is interested primarily in cash return and is in no position to investigate carefully should emphasize first and foremost, and perhaps exclusively, quality of the issuer. The definition of high quality entails two factors: first, there should be a general recognition by others such as bond-rating services that the issue is high quality; and second, the investor should reach a similar conclusion after independent analysis, however cursory. If there are any doubts about the safety of the cash payments to be made to owners of the cash-return security, then that security should not be bought; if owned, it should be sold.

In most cases, a strictly cash-return investor should limit his portfolio investments largely to debt securities. This is because the holder owns a legally enforceable right to be paid principal and interest by the issuer and any guarantors in accordance with speci-fied contractual terms, affording the cash-return investor a margin of safety.

In contrast, a workout- or special-situation investor emphasizes price of the issue rather than quality of the issuer. It is not that the special-situation investor sacrifices safety for yield, but rather that he finds safety in a low price. This approach, in contrast to the conventional one, involves hard work and a large degree of know-how. The basic philosophy is that as a result of study, the investor will know more about the particular situation than the market does. The workout-situation investor does not rely on general recognition. It is our view that the most successful of these investors tend to place important, but never sole, emphasis on the four essential elements of the financial-integrity approach.

DISCLOSURES AND INFORMATION

Chapter 6

Following the Paper Trail

ہؤ

*It shall be unlawful for any person, directly or indirectly . . . (b) to make
any untrue statement of a material fact or to omit to state a material fact
necessary in order to make the statements made, in light of the circumstances under which they were made, not misleading . . . in connection
with the purchase or sale of any security.*

A SUMMARY OF A PORTION OF SEC REGULATION 10(B)5
AS IT PERTAINS TO DISCLOSURE

I N THE UNITED STATES, as nowhere else in the world, written disclosures are comprehensive and reliable. As a matter of fact, the
very comprehensiveness and reliability of these disclosures make
them essential working tools for all types of creditors and investors,
from commercial-bank lending officers to individual common-stock
investors. The key disclosure documents for creditors of, and investors
in, public companies are those issued pursuant to rules and regulations
promulgated by the Securities and Exchange Commission.*

---

*Although SEC disclosures are crucial for most analyses of public companies,
they are far from the only disclosure documents that may be important in a given situation. The others, however, are beyond the scope of a book as short as this one.
Chapters 32, 33 and 34 of Volume II of the *Financial Analyst's Handbook* (Sumner

These frequently crucial documents disclose information in two forms—financial statements and narratives. Financial statements are discussed in the next two chapters, "Financial Accounting" and "Generally Accepted Accounting Principles." Our primary interest in this chapter is in narrative disclosure.

Principal documents of the paper trail are as follows:*

Form 10-K is the official annual business and financial report that must be filed by most companies with the SEC.

Form 10-Q is the quarterly financial report filed by most companies with the SEC that includes disclosure of certain material and extraordinary events that occurred during the reported three-month period.

Form 8-K is a report to the SEC, within fifteen days of the occurrence of a reportable event, of unscheduled material events or corporate changes.

Annual reports to stockholders are the most important way most public corporations communicate directly with stockholders.

Quarterly reports to stockholders are statements many companies mail every three months directly to their stockholders.

Annual-meeting proxy statements are documents mailed to stockholders soliciting their votes for election of directors and other matters, such as the appointment of independent auditors. If a company does not solicit "proxies," information that would otherwise have been disclosed in proxy statements is disclosed in Part II of Form 10-K.

Merger proxy statements are issued when stockholders are to vote on an asset-conversion matter—for example, merger, consolidation, sale of assets or liquidation. If new securities are to be issued as part of the asset-conversion event, the merger proxy statement also

---

N. Levine, ed., Homewood, Ill.: Dow Jones-Irwin, 1975, p. 852) are excellent overviews of the types of public non-SEC disclosures that are generally available. Chapter 32, by Dorothy Hennessey Sussman, is entitled "Information Sources—An Overview." Chapter 33, by Sylvia Mechanic, is entitled "Key Reference Sources." Chapter 34, "A Guide to Industry Publications," is a reprint of a brochure originally issued by the New York Society of Security Analysts.

*A good pamphlet describing the principal documents filed with the SEC is included here as Appendix III with the permission of Disclosure Incorporated.

serves as a prospectus for the new issue of securities, and is registered as an S-14 Registration.

Prospectuses are part of registration statements and are issued
when securities are to be offered publicly, either for cash or in an
exchange-of-securities transaction where no stockholder vote is
sought. Principal registration forms are the S-1 (a generalized form)
and the S-7, a short form used by seasoned companies with relatively
healthy operating histories. Preliminary prospectuses are known as
"red herrings."

Cash tender offer circulars are sent, or otherwise made available,
to stockholders when a publicly announced offer is made to buy shares
for cash from the general list of stockholders.

The use of SEC disclosures is the key to our financial-integrity
approach. Indeed, there seems to be an almost symbiotic relationship
between SEC-prescribed disclosures and our approach in that the
SEC seems to make special efforts to provide the types of information that are most important to us, as is demonstrated by the examples of actual disclosures that are contained in Appendix IV.

The presence or absence of encumbrances is almost always
spelled out in SEC documents to those who carefully read financial
statements (including footnotes), especially audited financial statements. SEC disclosures also permit insights into management character, at least insofar as their relationships with security holders are
concerned. Information about these matters is contained either in
proxy statements for annual meetings, or when proxies are not solicited, in Part II of Form 10-K, the company's annual report filed
with the SEC. The proxy statement and Part II of the 10-K contain
descriptions of management remuneration, certain transactions with
insiders, and in proxy statements where shareholder votes are solicited, proposals designed to insulate management in office.* Also,

---

*The SEC, as of the time of this writing in early 1979, is deeply involved in
studying methods for improving these proxy-statement and Part II disclosures. One
recent change made in management remuneration is to require, for fiscal years ending after December 25, 1978, disclosure about remuneration for the *five* highest-paid
executive officers or directors whose annual compensation exceeds $50,000, instead

financial statements, Form 10-K and Part II of Form 10-Q (the quarterly report filed with the SEC) contain disclosures on litigation. All these items give evidence to analysts about management attitudes and management character.

Neither academics, whether economists or finance professors, nor securities traders seem to appreciate just how useful these documents are. This failure can perhaps be explained by the fact that most of the critics have had virtually no experience in preparing the documents required by the SEC. Document preparation has been left largely to investment bankers, practicing lawyers, accountants and members of corporate managements. Although firsthand experience as a document preparer is not essential to understanding the uses and limitations of the paper trail, an investor (or critic) ought to comprehend how the preparers go about composing the materials that they must file with the SEC or mail to securities holders.

The first thing to remember is that there are few liars among document preparers. Virtually no professional accountant, lawyer, investment banker or, especially, independent auditor wants even to be suspected of misleading investors, much less of fraud. The professionals whom we know and work with do not wish to risk their livelihoods and reputations for the benefit of third parties, such as managements and large stockholders.* As a general rule, the information gleaned from the paper trail is truthful and reliable in stating whatever it purports to state.

---

of (formerly required) disclosures about compensation to directors and the *three* highest-paid officers whose annual compensation exceeded $40,000. Also, the remuneration table will contain three types of information about remuneration for these five executive officers and all directors and executive officers as a group: (1) salaries and similar amounts actually distributed or accrued during the fiscal year; (2) other forms of contingent remuneration, such as insurance premiums and other benefits; and (3) contingent remuneration. (See Exchange Act Release 15380, dated December 4, 1978.)

*We are convinced this remains true despite what we consider to be the Supreme Court's unfortunate language in regard to Section 10(b)5 in *Ernst and Ernst* v. *Hochfelder* (see supra). The vast majority of financial professionals appear to us to be honest and ethical because they want to be, not because they have to be.

This is not to say that all these documents are complete and accurate; there is short-cutting, but much of it is inadvertent. It is sometimes difficult for competent and honest document preparers to make appropriate judgments as to what are material disclosures. However, in our experience, important nondisclosures do not occur frequently. Some short-cutting is undoubtedly deliberate, but the outright frauds or possible frauds—Equity Funding, Stirling Homex, National Student Marketing, and Westec—are few and far between.

Second, in preparing documents, there are two well-established rules: Follow the required form so that specific regulations are complied with, and *don't* run afoul of antifraud provisions of the securities laws. These antifraud provisions make it unlawful in connection with the purchase or sale of any security for any person, directly or indirectly, "to make any untrue statement of a material fact or to omit to state a material fact necessary in order to make the statements made, in light of the circumstances under which they were made, not misleading."[21] The typical preparer of documents, therefore, is going to try to disclose, as truthfully as possible, everything he thinks is factually relevant. He will do this to avoid trouble, both from government regulators and from private securities holders whose attorneys may bring class-action suits, either derivatively or directly, to redress their grievances.

Understanding this is a large part of understanding why the paper trail is so useful. In most commercial and economic transactions, any sensible participant has to worry about the truthfulness of the other parties to the transactions. This is rarely a consideration for followers of the paper trail who rely on written disclosures. It is as if the person contemplating the purchase of a used car could know that the salesman who says "This auto was only driven on Sunday by a little old lady

---

[21] 10(b)5 is part of the Securities Exchange Act of 1934 as amended. Prospectus preparers operate under similar and additional strictures growing out of Section 17 of the Securities Act of 1933 as amended. In addition, there are similar strictures existing under other parts of the Securities Exchange Act of 1934 as amended. But 10(b)5 is the catchall of the antifraud regulations, covering situations not otherwise enumerated specifically.

going to church" is telling the truth. Being able to rely on the truthfulness of disclosures about publicly held corporations is of enormous help to any creditor or investor in coming to financial judgments.

THE DOCUMENTS AND HOW TO READ THEM

In order to take full advantage of disclosure, the reader ought to have an understanding of what is contained in principal disclosure documents. The first and most important thing to do is to read them. Almost anyone, after carefully reading, say, five 10-K's and four merger proxy statements, will have good insight into how their contents can help him in an investment program. Second, the reader should obtain copies of the forms and the general regulations for the preparation of forms. Reading such materials will give good insight into what preparers go through to produce the various key documents. Investors pursuing an in-depth study of these forms can obtain copies of them as well as general instructions and guides for their preparation from the SEC itself, from other sources, including the *Federal Securities Law Reporter* (a loose-leaf service published by Commerce Clearing House in Chicago), and from financial printers such as Bowne and Appeal.

There are other SEC filings that are occasionally important, but these are beyond the scope of this brief chapter. These include offering circulars under Regulation A; filings by insiders concerning their shareholdings and changes in holdings (Forms 3 and 4); and Form 144, filed by holders desiring to sell restricted stock under Rule 144. Form 13F, to be filed quarterly commencing in 1979 by institutional investment managers exercising discretion over accounts holding more than $100,000,000 of marketable equity securities, describes the securities held in those portfolios. Notices of various filings can be found in the *SEC News Digest*, a daily summary of SEC activities, including rules and related matters, announcements, registrations and filings in connection with tender offers and 5 percent ownership; the *SEC Docket*, a weekly compilation of the full text of SEC releases; and the *Official Summary*, a monthly summary of securities transactions and holdings reported by insiders, taken from Forms 3 and 4 as filed.

OBTAINING THE DOCUMENTS

Some documents—for example, annual reports, annual-meeting proxy statements, prospectuses and cash tender offers—are publicly distributed. The investor who wants to study any of these can easily pick up a copy from a broker. He can also obtain copies by writing to the issuer.

Writing to the issuer is probably the easiest way of obtaining copies of materials that are filed with the SEC but are not publicly distributed, such as 10-K's, 8-K's, 10-Q's and Schedules 13D and 14D. Schedules 13D are filed within ten days by persons who have acquired 5 percent or more of an outstanding security issue (or who, once having acquired 5 percent, acquire an additional 2 percent within a twelve-month period).* Schedules 14D, whose informational requirements are similar to those of Schedules 13D, are filed by offerers prior to the making of a cash tender offer for 5 percent or more of a class of securities. There are other ways to obtain these documents, however. The SEC has copies of materials filed on microfiche cards, in its main office in Washington and (except for Schedules 13D and 14D) in its regional offices, that are available to the public in public reference rooms. There are also services that, for a fee, will acquire and mail these materials.[22]

---

*Prior to the end of 1978, there were no necessary Schedule 13D disclosures for certain beneficial owners of 5 percent or more of an issue, to wit, if beneficial ownership of the securities was acquired prior to December 22, 1970; or if the acquirers had not been "rapid accumulators" and had never obtained more than 2 percent within a twelve-month period; or if beneficial ownership was acquired in certain stock-for-stock exchanges. Filing by these beneficial owners will, after 1978, be made on Schedule 13G, required to be filed once a year within forty-five days after the end of a calendar year. (Securities Act Release 15317, November 9, 1978.)

[22]Four leading services are Disclosure Incorporated, Washington, D.C. (301-951-0100); The National Investment Library, New York (212-982-2000), Boston

WHAT THE PAPER TRAIL DOES
FOR THE OUTSIDE INVESTOR

Once all this information has been gathered, how useful is it? How limited? Though it is not particularly useful for the trader who seeks immediate market performance, we think it is extremely useful for all other investors, whether they be control buyers or passivists, who have a modicum of training in what to look for. The paper trail is especially useful in allowing those using the financial-integrity approach to arrive at very meaningful judgments most of the time.

This does not mean that the paper trail is perfect. Certainly it will not tell the creditor or investor everything he wants to know. Even so, unless the outsider has some special know-how or know-who, we think it is so good that he would do well to restrict his investments to securities covered by the paper trail. In fact, when we advise European clients about U.S. investments, we frequently recommend securities to them, rather than, say, real estate, precisely because the paper trail exists, and the disclosures it provides mean that other things being equal, an investment will involve a lesser element of risk than one in any non-SEC filing enterprise.

For the followers of the financial-integrity approach, the paper trail is excellent, as we noted above, for pointing to securities that because of poor financial position or insider avarice are unattractive at any price. But it is also highly useful in a more positive sense: an investor can obtain quite reliable assurances that a company's financial position is strong and that insiders are not overreaching, or based on past performance, are likely to overreach in the future.

In effect, much of the entire SEC narrative-disclosure process and many of the disclosures of financial accounting are directed toward informing investors about corporate obligations. Stockholder annual reports, 10-K's, 10-Q's, 8-K's, and where issued, other documents will give investors strong clues to the encumbrances attached

---

(617-227-6666) and San Francisco (415-398-6900); Stock Research Corporation, New York (212-964-2440); and the Washington Service Bureau, Washington, D.C. (202-833-9200).

to a business entity. Particularly important in this regard are audited financial statements, including the auditor's certification and the footnotes to the financials. Descriptions of on-balance-sheet debt and footnote descriptions of encumbrances, including balance-sheet items, pension-plan obligations and contingent liabilities, tend to be carefully and accurately done.*

Auditors' certificates are particularly important as attestations that have become increasingly carefully worded in recent years. Such attestations are either "clean"—presented without qualification—or "subject to" certain conditions. Additionally, there are what in effect are nonattestations, namely "adverse opinions" or "disclaimers of opinions." Clean opinions, as distinct from certain but not all subject-to opinions, adverse opinions or disclaimers of opinions, are important in giving comfort to investors following the financial-integrity approach; such investors are unlikely to be interested in a junior security on the basis of an opinion subject to a serious qualification (such as "subject to the ability to continue as a going concern"), or on the basis of an adverse opinion or of a disclaimer of opinion.

The encumbrances that are missed by the paper trail tend to be those that sometimes even the insiders are unaware of. One example is a business that enjoys a strong financial position only because it fails to make needed expenditures to modernize, expand or replace outdated facilities. In such cases, a strong financial position is deceptive, and the strong balance sheet will tend to be dissipated in future years as the business suffers large operating losses, embarks on massive catch-up capital-expenditure programs, or both. (This is precisely what happened in the cement industry in the late 1950's and early 1960's.) Nonetheless, it has been our experience that most of the time, the paper trail does disclose enough, so that the investor's estimate of what the total encumbrances will prove to be are relatively accurate.

*Though perhaps not part of any glossary, "on-balance-sheet items" commonly refers to assets or liabilities stated directly on a balance sheet, whereas "off-balance-sheet disclosures" usually refers to information about balance-sheet items disclosed in footnotes to financial statements.

The paper trail is also fairly good in giving clues about insider overreaching. Proxy statements for annual meetings at which directors are elected contain disclosures about management remuneration,* about borrowings by insiders from the company, and about certain transactions—dealings and participations between the company and its insiders. In addition, the long-term record of management is revealed, and this is helpful to analysts who tend to believe that behavior patterns probably do not change much, if at all. For example, since the management of Rapid American Corporation forced out minority shareholders of Schenley Industries in 1971 at what we believed, from examining the 1971 proxy material, was a grossly unfair price (as one of us testified in court), we have concluded that we would rather not be an outside investor or creditor in any company controlled by the Rapid American management, albeit there was nothing illegal about the Schenley Industries force-out.

True, much past insider overreaching may escape disclosure in the documents of the paper trail. Certainly the documents as they exist today leave few clues concerning such matters as the prevalence of widespread nepotism at levels below parent-company officers and directors. Yet, there appear to be sufficient data, so that the outside investor can make reasonable judgments about the character of the insiders, at least insofar as it affects actual or proposed investments.

An investor may decide that a security meeting the criteria of a financial-integrity approach is attractive because of additional considerations. The paper trail will help him uncover these other attractions, perhaps providing hints that future earnings might increase dramatically; that large cash distributions to stockholders are likely; that a company is a takeover candidate; that it is likely to be liquidated or recapitalized in whole or in part; or that a security is priced inexpensively compared with other companies, based on its history.

---

*The management remuneration section of a proxy statement (or Part II of a Form 10-K) will contain information not only about salaries, but also about all other types of remuneration, such as stock options, stock-appreciation rights, pension-plan benefits, bonuses, profit-sharing plans and employment contracts. The SEC is considering requiring that information about management perquisites, such as company hunting lodges or the use of company planes for private purposes, be disclosed.

The paper trail can provide information that is crucial to assessing each of these factors. The knowledge gained from it about a company's business and operations provides a reasonable basis for making judgments about future earnings, cash returns and risk. Information about who owns the company's stock, who is acquiring it and what resources the company has may tell whether or not it is a likely candidate for a takeover, or for a liquidation or recapitalization.

Finally, data on the existing asset base, historic earnings, cash returns and percentage yields on the security are essential to a determination of whether the security is underpriced on a comparative basis. True, the paper trail does not provide all the necessary information for this last determination; it does not tell the price of the security relative to others, nor does it generally identify other comparable securities. Such information is readily obtainable from other sources, though, including trade association directories, Moody's, Standard and Poor's and the *Directory of Companies Filing Annual Reports with the Securities and Exchange Commission.*

As we stated before, the paper trail enables an investor using the financial-integrity approach to pinpoint those securities that are unattractive at any price. The statement that everything has a price at which it is a bargain is, as a practical matter, simply not true when it comes to investment. Junior securities—especially those that are pure residuals, such as common stocks and warrants—may be in such a hopeless position that they are likely never to have a value high enough to compensate for the costs of ownership. This may happen in one of two situations. The first is where the financial position of the company is so bad that whether the company is in bankruptcy or not, the entire business has to belong to the creditors.* For reasons that are examined in Chapter 16, even a tax-loss carry-forward will not impart value to junior securities in such a situation unless it exceeds the creditor

---

*However, because of fraud, junior-security holders can sometimes become at least general creditors. The Equity Funding Corporation Chapter X bankruptcy is one example of this. Here, the common survived the Chapter X bankruptcy reorganization as a creditor class with the common's creditorship position arising out of the fraud claim. It is our view, however, that Equity Funding types of frauds are rare among public companies.

claims. The second situation in which equity securities should be avoided at any price is that of a going concern with an entrenched management whose prime objective is to milk the company for personal benefits at the expense of the security holders. By far the best way to pinpoint such a situation is to follow the paper trail.

WHAT THE PAPER TRAIL DOESN'T DO

The principal shortcoming of the paper trail stems from the fact that it is designed and used to provide material disclosures of hard information. Soft information, such as company forecasts, company budgets and valuation appraisals of assets—for example, possible and probable petroleum reserves or real estate holdings—are rarely disclosed.* This is principally because much soft information is a tool for stock market manipulation.

*We note what appears to be a trend in recent years toward improved disclosure of soft information without any changes in laws, rules and regulations about such disclosures. For example, see the S-14 Prospectus and Merger Proxy issued in 1975 in connection with the acquisition of General Crude by a subsidiary of International Paper. An exhibit to that document gave values for all of General Crude's oil properties—not only proved reserves, but also probable and possible reserves as well as undeveloped acreage. We are not aware that such soft information had ever been disclosed previously in any SEC prospectus, proxy statement, or 10-K.

The SEC, however, is now intensively examining the question of expanding the promulgation of soft information through new rules and regulations. A breakthrough in requiring soft information probably occurred in 1976 when the SEC, for the first time, required companies with inventories and gross property, plant and equipment aggregating more than $100 million and comprising more than 10 percent of total assets to provide supplementary data in the 10-K about estimated replacement costs. (Accounting Series Release 190, dated March 23, 1976.) In 1978, the SEC proposed guides that would permit and encourage projections of financial information by companies. These forecasts were to be made voluntarily and forecasters were to be given a "safe harbor," that is, they generally would not be held liable under the federal securities laws for reasonably based projections that did not work out (Exchange Act Releases 15305 and 15306, dated November 7, 1978). Also, in Accounting Series Release 253, dated August 31, 1978, the SEC adopted requirements for supplemental disclosures for fiscal years ending after December 25, 1979,

Sometimes this soft information may be vital to understanding a business, either as an asset-conversion enterprise or as a going concern. For example, in early 1976 Tishman Realty announced liquidation plans. Without knowing the prices at which Tishman's real properties could be sold, there was no realistic basis for judging the merits of Tishman as an investment; and without real estate appraisals of the individual properties, it was extremely difficult to approximate these prices. Another example is Duplan Corporation, which in early 1976 found itself in serious financial trouble, its very viability threatened unless it could become profitable in six months to a year. Here, management forecasts and budgets were crucial to anyone contemplating becoming an investor in or creditor of Duplan.

There are many other kinds of information besides management forecasts, budgets and asset appraisals that the paper trail fails to disclose. For example, there are no disclosures of merger and acquisition discussions that never reach a definitive state. There rarely will be information about comparative cost analysis, comparative security prices or comparative market penetrations within an industry. Ordinarily, outsiders do not know what a company ought to spend on plant equipment or inventory in order to remain competitive. The paper trail rarely includes disclosures of detailed special studies in areas such as marketing or engineering. Nor will there be information about long-festering internal disputes among management. Occasionally, even obviously material hard information may be lacking: for example, companies may provide only consolidated financial statements in situations where such statements would be less informative than consolidating or company-only statements. (In consolidating or company-only statements, information about the parent company and individual subsidiaries

---

of the valuation (and changes in valuation during the year) of certain companies' proved oil and gas reserves; this is a method of accounting the SEC calls reserve recognition accounting, or RRA. RRA was adopted despite SEC reservations that "the feasibility of developing RRA, however, is not assured at the present time because of the inherent imprecision of estimates of proved oil and gas reserves and the need to establish standards for valuations of these reserves in order to achieve an acceptable degree of reliability."

is disclosed, whereas such information is not shown separately in consolidated statements.)

There may even be situations that the paper trail misses entirely. An example would be a very small acquisition that does not require a stockholder vote. If such a vote were required, proxy statements would be mailed to shareholders. Without a proxy or 8-K filing, the financial statements and descriptions of the companies being acquired would not be available at all from SEC filings. Skimpy information about small transactions involving the listing of newly issued securities can be obtained from the acquiring company's stock exchange listing application, which is available from the exchange itself or from brokerage-house libraries.

It is important to note, of course, that the lack of soft information on the paper trail is a much less serious shortcoming for the long-term investor than it is for the trader. For the trader, a near-term earnings forecast or dividend action may be the only disclosure of interest. The long-term investor, especially the investor whose analysis rests on the financial-integrity approach, is resource-conscious; the hard information disclosed by the paper trail is of great importance to him in virtually all his evaluations. Furthermore, for this investor an apparent low price relative to an estimate of the resources in the business can compensate for the risks inherent in knowing less about a company than would be optimal. This safety valve does not exist for the trader who is seeking the best possible near-term market performance.

HOW GOOD IS THE PAPER TRAIL?

The SEC paper trail provides the investor with a stereotyped format. The disadvantage of the stereotyped format, of course, is that following a form frequently results in inadequate descriptions of reality and inadequate weighting of what is important. The principal advantage is that the reader can be assured that the professional preparers are striving to see that the documents do not omit material statements and do not contain material misstatements. In addition, the investor who uses stereotyped documents becomes a very practiced reader and can obtain vast quantities of information merely by skimming, because he knows what to look for and where to look for it.

On balance, our appraisal is that most of the time the paper trail is excellent. We have reached this conclusion in large part on the basis of our experience in conducting in-depth analyses for companies that retain us. In these situations, the companies provide all the data we want and do studies to generate any necessary data that is otherwise unavailable. Invariably, these in-depth analyses have been materially easier to do and more meaningful for users when we have had SEC documents available as a source of information and as a check against other information received. We are sure this holds true also for virtually all other analysts doing comparable studies. This points up, incidentally, one of the more important social and economic benefits to the United States from the paper trail: It has uplifted the standards of analysis, making it infinitely easier to conduct meaningful analyses for all sorts of appraisers, from commercial-bank lenders to government officials, who may not be interested in securities markets per se or common stock investing at all.

Of course, the paper trail is always going to be more useful for some kinds of companies than for others. For example, for large, stable, dividend-paying companies, such as Graham and Dodd's theoretical list of the one hundred highest-quality issuers, the paper trail probably imparts more information to outside investors than they care to know. On the other hand, in areas where Generally Accepted Accounting Principles are not an overly useful tool—such as in the analysis of extractive industries, real estate development companies and emerging issuers—the nonaccounting disclosures of the paper trail are not going to be too useful either. For the whole range of companies in-between, however, the paper trail is a godsend.

Anyone who follows the paper trail must, of course, appreciate what it cannot do for him. First and foremost, much of the world is unknown and unpredictable. Thus, forecasting will always be an art. Second, the paper trail is probably not of much help in gaining insight into immediate timing and immediate performance in the stock market. Obviously, there is no way the paper trail is going to disclose intimate secrets of activists and their plans, which are frequently formulated no place else but in their minds. Nor does it provide anyone with know-who, even though it does tend to give the background that makes it easier to obtain.

The paper trail does *not* provide full disclosure, and never can. Like any other analytical tool, it has its limitations. But for the investor who concentrates on our approach, the paper trail is going to be the essential starting point for his analysis almost all of the time. In some instances, the paper trail is all he will ever need.

Chapter 7

Financial Accounting

❦

Manager to Accountant: "How much is two plus two?"
Accountant (cautiously): "How much do you need it to be?"

TYPES OF ACCOUNTING

THERE ARE THREE separate and distinct types of corporate accounting: *cost* (or *control* or *managerial*) accounting, *income-tax* accounting and *financial* accounting. While these three are interrelated, the differences among them are at least as important as, and perhaps more important than, the connections.

Because this is a book about securities, we keep emphasizing—and with good reason—the uses and limitations of financial accounting in corporate and securities analyses. The importance of understanding financial accounting cannot be overestimated by businessmen and investors unless they wish to restrict their activities to the very few fields where it may be occasionally inapplicable or of minor relevance—say, in promoting or being promoted for new inventions or new discoveries.

Why is accounting in general, and financial accounting in particular, so important? First, it tends to be the single most important tool in making sense out of most business situations most of the time. In fact, much of this book is concerned with helping the reader understand how to use—and how not to use—financial accounting.

Second, financial accounting relates very much to the world at large. It is, more than anything else, the language of business. Furthermore, it is much more the language of corporate law and economics than people in those professions sometimes seem to realize. Corporate financial accounting as a language is frequently used, virtually untranslated, in money and banking, much of government accounting, corporate litigation and social accounting. Such concepts as budgets, surplus and deficits, and balances—whether of trade or payments, income, inventory, payables or accruals—are best defined and understood as corporate accounting items.

Finally, financial accounting is of vital importance because it is the cornerstone of disclosure in connection with each and every security or securitylike transaction. This holds true whether it is the Manufacturers Hanover Bank considering the basic financial statement disclosure submitted by Union Carbide Corporation to obtain a $100 million line of credit, or an individual investor who purchases 100 shares of Union Carbide common stock for $4,000 on the New York Stock Exchange after reading the company's annual report and, perhaps, Union Carbide Forms 10-K and 10-Q.

There are a number of definitions of financial accounting. The one we like best was formulated in 1941 by the Committee on Accounting Procedures of the American Institute of Certified Public Accountants.

Accounting is the art of recording, classifying and summarizing in a significant manner and in terms of money, transactions and events which are, in part at least, of a financial character, and interpreting the results thereof.[23]

---

[23]*Accounting Research and Terminology Bulletin—Final Edition* (New York: American Institute of Certified Public Accountants), p. 9.

HOW TO UNDERSTAND
FINANCIAL ACCOUNTING

There are five common misconceptions about financial accounting that must be eliminated if the users of financial statements want to appreciate how financial accounting can be used as an evaluation tool and what its practical limits are. Three of these misconceptions are discussed in this chapter; the last two, which are specifically related to Generally Accepted Accounting Principles, are discussed in the next chapter. These misconceptions are

1. That there is no need to distinguish between financial accounting on the one hand, and income-tax and cost accounting on the other.
2. That financial accounting has precisely the same function in corporate analysis as in stock market analysis.
3. That accounting can be made distortion-free and/or uniform and/or realistic.
4. About the meanings of Generally Accepted Accounting Principles.
5. About the shortcomings of the corporate audit function and the ethical standards of independent auditors in the United States.

Misconceptions that There Is No Need
to Distinguish between Financial Accounting on the One Hand
and Income-Tax and Cost Accounting on the Other

The purpose of cost accounting is to tell a management what its costs are. Such accounting is internal and is essential to the operation of all businesses, although the most refined techniques are probably best applied to manufacturing entities. General Motors could hardly produce, price and sell one or one million Chevrolets without effective sources of information that give management insight into each factor and component of the cost of the cars, as well as the cost of possible alternatives. Cost accounting has a hard-nosed economic reality to it; most companies had better be able to know or estimate their costs with a high degree of reality if they hope to become or remain viable.

Unlike cost accounting, income-tax accounting is not supposed to measure economic reality. Rather, income-tax accounting is designed to create an economic reality (a tax bill) and is based on the use of relatively rigid rules (the Internal Revenue Code), which may or may not be related to other facts of commercial life. This code ordinarily is used in two ways by law-abiding individuals or corporate taxpayers. First, the rules are bent so that the minimum tax payable may be computed, and second (and far less important), the rules are then used for the actual computation of the tax liability.

Sandwiched between cost accounting and income-tax accounting is financial accounting, the type with which we are most concerned. According to *Accounting Principles,*[24] "The basic purpose of financial accounting and financial statements is to provide quantitative financial information about a business enterprise that is useful to statement users, particularly owners and creditors, in making economic decisions." Although both cost and income-tax data are useful to statement users in making economic decisions, they are designed to be used not by owners and creditors, but rather by managements and tax collectors. The purposes of financial accounting, on the other hand, are clearly stated in auditors' opinion certificates, which accompany certified financial statements. They are to

Present fairly the financial position of ——— Company and the results of operations and changes in financial position in conformity with generally accepted accounting principles applied on a consistent basis.

In cost and tax accounting, there is no requirement to present matters "fairly." And cost and tax accounting are not derived in accordance or conformity with Generally Accepted Accounting Principles (see Chapter 8). Insofar as cost accounting is derived from principles, the most applicable ones come from engineering and economics. The principles from which tax accounting is derived

[24]American Institute of Certified Public Accountants, *op. cit.*

are those of the Internal Revenue Code and its related rules and regulations.

These distinctions should put to rest two common errors in security analysis. The first relates cost to financial accounting. Some security analysts think one can accurately gauge the comparative efficiencies of companies, especially manufacturing companies, on the basis of the disclosures required by Generally Accepted Accounting Principles. In truth, it cannot be done without access to all sorts of internal records. Any analysis of an operating company by a security holder with access only to public financial statements is bound to be limited in scope. Not only is there frequently a lack of access to internal cost data, but when such data is available, many analysts are not qualified to use it. Sometimes the lack of internal material may mean that one cannot do a reasonable job of analysis. More often, the drawback is not that serious. In general, such cost analysis is least important for large, stable, well-financed businesses and for analysts oriented toward the financial-integrity approach.

The second error is a tendency in financial accounting to place undue stress on the income account in the mistaken belief that it should be stated more fairly than other statements. To quote *Accounting Principles:*

The fairest possible presentation of periodic net income with neither material overstatement nor understatement is important, since the results of operations are significant not only to prospective buyers but also to prospective sellers. With the increasing importance of the income statement, there has been a tendency to regard the balance sheet as the connective link between successive income statements; however, this concept should not obscure the fact that the balance sheet has significant uses of its own.[25]

Under the financial-integrity approach, or virtually any nontrading approach, a fair presentation of net income is not the factor of primary importance.

[25]*Ibid.,* Sec. 510.03, p. 31.

Misconceptions that Financial Accounting Has Much the Same Role in Corporate Analysis as in Stock Market Analysis

There are two fundamental differences in the uses made of financial accounting in corporate analysis and in stock market analysis.

1. In corporate analysis, primary emphasis is placed on what the numbers *mean* rather than (as in the case of stock market analysis) on what the numbers *are*. What the numbers *are* is, of course, what actually is reported.
2. In corporate analysis, there is no a priori rule that one accounting number is more important than any other, but, rather, there is a realization that each accounting number is derived from, is a function of and is modified by all the other accounting numbers involved in income accounts, balance sheets and cash reconciliations. In contrast, in stock market analysis primary emphasis tends to be put on one number—net income—and its corollary, earnings per share.

These differences in the uses of accounting are understandable when viewed against the background of the different emphases in corporate analysis and in stock market analysis. In corporate analysis, whether for a bank loan, a merger or the purchase of a hundred shares of common stock, the profit is sought primarily from factors that are present within the business itself. In contrast, in stock market analysis the profit is sought primarily from believing that others will buy that security at higher prices, which currently exist regardless of the factors within the business.

In many instances, the variables that go into a corporate analysis will be similar to those that go into stock market analysis, but they will rarely if ever be identical. Sometimes they will be totally unrelated. For example, as we pointed out in Chapter 3, "The Significance of Market Performance," many investors seeking cash return through the purchase of corporate indebtedness could not care less about market price. Their analysis concentrates on corporate factors: What are the terms of the issue, and will the debtor be able to service it with a margin of safety? This is pure corporate analysis in the context of a "creditor mentality." On the other hand, many investors interested in near-term market performance will not purchase any issue, regardless of the value they believe it represents at its current price, unless they believe that buying interest will come into the issue—that is, that it will obtain "sponsorship." This is pure stock market analysis in the context of a "trading mentality."

In terms of accounting, stock market analysis dwells on earnings, and more particularly, on changes in near-term recurring accounting earnings from operations as reported. The underlying belief is that changes in operating earnings will have a direct and significant impact on stock prices. Since short-term time horizons are crucial in stock market analysis, great emphasis is placed on earnings reports for such short intervals as the single quarter (or three-month period). Insofar as the accounting profession and regulatory authorities tend to believe that security analysis should be mainly stock market analysis, there are considerable pressures on the accounting profession and issuers to have quarterly reports not only relatively complete (a good thing for corporate analysts), but also accurate and reliable (an impossible undertaking in the case of the vast majority of issuers).*

In contrast to the emphasis on changes in short-run accounting earnings as reported, corporate analysts use accounting figures as tools. Financial position and access to finance are viewed frequently in corporate analysis as more important than earnings, whether or not those earnings are accounting earnings as reported or accounting earnings as adjusted by the analyst. Corporate analysts also are cognizant of book net asset values most of the time, a factor all but ignored in most stock market analysis.

Within the earnings figures, sometimes recurring earnings from operations are emphasized by the corporate realist, and sometimes other aspects of the income account are emphasized, such as cash generated from the use of tax-loss carry-forwards (an "extraordinary

---

*The Financial Accounting Standards Board is currently studying interim financial reporting and expects to issue a draft in early 1979.

item," in accounting parlance). In most corporate situations, earnings emphasis is based on looking at results over a number of years to obtain an understanding of how a business operates under a variety of conditions. In stock market analysis, on the other hand, long-term earnings tend to be significant only if there can be an extrapolation of a growth trend, because in good markets growth trends are apt to be sponsored into high price–earnings ratios regardless of the underlying economics of the business. Indeed, in bull markets the price–earnings ratio that the market assigns to a common stock seems to be derived exclusively from two factors: (1) the growth trend of earnings per share, and (2) the industry identification of the issuer. In the latter case, a glamour name for a company in a glamour industry tends to be worth millions in terms of stock market appraisals.

It seems unlikely to us that outside investors without great psychological insights are going to have much success in predicting the direction of the general market. The appraisals the market will give to companies identified with certain industries and to the near-term earnings performance for most companies are not the subject of factual corporate analysis. (Electric utilities' profits are highly predictable; manufacturing companies' in general are not.) Yet, whereas stock market analysis is mostly myth to us, it is easy to understand why it is reality, not myth, for those who regard themselves as "market players."

First, outside investors, whether individual or institutional, gravitate toward stock market analysis when they have neither access to information nor control of corporate situations, or when they do have information or control but they lack the training for using it. In this situation, the reality is, The market knows more than I do.

Second, insofar as investors have limited resources, there is a natural desire to make gains fast and avoid losses. Thus, short-run market analysis becomes supreme. In stock market analysis the maxim is, Don't try to buy at the bottom. Yet almost everybody tries to. In part, this is because each stock purchaser feels that he has special luck and limited exposure; the laws of chance do not apply to him. Furthermore, even if things turn sour, he will be able to sell out at only a small loss if the security declines a small amount.

Third, in a certain sense it is logical in stock market analysis to emphasize net income rather than the resources, financial or otherwise, of a business that is either strictly a going concern or a candidate for asset conversion. The outsider, having no control over the way resources are used, feels more assured that favorable earnings reports will cause a common stock to sell at higher prices than if almost any other event occurred. Events other than earnings that might cause the stock to sell at higher prices—such as a merger, takeover or new discovery—may be far less predictable than earnings.

Fourth, many advisers, ranging from analysts at mutual funds to customer's men, tend to be judged on near-term performance by both their peers and their customers. Being right about the market has an importance all its own, so that many have to try to predict the market whether they can and want to do so or not.

Fifth, the financial position of a securities holder may be viewed by him as crucial, causing him to strive mightily for near-term performance. (Borrowed money in the spring of 1978 cost between 7 percent and 8 percent, for better credit risks.)

Stock market analysis and even stock market reality can be important to activists who are not stock market players. For example, stock market considerations are very important tools that the active investor or promoter has to be cognizant of if new money is to be raised by issuing equity securities to the public. This is pointed up in Appendixes I and II.

One final note about a difference between corporate reality and stock market reality when it involves the use of financial accounting. Since in stock market reality there is no attempt at a deep-down understanding of a business, success is sought elsewhere. Commonly, it is in numerical precision. Thus, great weight is given to precise figures, such as earnings as reported, dividends, the closing price of a stock and—almost exclusively in the case of registered investment trusts where asset-conversion values are always given great weight by all investors—net asset value as measured by market prices. In contrast, the only time such weight is given to precise numbers in corporate analysis is in situations where there is to be realization rather than measurement of value. Precise market prices become important in corporate reality only when they are to be used to buy or sell or to collateralize securities. Interest and dividends are also realization, not valuation, figures.

Misconceptions that Accounting Can Be Made Distortion-free and/or Realistic and/or Uniform

Financial accounting is based on a not too precisely defined, but still relatively rigid, set of assumptions known as Generally Accepted Accounting Principles, commonly referred to as GAAP. In order that financial accounting be a useful tool in providing objective bench marks, it is important to have a good idea of what GAAP is and is not. This is discussed in the next chapter. Suffice it to say for purposes of this section that because of its relatively rigid assumptions, GAAP cannot accurately encompass, describe and measure all business stiuations.

Included among the rigidities that tend to limit GAAP are the following principles:

1. An attempt is made to match revenues with costs on an accrual basis to the exclusion of matching cash inflow with cash outflow.
2. An attempt is made to view businesses on a going-concern basis, even though that concept is frequently put aside in the desire to make accounting universally "truthful."
3. Financial-accounting measurements are primarily, but not exclusively, based on exchange prices—that is, the cost or proceeds from transactions are measured, in this country, in U.S. dollars.
4. Financial accounting is primarily based on historical costs, even though all going-concern audits have to contain a large number of judgments about, and estimates of, future events.
5. Financial statements are designed to be general-purpose: as is stated in *Accounting Principles,*[26] they "serve the common needs of a variety of user groups with primary emphasis on the needs of

[26]American Institute of Certified Public Accountants, *op. cit.*

present and potential owners and creditors," even though the same items tend to have quite different meanings when they are part of American Telephone's financial statements, compared with when they are, say, part of Tishman Realty's.

Because of the various limiting rigidities, GAAP cannot be distortion-free, realistic or uniform for all users. Much of the scorn presently heaped on the accounting profession is based on views that financial accounting can in fact achieve such goals. We, on the other hand, feel that corporate accounting as it has developed in the United States has attained an unusually high degree of social and economic usefulness as a professional service. This certainly seems true compared with, say, stock brokerage, management consulting, economics, tax accounting or corporate law. With a number of others, such as Robert A. Kleckner of Alexander, Grant and Company and Samuel Gunther of Richard A. Eisner and Company, we feel that continued attempts on the part of the profession to make accounting distortion-free, realistic or uniform are bound to be counterproductive, since they will make financial accounting a less useful objective benchmark for creditors and long-term investors than it now is.

Financial accounting is not very useful in corporate analysis for those who are untrained or unwilling to use it, nor can it be designed to help traders primarily interested in stock market reality without detracting from its essential role in corporate analysis as a tool for creditors and investors. In this we are in agreement with one of the promulgations of GAAP, namely, "Financial statement users are presumed to be generally familiar with business practices, the technical language of accounting and the nature of the information reported."[27] Many critics of accounting, however, believe that financial statements should be directed exclusively toward average investors— outsiders and traders caught up with day-to-day stock market fluctuations.

As a measuring tool, accounting results are more meaningful, more accurate and more important for certain types of companies than

---

[27]*Ibid.*, Sec. 1022.27, pp. 138–39.

for others, especially when financial accounting is used to measure economic results and values rather than the solvency of a business.

At the one end of the scale are strict going concerns—for example, operating utilities—where the periodic report of net income may be a fairly accurate indicator of how the business performs, and the balance sheet may give a reasonably reliable indication of economic assets and economic liabilities. This is true even though such results may fail to reflect the ravages of inflation on plant replacement costs and their inadequate depreciation charges, or the ravages of higher interest rates on refinancing costs, or the ravages of energy shortages on future fuel costs. On the other end of the scale from utilities are a series of industries where financial accounting tends to be less important (though it is always essential), a less accurate measure of economic events, and less meaningful: these are industries that are largely involved in natural resources, real estate and life insurance, as well as companies actively engaged in mergers, acquisitions and imaginative financing and refinancing.

GAAP is better able to measure certain types of economic phenomena than others. The following table shows the characteristics of companies where GAAP is more useful compared with those where GAAP is less useful.

	GAAP *More Useful*	GAAP *Less Useful*
Object of business is to create wealth through	Going-concern operations only	Going-concern operations or asset-conversion activities that result in realized or unrealized capital gains
		Going-concern operations frequently are the least desirable method of wealth creation
Cycle to complete economic transaction	Short	Long or indeterminate
Opportunities for tax shelter	Nonexistent	A prime incentive governing economic actions

	GAAP More Useful	GAAP Less Useful
Asset value can be measured with some degree of precision	Yes	No
Differing accounting choices within the industry	No	Yes
Corporate actions limited by regulation	Yes	No
Physical operations within the industry tend to be unique	Yes	No
Opportunities for diversification exist	No	Yes
Management is merger- and acquisition-conscious	No	Yes
Financial techniques used are imaginative	No	Yes

Also, on an interindustry basis, distortions have to be present in GAAP. The same words mean different things applied to different industries. For example, in certain areas of real estate accounting, depreciation charges are an economic fiction; much of well-maintained, well-located real estate does not depreciate over time, even though for financial accounting and tax purposes the property is depreciated. In other spheres, accounting depreciation charges against property may also be an economic fiction, but only because they are woefully inadequate compared with the economic depreciation caused by obsolescence, misuse and inflation. Examples of inadequate depreciation include charges against income for depreciation before 1972 by certain lessors of IBM 360 computers, namely Rockwood, DPF, DCL, Boothe, and Greyhound. All these companies assigned an eight- to ten-year useful life to the 360, in contrast to IBM, which assigned it a five- to seven-year life. Some of the "big bath" write-downs in the last several years reflect a realization that past depreciation charges were inadequate.

Further, there are interindustry distortions based on GAAP that come about by calling very similar economic events "permanent differences" in one context and "timing differences" in another.

Under GAAP, timing differences are defined as "differences between the periods in which transactions affect taxable income and the periods in which they enter into the determination of pretax accounting income. Timing differences originate in one period and reverse or 'turn around' in one or more subsequent periods. Most timing differences reduce income taxes that would otherwise be payable currently, based on financial accounting."*

Under GAAP (according to APB Opinion 11, Paragraphs 13e and f, issued December 1967), permanent differences are defined as follows: "Differences between taxable income and pre-tax accounting income arising from transactions that, under applicable tax laws and regulations, will not be offset by corresponding differences or 'turn around' in other periods." It is permissible to classify percentage depletion as a "permanent difference."

In brief, accelerated plant depreciation under GAAP gives rise to a liability for future income taxes called deferred income tax, and thus has to be accounted for at the time the actual tax savings are realized. Percentage depletion under GAAP also results in current tax savings, but there is no necessity for setting up a reserve for any future tax expenses, simply because no tax liability ever will be created out of an excess of statutory depletion over cost depletion. One realistic theory of percentage depletion, though, is that the natural resource recovered is a wasting asset, and that the tax savings created by the percentage-depletion allowance will have to be invested in costs for discovering new reserves. Under this theory, GAAP might have concluded that if it did not want to distort relative to accelerated plant depreciation, the current tax savings, instead of being flowed through to net income, could result in an equivalent charge to net income for a reserve for future exploration and development costs.

*Paragraph 13 of Statement of Financial Accounting Standards 9 (issued in October 1975 by the Financial Accounting Standards Board) gives oil- and gas-producing companies an election as to whether a company desires to "flow through" or "normalize" excess statutory depletion.

Analogously, under the going-concern concept GAAP could have fairly concluded, also, that the tax savings arising out of accelerated depreciation would be reinvested in more depreciable assets with their accompanying tax deductions, and thus the deferred taxes would never in fact become payable. Such a flow-through treatment would put accelerated plant depreciation on the same footing as statutory percentage depletion.

The basic point, however, is that a logical argument can be made that current tax savings virtually always result in permanent differences in the real world of tax shelter, and certainly when there is accelerated depreciation taken by going concerns. An equally logical argument can be made that what are now called permanent differences—percentage depletion, investment credit, savings and loan reserves, and life insurance company policyholder surplus—are no more permanent in economic fact than are many other tax savings where GAAP requires that reported income be reduced by a charge for a reserve for future expenses (usually income taxes). But GAAP has to take a yes-or-no stand somewhere. Accordingly, it can never be distortion-free in matters such as these. This does not mean that GAAP is not useful. It is particularly useful when it is reconcilable. But reconciliation means work for the user of accounting statements, not for the preparer of financial statements.

Perhaps an even stronger point can be made that deferred taxes should not be charged against income at their face value, but, rather, should be discounted to present value to reflect the fact that the reporting company has the use of the tax savings until some future date, as well as the possibility that the tax may never become payable. Insofar as this is done, GAAP tends to lose objectivity and therefore some usefulness. It is our view that the discounting to present value in the vast majority of instances is something that should be done by the user of financial statements, not the preparer.

On an intra-industry basis, there is an inherent conflict between wanting GAAP to be uniform and wanting it to be realistic. Most companies in most industries, and virtually all companies in nonregulated industries, have marked differences in the way they do things, whether in regard to engineering practices, sales methods, advertising techniques, diversification, renting versus owning, executive compensation or product mix. To make their accounts uniform would be unrealistic. The most one can hope for is reconcilability.

On the other hand, making GAAP largely realistic would limit its main function as the provider of understandably limited bench marks to the users of financial accounting (principally securities holders and creditors), who, if they wish, can make their own corrections.

Accounting for lessors engaged in finance leasing serves as one good example of how GAAP has to distort. GAAP provides in this instance a fair statement of the lessor's net income during each of the periods being accounted for, insofar as the accounting refers only to the one asset being leased. Thus, a distorted view is received by the user of the lessor's cash-in and cash-out, and also of the lessor's periodic net income, if one assumes (as is almost always realistic) that differing amounts of assets will be leased out in each period.

To begin with, the financing method of leasing results in a fair statement of a lessor's periodic net income on a per-lease basis only. In order to accomplish this, GAAP requires a front-end load in the realization of revenues, so that in earlier periods the reported rental revenues will usually be greater than the cash collections. Thus, when enough new leases are written in each period to increase the initial recording of earned income, the lessor's reported profits in each period will exceed its cash collections. If these increases in leasing activity continue indefinitely, a distortion will result in reports to outside stockholders because of the disparity between reported earnings and the cash experience. This distortion will occur even though there is a fair statement of periodic net income on a per-lease basis.

There is a corollary to this: the financing method does not adequately measure discounts to present value. For example, dollars to be received in the future, such as from estimated residual values, are worth less than dollars to be received today.

It should be noted too that if the financing method were changed so that it would be more closely related to a lessor's actual cash experience, other distortions would still result. This follows because, first, a lessor's net cash collections during the initial year that a profitable lease is put on its books will not reflect the lessor's earnings in the form of equity in future rentals to be collected. Next, the return on the equipment being leased will be distorted at the initial stages; the lessor has a greater capital investment in the equipment being leased, and thus should be able to report higher earnings in earlier years, in part to cover higher charges on borrowings.

Specifically, the Accounting Principles Board, or APB (the predecessor group to the Financial Accounting Standards Board, or FASB, which has the primary responsibility for determining appropriate accounting principles), promulgated in 1966 APB Opinion 7, "Accounting for Leases in Financial Statements of Lessors." In Paragraph 5 of that opinion, the APB stated:

Under the financing method, the excess of aggregate rentals over the cost (reduced by estimated residual value at the termination of the lease) of the leased property is generally designed to compensate the lessor for the use of the funds invested. Since this excess is in the nature of interest, it is recognized as revenue during the terms of the lease in decreasing amounts related to the declining balance of the uncovered investment or, in other words, as an approximately level rate of return on funds not yet recovered. When rentals are level, this results in a decreasing percentage of each succeeding rental being accounted for as revenues and an increasing percentage as recovery of investments. This is comparable to the method followed by most leading institutions in accounting for level payment plans.

In November 1976 the Financial Accounting Standards Board issued the Statement of Financial Accounting Standards 13, "Accounting for Leases." FASB Statement 13 does not alter materially the method usable by lessors to account for direct financing leases.

The comparable language in the Statement of Financial Accounting Standards 13 is contained in Paragraph 18b.

The difference between the gross investment in the lease in (a) above and the cost or carrying amount, if different, of the leased property shall be recorded as unearned income. The net investment in the lease shall consist of the gross investment less the unearned income. Initial direct costs (as defined in paragraph 5(m)) shall be charged against income as incurred, and a portion of the unearned income equal to the initial direct costs shall be recognized as income in the same period. The remaining unearned income shall be amortized to income over the lease term so as to produce a constant periodic rate of return on the net investment in the lease. However, other methods of income recognition may be used if the results obtained are not materially ·different from those which would result from the prescribed method in the preceding sentence.

Let us look at how Paragraph 5 used to work in practice (and how FASB 13 would work now).* Leasco Corporation's accounting practices under the financing method seem fairly typical. According

*Since FASB 13 is being phased in at the time of this writing, we have not yet uncovered any footnotes to financial statements covering the finance method for lessors that is as specific as the language used by Leasco. The best FASB 13 language we found was contained in the 1977 financial statements of ACF Industries Incorporated. ACF's accounting practice for finance leases under FASB 13 appears to be substantially similar to Leasco's under APB Opinion 7. See the ACF footnote on the opposite page.

In addition, certain railroad cars were leased in 1976 and 1977 under the finance method. The Company recognized the applicable manufacturing revenues, costs and profit and recorded the aggregate rental receivable net of the amount of unearned financing charges. The unearned financing charges are to be recognized in decreasing amounts over the life of the lease which will provide a level rate of return on the unrecovered investment. A summary of the amounts outstanding resulting from the finance leasing of railroad cars is as follows:

	December 31	
	1977	1976
Aggregate rental receivable	$20,750,000	$22,398,000
Unearned financing charges	(10,219,000)	(11,303,000)
Net receivable from finance leasing	10,531,000	11,095,000
Portion to be recovered within one year	(623,000)	(564,000)
Balance, receivable in installments through 1992	$9,908,000	$10,531,000

At December 31, 1977, minimum future rentals to be received from finance leases for each of the five succeeding years are as follows: $1,648,000 in 1978 and 1979; $1,653,000 in 1980; $1,645,000 in 1981; and $1,493,000 in 1982. The estimated residual value of $751,000 of these railroad cars is included on the consolidated balance sheet with specialized railroad cars leased to others.

to the footnote in a 1973 Leasco prospectus, its accounting under the financing method was described as follows:

For leases where costs will be recovered during the initial term, the finance method of accounting for lease income is used. The excess of gross rentals, plus the estimated additional amounts at the end of the lease (defined below) over the cost of the equipment leased represents unearned income. During the first months of each lease, a portion of the unearned income is transferred to earned income to offset the costs incurred in acquiring and consummating the lease, which costs are expended as incurred. These transfers ... were 13% of the income—Commencing with the second month, the balance of unearned income is transferred to earned income over the terms of the lease by the sum of the years-digits method. The estimated additional amounts represent the residual value at the end of the lease term determined on one of the following bases not to exceed in most instances 10% of the original equipment cost: (a) at the stated option prices, if any, in the lease contract; or (b) the estimated renewal payment to be received after expiration of the original lease term; or (c) at the estimated salvage value if lower than the foregoing.

(Unearned income is a balance sheet debit and earned income is an income account credit, i.e., profit.)

Applying this Leasco paragraph on an annual rather than a monthly basis to a theoretical yet practical lease situation, one can construct both income accounts and cash-collection accounts. The purchase, lease and financing of the equipment is assumed to be as follows:

1. Purchase equipment for $4.5 million
2. Lease equipment for five years at $1.2 million per year
3. Estimated residual value of equipment—$400,000
4. Cost of acquiring lease—$200,000
5. Borrow $4 million to purchase equipment, repayable over five years based on level debt service of $950,000 per annum. Of annual level debt service, $250,000 of the first year's payment is attributable to interest, as is $200,000 of the second year's, $150,000 of the third, $100,000 of the fourth and $50,000 of the fifth

Given these assumptions, simplified five-year summaries of income accounts using the financing method and as compared with the cash-collection experience would be as follows:

INCOME ACCOUNT — FINANCING METHOD

	Year 1	Year 2	(000) Year 3	Year 4	Year 5	Aggre- gate
Acquisition expense (credited to income)	200					200
Revenues—booked on sum-of-the-year's-digits method	567	453	340	227	113	1,700
Earned income	767	453	340	227	113	1,900
Acquisition expense (debited to income)	200	—	—	—	—	200
Operating income	567	453	340	227	113	1,700
Interest expense	250	200	150	100	50	750
Income before taxes	317	253	190	127	63	950*

CASH-COLLECTION EXPERIENCE

The initial cash deficit is $500,000, equal to the excess of the cost of equipment, $4.5 million, over borrowings of $4 million.

	Year 1	Year 2	(000) Year 3	Year 4	Year 5	Total
Rent collection	1,200	1,200	1,200	1,200	1,200	6,000
Acquisition expense	200					200
Debt service	950	950	950	950	950	4,750
Cash generated	50	250	250	250	250	1,050
Cumulative cash (deficit) or surplus	(450)	(200)	50	300	550*	

*The difference between this $950 profit reported under GAAP and $550 cash generated is attributable to the estimated residual value of $400.

As long as an increasing volume of leases can be obtained, first-year results will dominate reports to stockholders, that is, reported profits will be at their maximum, as will cash deficits. Just by increasing lease volume (even if leases are not very profitable), lessors can report relatively large profits. For example, assume in the above example that annual rental payments were only $1,050,000 per annum. Such a rental schedule means a loss over the five-year life on each lease of $200,000 before allowing for the $400,000 profit in the estimated residual value of the equipment. In that instance, pretax profits accounted for under the financing method would be as follows:

INCOME ACCOUNT — FINANCING METHOD

	Year 1	Year 2	(000) Year 3	Year 4	Year 5	
Earned income	217	253	190	127	63	950
Interest expense	250	200	150	100	50	
Income before taxes	67	53	40	27	13	200*

CASH COLLECTION

	Year 1	Year 2	Year 3	Year 4	Year 5
Rental income	1,050	1,050	1,050	1,050	1,050
Acquisition expense	200				
Debt service	950	950	950	950	950
Cash generated	(100)	100	100	100	100
Cumulative cash (deficit)	(600)	(500)	(400)	(300)	(200)

*Based on $400,000 residual value less $200,000 loss exclusive of residual value.

We believe that the financing method distorts because the front-end load on revenues results in an overstatement of profits relative to cash collections when the business is expanding. It results in "Ponzi accounting."* However, a cash-collection method of accounting distorts too because while a business is expanding, cash collections fail to reflect the equity the lessor has in the probability that future rentals will be collected. We believe that no accounting method could be promulgated that would not distort in one or more meaningful contexts. Finally, we believe that outside investors are entitled to sufficient disclosures, so that they can—if they are willing to work—obtain reasonable insights into what the reported accounting numbers really mean. Without such disclosures and a willingness to use them, financial accounting, we think, is not likely to provide useful tools much of the time.

Another area where GAAP becomes very difficult to apply in an undistorted manner is in mergers and acquisitions—whether the accounting used should be purchase or pooling of interests. Both distort, compared with economic reality. The implicit assumption in purchase accounting is that the stock market price and/or value—whether real or imputed—of senior securities measure the economic value of a business. The implied assumption in pooling is that book values measure economic value. As far as we are concerned, neither market prices nor book values alone measure real values for most businesses in most contexts.

Accounting based on historic cost tends to be distortion-free in disclosing to the user what has actually happened. It is highly distorted in terms of measuring what the future experience will be for going concerns based on probable replacement costs. The Securities and Exchange Commission's Accounting Series Release 190, which requires certain issuers to provide supplemental financial statements based on replacement costs, may give valuable new supplementary

---

*Charles Ponzi was a notorious Boston swindler in the 1920's. He borrowed money from unsuspecting persons, promising them inordinately high returns. He obtained funds to repay his early investors their principal and interest by inducing increasing numbers of people to invest with him. Eventually, this chain-letter scheme collapsed when new investors could not be found fast enough to keep old investors satisfied. What survived was a description of this method of operations, commonly called a Ponzi scheme or a Ponzi game.

disclosures to investors, even though it is our experience that it will not be very helpful to know what estimated replacement costs are if there are no disclosures about what capital expenditures will be. However, replacement-cost disclosures viewed alone distort, despite their possible value, because in most analysis it is important to have knowledge of actual past costs and experience.

Other new proposals for supplementary accounting information are valuable and useful, but they, too, distort. For example, much of present-value accounting distorts because the discount factor is not derived from sufficiently objective standards. Furthermore, whereas present value may be applied to certain of an issuer's accounts, such as receivables on the installment sale of real estate, present-value concepts may not be applied to such other accounts as a long-term debt at a well-below-market interest rate.

General price-level accounting distorts too because it is based on the underlying assumption that the value of money depreciates as inflation increases, as measured by such indexes as the Bureau of Labor Statistics' Wholesale Price Index. However, insofar as inflation is accompanied by increasing interest rates, money does not necessarily depreciate in value, at least for those who have surplus cash that they invest in short-term money-market instruments, such as U.S. treasury bills, bank certificates of deposit or commercial paper. If an issuer had cash in 1974 that it could invest in 10 percent money-market instruments, in that context the cash is much more valuable than it was five years previously, when it would have been invested in comparable instruments for only a 5 percent return.

From the point of view of most parent-company stockholders of solvent going businesses, the key financial statements upon which to rely are consolidated financial statements, since they provide an overview of how the whole company is doing and what its position is to the outside world. However, if you are a security holder of a shaky parent company, or even a secured senior lender, and the parent has to obtain distributions from its subsidiaries in order to service its obligations, then the key financial statements are not the consolidated statements. Primary financial data here would come from examination of the parent-company financial statements. This does not mean that either consolidated financial statements or parent-company-only financial statements necessarily distort. It does mean that both are useful, depending on who is using them for what purposes, and that either type can distort if the user is unaware of its uses and limitations.

Progress in improving accounting disclosures for investors and creditors has been fast and dramatic in recent years. In fact, since around 1972, many of the new rules and proposals promulgated by the accounting profession through both the former Accounting Principles Board and its successor, the Financial Accounting Standards Board, have resulted in quantum leaps in new disclosures given to investors. Also, the Securities and Exchange Commission, through its Accounting Series Releases, has contributed importantly since 1972 in requiring issuers to provide valuable new disclosures to public investors. Important new disclosures of general usefulness that have become available through these sources include the following:*

*In addition, there have been a number of pronouncements about particular industries that have proved especially helpful to investors. These are contained in the Industry Audit Guides, published by the American Institute of Certified Public Accountants, and in the SEC Accounting Series Releases.

Release	*Short Title*	*Date*	*Contents*
Accounting Principles Board Opinion 22	Disclosure of Accounting Policies	April 1972	Each audit statement now contains a review of the issuer's specific accounting principles and the methods of applying those principles
Financial Accounting Standards Board Statement 13	Accounting for Leases	Nov. 1976	Established standards of financial accounting as reported for leases by lessees and lessors

Release	Short Title	Date	Contents
Financial Accounting Standards Board Statement 14	Financial Reporting for Segments of a Business Enterprise	Dec. 1976	Requires that the financial statements of a business enterprise include information about the company's operations in different industries, its foreign operations and export sales, and its major customers
Securities and Exchange Commission Accounting Series Releases 148 and 172	Disclosure of Compensating Balances and Short-Term Borrowing Arrangements	Nov. 1973 (supplemented June 1975 to conform to Financial Accounting Standards Statement 6)	Issuers now disclose in footnotes important information about the terms of short-term borrowings
149	Improved Disclosure of Income-Tax Expense	Dec. 1973	Issuers now provide footnote reconciliation between theoretical tax rate and actual tax rate booked for financial-statement purpose
150	Disclosure of Inventory Profits	Jan. 1974	SEC encourages but does not require footnote disclosure of effect on profits of rapidly rising costs of inventory which may not be compensated for by sales-price increases
159	Adoption of Guide One of the Guides for the Preparation and Filing of Reports under the Exchange Act	Aug. 1974	Requires the inclusion of a narrative explanation of changes in sales and expenses from one reporting period to another
164	Improved Disclosures Related to Defense and Other Long-Term Contract Activities	Nov. 1974	Improved disclosures in statements and footnotes for certain types of contracts

Release	Short Title	Date	Contents
165, 194 and 250	Disclosure of Relation between Registrants and Their Independent Public Accountants	Dec. 1974, April 1976 and June 1978	Requires adequate disclosure of reasons for changes in auditors—filed as Form 8-K rather than as part of financial statements
166	Disclosure of Unusual Risks and Uncertainties in Financial Reporting	Dec. 1974	Encourages disclosure of potential problems that otherwise would not be required in financial statements
177	Interim Financial Reporting	Sept. 1975	Requires more comprehensive disclosures in interim financial statements
226 and 237	Disclosure by Commercial and Industrial Companies of Investments in Marketable Securities and Other Investments	Sept. 1977 and Dec. 1977	Requires detailed disclosures regarding each issue of securities of any issuer held in a registrant's portfolio where the greater of the aggregate cost or market value of the securities of the issuer constitute 2 percent or more of the total assets of the registrant
253	Financial Accounting and Reporting Practices for Oil- and Gas-Producing Activities	Aug. 1978	Requirements for reporting periods after calendar 1979 of supplementary data giving valuation of, and changes in valuation of, proved oil and gas reserves for oil and gas companies

Chapter 8

Generally Accepted Accounting Principles

❧

"When I use a word," Humpty Dumpty said, in rather
a scornful tone, "it means just what I choose
it to mean—neither more nor less."
"The question is," said Alice, "whether you can make
words mean so many different things."

— LEWIS CARROLL,
Through the Looking Glass

MYTHS AND REALITIES ABOUT THE
MEANING OF GENERALLY ACCEPTED
ACCOUNTING PRINCIPLES (GAAP)

THE CODIFICATION of rules and regulations under which managements prepare financial statements that are reviewed and frequently certified by accountants is known as Generally Accepted Accounting Principles, or GAAP. The primary users of statements prepared in accordance with GAAP are securities holders of all sorts—bank lenders, outside investors in common stocks, private-venture capital investors and property owners who lease facilities to users on a net, net, net basis.* However, virtually all other segments of our economy

*"Net, net, net" refers to the complete passivity of a landlord. The landlord holding a net, net, net position is responsible for no function in the operation of a property. The landlord merely is a recipient of rents.

are readers of GAAP-prepared financial statements, including company customers, vendors, labor unions and even the Internal Revenue Service, which has some relatively precise (though not necessarily logical) rules as to when financial statements prepared in accordance with the Internal Revenue Code have to comport with those prepared in accordance with GAAP, and when the two need not have any discernible relationship to each other. Every investor interested in corporate reality ought to know what GAAP is, its uses and its limitations.

There are three prevalent myths about GAAP. The first is that GAAP tends to, or ought to, be rigidly codified with a series of well-articulated do's and don'ts. Fortunately, GAAP is still not as highly rigid as is that other major United States accounting system, the Internal Revenue Code. It is to be hoped that GAAP never will become that way. If it does, it will no longer be useful for its principal purpose, which is to serve as an objective bench mark for those who appreciate its uses and limitations.

The second myth is that GAAP is all-encompassing and is, or should be, designed to measure all sorts of corporate events and phenomena. GAAP in fact measures only a limited number of events in limited ways.

The third myth about GAAP is the one expounded by its most vociferous critics, such as Abraham Briloff[28] and David Norr.[29] This myth is centered on a belief that GAAP ought to tell the Truth, that somehow it can be made more realistic for average investors while still becoming more informative and more useful for all of its users. The goal of reality-for-all through GAAP is a mirage. Corporate life is too complicated to expect any system of measurement to reflect more than a few pertinent objective bench marks; it cannot accurately—that is, realistically—report on all events and positions, especially since what is realistic frequently depends on the subjective interpretation of individual users of GAAP, as, for example, whether

[28]Abraham J. Briloff, *Unaccountable Accounting* (New York: Harper & Row, 1972).

[29]David Norr, *Accounting Theory Illustrated*, Vol. II, 1974 reports (New York: First Manhattan Co., 1975).

the first approach to valuation should be a going-concern approach or an asset-conversion approach. Within very wide limits, the way to make GAAP more useful is to make it more informative, regardless of whether it becomes more realistic. Fortunately, nearly all critics of GAAP, whatever else they disagree on, think it should be made increasingly informative. As a result of this, improvements in GAAP disclosures during the past ten years have been dramatic, as we pointed out in the previous chapter.

The formal definition of GAAP, as it appears in *Accounting Principles,* is as follows:

GAAP incorporates the consensus[1] at a particular time as to which economic resources and obligations should be recorded as assets and liabilities by financial accounting, which changes in assets and liabilities should be recorded, when these changes should be recorded, how the assets and liabilities in them should be measured, what information should be disclosed and which financial statements should be prepared.

(1) Inasmuch as GAAP embody a consensus, they depend on notions such as *general acceptance* and *substantial authoritative support* which are not precisely defined.[30]

Opinions of the Accounting Principles Board (APB) and its successor, the Financial Accounting Standards Board (FASB), constitute substantial authoritative support. Theoretically, substantial authoritative support can exist for principles that differ from those of APB and FASB, but the burden of proof for departing from their dicta lies with the accountant preparing the financial statements in question. Such departures must be disclosed, but they are extremely rare.

Because GAAP is derived from general acceptability and substantial authoritative support, the emphasis has been on functionalism—whether particular rules will be useful and will work. The use of these standards has been fortunate in that it has enabled GAAP to reach its present status as an extremely useful tool for corporate

---

[30]American Institute of Certified Public Accountants, *op. cit.* Secs. 1022.18 and 1026.01, p. 136.

analysis. However, the level of abstraction involved in deriving GAAP is not at all deep; rather, it is relatively superficial. There is very little in accounting literature that is deeply abstract, at least insofar as trying to explain why GAAP has developed the way it has or what GAAP is designed to do.

In the following pages, we review various underlying abstractions out of which GAAP evolved that we believe are important in helping investors understand how GAAP is useful and where it is limited. Because GAAP grew out of general acceptability, the assumptions underlying GAAP reflect the economic, legal and social mores that prevail in the United States. Indeed, because GAAP is based on commonly granted realities, it tends to be more useful than a code based upon abstract theorizing in a vacuum.

We believe that there are eleven underlying, unarticulated assumptions, an appreciation of which gives creditors and investors good insights into the uses and limitations of GAAP.

UNDERLYING GAAP ASSUMPTION I

Ownership of—that is, title to—tangible assets is the basis of value and the means of creating income.

Although it may seem to be a natural outgrowth of free-enterprise economics that value and income are created out of ownership of title to tangible property, there are no necessary reasons why an accounting system has to be based on such concepts. These concepts result in defining value or income as the excess of cash, receivables, inventory, investments and fixed assets over liabilities, with liabilities being defined strictly as obligations incurred to create assets, either tangible or intangible, that appear on a company's balance sheet, where the only assets that normally appear are those to which the company has title.

Rather than basing a corporate accounting system upon title to tangibles, a system could be based on "rights to use" as a definition of assets, and "increases (or decreases) in rights to use" as a definition of profit (or loss). Because title to tangible assets is an underlying ownership concept of GAAP, any attempt to fit the right-to-use phenomena into it is awkward. Thus, there are various difficulties in accounting for leases by lessors and lessees.

GAAP could also have been grounded in other underlying assumptions. For example, one might argue that value and income are best measured by estimating future benefits for the corporation. This is the assumption underlying the capitalization of expenditures, which would otherwise be expensed by charges to income; the GAAP treatment or nontreatment of capitalized expenditures, especially for intangibles such as research and development, has always been awkward.* Also, it would be logical in a mixed or nonfree enterprise system to base accounting rules on estimated social cost rather than on historic cost; many such proposals are extant today.

GAAP, as it must be, is a limited tool in measuring value and income, albeit an essential tool. It is limited in its measurements by economic data that fit into a bookkeeping cycle, which in turn is limited, by and large, to tangible assets to which a company has title. There are, however, all sorts of economic phenomena that create value and income that are not part of GAAP. Analysts, lenders and equity investors can ignore these non-GAAP variables only at their own peril, even though each and every one is an intangible. These key intangibles include the following:

- The first intangible involves debt finance. A lack of debt or an ability to create new debt is frequently a most important asset. In principal areas of corporate finance—such as underwriting, private placements, and mergers and acquisitions, as well as in the financial-integrity approach to fundamental analysis—a key variable almost all practitioners focus on is a lack of debt. The quality

---

*Since the effective date of FASB Statement 2 (January 1, 1975), corporations have been required to charge all research and development costs to expense when incurred.

of the balance sheet tends to be a far more important consideration in corporate finance than the quantity of net assets on the balance sheet, or reported net worth, as is pointed out in Chapter 12, "Net Asset Values." Yet lack of debt is largely ignored or played down in conventional fundamental security analysis, in part because, we suspect, unlike earnings and book value, GAAP does not measure an absence of obligations per se.

- The second intangible involves equity finance. The price at which its common stock sells can be a highly important company asset (or liability), especially to any company planning to issue its stock either to raise new money or to obtain additional assets via merger and acquisition. (An acquisition-hungry company using its stock when it is selling at one hundred times earnings and ten times book value to acquire a solidly financed, profitable firm selling at, say, close to book value is said to be trading with "Chinese dollars" or "funny money."*) The stock price conceivably can be important, too, to almost any company planning new financing, even if only short-term bank loans, since there is sometimes (though far from always) a tendency by outsiders to give considerable weight to the stock price in determining how much a company's equity is worth.

Financial strength does not arise solely out of a lack of existing debt or an ability to create new debt, but may also exist because of the presence of low-cost long-term debt. For example, one of Madison Square Garden's principal assets is the ownership of an 80 percent interest in 2 Penn Plaza, an office building in New York City financed by the issuance of a twenty-five-year (or three-hundred-month) level-debt-service mortgage loan bearing 5¾ percent interest. (*Level debt service* refers to a method of loan repayment, under

---

*See Appendix II, "Creative Finance Applied to a Corporate Takeover," where the acquisition of Reliance Insurance Company, a solidly financed, profitable firm, was financed because the acquirer, Leasco Data Processing, was able to issue its high-priced glamorous equity securities for Reliance stock.

which total monthly payments are a constant amount and include both interest and debt repayment. In the early months, most of the payments constitute interest, while as time passes interest payments decrease and principal repayments increase.) If such a mortgage were to be issued under current conditions, the interest rate probably would be at least 9 percent. Since Madison Square Garden can sell its interest in 2 Penn Plaza subject to the 5¾ percent mortgage loan, the buyer would be willing to pay much more to acquire the building than would otherwise be the case, because a major part of the purchase price involves the assumption of a 5¾ percent mortgage loan. Based on this mortgage-rate factor, the net value of 2 Penn Plaza, using an asset-conversion analysis, is understated on Madison Square Garden's books—that is, liabilities are overstated based on present values for the 5¾ percent mortgage. On a going-concern basis, though, assuming the mortgage will someday have to be refinanced and earnings are currently being overstated because of the need to replace the existing 5¾ percent mortgage, interest charges against income are too low.

By the adoption of an asset-conversion type of present-value accounting, a 5¾ percent loan could be reflected in Madison Square Garden's books so that the mortgage liability, instead of being in the balance sheet at its face value of $25 million, might be reflected in the balance sheet at 90 percent of face value, or $22.5 million, equal to a yield to maturity of 9 percent. But under GAAP this raises all sorts of problems. Should the amount of the mortgage liability be changed periodically to reflect changes in interest rates? Should other accounts—the building itself, for example—also be adjusted to present value, even though there may be only very imprecise measures of present value for other accounts? We fear the widespread adoption of present-value accounting would get too far away from GAAP's underlying assumptions and would result in more confusion than it is worth. Present values, by and large, are something for creditors and investors to determine themselves, using GAAP disclosures as objective bench marks. Present-value accounting has thus far been made part of GAAP in only those limited areas where it seems to have elements of objectivity—in pension accounting and accounting for certain long-term real estate receivables. We do not think present-value accounting should be extended much further.

One concept that pervades this book is the importance, in the appraisal of any corporation or any investment situation, of financial integrity, which is, of course, an intangible that is more or less outside the GAAP scheme of things. There are myriad other intangibles that are not part of GAAP but that are frequently important and even crucial in security analysis and corporate finance. In brief, these other intangibles can include the following:

1. Long-term, favorable (or unfavorable) contracts with key employees, customers and vendors
2. Trade names and patents
3. Distribution channels, such as dealer organizations
4. Manufacturing know-how
5. Licenses to do business
6. Tax-loss carry-backs (worth cash) and tax-loss carry-forwards (which we believe tend to be worthless unless they are usable in clean, or relatively debt-free, shells; see Chapter 16)

There is a final point about intangibles that is almost an aside. GAAP becomes increasingly less descriptive of phenomena in our economy as intangibles become more important as the principal elements of value and the principal sources of income. Intangibles are becoming increasingly prevalent as more and more of the United States' Gross National Product is derived from personal services. GAAP provides good objective bench marks to value the output of steel mills; GAAP does not provide equally good bench marks at all to value the worth of a citizen's medical degree.

UNDERLYING GAAP ASSUMPTION 2

Corporate asset items have independent values unmodified by their inclusion as but one small part of a going concern.

This is the one underlying assumption of GAAP that appears to be at wide variance with reality for going concerns. Indeed, it appears to be in conflict with the pervasive principle of GAAP that financial statements reflect the operations and position of a going concern.

As a practical matter, there are few assets that are part of a going concern that have values independent of the going concern. Independent values for classes of assets exist only in asset-conversion, not going-concern, contexts. No business can have title to or rights to use assets without at the same time assuming substantial encumbrances, de jure or de facto, that involve obligations that might include some liabilities recognized as such by GAAP, but almost certainly will include many others that are not part of GAAP. For example, a company, through ownership of assets, assumes obligations to pay property taxes, to treat its employees fairly, to avoid default in servicing its creditors, to deliver on time to its customers, to not pollute the environment and so on. As a matter of fact, the ownership of or right to use assets can give rise to such onerous non-GAAP liabilities as to bankrupt a business: witness the Chicago, Rock Island and Pacific Railroad's bankruptcy in 1975, caused in great part by the Road's legal obligations to continue operating unprofitable branch lines that it either owned or operated under long-term leases.

About the only situation where the ownership of assets seems to be purely passive and not giving rise to the assumption of material encumbrances is where public, noninstitutional security holders—that is, pure outside investors—hold small amounts of highly marketable securities or cash. Passivity and liquidity are highly interrelated. The more liquid the assets, the less the responsibilities for managing those assets. The speculator who buys egg-futures contracts is rarely looking for the responsibility that goes with owning eggs.

The fact that assets in going concerns do not have a value independent of their relationship to the going concern figures importantly in security analysis. For example, our valuation of deferred income taxes in Chapter 7 is based on a nonindependent, going-concern view of a depreciable asset, in contrast to the independent value assumed under GAAP. Under GAAP, if accelerated depreciation is taken on a piece of machinery for tax purposes, and on regular depreciation for stockholder purposes, income is charged with deferred income taxes, whereas actual tax payments are now reduced because of the accelerated depreciation. Over the life of the piece of machinery, the total tax bill will be the same regardless of the depreciation method used. Our analysis, on the other hand, assumes that it is probable or possible that the cash saved in the early years of use of the piece of machinery because of accelerated depreciation for tax purposes will be reinvested in other depreciable assets. As a consequence, the deferred tax charge is something less than the 100 percent expense GAAP makes it out to be, and indeed the deferred tax may never have to be paid at all. Rather, on a going-concern basis, deferred tax charges have elements of both profit and expense, with the percentage of breakdown between profit and expense best left to analysts rather than to accountants.

UNDERLYING GAAP ASSUMPTION 3

Changes in accounting rules should not be disruptive of important existing practices unless there is conflict among establishment members.

This underlying assumption was considerably more valid before the 1974 pronouncement of the FASB, under which a rule was promulgated requiring that all research and development expenditures be expensed. Nonetheless, it still remains true that GAAP is an establishment tool, and there is implicit recognition that its basic purpose is to aid, not to fight or alter, an existing economic system.

We may expect changes in GAAP to be evolutionary rather than revolutionary or radical. Revolutionary or radical changes rarely if ever reflect a consensus or have general acceptability, at least in the United States as it exists today. And consensus and general acceptability are the stuff out of which GAAP is made.

Thus, the great body of accounting-rule changes tends to be nondisruptive, and if they prove to be disruptive, such changes are either amended or ignored. When accounting rules change, harmful changes are virtually never retroactive, and important exceptions to the new rules tend to be made to accommodate sectors of the establishment that would be harmed if such changes had to be complied with. For example, Opinion 20 of the Accounting Principles Board, entitled "Accounting Changes" and issued in 1971, states that with *one exception,* when accounting principles are changed there should always be disclosure, in one fashion or another, of what the financial statement looked like before the accounting change and what it looked like after. The one exception is contained in Paragraph 29, "Special exemption for an initial public distribution," which refers to companies going public for the first time, in which case there need be no disclosure of what reported net income was before the change in accounting principle. When companies are private, they tend to adopt accounting principles that minimize reported net income and therefore income taxes; when companies go public, they tend to opt for accounting principles that maximize reported net income and, it is hoped, the price at which new issues can be marketed to the public. It could put quite a damper on the new-issue market to require of companies going public for the first time the disclosure of their earnings as reported when the businesses were private. A good argument can be made that such disclosures would serve broad economic interests, either by discouraging certain new issues from ever seeing the public light of day or by making it likely that new issues would be priced lower than they now are. But GAAP tends to be an inappropriate vehicle through which to discourage the financial community's underwriting of companies going public for the first time—which at times has been a significant Wall Street subindustry. This is discussed in some detail in Appendix I, where the F. & M. Schaefer public offering is described.

The one area where there are likely to be radical changes in accounting rules is where one establishment group needs protection against another. The best example of this was the issuance in 1970 of Opinions 16 and 17 of the Accounting Principles Board, severely limiting, and in many cases eliminating, the use of pooling-of-interests accounting for acquisitions. Opinion 16 lays down nine criteria that have to be followed to use pooling accounting rather than purchase accounting. Opinion 17 requires amortization of purchase premiums over periods not to exceed forty years when purchase accounting is used. Acquisitions can be made using either pooling or purchase accounting. Pooling accounting is helpful to earnings-per-share-conscious acquirers whose stocks are selling at substantial premiums above book value and who issue stocks whose market prices represent a substantial premium over the acquired company's book value. In a pooling, two companies merely combine their books; no premiums need be amortized by periodic charges against profit. In purchase accounting, however, a purchaser who issues stock in an acquisition has to account for that acquisition at a price related to the number of shares issued in the acquisition times the market price of the stock issued.

Insofar as that market-derived value exceeds the book value, or appraisal value, of the acquired company, the difference has to be set up in the balance sheet as purchase good will and must be amortized for financial-statement purposes—but not for income-tax purposes—by periodic charges to net income.

Insofar as reported earnings are the name of the game in the stock market, an inability to use pooling discourages many issuers from acquiring companies at values representing premiums over the acquired companies' book values. Such a development has ensued since 1970 and has been warmly greeted by the managements of many staid, solid, conservative companies, which would rather not be taken over by a company run by aggressive financiers anxious to issue Chinese dollars in merger and acquisition transactions.

Opinions 16 and 17 have radically altered the arithmetic and structure of mergers and acquisitions by public companies, and the effects of 16 and 17 would no doubt have been even more dramatic if the 1971–75 bear market, which dropped many stock prices below book value, had not occurred. To us, it seems probable that had a sizable body of influential members of the corporate community—and the antitrust political community as well—not thought that the pace of mergers and acquisitions should be dramatically slowed, there would have been no 16 and 17. The FASB is now restudying 16 and 17 with a view to modifying these opinions, because many believe that they went too far in eliminating the use of pooling and thereby discouraging many mergers and acquisitions that would otherwise be feasible and desirable.

UNDERLYING GAAP ASSUMPTION 4

A puritan work ethic is desirable; hence achievements through going-concern operations are far more desirable than achievements through asset conversions—mergers and acquisitions, reorganizations or refinancings.

It seems implicit in financial accounting and its going-concern standards that businesses are run for the purpose of making profits from operations and that these results are reflected in successive income accounts. With the exception of investment trusts, businesses that attempt to create wealth by refinancing, reorganizing, acquiring, disposing of, or creating realized or unrealized capital gains are aberrational. In part, this is attributable to the fact that businesses that do not strive for operational profits are harder to fit into GAAP standards than those that do. However, there is a universality of the concept that the goal of businesses should be to produce profits from operations rather than to create wealth by fostering capital gains, realized or unrealized. Such a concept is central not only to GAAP, but also to virtually all the literature on security and corporate analysis, ranging from Dewing,[31] Bonbright,[32] and Graham and Dodd,[33] to

[31]Arthur S. Dewing, *The Financial Policy of Corporations* (New York: Roland Press, 1920).

[32]J. C. Bonbright, *The Valuation of Property* (New York: McGraw-Hill, 1937).

[33]Graham and Dodd et al., *op. cit.*

Mauriello[34] and Bogen.[35] It is also an underpinning of our antitrust laws, which tend to deem that expansion by opening new operations is competitively good, whereas expansion by acquisition decreases competition and is ergo bad.

The final seven underlying GAAP assumptions are derived from the accountant's views of what should be done in order to enable a *fair presentation* to be made to readers of financial statements. Most often, but not always, it is thought that a fair presentation ought to be made to average investors. Typically, "average investor" seems to be defined as someone who is (a) not too bright, (b) not trained in the uses and limitations of GAAP and (c) vitally affected by day-to-day fluctuations in stock market prices. We again emphasize that it is impossible, a will-o'-the-wisp, to even attempt to make GAAP comprehensible, much less fair, to an average investor or trader as defined.

UNDERLYING GAAP ASSUMPTION 5

The medium is the message.*

Immediate stock market impact is what financial statements are directed to. What the numbers, especially the net-income figure, are reported as is more important than what the numbers mean. As a corollary to this, there are twin goals that most accounting critics desire—that is, that GAAP should represent Truth and be both realistic and informative. We disagree. We do not believe that much more should be asked of GAAP than that it be informative to people trained to use it.

[34]J. A. Mauriello, *Accounting for the Financial Analyst* (Homewood, Ill.: Irwin, 1967).

[35]Jules I. Bogen, ed., *Financial Handbook,* 4th ed. (New York: Ronald Press, 1964).

*Marshall McLuhan's original statement was "The Medium is the Massage."

UNDERLYING GAAP ASSUMPTION 6

Precise definitions are a desirable goal.

Insofar as possible, items are to be neatly defined as expense or income, liability or proprietorship. Except for insurance-company accounting, there is no recognition that many items—for example, deferred income taxes, unexpired subscriptions and low-interest-rate mortgage loans—have elements of both expense and income, of liability and proprietorship. In other words, there are meaningful equities present in all sorts of liabilities and expenses that are unrecognized under GAAP. To us, this is all to the good; precision helps GAAP perform its function of providing objective bench marks for its users. What these equities are, or if they exist at all, should be determined by GAAP users.

UNDERLYING GAAP ASSUMPTION 7

GAAP is designed primarily to protect the cash buyer of securities.

This underlying assumption, probably the most important, is articulated in GAAP's modifying convention of conservatism. By far the great bulk of cash buyers of corporate securities are lending institutions—banks, insurance companies, pension trusts and finance companies. They could hardly function if they did not rely on GAAP, and GAAP with a conservative bias at that.

As far as the cash buyer of equity securities is concerned, GAAP tends to deliver him a message: how bad things are if you give up your cash for this security. This is a conservative bias. However, GAAP is less well equipped to deliver a message when a holder of equity securities is asked to give up his securities—either for cash or, more commonly, for another security—in a merger and acquisition situation. There, conservatism would involve telling an investor not how bad things might be if he gives up cash for a security, but rather how good things might be if the investor decides to continue holding the security he now holds. GAAP is not designed to provide protection through a conservative bias in situations where the investor is asked to give up securities, as it is in the more conventional situation where he is asked to give up cash.

It would be hard to overstate the importance of this conservative bias in making our economy viable. The investor being asked to give up securities probably is entitled to the same disclosure protection that exists in GAAP for the investor being asked to give up cash. We think such disclosure protections ought to come from narrative disclosure, not from altering GAAP so that the modifying convention of conservatism is altered.

UNDERLYING GAAP ASSUMPTION 8

Security holders tend to be monolithic: all have the same interests.

All stockholders are, according to GAAP, basically interested in the price of the stock they own, and all believe that the most profound influence that GAAP has on stock prices is caused by earnings as reported, and as a corollary, earnings per share. Thus, *Accounting Principles* has a modifying convention attesting to the primacy of the income account. Also, APB Opinion 15 consists of rigorous rules for the computation of earnings per share. There are no comparable rules for the computation of book value.

We, of course, do not believe that stockholders have monolithic interests, or that there is a universal primacy of anything except perhaps financial integrity.

UNDERLYING GAAP ASSUMPTION 9

Per-share market prices are per se important and are the single most significant indicator of the value of entire businesses.

GAAP invests market price with great importance, as indicated, *inter alia,* in the encouragement of the use of purchase accounting by APB Opinion 16. Under 16, the equity of whole businesses or major portions thereof are deemed, in transactions where common stocks are issued, to be worth the number of shares outstanding times the stock market price of the shares.

To us, this assumption is unrealistic. We believe GAAP and accountants would be better off if the importance of stock market values would be down-played in the preparation of all financial statements other than those in which the securities portfolios consist of stocks that are readily marketable, as is the case for investment trusts and fire and casualty insurance companies. To repeat, from most points of view—insiders, potential acquirers, senior lenders—stock market prices do not measure the value of securities that are not readily marketable, even though the same issue has a market price.

UNDERLYING GAAP ASSUMPTION 10

In classifying assets or liabilities, physical substance and legal substance are deemed to be more important than economic substance.

GAAP cannot be flexible enough to recognize that economic substance frequently differs from physical fact and legal definition. For example, many noncurrent, fixed assets are in reality subject to asset conversion and thus are highly liquid and very marketable, whereas other assets defined as current cannot as a practical matter be turned into cash; these current assets are locked up, dedicated to the continuing operations of going concerns.

Examples of fixed assets that are relatively easy to convert into cash abound, and such assets are the basis of considerable tax shelter, as is particularly pointed out in Chapter 12, "Net Asset Values." Fixed assets that are quite current can include domestic oil reserves in the ground; an office building or shopping center producing income from AAA tenants on long-term leases; and an old building with a large book value used in a trade or business where a profitable company owning it can virtually abandon the building and obtain cash tax refunds through the device of creating a tax-loss carry-back.

On the other hand, the aggregate amount of revolving charge-account receivables and inventories held by, say, Sears Roebuck is hardly a current asset in any going-concern sense of the term. Any attempt to reduce the amount of such current assets in existence would virtually put Sears Roebuck out of business; it would be out of either merchandise or customers who are able to buy only because Sears provides them with financing.

The same type of rigidity has to govern GAAP on the liability side of the ledger. From the point of view of senior lenders, subordinated debentures are equity; from the point of view of common stockholders, subordinated debentures are debt. GAAP tends to adopt the common shareholders' point of view. For the creditor or investor, however, neither the common stockholder nor GAAP is necessarily realistic, though both are legally correct. In the case of companies heavily in debt and with little or no equity—say, Cadence Industries in 1975 or Rapid American in 1971—the analyst concentrating on economic substance would view the outstanding subordinated debentures as the common stock, and the company's common stocks as voting warrants. Such a change in approach, which is impractical for GAAP, may make appraisal much simpler and more feasible for the analyst.

UNDERLYING GAAP ASSUMPTION II

There is a basic identity of interests between a company and its various stockholder groups.

We think it is much more realistic to view the relationships between a company and its stockholders and between the company and various stockholder groups as combinations of communities of interest and conflicts of interest. This is discussed further in the next chapter. To provide objective bench marks, however, GAAP assumes implicitly that companies are run in the best interests of all stockholders. Though not realistic, such an assumption provides a good objective bench mark or starting point for an analysis. Conflicts of interest, for example, between companies and stockholders arise out of such things as appropriate dividend policies: whether operations should be directed toward maximizing near-term reported profits or toward minimizing near-term federal income taxes, or whether management should have better ways to spend time than promoting the price of the stock.

MYTHS ABOUT THE SHORTCOMINGS OF THE CORPORATE AUDIT FUNCTION AND THE ETHICAL STANDARDS OF THE U. S. INDEPENDENT AUDITING PROFESSION

Few people, including practicing accountants, realize how relatively well the accounting profession performs the audit function. By and large, when an outside investor or creditor looks at accounting figures attested to by an unqualified certificate audit, he can be confident that those accounting figures represent a reliable tool usable in making judgments. This does not mean that the tool is not sometimes unreliable and sometimes not very usable. However, for the creditor or investor, analysis would be infinitely more difficult without the U.S. audit. There are securities markets where these high standards do not exist—as, for example, in domestic, tax-free general obligations and in foreign securities not registered with the U.S. Securities and Exchange Commission.

One indication of the value of high U.S. auditing standards is that in the past twenty-five years, at any rate, most speculative bubbles have been in industries or issues where GAAP is either nonexistent or of little significance in appraising a business or a stock. This explains in great part why Equity Funding is such a shocker. Put simply, "bad audits" such as Equity Funding's are a rarity. In fact, unscrupulous promoters consciously or unconsciously seek to promote in those areas where there is little or no investor reliance on GAAP. Thus, where have most of the recent speculative bubbles been? In exploration ventures and in new discoveries, new inventions, new industries and such industries as life insurance.

Financial accountants today are embattled, involved in litigation, and clamor for reform, much of which involves not bad audits, but, rather, trying to define and redefine the words *fair presentation*. No profession is perfect, but we submit that what accountants have done in providing users with GAAP and high-quality audit standards is deserving of the highest praise, certainly at least compared with what has been accomplished in other areas of professional financial services, such as law, tax, securities analysis, independent appraisals by investment bankers, management consulting and economics.

THE FINANCIAL AND INVESTMENT ENVIRONMENT

Chapter 9

Tax Shelter (TS), Other People's Money (OPM), Accounting Fudge Factor (AFF) and Something off the Top (SOTT)

P EOPLE AND COMPANIES rarely act unless they expect a resulting benefit, either for themselves or for others with whom they have identities of interest. This is equally true whether what is involved is a $600 million decision by General Motors to produce and market the Vega, or a $6,000 decision by John Doe to buy 100 shares of American Telephone common. In making such decisions, the actors aim to take advantage of certain profit-maximizing and risk-minimizing factors in order to tip the profit-risk ratio as far in favor of profit as possible.

The first of these factors, and the one that probably has the single most pervasive influence on our economy, is tax considerations. Actors seek to maximize profits by minimizing their tax liabilities. In its ultimate form, tax shelter, or TS, exempts the taxpayer from tax altogether; but it may also involve structuring a transaction in special ways so as to achieve a preferential tax rate on the profits realized or to allow the taxpayer to control the timing of the tax liability.

A second factor is other people's money, sometimes called Opium or OPM. OPM can take many forms. The most familiar of these is, of course, the conventional borrower-lender relationship, where a person pays fees for the privilege of using someone else's money. The user of other people's money may, however, obtain his money without direct payment of fees. For example, commercial banks obtain demand deposits without paying, or in fact being allowed to pay, interest on them; insurance companies obtain pre-payment of premiums on the policies they issue. The users of other people's money may even obtain profits from the very providers of funds. This is so, for example, in the case of insurance companies that make money not only by investing the cash created by the pre-payment of premiums, but also from the operations of the insurance business itself for which the premiums are paid.

Besides tax considerations, the use of funds provided by others in one form or another is part of almost every business transaction that takes place. Many people involved with corporations try to obtain other benefits out of the association for themselves or for the corporation. We characterize all such benefits as something off the top, or SOTT, which means different things to different users of it. For example, to a company, something off the top may mean diversi-fied income, freedom from regulation, and political clout. To a pub-lic company, it may also mean control of the registration process, together with an ability to sell equity securities at an ultrahigh price, so that new productive assets can be obtained on an advantageous basis via either a public offering or a merger and acquisition pro-gram. To management, something off the top means not only salaries, bonuses, stock options, expense accounts and perquisites such as prestige and big offices, but also power and operating con-trol. In a public company, this includes control of the registration process and proxy machinery. Finally, not being an insider can occa-sionally even serve as a form of something off the top to those out-side securities holders who eschew any of the responsibilities that go with being an insider, and who want nothing more than absolute pas-sivity, liquidity and marketability.

These, then, are what businessmen and investors strive for when they engage in a deal. They may seek all of these factors, or they may use one to attain another—as, for example, granting something off the top in exchange for other people's money. This is what was done, for example, in the Schaefer transaction in which insurance lenders providing $65 million of financing through loans were given common stock for which they paid $1 per share several months before there was a public offering of newly issued stock at $26 per share.

Understanding tax considerations, other people's money and something off the top is thus important to an understanding of American business. There is yet another factor, however, that motivates decisions of managements of publicly traded companies. This we call the accounting fudge factor, or AFF.

The accounting fudge factor differs from the other factors enumerated here, because it is not an end in itself. Rather, it is a tool that companies manipulate to achieve tax benefits, an availability of funds on attractive bases, and something off the top. For the investor-owned public company whose stock prices are influenced to an inordinate degree by two numbers—net income as reported for accounting purposes, and its corollary, reported earnings per share—the accounting fudge factor is used primarily to obtain a high trading price.

Tax considerations, other people's money, something off the top and the accounting fudge factor are facts of commercial and bureaucratic life, the underlying factors that motivate decisionmakers to act as they do.* We are not concerned here with whether they are "fair" or socially beneficial; such considerations are counterproductive to achieving an understanding of the way our system operates. They are there; they are useful to different groups in different ways; and as

---

*One of our students at Yale University, Philip Bareiss, coined a related acronym, CIX—meaning contacts, information and experience—to describe what Joseph Kennedy did to achieve such great success as an investor and promoter. CIX offers an explanation of how many people approach business and investments, and why those who can combine CIX with good judgment turn out to be Joe Kennedys, or reasonable facsimiles. It is a *sine qua non* for obtaining the most valuable types of SOTT and OPM.

long as people do not all have absolutely identical wants, no system can be designed without them.

TAX CONSIDERATIONS

Volumes have been written about tax considerations and tax shelters, and many more will be forthcoming. Obviously, any in-depth analysis of the area is beyond the scope of this book. For our purposes, it is sufficient to recognize that business decisions are motivated to a great extent by a desire to achieve beneficial tax postures and to avoid negative ones.

There are three important tax considerations that influence taxpayers. The worst possible tax posture is (1) to be subject to taxation at maximum rates, (2) to be unable to control the timing of the tax liability and (3) to be in a situation where the transaction that gives rise to the tax does not also provide the cash with which to pay it. An example of such a negative transaction can be the receipt of certain nontransferable stock options that would be treated for IRS purposes as income at the time of receipt and taxed as ordinary income.

Tax reform will never eliminate tax shelters, which will continue to be a motivating factor in business decisions. There is no way that taxes can be fair and equitable to every taxpayer, or neutral in their effect on commercial activities. As long as people have different preferences, any tax will be deemed unfair or inequitable by someone. Likewise, as long as commercial transactions have different economic results, they will have different tax impacts; and since the businessman will consider the tax liability in evaluating the transaction, the tax will not be neutral in its effect.

For example, consider the event that requires the payment of a tax on income. If someone earns $10,000 in salary or commissions, he must pay income tax on that. The same is true if he sells something for a $10,000 profit. If, on the other hand, he buys a piece of land for $1,000 and watches it appreciate in value to $11,000, he pays no income tax on the $10,000 gain so long as he holds the property, because there has been no taxable event. There is an obvious inequity in taxing realized profits while allowing the holder of appreciated property to escape or indefinitely postpone taxation. On the other hand, taxing the holder of appreciated property on his unrealized gain is also inequitable, not only because the value of property is extremely hard to measure and will fluctuate, but also because any appreciation in value that is being taxed does not give the person who is allegedly benefiting from it the cash with which to pay his taxes.

Even aside from such problems as the differential treatment accorded realized and unrealized profits, there are conflicts about the kinds of reforms that would make income taxes fair and equitable. Should taxes be regressive or progressive? Should the tax rate depend on wealth instead of income, or on some combination of the two? What is the definition of "expense"? Should some people—for example, athletes—be granted a depletion allowance to reflect the decrease in the value of their professional skills, whereas others—such as college professors, lawyers and consultants, whose talents may create additional values each year over and above their reported incomes—be subject to an added-value tax? We do not know the answers to these questions. Nor, we suspect, does anyone. Society tries to make taxes fair and equitable by using ad hoc legal definitions of fairness that are modified from time to time by social and political pressure. Some degree of differential tax treatment will always be dictated, though, by common sense and economic reality. And as long as this remains, people will engage in tax avoidance. The tax laws can be made over in many ways, but they cannot be made neutral. Tax considerations are a fact of economic life. Ergo, they are a fact of life in investments and finance.

OTHER PEOPLE'S MONEY

Other people's money comes in all forms. It may be clearly reflected in accounting reports—so-called on-balance-sheet liabilities—or it may be in the form of off-balance-sheet liabilities. Depending on who is the user of other people's money, it takes varied forms. For commercial banks, OPM is primarily demand deposits; for American

Express, other people's money is the float arising out of the issuance of traveler's checks that consumers have already paid for but have not yet cashed; for insurance companies, it includes unearned, prepaid premiums; and for mutual-fund managers, whose fee is based on the market value of the fund's stockholdings, other people's money is what the public has invested in mutual funds under management. In the majority of instances, however, other people's money probably takes the form of a conventional loan. The interest payments are the price paid for the use of such funds.

Outside investors tend to underestimate the importance of other people's money to a company in appraising the investment merits of its common stock. Instead, operating on a theory that assets are useful only if they can be used to create earnings, many emphasize net income, earnings per share, and particularly, the price–earnings ratio, or PE. The PE is the multiple arrived at by dividing the price of a company's stock by its reported earnings per share. For example, American Telephone and Telegraph reported earnings of $6.97 per share for 1977, at a time when its common stock was selling at 61; its PE, therefore, was 8.8 (or 61 divided by 6.97). To justify a PE, outsiders generally look at such elements as reported earnings for the latest period, the historic trend of earnings, the industry position of the particular company and its industry identification—usually a key factor. You hear, for instance, that drug stocks should sell at about 20 times earnings, steels at 6 times, finance companies at 10 times and grocery chains at 8 times.

In thus de-emphasizing a business's general financial position and access to resources, these outside investors are overlooking an important source of wealth creation for the company. As successful insiders and promoters know, the availability of financial resources and the production of net income are each a needed condition for the other; you really cannot have income without resources, nor can you have resources without income. In fact, the cliché that assets are useful only if they can be used to create earnings is no more than a half-truth. The whole truth is, Assets are useful only if they can be used to create earnings, and earnings are useful only if they can be used to create assets, some of which may be distributed to stockholders and others of which will be retained in the business.

Ironically, the tendency of unaffiliated investors to place undue emphasis on the earnings and earnings ratio at the expense of concentrating on financial position provides promoters who have access to other people's money with the classic opportunity to enrich themselves.

Take a simplified example that ignores underwriting commissions and the expenses involved in making a deal. Suppose that most publicly owned companies in the widget industry are selling at around 10 times earnings. Joe Promoter has his eye on Eastern Widget, a privately owned company that earns $2 million before taxes and $1 million after taxes. The company has a net worth of $5 million, no debt of any sort and a ratio of current assets to current liabilities of 3 to 1. Thus, it can be used as a source of other people's money. The owners of Eastern want to sell because they are getting older; to their way of thinking, they would be willing to sell their company for $8 million cash, equal to 8 times earnings and a 60 percent premium over book value. Joe Promoter has reason to believe the public will pay 8 times earnings for Eastern Widget, because it is a good company in an industry where the common stocks of other companies are selling at a somewhat higher price–earnings ratio.

Joe wants to buy Eastern Widget for $8 million cash (using other people's money), turn the company into a public company and end up owning at least 30 percent of the common stock. If this public-company stock were to sell at around 8 times earnings, the market value of Joe's interest would be about $2 million—although he has invested virtually nothing other than his promotional efforts.

How does Joe accomplish this? He incorporates a new company, Midlantic Widgets. Midlantic is to be used to acquire Eastern. Midlantic initially has 250,000 common shares outstanding, all owned by Joe. Based on Eastern's strong balance sheet and record of profitability, as well as on Joe's plans to create a public company, Midlantic raises $8 million (none of which is invested by Joe); it borrows

$6 million from banks and insurance companies by selling 8 percent notes at par; and it sells to private individuals and venture capital firms, for $2 million cash, units consisting of debentures and common stock. The sale of these units results in Midlantic's issuing $2 million of 5 percent subordinated debentures and 137,500 common shares.

Using these $8 million of funds, Midlantic acquires Eastern. It can now report Eastern's earnings as its own. Midlantic's *pro forma* net income and earnings per share at this point will look like this:

Eastern's net income before taxes	$2,000,000
Less interest on bank and insurance loans—8% on $6,000,000	480,000
Interest on subordinated debentures—5% on $2,000,000	100,000
Amortization of purchase good will over 40 years	75,000*
Adjusted pretax net income	$1,345,000
Less income taxes at 50% without deduction of good-will amortization	710,000
Net income	$635,000
Earnings per share on 387,500 common shares (of which Joe owns 250,000 and the private placement investors 137,500)	$1.64

*The amortization of purchase good will is required by Accounting Principles Board Opinion 17 over periods not to exceed 40 years: 40 years times $75,000 equals $3 million, the amount over net worth that Joe paid for Eastern Widget.

Midlantic now has a public offering via an underwriting. It markets 375,000 newly issued Midlantic common shares at $8 per share, for proceeds of $3 million. These proceeds are then used to retire at par all of the 5 percent subordinated debentures and to pay down the $6 million of bank debt by $1 million. Midlantic's *pro forma* net income and earnings per share now look somewhat different:

Eastern's net income before taxes	$2,000,000
Less interest on bank and insurance loans—8% of $5,000,000	400,000
Amortization of purchase good will over 40 years	75,000
Adjusted pretax net income	$1,525,000
Less income taxes at 50% without deduction of good-will amortization	800,000
Net income	$725,000
Earnings per share on 762,500 shares (375,000 shares owned by the public, which paid $8 per share; 250,000 shares owned by Joe Promoter, who now has no cash investment in Midlantic; and 137,500 shares owned by the private placement group, which now has no cash investment in Midlantic either)	$0.95

Joe Promoter bought a company at 8 times earnings and then put other people's money into it. He turned around and sold an interest in the same enterprise (but a different company) to the public at about 8 times earnings. For his efforts, Joe ended up in control of a public company, with a 32.8 percent interest in its common stock, which has a market value of $2 million and for which he made virtually no cash payment. Is what Joe did easy? No. But a lot of promoters have done and are doing what Joe did, and indeed have accomplished much more. Is this use of other people's money a lot more complicated than is supposed in our oversimplified example? In many ways not really, though of course it's not quite that easy, as should be apparent after reading Appendix I, which describes a not dissimilar transaction in detail. But for purposes of this discussion, Joe's experience brings home forcefully the power of other people's money in creating wealth for people within our system.

A word of caution is needed at this point, even granting that Joe's use of other people's money was highly judicious because he was an active investor combining knowledge and control. Every financial practice that is useful is also subject to abuse. This may be truer of the use of other people's money than of any other financial practice; injudicious use and overuse of other people's money abound.

The use of other people's money by outside investors—that is, margin accounts—may be especially risky, because such investors frequently are not knowledgeable about the securities in which they are investing, and by definition, there is no control whatsoever attaching to ownership of the asset. The risk occurs when the investor borrows money to trade marketable securities "naked," with the object of profiting from security-price movements. For example, let's say you borrow $4,000 to purchase 200 shares of Xerox at a cost of $8,000, or $40 per share, because you think Xerox will appreciate to 60, 80, 100 or 300. Your position is naked, or unarbitraged, because there is no offset, such as simultaneously selling Xerox convertible debentures short (a so-called convertible arbitrage).

Our bias toward the financial-integrity approach prejudices us against playing the stock market on margin for two reasons. First, we think it is nearly impossible for any outsider to predict or influence short-term to intermediate-term stock-price movements. Second, there is a danger of loss where there is a lack of positive cash-carry— that is, a positive cash-carry occurs when the cash interest payments on a loan are exceeded by the cash income from the investment.

SOMETHING OFF THE TOP (SOTT): SOME PRELIMINARIES

Every economic entity—corporations, managements, securities holders—tries to obtain something off the top, even though various recipients of SOTT may not regard themselves as having obtained special advantages. Most unaffiliated security holders are unaware of possible beliefs by managements that outside stockholders are taking unfair advantage of insiders. The insider, on the other hand, may say, as many do, "Isn't it a shame that I have to break my back to make my sixty percent of the company valuable while the other owners do nothing but obtain a free ride?" From his point of view, the stockholders *may* be getting a free ride.

Certainly, outside investors have a form of SOTT that appears to be almost unique in our society. Ownership of assets in any form usually entails considerable responsibilities—whether it is keeping the lawn in front of the house you own mowed, or the customers and employees of the business you control satisfied. Not so the passive, individual investor. His ownership of assets carries with it no obligations or responsibilities to others. Moreover, unlike the insider, he is free to sell his securities without restriction, and does not have to comply with Securities and Exchange Commission rules and regulations, or to deal with lawyers and accountants.

Yet, make no mistake, public shareholders pay a high price for the luxury of passivity. They cannot obtain the information available to insiders. They have little or no influence on how the resources in which they have invested are used. Above all, they get no return from the company for their ownership interest other than that to which their security holding entitles them.

Contrast this with the position of the insider. To him, security ownership may be of only incidental value compared with all the benefits he can obtain from his relationship with a company—not only salaries but a myriad of perquisities ranging from well-appointed offices to opportunities to buy cheap stock. The insider can obtain PPM—power, prestige and money.

The value of control, whether positive or negative, has to be appraised on a company-by-company basis. The responsibilities a control group must assume may outweigh any possible benefits—especially when the enterprise is truly a sick company. In that situation, the outsider may tend to be the one with the SOTT; the control should carry a discount. Thus, like anything else, control that is a plus in one context may turn out to be a minus in another.

In any economic activity, the relationship among various economic groups and individuals will be marked by areas where there are conflicts of interest and areas where there are communities of interest. SOTT is an area where conflicts of interest seem dominant, as a general rule. More specifically, there tends to be an inherent conflict between management SOTT on the one hand and stockholder well-being on the other.

Most managements undoubtedly feel a responsibility to their securities holders most of the time, even if improving returns to these holders results in reducing management SOTT. The woods seem to be full of corporate "milkers," however, for whom the realization of personal benefits off the top is a sole goal, and who believe that giving benefits to outside stockholders will detract from the realization of this goal.

Even aside from these milkers, the inherent conflict between management SOTT and investor well-being poses a problem for the outsider. Admittedly, SOTT is generally created at someone else's expense. The obvious target is an amorphous outside group with whom management has no personal acquaintanceship or dealings. Thus, we have observed that a corporation or a corporate insider tends to create SOTT at the expense of public stockholders and the IRS, rather than at the expense of groups such as labor unions, vendors or customers with whom they have daily relationships.

This inherent conflict becomes especially important when looking at small companies. It is of real concern to every outside security holder—even such a one as a commercial bank whose holding is a senior loan. After all, no matter how senior the loan, interest and amortization payments on that loan will be made at any given point in time only after management salaries have been paid.

An important caveat for public investors is to try to avoid ownership of shares in companies where the insiders have a basic disdain for public stockholders and are in a position to create SOTT at their expense. This is, of course, an essential element of the financial-integrity approach.

SOME PRELIMINARIES ON THE ACCOUNTING FUDGE FACTOR (AFF)

Accounting appears to be an exact science: it just reports a set of numbers, occasionally showing in a footnote or textual exposition how the numbers would have been different if another method of calculation had been used. Yet in reporting business events—which is part of what accounting does—there is no "right" way of describing anything; it depends on the angle from which you are viewing the transaction, as we pointed out in the two previous chapters. Are you a senior lender, a common stockholder or the president of the company? Are you interested in cash returns, the build-up of intrinsic value, the price of the stock, or some combination of the three? Are you viewing the accounting transaction singly or as part of the overall operation of a business? Here, we merely wish to emphasize the extent to which the accounting fudge factor can and will continue to be used in describing business transactions. A simple example demonstrates this.

Assume a bank lends you $4,000 for five years, at the end of which you are to repay it $5,000.* Assume further that it costs the bank $150 to create the loan in the first year, and $10 per year to carry it for each of the five years that the loan is outstanding. On a cash basis, the bank's "income account" will look like this:

INCOME ACCOUNT RELATED TO FIVE-YEAR LOAN ON CASH BASIS

	Year 1	Year 2	Year 3	Year 4	Year 5	Total
Income	—	—	—	—	$1,000	$1,000
Expense	160	10	10	10	10	200
Profit (or loss)	(160)	(10)	(10)	(10)	$990	$800

If, on the other hand, the bank chooses to "accrete discount" (meaning it allocates the revenue from the loan among the years for which it is outstanding), its income account related to this loan would look quite different:

INCOME ACCOUNT RELATED TO FIVE-YEAR LOAN ON SIMPLE ACCRUAL BASIS

	Year 1	Year 2	Year 3	Year 4	Year 5	Total
Income	$200	$200	$200	$200	$200	$1,000
Expense	160	10	10	10	10	200
	$40	$190	$190	$190	$190	$800

*For simplicity of discussion, we ignore both the bank's taxes and the finer points of compound interest. Here the customer is paying 5 percent simple interest.

Of course, this picture is not quite accurate either, since if the bank collected cash equal to ⅕ of the income from the loan in each of these years, it could reinvest these funds.

There is yet another school of thought on how this transaction should be reported on an accrual basis. Assuming a more or less constant level of business, loans will be repaid constantly. Thus, this account should reflect a constant return on the capital invested. Under this view, revenue is booked on the basis of the sum-of-the-years'-digits or some variation thereof.* In the case of a five-year loan, the sum of the digits is 15 (1 + 2 + 3 + 4 + 5); ⁵⁄₁₅ of the income is booked the first year, ⁴⁄₁₅ the second year and so on. Of course, the first year should not be burdened with all the acquisition costs any more than the last year should enjoy all the revenues. Rather, these should be spread over the life of the loan. This can be accomplished by subtracting the $150 from $1,000, then applying the sum-of-digits to $850, and adding back $150—the acquisition cost—to the first year's revenues. The income account, then, would look like this:

ACCRUAL—SUM-OF-YEARS'-DIGIT ALLOCATION OF ACQUISITION EXPENSE

	Year 1	Year 2	Year 3	Year 4	Year 5	Total
Income	$433	$226	$170	$114	$57	$1,000
Expense	160	10	10	10	10	200
	$273	$216	$160	$104	$47	$800

Thus, on the same economic facts, the bank that reports on a cash basis shows a loss of $160 for the first year, whereas a bank that accretes discount and allocates acquisition costs shows a profit of $273. Both are reasonable approximations. Both banks come out the

---

*One such variation is the so-called Rule of 78, a sum-of-the-digits formula based on using twelve accounting periods: 1 + 2 + 3 + 4 + 5 + 6 + 7 + 8 + 9 + 10 + 11 + 12 = 78. The first period's accrual is 12/78, the second's 11/78, the third's 10/78 and so on.

same on a per-transaction basis: at the end of five years each has earned $800 on the loan. But they look very different year by year.

This apparent difference is exacerbated if differing amounts of business are booked each year. If the bank is expanding and writing increased amounts of loans like this one, the early years will be heavily weighted. The bank accreting discount will report huge profits relative to the bank that does not accrete. Suppose, however, that business is decreasing. Then, the fifth year of these loans will be more heavily weighted in the overall profits of the bank than will the early years. In that case, the bank that does not accrete discount will seem proportionately more profitable than the bank that does.

This is but one simple example of how a single transaction can be reported in a myriad of ways, each of them reasonable. Similar examples could be shown for the treatment of development costs, deferred taxes and a host of other items. Whenever accounting figures are to be used for more than a single purpose, one set of figures will be better suited for one of these purposes, another set for another. Thus, the conditions for AFF will exist.

HOW IT ALL MESHES

Investment realists try to understand relevant behavior. The various participants in our system's economic life seek to obtain edges which benefit them and/or those most closely associated with them. We suggest that those edges in our commercial activities are best understood when viewed as tax considerations, other people's money, something off the top and the accounting fudge factor.

Chapter 10

Securities Analysis and Securities Markets

෴

If after ten minutes at the poker table
you do not know who the patsy is—you are the patsy.

POKER PROVERB

COMPANIES OR SECURITIES can be analyzed only in context. No particular variable taken by itself is either good or bad. What is good in one context or time becomes bad in another. Simplistic views may be helpful in making one a successful trader. Simplistic views, however, hamper the attainment of understanding about corporations and about financial situations in general. In this and the next chapter, we review several of the more important variables that cannot be classified as good or bad. The variables discussed in this chapter are relevant to decisions for acquiring and holding securities. They are as follows:

- Profit margins
- Size
- Liberal accounting policies
- Low net asset value

- Wall Street sponsorship
- The trading assumption versus the investment assumption
- Convertible securities
- Limitations of comparative analysis

REASONS FOR ACQUIRING AND HOLDING SECURITIES

It is usually believed that in some absolute sense there are good reasons for acquiring and holding certain securities, such as common stocks of companies with high profit margins, high returns on investment, aggressive managements and high book value; and that correspondingly, there are good reasons for avoiding the ownership of other securities, such as common stocks of companies with low profit margins, low returns on investment, nonaggressive management and low book value.

The reality, however, is that any of these characteristics may be a reason for being attracted to a company's securities in one context and avoiding them in another. Financial characteristics are related to each other and modify each other, so that by achieving one thing that might be defined as good, there may be a strong probability of having something else at the same time that is bad. For example, companies with aggressive managements usually utilize liquidity fully, and such companies generally have weak financial positions. A high book value relative to market price at a time when price–earnings ratios are also high translates into a low return on investment. Companies with high profit margins, high stock prices, low book values and high returns on investment tend to attract competition; companies that survive and prosper in highly competitive, highly cyclical, unprotected industries tend to be run by able, dedicated managements.

Let us review various characteristics of securities and corporations, and see how they can provide reasons to acquire, or not to acquire, certain securities.

PROFIT MARGINS

Low profit margins can be a strong reason for purchasing a security if there are grounds for believing that they will improve. Small improvements in low profit margins can result in dramatic increases in earnings, whereas the same improvements for a high-profit-margin business would have only a modest impact on earnings.

A good argument can, of course, be made for investment in the stocks of companies that have had consistently high profit margins on the basis that such good results over the long term are likely to persist indefinitely, and that companies in such a position will continue to profit from their competitive muscle.

But slavish adherence to the high profit margin as the central guide to equity investment can be dangerous for two reasons. First, because constantly high profit margin firms are viewed by the investing public in general as good, stock market prices for such companies tend to be high. Second, it happens not infrequently that high profit margins that have persisted for many years suddenly become nonexistent. Companies to which this happened in recent years include NCR, Pitney Bowes, General Foods, Litton Industries, Union Carbide and Aluminum Company of America.

It certainly is true that each of today's high-profit-margin giants faces special problems. For General Motors, smaller cars with lower profit margins may be an increased part of the product mix in an overall market where General Motors' market penetration has been decreasing, at least as measured from the dates that foreign imports seized a 15 to 20 percent penetration of the U.S. market; Avon has spawned a host of imitators; American Telephone faces the specter of new competition on various fronts from both large and small companies; and both Kodak and IBM face antitrust problems as well as increasing competition.

SIZE

Much the same argument can be made for investment decisions that are based on the size of the enterprise. Smaller companies should be chosen because of the appreciation potential inherent in their prospects for growing into giant businesses. A prime example of this was Tokio Marine and Fire Insurance Company, Japan's leading fire and casualty insurer. In 1965, when its premium volume was $150 million, Tokio Marine and Fire seemed to have unusually good prospects for growth; because the Japanese economy was highly underinsured and Tokio Marine had considerable excess capital, it could easily, if it chose, finance almost any foreseeable expansion without recourse to outside financing. By fiscal 1975 Tokio Marine's premium volume had increased to $817 million with earnings-per-share growth over the period generally comparable to the increase in premium volume. The price of Tokio Marine common stock increased from around 20 to 170 in the eight-year period. Much the same story could be told about the purchase of the securities of other companies when they were moderate-sized and poised for growth— Xerox in 1956, Polaroid in 1953, Winnebago in 1965 or McDonald's in 1963.

Many small to medium-sized businesses are well financed and effective competitors—that is, they are reasonably good quality to extremely high quality issuers, even if they lack general recognition as such. Names that we believe provide examples of this at this writing include Ametek, American Manufacturing, NN Corporation, Orion Capital Corporation, Standard Shares and Stewart-Warner.

Yet there is merit to the viewpoint that restricting investments to very large and well-known companies (Graham and Dodd's top one hundred or the institutional investors' so-called nifty fifty) is a satisfactory and highly comfortable road to modest investment success, even though it is probably not the road to outstanding success. These large companies are generally recognized as high-quality issuers that combine good earnings records with reasonable finances. In fact, we concur that it is a good policy to opt for large firms that are generally recognized as first-class when the investor is unable for any reason to obtain a fair degree of know-how about the company whose securities he desires to own.

In general, it is true that the smaller the business, the riskier. However, it is our view that diligent, long-term outside investors using the financial-integrity approach can obtain sufficient knowledge (at least about some smaller companies) to make investing attractive and relatively safe. They can become informed through a combination of making use of their own personal experience and contacts, and a careful reading of the voluminous number of key documents that are now publicly available (see Chapter 6 and Appendix III). In particular, we recommend that the individual investor combine the financial-integrity approach with his own special knowledge. (If, for example, you have been in publishing all of your life, you might be in a better position than most to evaluate publishers.)

Furthermore, depending on price, there probably will be times when investment in very large, solid businesses may actually be riskier than investment in run-of-the-mill, but not wildly speculative, secondary companies. This is especially true if the investor understands them.

LIBERAL ACCOUNTING POLICIES

Certain investors have been enjoying great success by purchasing equities in companies that follow ultraliberal accounting policies. For example, it is generally agreed that in the 1960's, computer-leasing companies were following liberal accounting policies. Leasco Data Processing Corporation was one of these. A purchaser of Leasco common stock at the high in 1966 would have paid 40½ per share; the shares could have been sold at the low in the last part of 1968 for 90¼.

Much of this spectacular price performance for Leasco common probably was attributable to Leasco's liberal accounting policies, which permitted the reporting of practically maximum earnings per share. These policies are discussed in Chapter 7 insofar as they refer to finance leasing. In addition, the company obtained additional reported earnings by flowing through its investment credits. Under the Internal Revenue Code as it has existed in recent years, purchasers of most types of equipment could take as a credit against their income taxes up to 10 percent of the cost of the new equipment.

For accounting purposes, a minority of companies booked profits from this investment credit each year over the life of the equipment; others, like Leasco, booked all the profits from the tax credit in the year the equipment was purchased. (The former practice of deferring profit for accounting purposes is called normalization, whereas the immediate booking for all profit is called flow through.) Leasco's estimated useful life for purposes of depreciating computer equipment was anywhere from 50 percent to 100 percent longer than the lives used by IBM for the same equipment.

Also, Leasco dressed up its accounts by using the pooling method for its major acquisition. (Under an exchange offer, Reliance Insurance had become a 97-percent-owned Leasco subsidiary in 1968.) The apparent result of all this liberal accounting was not only that the Leasco stockholders did very well, but the use of liberal accounting policies was an important benefit to the corporation itself. Because Leasco's reported earnings increased and because the Leasco stock was so well sponsored, the shares achieved a market price that almost everyone would consider ultra-high based on corporate reality. Leasco used this ultra-high-priced stock to obtain productive assets on an ultra-attractive basis by both (a) selling new issues publicly and (b) acquiring via an exchange of securities a 97 percent interest in a large, first-class enterprise.

When stock market investors overemphasize earnings as reported rather than business reality, there are attempts to utilize liberal accounting—that is, to report as much profit as possible for financial-accounting purposes, frequently as soon as possible, especially if such a reported profit means an increase from the prior year.

We do not believe that liberalized accounting will ever be legislated out of existence. We would never have purchased or recommended Leasco to outside investors, regardless of price, because we concluded that Leasco did not at any time enjoy a strong financial position. But despite our relatively rigid standards, there was a period when a key variable for Leasco was its liberal accounting, which made Leasco a buy during much of the 1960's for many, even if not for us. Obviously, the Leasco management was dedicated to realizing as high a market price as it possibly could for its stockholders, something many outside investors justifiably feel is a bullish factor.

It has been said, What goes up must come down. Both in modern rocketry and finance, this is no longer always true. If a stock goes up far enough and its management is astute, it may use the Chinese dollar, or puffed value, to buy economic value elsewhere at a discount. Many of the late 1960's "conglomerateurs"—for example, Gulf and Western, Walter Kidde, Teledyne, and City Investing—succeeded in doing just that. Real values were built into their stocks and the company by issuing common stocks that were overpriced relative to corporate reality to acquire real corporate values.

We believe that the financial-integrity approach is highly satisfactory for many investors; we also think a "nifty fifty" approach makes sense, too, for those less diligent or less dedicated. Yet, under either of our recommended approaches, many attractive opportunities will be missed by the outside investor. For 1965 through at least early 1969, the holding of Leasco equity securities did make sense for many.

The standard of investment behavior for passivists as well as activists should be, Don't worry about the investments you did not make. Rather, concentrate your worries on the ones you made, but which you should not have made. The only people who logically ought to worry about investments they did not make are total-return traders who are attempting to maximize or beat the market. This book is not directed to them.

Giving managements some leeway in the accounting practices they follow affords analysts and investors a reasonable disclosure tool. For example, a study of Leasco's liberal accounting policies told volumes about Leasco's management and what they were trying to achieve for Leasco stock—much more, we believe, than might have been obtained from intensive interviews with the management (though studies of accounting practices are not necessarily a substitute for field work, or vice versa). As we pointed out, such a study could have been a reason for buying or not buying Leasco, depending on who the investor was.

In a different way, a study of American Telephone's pre-1968 accounting practices told volumes to the investor. It showed that the company was consciously refusing to take the maximum depreciation allowances available to it for income-tax purposes, and it was obvious that the reasons for this were based on management's complete misunderstanding of what deferred income taxes really meant, either in the accounting sense or in a rate-regulation sense. The results of such a study could also give rise to decisions to buy or not buy American Telephone common, depending on whether the buyer concluded that the management would remain unsophisticated or would reform its financial practices, which American Telephone has done to some extent since 1969.

It should be noted that liberal accounting policies in one context become conservative in the next. Pooling-of-interests accounting is liberal accounting when a company is acquired at a premium over book value; purchase accounting becomes liberal when the acquisition is obtained at a discount from book value, because the acquirer, for stockholder financial-statement purposes, will increase income by crediting the profit-and-loss statement to reflect the amortization of "negative good will." (Negative good will represents the excess of book value acquired over the price paid.) There are no strict rules about the period over which negative good will should be amortized, and an acquirer might amortize it over, say, a five- to ten-year period.

ADVANTAGES OF A LOW NET ASSET VALUE

Lack of net asset value, or low book value, can be advantageous for a corporation and for the price of its stock when the company is strictly a going concern without asset-conversion possibilities. This can be seen by comparing two companies that are similar, except that Company A has a smaller net asset value than Company B.

As far as Wall Street practice is concerned, many analysts who claim that book value is relatively unimportant claim also that return on investment (ROI) is a key factor in business valuation. Arithmetically, the lower the book value, the greater the ROI. A simple example should suffice for two debt-free companies:

COMPANY A			COMPANY B		
Net Income	*Net Asset Value*	*ROI*	*Net Income*	*Net Asset Value*	*ROI*
$1,000,000	$5,000,000	20.0%	$1,000,000	$15,000,000	6.7%

There is considerable business merit to this assumption for strict going concerns. First, some companies may literally be more efficient than others and can earn as much or more with lower-cost assets. Second, the view has merit not only where companies are viewed strictly as equally efficient operations, but also where the company with surplus assets is unable to utilize, dispose of or otherwise convert the assets owned.

As we have pointed out, the mere ownership of assets (except in the case of individual ownership of securities and pocket-holding of cash) entails incurring obligations and expenses for the ownership of such assets. Taxes have to be paid on idle property, inventories have to be stored, assets have to be insured, skeleton work forces have to be paid, and where a property is operated, a company may be required to spend vast sums for, say, pollution control, which adds to book value but not to profits. Thus, a company owning many nonproductive assets that it is unable or unwilling to utilize or convert to other uses may indeed be worth less than a company with the same current earnings and less asset value. This fact is reflected in ROI data.

The limitation to this ROI approach, though, is that frequently the company with the higher asset value has asset conversion opportunities and can convert assets, as, for example, by disposing of the excess assets on a quite profitable basis. This, of course, is not necessarily true, as is evidenced when railroads are forced to maintain operations on unprofitable mileage.

WALL STREET SPONSORSHIP

A sponsored security is an issue that is recommended and/or purchased by people in the financial community who are able to lure or influence others to acquire that security. Any outside investor interested in immediate performance or timing or in owning a highly marketable, actively traded security (except in the case of the largest U.S. corporations) is well advised to be interested in sponsorship. The Securities and Exchange Commission has, since 1972, given implicit recognition to the importance of sponsorship by revising prospectus regulations, so that investors obtain more background information about the individuals promoting a company or an issue.

We have for many years counseled corporate clients who contemplate going public via a small underwriting that the proposed managing underwriter—who, after all, will be the principal sponsor of the issue—pass an acid test before being accepted. This test consists of looking at his last three underwritings to see what kind of Wall Street sponsor he has been. Has the firm been able to market what it proposed to market? And where the underwriting was consummated, was the underwriter a good-enough sponsor, so that the issue sold at a premium over the offering price?

One problem with companies in sponsored industries is that capital-raising opportunities are so attractive that inordinate amounts of new competition are attracted to the industry. Witness the tremendous amount of overcapacity visited on the computer components, computer leasing, electronics, food franchises and nursing-home industries during the 1960's. The very sponsorship of these industries assured that over the long term most companies would fare poorly, if for no other reason than that too much competition would be attracted.

Buying poorly sponsored or unsponsored equity securities has advantages in that they are where the bargains lie for long-term investors, especially for those adhering to the financial-integrity approach. Unsponsored securities, especially during bear markets, frequently sell below unencumbered asset values at, say, two to four times increasing earnings, or on a basis where the cash return to maturity may be 15 percent to 20 percent per annum with reasonable safety. The principal problem with unsponsored securities is that they require know-how to be analyzed so that their true bargain status can be estimated in an always uncertain environment. Also, the timing is indeterminate. There usually is no basis for making judgments that the market price for the securities will react favorably over the near term. If there were, the security would probably already be sponsored, because even in bear markets, there are any number of dedicated, hard-working individuals concentrating on finding securities they believe will perform well over the near term.

THE TRADING ASSUMPTIONS VERSUS THE INVESTMENT ASSUMPTIONS

There is a great amount of conflicting standard stock market advice that is good or bad, depending on the investor's underlying assumption. For example, "The market knows more than I do about the security I hold" may be contrasted with "I know more about the security I hold than the market does." The unstated assumption of a vast number of stock market books is that the market knows more than any investor does; thus, much of the advice given in the standard books makes sense only against the background that the investor is relatively uninformed about the companies in which he invests.

CONVERTIBLE SECURITIES

There is no magic in owning any particular form of security. For a while, there was a school of thought that investments in convertible debentures were the royal road to investment success. The special appeal was that if the common stock appreciated, the convertible would participate; that if the common depreciated, the loss in the convertible would be limited, because it would sell only as low as its investment value; that trading costs for convertible debentures would be less because of lower commission rates; and finally, that a security holder would be able to borrow more money by using convertible debentures as collateral than by using the underlying common stock.

All of these reasons have elements of validity except, perhaps, for the last two. Negotiated commissions, in effect since May 1975, have dramatically reduced commission costs for investors in common stocks. Also, Federal Reserve Board margin requirements limiting the amount that can be borrowed to carry securities are now the same for convertibles as for common. (Convertibles probably still are better collateral where the borrowing is "nonpurpose"—that is, for some reason other than carrying securities.) However, the elements of validity are limited. The concepts of participating in common appreciation and of limiting loss to investment value are functions of the price of the convertible measured by premium above conversion parity and by premium above investment value. For example, at this writing Burlington Industries common stock is selling at 20. Burlington Industries has outstanding a 5 percent convertible subordinated debenture due to mature in thirteen years and convertible into common at 39—that is, each $1,000 debenture is convertible at the holder's option into 25.64 common (or 25.64 shares times $39 equals $1,000). The investment value of straight subordinated bonds is, in our view, around 60, equal to about a 10.5 percent yield to maturity. The convertibles sell at around 75, or at a 46.3 percent premium over conversion parity and a 25 percent premium over an investment value of 60. Conversion parity is calculated by relating the price of the debentures, $750, to the value of the debenture, here based on looking only at the market value that the debentures would have if they were converted to common stock (that is, 25.64 common at $20 equals $512.80). Thus, $750 divided by $512.80 equals 146.3 percent, or a 46.3 percent premium above conversion parity.

Concentrating on convertible programs can stop investors from looking at the securities of attractive issuers, especially those with strong, simple capitalizations, such as common stocks only. In addition, convertible issuers themselves are a biased sample of all issuers and may, as a group, be weaker than comparable companies, though this would be impossible to prove. Issuers of convertible debentures are frequently, though far from always, second-rank companies that market convertible debentures because the particular business has capital needs; the conversion feature is included because either (a) the issue could be sold only with a "sweetener" or (b) the underlying common stock is selling at such a high price that selling equity in the form of a convertible issue becomes attractive for the company, simply because the public is willing to pay such a high price.

Convertible preferreds with voting rights are generally issued in merger and acquisition transactions where voting securities have to be exchanged for voting securities in order for a transaction to be a tax-free reorganization. Before October 1970 the issuance of convertible voting preferreds in mergers and acquisitions would permit both a tax-free reorganization for tax purposes and a pooling of interests for financial-accounting purposes. Since October 1970, if any security other than common is issued in a merger or acquisition, the transaction has to be accounted for, for financial-accounting purposes, as a purchase, not a pooling.

There is also no necessary magic in issuing convertible debentures, from the point of view of companies. Many feel that issuing convertibles represents a means of selling common publicly at a price over the market. (New issues of convertibles are usually priced at a premium of 10 percent to 15 percent above the market for the common.) It also represents a method of raising long-term money on a subordinated basis and at a low interest rate. (A medium-grade issuer will normally attach a coupon on a convertible of 100 to 200 basis points below the prime rate; for example, if the prime rate is 7 percent, a convertible might have a coupon rate of 5 percent or 6 percent.) Finally, costs of marketing the convertible through an underwriting probably would be less than the costs of selling comparable amounts of common, even including expenses over the life of the debentures for the indenture trustee, which is required by the Trust Indentures Act of 1939 for publicly held debt obligations.

These attractions in marketing convertibles are real, but limited. If the underlying common pays no dividend, there will be a comparative cash drain on the corporation, even on an after-tax basis, because it will be required to pay interest on the convertible debenture until maturity or until conversion can be forced. For conversion to be forced, the debentures have to have a conversion parity that represents a premium over the call price.

For example, Data 100 convertible debentures, which are

callable or redeemable at 110 at the option of the company, are selling at the time of this writing at 160. Each $1,000 debenture is convertible into 100 shares of common stock, which is selling around 16. If Data 100 calls the debentures, conversion is forced, because the holder would stand to lose money if he did not convert all his debentures and sell the underlying common stock at 16, or sell the common stock first at 16 and then convert and deliver the Data 100 shares sold. The holder could, of course, just convert and hold the underlying stock—but he is still forced to convert. A simple example will show the loss to a Data 100 debenture holder who fails to convert at this time.

Cash proceeds to $1,000-debenture holder from sale of 100 Data 100 common at 16	$1,600
Cash proceeds to $1,000-debenture holder if Data 100 convertible debenture is redeemed at its call price of $1,100	1,100
Loss by failing to convert	$500

If an issuer already has convertibles outstanding and cannot force conversion or redeem those issues, it may be difficult to sell additional indebtedness. Thus, there is a tendency for outstanding debentures to use up part of a company's "borrowing base." Conversion results in an increase in a company's net worth and, therefore, in its underlying borrowing base.

Finally, concerning convertibles, there is no prima facie reason for assuming convertible debentures are higher-quality issues than convertible preferreds. Almost all convertible debentures are subordinates, which means that, in effect, if a business gets in trouble, all other creditors are paid first before anything is available for the subordinates. If there is a default in servicing subordinated debentures, the debenture holders, usually acting through the indenture trustee, have a right to declare all interest and principal on the debentures due and payable.

In contrast, in the typical convertible preferred there is only the right to accumulate arrearages, and if more than four or six quarterly dividends are passed, the preferred can elect a minority of the board of directors. This preferred stock's right to elect a minority of the board in the event of dividend arrearages is meaningless. However, much of the time the debenture's right to declare an event of default is nothing more than the right to commit suicide. Exercising the debenture holders' rights in the event of default spells bankruptcy. In light of the position of other creditors, subordinate holders are very likely to be wiped out, especially since U.S. bankruptcy is a very expensive, very protracted procedure.

Occasionally, however, publicly held convertible subordinated debentures can be de facto senior to the most senior debt of a company where that senior debt is privately held. This occurs when an issuer desires to recapitalize without recourse to the bankruptcy statutes. In that instance it may be able to negotiate modifications of loans with just a few senior debt holders, but not with thousands of subordinated debenture holders. Also, the issuer may be able to bind all preferred and common shareholders by causing a vote. Such an option, though, would not be available in dealing with debt holders. In that case a troubled company might be able to renegotiate terms with senior lenders in order to avert bankruptcy, but would be unable to restructure subordinated debt, simply because there are too many public bondholders who would withhold consent. It has even happened (as, for example, in some real estate trusts in 1975 and 1976) that senior lenders not receiving service on their debt have invested new funds into borrowers, part of which have been used to service subordinated debentures.

LIMITATIONS ON COMPARATIVE ANALYSIS

Comparative analysis is an essential tool in much of security analysis. We are always comparing one company with another and one investment opportunity with another. Comparative analysis of companies is limited by the availability of information and by time strictures. Comparative analysis of investment opportunities is also limited by knowledge and time. In virtually every comparative analysis, the goal cannot be completeness; it has to be "good enough." Where the four standards of the financial-integrity approach—strong financial position, reasonably honest control groups, reasonable amounts of information available and low price relative to estimates of net asset value—are the *sine qua non* of investment, comparative analysis tends to become secondary.

"Good enough" also has to be the standard for measuring market performance or business performance. No one can be best all the time or own all the resources in the world.

Chapter 11

Finance and Business

*Biting the bullet is great
if it's someone else's teeth.*

THE MATTERS listed below are discussed in this chapter.

- Heavy debt load
- Large cash positions
- Diversification versus concentration
- Management incentives
- Highly cyclical companies in competitive industries
- Going public and going private
- Government regulation
- Who runs most companies
- Consolidated versus consolidating financial statements
- Ownership of assets with negative value

HEAVY DEBT LOAD

Like liberal accounting policies, a heavy debt load can be viewed as a good contributory reason for acquiring a common stock, even though we, in following the financial-integrity approach, tend neither to buy nor to hold such common stocks. Heavy debt loads are frequently signs of aggressive management utilizing productive assets to the utmost. As far as stock market impact is concerned, there has been a strong tendency in Wall Street, at least up until the mid-1970's, to equate aggressive management with good management, especially in bull-market periods. Companies that had been well regarded in recent years in part because they incurred so much indebtedness were Boise Cascade, Coastal States Gas, Wilson Brothers and F. & M. Schaefer Corporation. Each, of course, eventually suffered, with a contributory factor being high fixed costs at a time of a business downturn. This, however, need not necessarily have been the case. For example, senior securities have, for many years, made up approximately 65 percent of the invested capital of electric utilities. To date, most U.S. companies in the industry have enjoyed some forty years of steady growth.

A high debt load can be an asset in a business sense as well as in a stock market sense. This occurs where the indebtedness had been incurred on an attractive basis that could not be duplicated under present conditions, no matter what the quality of the deal. For example, see the discussion of Madison Square Garden Corporation's mortgage debt in Chapter 8.

LARGE CASH POSITIONS

Large cash holdings can sometimes be a sign of unattractiveness in a company and its common stock, either where entrenched and non-raidable managements refuse to make productive use of the funds, or where management has refused to use the funds to undertake necessary expenditures. A classic example of cash holdings being unattractive for investors is Montgomery Ward's huge cash hoard after

World War II. As an operation, Montgomery Ward fell steadily and dramatically behind its arch rival, Sears Roebuck, as Sears continued to expand by opening new stores and by entering new businesses.

In the same manner, in the late 1950's and early 1960's labor costs had risen so sharply in the cement industry that in order to remain competitive, it was essential for companies in the industry to undertake relatively massive capital-expenditures programs, especially for large automated kilns. In the mid-60's, it was almost axiomatic that cement companies with strong financial positions were companies with obsolete, noncompetitive plants, whereas companies that were competitive operationally had heavy debt loads.

DIVERSIFICATION VERSUS CONCENTRATION

Corporate diversification can be viewed as a contributory reason for acquiring an equity as well as for not acquiring one. Certain managements in certain situations seem to do extremely well by having a singleness of purpose—that is, by pouring all their resources into one industry. McDonald's is a good example of a highly successful, primarily single purpose business. Other companies that have concentrated on one line of endeavor seem to have suffered mightily for having done so. Companies in the cement and steel industries provide examples of businesses that might have fared much better had they diversified. Correspondingly, certain companies have been highly successful because of aggressive diversification into other businesses and industries. Examples include such diverse businesses as Sears Roebuck, Procter and Gamble, R. J. Reynolds and Stewart-Warner. But attempts at diversification have been anywhere from unsatisfactory to disastrous for such others as Boise Cascade, Beck Industries, Commonwealth United, Litton Industries and RCA.

There is no a priori way for concluding that corporate diversification is per se good or bad. Diversification usually requires a high order of managerial ability, in operations as well as in investing.

Many authorities apparently believe that concentration on diversification was a prime cause of the Penn Central bankruptcy. The facts are that the Penn Central management had some degree of success as investors on behalf of the railroad; they apparently were abominable at operating a railroad. The contribution of cash to the railroad operations generated by Penn Central's investments kept the business alive longer than otherwise would have been the case. The theory that the Penn Central management would have been better railroad operators had they not concentrated so much on investments may have some validity. Nonetheless, the subject seems much more debatable than one would gather merely by reading statements in the financial press.

MANAGEMENT INCENTIVES

Generous incentives may be extremely important in attracting management that can turn an unprofitable company around, but they can also be used to enrich management without any benefits to securities holders.

In one context, management compensation is a use of funds that competes directly and effectively with the interests of securities holders. Managerial salaries and expense accounts are paid before anything is used to service any securities, including such senior securities as first mortgages and commercial-bank loans. In the case of the vast majority of publicly owned companies which are profitable and which have annual sales volumes of over, say, $25 million, this is not a real problem. In most instances, management salaries and expenses are not large enough to constitute meaningful looting. However, such looting does occur often enough and is significant enough so that no stockholder in a publicly owned company should assume that securities holders have an absolute community of interest with company management. At best, and as is pointed out in Chapter 9, they have only partial communities of interest and partial conflicts of interest.

ADVANTAGES OF HIGHLY CYCLICAL
COMPANIES IN COMPETITIVE INDUSTRIES

There is a tendency for companies in industries subject to adversity to attract more capable operating management, and for less dedicated personnel to run companies in basically stable industries. We remember being impressed in the late 1950's with certain machine-tool and metal-processing company managements who had to compete in an environment marked by increased competition, large-scale technological innovation and sharp cyclical downturns in overall demand. We compared these people with managements of certain telephone companies insulated behind government-granted monopolies. The comparison was such that a good argument could be made for tending to prefer investment in going-concern operations in highly competitive, highly cyclical environments despite their obvious other faults, especially where the common stocks of these companies appeared attractive based on the four standards of the financial-integrity approach.

It is true also that companies in highly cyclical industries tend to be well financed and relatively liquid. They cannot afford not to be. This seems particularly true for second-level American companies in basic manufacturing industries.

GOING PUBLIC AND GOING PRIVATE

It is important to remember that what a business is worth as a private enterprise is different from what the equities will be valued at in the stock market when the issue is public. Sometimes the market values the public will attribute to a business are well in excess of what the company would be worth as a private enterprise. There is a tendency to take advantage of this by making private companies go public through the issuance to outside investors of equities—common stock, convertibles and warrants. (When a company goes public for the first time, it almost always has to market common stock, since for convertibles or warrants to be attractive, they have to give holders the right to convert into or to purchase a public issue.)

There are two ways for a private company to go public. The first is by the sale to the public of equities via registering an issue with the Securities and Exchange Commission and then offering shares to the public, usually by means of an underwriting. Some of the techniques of doing this are discussed in detail in Appendix I. The second method for going public is to sell out to a company that is already public for cash, equities or other securities in either a taxable transaction or a tax-free reorganization. Examples of companies that have gone public this way, in whole or in part, include Martin Processing merging into HCA Industries (now Martin Processing) and Coroon and Reynolds being acquired by Reliance Insurance in exchange for Class A Reliance common.

Frequently, however, public businesses may be worth much more as private enterprises than as public companies. In these instances the companies go private, usually (though not always) by giving the stockholders a premium over the then current market price for the stock of the company going private. Unlike private companies going public where cash, equities or other securities can be involved, going private most frequently entails compensating the outside shareholders with cash in a taxable transaction. Companies can go private in whole or in part. Those going private in whole do so by using the proxy machinery, usually in cash transactions. Those going private in part, or semiprivate, do so either through voluntary purchases for cash or through the issuance of senior securities in exchange for common stock. Public companies that repurchase their own shares are, in effect, going private in part. Share-repurchase programs, which are briefly discussed in Chapter 15, have been undertaken by literally hundreds and perhaps thousands of companies in 1977 and 1978 alone.

GOVERNMENT REGULATION

Government regulation, especially regulation by the Securities and Exchange Commission, is also two-sided for the investor—partly beneficial, partly harmful. It appears to us that the most emphasized thrust of SEC regulation in the disclosure area has been to prevent manipulative practices (such as the use of inside information for trading purposes) and also to control trading practices effectively. However, one should realize that a truly outstanding job has been done in providing meaningful disclosures to diligent, long-term serious investors, and that the SEC has been the major agent in causing these disclosure improvements during the last ten to fifteen years for all filing companies. All U.S. companies engaged in interstate com-

Regulatory Action	Regulatory Objective	Secondary Effect
Restrict investment advisers from purchasing securities they recommend to advisees	Prevent advisers from taking unfair trading advantage of advisees	Prevent advisees from getting advice from best possible sources—advisers who put their money where their mouth is
Simplify accounting procedures for benefit of average investor	Make financial statements more understandable for neophytes. Prevent financial statements from being used to manipulate in trading situations	Prevent sophisticated investors from obtaining adequate disclosures. Lend a measure of regulatory blessing to having investors trade speculatively (thereby discouraging upgrading of investor mentalities)
Prevent markets from being "conditioned" at certain critical times	Protect investors when big sales pushes are being made	Ensure that unauthorized information will be given out under the table. Deny written disclosures to those responsible enough to handle them
Require considerable disclosure before 5 percent or more of stock can be purchased in contested situations	Create "fair" trading environment. Protect incumbents?	Discourage contests for control, especially via stock purchases. Protect incumbents?
Prevent sale of nonregistered stock	Protect investors from buying securities about which disclosures haven't been made. Prevent insiders from converting gains to cash?	Encourage the continuation of speculative bubbles by restricting the supply of overpriced stocks coming on the market

merce with over five hundred shareholders and $1 million of assets (except those in certain regulated industries) have, since 1966, been filing companies.

It should be realized, though, that SEC rules and regulations are a two-edged sword. It seems as if each regulation promulgated for some primary purpose always has an unintended secondary purpose.

Examples of desirable primary effects and perhaps not so desirable secondary effects growing out of Securities and Exchange Commission rules and regulations can be seen from the table on page 182 showing various regulatory actions, the regulatory objective that gave rise to those actions, and the frequently unexpected and undesirable secondary effects of those actions.

WHO RUNS MOST COMPANIES?

One myth particularly prevalent in law is that directors run companies. Almost without exception, functioning companies are really run by their day-to-day management. Because of this myth, outside directors are finding increasingly that the liabilities they assume by being directors far outweigh the benefits they obtain. They sometimes find themselves responsible for matters in law that they cannot be responsible for in practice.

Both the theory and practice of directorships need a thorough reconsideration.

CONSOLIDATED VERSUS CONSOLIDATING FINANCIAL STATEMENTS

In Chapter 8, "Generally Accepted Accounting Principles," we commented that there are times when GAAP places form over substance. This can occur when questions arise as to which is more meaningful for an investor—consolidated financial statements or consolidating statements that are broken down to show separate financials for the parent company, each subsidiary and the consolidated entity.

This problem is brought home if one addresses the question of when a common stock is really a senior security. Take the case of Mountain States Telephone common, 88 percent of which is owned by American Telephone. For the parent company to obtain cash to service its debt and pay dividends on its common, it has to receive dividends from the operating subsidiaries, of which Mountain States is one of the more important. Thus, in economic fact Mountain States common has most of the key attributes of being an American Telephone senior security, though it does lack one attribute—there is no legally enforceable right of Mountain States stockholders to receive dividends. Accounting recognizes this senior position of the non–American Telephone stockholders of Mountain States. In American Telephone's consolidated accounts, this minority interest is separated out and is carried as senior to American Telephone's capital and surplus. In economic fact the Mountain States common can, in a sense, be viewed as senior to the most senior parent-company obligations, simply because the minority shareholders have to receive dividends *before* such cash dividends to its other shareholder, American Telephone, can be used by American Telephone to pay interest and principal on its debt.

This same feature can be brought home even more forcefully in the case of Schenley Industries when it was 86 percent owned by Glen Alden between 1968 and 1971. Without distributions from Schenley, Glen Alden, the parent, would have been insolvent and probably could not have been made solvent by obtaining distributions from other subsidiaries; it was improbable that enough cash could be generated in short order from their other subsidiaries, either from operations or through the sale of businesses or parts of businesses. As such, the Schenley common represented by the minority interest was senior Glen Alden debt. Glen Alden had to cause Schenley to pay dividends, and the minority interest had to share in these payments on a pro-rata basis. The Glen Alden debentures, of which some $700 million were outstanding, could be properly viewed as Glen Alden's equity. The Glen Alden common, which was under water (that is, had no tangible net worth attributable to it), might best be viewed as a voting warrant. In any event, the legal and accounting definitions of what these securities were did not necessarily jibe with the realistic economic definitions of what they were.

In much of securities analysis, consolidated statements are all that is needed. Frequently, though, consolidated statements are insufficient for an analysis. SEC-required disclosures tend to be fairly good in providing parent-company and subsidiary financial statements when these are important for understanding 10-K's, merger proxy statements and prospectuses.

NEGATIVE VALUES IN OWING ASSETS

Two Wall Street clichés conflict. One states, "Everything's got a price," meaning a positive price. The other states, "I wouldn't own that asset if you gave it to me." Since we believe that the ownership of most assets entails obligations and expense, we think the second cliché frequently tends to be truer than the first.

TOOLS OF SECURITIES ANALYSIS

Chapter 12

Net Asset Values

❧❦❧

The race is not always to the swiftest
nor the battle to the strong . . . but that's
the way to lay your dough.

DAMON RUNYON

BOOK VALUE is defined as a corporation's net asset value per share
as shown on the business's financial statements at a given date. Tangible book value is defined exactly as is book value, except that
intangible assets (patents, copyrights, purchase good will and so on)
are excluded from assets. Book value is calculated by dividing net
assets—that is, total assets minus total liabilities and outstanding
preferred stocks taken at redemption value—by the number of common shares outstanding.

Book value, unlike reported accounting earnings, seems to play
little or no apparent role in influencing day-to-day stock market
prices. This is probably the principal reason why nearly all writers
about financial accounting and security analysis have denigrated the
importance of book value as a tool of valuation, emphasizing instead
a primacy of earnings. We, on the other hand, believe that in almost all
analysis outside of the day-to-day stock-trading environment, book

value is a highly useful tool of analysis for a variety of purposes, including predictions of future accounting earnings. In this chapter, we detail reasons why we think attention to book value should be useful for creditors and investors.

A second reason why others treat asset values as less important than we do here is that they approach valuation solely from the point of view of outside investors examining strict going concerns. Our interests, in contrast, are much broader, covering all securities holders, creditors, activists and passivists. In addition, the businesses we analyze may not merely be strict going concerns, but may also be engaged in asset-conversion activities.

Insofar as the approach to analysis is restricted to the evaluation of the securities of strict going concerns by outside investors, it is understandable that there should be an emphasis on accounting earnings at the expense of net asset value. After all, in this situation the investor is not going to influence the way resources in a business are used, and indeed, by the definition of strict going concern there is every expectation that these resources will be used in the future just about the same as they have in the past. In such a situation, it is fair to conclude that the past earnings record is the best indicator of what is likely to happen in the future. The problem with this approach, it seems to us, is not that it is not applicable in certain situations (for example, with an electric utility), but that it may be applied where it does not belong, as, for example, in the analysis of a domestic crude-petroleum producer.

Before presenting our views about the importance of book value in security analysis, its uses and its very real limitations, it may be helpful to review briefly the conventional views about the relationship between book value and accounting earnings in security analysis and financial accounting. Typical among these conventional views are those contained in the books *Security Analysis; Accounting Principles; Corporate-Financial Reporting in a Competitive Economy,* by Herman Bevis; and *Valuing a Company,* by McCarthy and Healy.

Graham and Dodd, in *Security Analysis,*[36] recognize that book

---

[36]*Ibid.;* see, especially, pp. 551–52.

value is useful in certain cases. Nevertheless, in the analysis of most companies and in explaining stock market price behavior, Graham and Dodd place book value in a decidedly secondary position, concentrating on earnings and dividends as the prime measure of management performance and company value. The Graham and Dodd views about asset value are most definitively articulated in Chapter 41 of *Security Analysis,* "The Asset-Value Factor in Common Stock Valuation."

In describing stock market behavior, Graham and Dodd point out that book values "lose virtually all significance." Specifically, book values appear to them to have no relevance in determining earning power for industrial companies or railroads. Their studies show that market prices for rail and industrial common stocks had no correlations with book values: some were sold at high multiples of book value, others at discounts. Rather, Graham and Dodd found that market prices for these common stocks depended on the earning power and dividend payments of the company.

For Graham and Dodd, asset value is significant in special cases, not as a norm. For example, they find that book value is a significant predictor of future earnings and stock prices for some companies; book value is seen as an important stock-price determinant for financial enterprises such as banks, insurance companies, and savings and loan holding companies, because assets used in these businesses tend to be highly liquid and readily turned into cash. Similarly, asset values are important in public-utility companies, where rates are set at least in part on the basis of asset value, so that the larger the company's assets, the higher its potential earning power.

As a special case Graham and Dodd recommend that in evaluating risk or spotting unique opportunities, common-stock investors should use book value as a bench mark. They warn against common stocks selling at many times book value as carrying inordinate risk. On the other hand, they point out that a common stock selling at only a "small fraction" of its book value may have "speculative possibilities—especially so if there is no substantial debt." Common stocks selling at a price well below book value, earning-power value and past average market prices can be very promising, according to these authors. And if the stock price is below the value of the current assets alone, then "it is almost an axiom either the price is too low or the management should change its policies in some respect."

Financial accountants universally seem to subordinate book value to accounting earnings. Their definition of a "fair presentation" bottoms on a view that earnings ought to accurately reflect results of the accounting period. In *Accounting Principles* it is stated, "The information presented in an income statement is usually considered the most important information provided by financial accounting because profitability is a paramount concern to those interested in the economic activities of the enterprise."[37] Herman W. Bevis, former senior partner of Price Waterhouse and Company, states in his book, *Corporate Financial Reporting in a Competitive Economy,* "If one were forced to choose from among the financial statements that which bears most directly upon the stockholder's primary interest, it would, of course, be the income statement."[38] And McCarthy and Healy, in their book, *Valuing a Company: Practices & Procedures,* cite studies in a section titled "Lack of Significance of 'Book Value' " which conclude that book values, or net equities, "lack . . . significance . . . as a valuation factor."[39]

We have a different emphasis than Graham and Dodd and the financial accountants. To us, book value, in virtually all analysis other than predictions of common-stock prices for the immediate future, is at least as significant as accounting earnings. And in practice, one is not a substitute for the other. But in choosing a starting point within financial statements for an analysis, book value seems to us to be the better starting point most of the time than accounting earnings.

In part, our different emphasis results from different perspectives. Unlike Graham and Dodd and the financial accountants, we

[37]American Institute of Certified Public Accountants, *Accounting Principles,* Section 1022.04, p. 132.

[38]Herman W. Bevis, *Corporate Financial Reporting in a Competitive Economy* (New York: Macmillan, 1965), p. 50.

[39]George D. McCarthy and Robert E. Healy, *Valuing a Company: Practices & Procedures* (New York: Ronald Press, 1971), pp. 103–4.

believe that a very large part of American businesses are engaged in asset-conversion activities: that is, they are not strict going concerns involved only in operations that result in recurring accounting earnings. Rather, many companies, in whole or in part, are engaged in asset-conversion activities that give rise to tax shelter, mergers and acquisitions, changes in control, liquidations, investment activities and major refinancings. The analysis of businesses so engaged involves assigning a relatively increased importance to book value, or in any event a marked decrease in the significance of accounting earnings from operations. In addition, Graham and Dodd and the financial accountants seem to view their constituency as outside investors who are relatively conscious of, and influenced by, day-to-day stock market price fluctuations that seem to be more influenced by accounting earnings as reported than by book value. We, on the other hand, view our basic constituency as creditors and investors, and insofar as we write for the outside investor, it is to recommend to him that he analyze securities in much the same way as do creditors and investors who are activists or promoters.

We also differ somewhat from Graham and Dodd and financial accountants because we have a different fundamental view about the relationship between book value and accounting earnings. We believe that whenever accounting earnings are significant in the fundamental analysis of a company, so is book value. Indeed, in most instances book value is intrinsically related to earnings and exists in great part because companies or their constituent parts have enjoyed retained earnings in the past. In fact, our studies of stock prices indicate that when common stock are selling at low price–earnings ratios relative to average historic earnings, the same common stocks are also selling at large discounts from book value; conversely, high price-earnings ratios based on average historic earnings correlate with common-stock prices that are at substantial premiums above book value. Of course, there are logical reasons why this should be so.

In the bookkeeping cycle, net income not paid out to stockholders becomes a balance-sheet account, called retained earnings or earned surplus. These past profits tend to be the principal component of book value.* Thus, as a rule of thumb, companies with large book values relative to market prices have net worths that consist in great part of retained earnings. Such companies tend also to be selling at very low prices when compared with average long-term earnings.

Table I lists thirty companies that comprise the Dow Jones Industrial Average, and shows the relation to the price for each company's common stock on May 28, 1976, of its book value and ten-year average earnings.[†] Note that six of the seven common stocks selling at the highest premiums above book value—Eastman Kodak, Procter and Gamble, General Electric, International Paper, DuPont, and Sears Roebuck—were also selling at the highest price–earnings ratios. Furthermore, six of the seven common stocks selling at the biggest discounts from book value—American Can, Woolworth, Westinghouse Electric, International Harvester, Chrysler and Anaconda—were selling at the lowest price–earnings ratios.

This correlation between price–earnings ratios based on accounting earnings and the relation of market price to book value has not always been fully appreciated. For example, see the comments of McCarthy and Healy cited on page 184. Yet, we have found that there is a strong tendency for stocks selling at high multiples of historic earnings also to be selling at substantial premiums above book value. This correlation between price–earnings ratios and the spread between market price and book value is not perfect, of course. The correlation does exist, however, as a general rule. Given the integral relationship between historic accounting earnings and book value, we would be surprised if it did not. To say, then, that earnings determine common-stock prices but that book value is irrelevant clearly makes no sense unless one is talking only about short-swing, trading, stock-price movements.

---

*A study of fiscal 1975 year-end statements shows that retained earnings for twenty-nine of the thirty industrial companies in the Dow Jones Industrial Average (excluding American Telephone and Telegraph) equaled 75 percent of the total of capital, capital surplus and retained earnings.

[†]The correlation between the series shown in Table I is strong, equal to .899.

TABLE I RELATIONSHIP OF PRICE MAY 28, 1976,
TO REPORTED TEN-YEAR AVERAGE
EARNINGS AND LATEST BOOK VALUE

By Premium over (Discount from) Book Value	Percent	By Price-Earnings Ratio	Times
Eastman Kodak	338.0	Eastman Kodak	34.0
Procter & Gamble	244.0	Procter & Gamble	30.5
General Electric	129.0	International Paper	24.5
International Paper	120.0	U.S. Steel	22.0
DuPont	95.1	General Electric	20.4
Sears Roebuck	93.6	Sears Roebuck	20.3
American Brands	79.8	DuPont	19.1
Inco Ltd.	70.6	Union Carbide	16.8
General Foods	63.1	Aluminum Co. of America	16.7
General Motors	53.1	United Technologies	15.7
Union Carbide	49.9	Esmark	15.3
Exxon	31.2	Inco Ltd.	14.9
U.S. Steel	30.5	Owens-Illinois	14.2
United Technologies	20.1	Exxon	12.8
Aluminum Co. of America	16.7	Allied Chemical	12.6
Esmark	5.0	AT&T	12.6
Allied Chemical	3.6	General Foods	12.3
Owens-Illinois	(3.8)	General Motors	12.3
Standard Oil of California	(4.0)	Johns-Manville	11.0
Johns-Manville	(13.1)	Standard Oil of California	10.7
AT&T	(16.0)	Bethlehem Steel	10.4
Texaco	(17.8)	American Brands	9.5
Goodyear	(19.6)	Goodyear	9.5
American Can	(20.1)	Westinghouse Electric	8.9
Woolworth	(29.0)	International Harvester	8.8
Bethlehem Steel	(30.6)	American Can	8.7
Westinghouse Electric	(32.0)	Chrysler	8.4
International Harvester	(48.1)	Woolworth	8.3
Chrysler	(53.4)	Anaconda	8.2
Anaconda	(56.2)	Texaco	7.6

THE USEFULNESS OF BOOK VALUE IN SECURITY ANALYSIS

Since we place more emphasis on book value as a tool of analysis than do most other commentators, it is only appropriate that in reviewing its values and uses we also comment briefly on its limita-tions. First, book value is an accounting number, and in its usefulness and reliability it has to be as limited a tool of analysis as financial accounting itself, the limitations of which are discussed in Chapters 7 and 8. Second, book value alone does not mean much; it has to be related to other numbers and other concepts in order to become sig-nificant. Finally, book value is a quantitative measure of net assets: it tells us how much. In using the financial-integrity approach, however, quality of assets tends to be more important than quantitative consid-erations. We discuss at the end of this chapter the characteristics that give assets desirable or undesirable qualitative characteristics.

The special merits of book value as a tool of analysis are as follows:

- As one measure of the resources available to a business
- As one measure of potential liquidity available to a business
- As a competitive edge in common-stock selection

BOOK VALUE AS ONE MEASURE OF RESOURCES

Even where the past earnings record of a company is a superior indica-tor of future earning power, we know of no instance in which it has been the sole indicator. The amount of resources a management has available to create future earnings remains an essential indicator of future earning power. And one measure of available resources is book value.

This approach is more commonly used in the context of corpo-rate takeovers (such as mergers and acquisitions) than it is in the con-text of passive investing by outsiders. Corporate buyers tend to be acutely conscious of how they plan to use the resources over which they gain control in order to maximize earning power. Outside investors, on the other hand, are not in a position to alter the way a corporation's resources are used, and understandably are thus less likely to use this asset-conversion approach in forecasting future earnings. It does not follow from this, however, that an outside investor should or can safely ignore book value in analyzing a cor-porate situation. If only because corporate acquirers are using book-value analysis in this fashion, the outside investor may be able to reap a substantial benefit from adopting this kind of approach.

Book value as a measure of resources is also crucial in any kind of return on investment (ROI) or return on equity (ROE) analysis.* ROI and ROE analyses are important tools in forecasting future earnings. For example, high ROI may mean that a company has a proprietary position that will allow it to continue to enjoy above-average profitability; alternatively, it may be an invitation for new competition to enter the industry and drive down profits for all. Conversely, low ROI may evidence an overvaluing of assets and inefficient management, or it may be an indication that the business has a large amount of unused resources that give it a margin of safety and the wherewithal to expand earning power.

Many analysts recognize the importance of ROI and ROE analyses and place considerable emphasis on them while disclaiming the importance of book value. But you cannot calculate a return on investment unless you know the amount of the investment; nor can you know the amount of the investment unless you know the amount of the net worth. Inasmuch as book value measures common-stock equity, which is a component of net worth, it must necessarily figure in this calculation.

BOOK VALUE AS ONE MEASURE OF POTENTIAL LIQUIDITY

Liquidity is a qualitative characteristic of assets, and as such is discussed later in this chapter. Conventional going-concern analysis focuses on balance-sheet liquidity by relating current assets—especially cash, marketable securities and other assets readily convertible into cash—to liabilities. Such analysis is appropriate in the strict going-concern concept. However, in the real world of asset conversion and the tax carry-back provisions of the U.S. Internal Revenue Code,

---

*"Return on investment" is usually defined as net income (before interest costs) as a percentage of net worth and funded debt. "Return on equity" is usually defined as net income as a percentage of capital stock and surplus; sometimes when preferred stocks are outstanding, ROE is defined as net income as a percentage of net worth (with the net-worth account including preferred stock, common stock and surplus).

large quantities of brick-and-mortar assets are frequently the raw material out of which a great degree of liquidity is created.

With variations to allow for differences between financial accounting and income-tax accounting, the book carrying basis for assets is usually close to the tax-cost carrying basis for those assets. If so and if certain other conditions prevail—namely, that a profitable business has been a taxpayer at relatively high tax rates, and the company's common stock is selling at a steep discount from a brick-and-mortar book value—then opportunities exist to use tax carry-backs to create benefits for the stockholders of a company that sells its assets, and for a buying entity and its stockholders.

Under the U.S. Internal Revenue Code, in many situations where a company sells to an unrelated party assets used in the trade or business (whether they are current or fixed, from an accounting point of view) for less than the tax basis of those assets, the selling company will have realized a loss for tax purposes subject to offsets, namely, possible tax recapture of investment tax credits and accelerated depreciation. This loss after offsets is usually treated under Section 1231 of the Internal Revenue Code as an ordinary loss, even though the assets are considered capital assets. With an ordinary loss, the company can then obtain a "quickie" refund under the tax-loss carryback provisions of the Internal Revenue Code. A quickie refund results in a cash payment to the company, within forty-five days after the end of the tax year, up to the income taxes paid for the current year and the three years immediately preceding.

This tax-loss carry-back feature is especially useful when a profitable business is available for acquisition at a price well below net asset value as shown on the tax records. In that case, the Internal Revenue Service will probably provide a substantial amount of the cash needed to finance the acquisition.

Examples of such transactions abound. They include the purchase of Cletrac by White Motors; of American Viscose by FMC; of New York Trap Rock by Lazard Freres and Lone Star Cement; and the 1975 sale by Indian Head of its textile operations to Hanson Trust. Budd Manufacturing bought Continental Diamond Fiber assets in the late 1950's, and Fiber used the tax carry-over to finance the expansion of the one small operation that Budd did not buy. That small operation became Haveg Industries, which was eventually valued at over $50 million when it merged into Hercules.

The mechanics of such a tax-loss carry-back transaction can be best explained by a relatively simple example that assumes there are no recapture offsets.

Assume that the common stock of Target Company, which has a book value for financial-statement and tax purposes of $45, is selling at $15, or 7½ times earnings. Target has earned an average of $4 per share before taxes ($2 per share after taxes, based on a 50 percent tax rate) for the last four years. The company's assets include $3 cash per share, and Target is virtually debt-free.

Let's say that Acquirer Company, which has had no prior relationship to Target, purchases after negotiations all of Target's assets except its cash, and also assumes all of Target's liabilities by paying to Target $23 cash per share. In order to accomplish this, Acquirer is able to borrow $18 of the cash per share from an insurance company.

Supposing that Target incurs $1-per-share expense for this transaction and its subsequent liquidation, Target's workout value for the common stockholders will be $33 per share. This is shown in Table II. Target's assets available for liquidation consist of $23 cash

---

TABLE II   TARGET COMPANY WORKOUT VALUE
ON LIQUIDATION

Item	Per Share
Cash not sold to Acquirer Company	$3
Cash received on sale to Acquirer Company of assets, subject to all liabilities	23
Carry-back of Target's current-year income taxes, plus 3 years' prior income taxes at $2 per share per year	8
Subtotal	$34
Less Target's liquidating expense	1
	$33
% premium of workout over market of 15	120%

received from Acquirer on the sale of its assets, plus $3 of Target's own cash, plus an $8 tax carry-back, minus $1 expenses. This amounts to a 120 percent premium over the market price of $15.

From the buying entity's point of view, Acquirer was able to purchase the Target business at a price to it of $31, using only $5 of its own resources. The rest of the purchase price was other people's money—$18 borrowed from an insurance company and $8 obtained from the tax refunds. The difference between the $31 paid by Acquirer and the $34 gross value for Target is accounted for by the $3 of cash that Target did not sell to Acquirer.

Consummation of this transaction and the subsequent liquidation would result in Target's stockholders receiving a substantial premium over the market value of their shares. If Target wants to liquidate, it can do so by distributing $33 in cash to its stockholders. This liquidation would have no tax consequences to Target itself, provided that under Section 337 of the Internal Revenue Code a liquidation was substantially consummated within twelve months after the adoption of a plan of liquidation. Rather, the liquidation would be a taxable event for the stockholders: each stockholder would have a capital gain or capital loss, depending on the cost basis each had for his common stockholdings. Target, however, need not necessarily liquidate. If management wanted to continue in business, Target might become an investment trust,* or it might be able to buy certain other businesses.

Target did not necessarily have to sell all its assets to Acquirer. It

---

*Target's becoming an investment trust is a principal component of a form of transaction that has come to be known as the most common type of leveraged buyout. In this type of leveraged buy-out, three elements are present. First, assets are purchased at, or below (hopefully below, so that tax refunds may be obtained), their tax cost basis, so that no tax liabilities are created regardless of how low the cost basis for common stock held by principal stockholders may be. Second, the acquiring company hires the operating management of Target, giving them attractive long-term contracts, to run the business represented by the assets the acquiring company has purchased. Third, Target converts into an open-end investment trust, that is, a mutual fund, whose investments are restricted to tax-free securities issued by city and state governments. Target then offers to redeem shares at net asset value ($33 per share in Table II), at which time most public shareholders redeem and principal stockholders do not. The principal stockholders then control a mutual fund which

could, for example, have retained one operation and offset taxes on profits from that operation against the loss carry-forward created by the sale of assets.

On a *pro forma* basis, Acquirer's equity bought Target's net assets at around three times earnings, based on Acquirer's equity investment of 5, although Target's price–earnings ratio as an independent company was 7.5. Table III shows a condensed *pro forma* balance sheet for Acquirer, based on the acquisition of Target's net assets. Acquirer, if it were a public company, might also benefit because its purchase of Target's net assets at a price below book value enables it to report higher earnings on the operations than Target had. This result is due to two factors: because Acquirer's cost basis for the assets is lower than Target's, Acquirer's annual depreciation charges will also be lower; in addition, Acquirer will be able to amortize negative good will.

TABLE III ACQUIRER PRO FORMA BALANCE SHEET
(ON A PER-SHARE BASIS)

Assets purchased from Target, say	$30	Assumption of Target liabilities, say	$7
		Insurance-company loan	18
		Equity investment	5
	$30		$30

Table IV on page 194 illustrates a condensed income account for Acquirer, based on its having the same operating earnings before depreciation from Target's assets that Target had actually experienced in the prior four years.

---

has invested in tax-free obligations and which flows through without taxation all interest received to the remaining shareholders of Target. In effect, then, principal shareholders have converted their active business interests into a portfolio of tax-exempt securities without incurring any income tax liabilities even though their cost basis for their common stock holdings may be zero or close to zero.

TABLE IV   ACQUIRER PRO FORMA INCOME ACCOUNT (ON A PER-SHARE BASIS)

Pretax earnings as reported by Target	$4.00
Reduced depreciation attributable to Acquirer (because assets are lower cost basis), plus amortization of minor amount of negative good will, say	1.00
Subtotal	$5.00
Deduct interest at, say, 7% on $18 million loan	1.26
Pretax earnings	$3.24
[A]Taxes at 50%	1.62
Net income	$1.62
Acquirer price-earnings ratio, based on equity investment of $5 and after-tax earnings of $1.62	3.1X

[A]Cash benefits to Acquirer would be even greater if Acquirer had a usable tax-loss carry-forward.

BOOK VALUE ANALYSIS AS A COMPETITIVE EDGE

Most people who trade common stocks (as opposed to those who hold common stocks) seem to be more interested in the near-term outlook than in anything else. They will not purchase a security if the near-term outlook seems bad or uncertain, regardless of the price at which it is selling. An investor who is able to take positions based on other factors increases his chances of finding outstanding long-term bargains, since there is a relative lack of competition in the market in which he is buying. Given that market values will be determined by future earnings, and given also that most investors rely primarily on the past earnings record of a company in predicting future earnings, a good past earnings record will probably be reflected in a high market price. However, although they may also be an indicator of good future earnings, large high-quality asset values will probably not be reflected in a high market price for the stock. Thus, by placing primary weight on present asset value rather than on past earnings, an investor should be able to realize higher appreciation potential and lower risk of loss in the long term.

The outside investor who purchases securities regardless of the immediate outlook will probably always be in a distinct minority among securities purchasers. Such an investor must be in a strong financial position. He must also be capable of curbing any tendencies toward greed in his investment: he cannot attempt to buy precisely at the bottom of the market or to maximize capital gains over short periods. Finally, he must be convinced that there are important values in the company whose stocks he holds that are not reflected in the market price and are not likely to be dissipated. Without such conviction, almost any investor can be expected to panic if the market price of the security he holds declines. It tends to be much easier for outsiders to gain some degree of conviction if a cornerstone of their analysis is the financial-integrity approach.

Changes in earnings can be sudden and violent, and changes in price–earnings ratios even more so. Changes in book value, on the other hand, by definition must be more gradual. A large, relatively unencumbered book value may be an anchor to windward, both for the company with honest and reasonably competent management and for the investor who holds its stock.

LIMITATIONS OF BOOK VALUE IN SECURITY ANALYSES

To repeat, we do not believe in acquiring securities solely on the basis of the earnings record of a company or on the outlook for its reported earnings. Neither do we think that an investment program based on acquiring securities simply because they are available at large discounts from book value would necessarily be well advised. Availability at a large discount from book does give a first approximation that a security may be a bargain, or even that it may be attractive according to the financial-integrity approach. But this first approximation ought to be tempered by a more thorough analysis. In order for book value to be a good indicator of the wealth or future earning power of a going concern, other factors must be considered as well.

A company's record of profitability is, of course, some indication that the book asset value actually reflects real operating wealth, in the sense of assets that provide the wherewithal for obtaining earnings. Earnings for the current and the three prior years may also be a potential source of liquidity if income taxes have been paid or tax liability has accrued on them. The investor should also consider such factors as the size of the company's operational overhead and the incentives for control groups to work against the interests of the outside stockholders. Also, since book value is only an accounting figure, it cannot be more useful than accounting figures in general. In our view, the most important limitation of the usefulness of book value as an analytical tool is that in itself, it does not measure the quality of a company's assets, which we believe tends to be significantly more important than the quantity of asset value. Unfortunately, quality is a less measurable and less precise concept than quantity, involving what is essentially a subjective judgment.

What do we mean by "quality of assets"? In short, financial integrity. We suggest that quality of assets is determined in a corporate situation by reference to three separate, but related, factors.

First, an asset or mix of assets has high-quality elements insofar as it approaches being owned free and clear of encumbrances. Conversely, the assets of debt-ridden companies tend to be of low quality. Note that though encumbrances that depress the quality of assets (such as long-term indebtedness) may be stated liabilities, they may also be off-balance-sheet items, some of which, of course, will be disclosed in footnotes to the company's financial statements. These include such items as pension-plan liabilities, and such contingent liabilities as litigation and guaranties of the debts of others. Others may be disclosed elsewhere. For example, a railroad may be obligated to operate unprofitable commuter services, or a steel mill may be required to install antipollution equipment that does not generate revenue. Still other off-balance-sheet encumbrances may not be disclosed in any public document. A common example would be the need to substantially overhaul outdated plants and equipment in order for the business to remain competitive enough to survive. Unless an investor has know-how, and perhaps even know-who, he may be unable to find out that such encumbrances exist.

The second factor to consider in evaluating the quality of assets of a going concern is its operations. Does it have a mix of assets and liabilities that appears likely to produce high levels of operating earnings and cash flows? Good operations are the most important creator of high-quality assets and are likely to contribute to a company's having a strong financial position. Lenders quite properly prefer to finance businesses whose operations are sound and who are likely to create the wherewithal for continuing debt service on a long-run basis. The most financially attractive going concerns are blue chips and near blue chips, such as IBM, General Motors, DuPont, Kraftco, and R. J. Reynolds.

The third factor the investor must consider is the nature of the assets themselves. An asset or mix of assets tends to have high quality when it appears to be salable at a price that can be estimated with a modicum of accuracy. In most going-concern situations, of course, no values can be assigned to specific assets as a practical matter, because they are useful only as a part of the operations of the company—as part of an overall mix. For example, although it is said that certain proved and readily recoverable domestic oil reserves have a present value of five dollars per barrel, it is not especially useful for a nonmanagement investor analyzing Exxon to value that company's assets according to this formulation as long as the company is likely to remain a going-concern operation. Exxon's domestic reserves in that instance are dedicated directly or indirectly to Exxon's refinery and marketing operations; for practical purposes they have no five-dollar-per-barrel independent value. By contrast, if the same proved reserves were owned instead by, say, General American Oil, the five-dollar-per-barrel valuation would tend to be meaningful as long as there was a likelihood that General American would sell the reserves to others in bulk or in the normal course of business, or that General American would be acquired by others.

First and foremost, then, for an asset to have independent value from the point of view of the outside securities holder, it must be available for sale apart from the operations of the going concern. It must be something that is not so related to the going-concern operation, or if so dedicated, is separable from it in a manner that will not have an adverse impact on the operating-earnings power of the going concern.

Aside from this freedom from a going-concern encumbrance, there are certain other characteristics that tend to make assets more attractive to lenders, and thus of higher quality. Assets that are liquid and marketable tend to be more attractive to lenders than those that are not. Liquid assets include cash and equivalent marketable securities, including restricted securities with meaningful rights of registration, proved oil and gas reserves, cutting rights and timberlands, and various types of real property. In order to be marketable, the assets must have a value that is readily measurable. In the case of securities that are traded in organized markets, the market provides a measure of value. Other assets may have readily ascertainable values even though not so traded—as, for example, income-producing real estate.

If an asset is one that third-party lenders or guarantors (such as financial institutions and governments) are experienced in lending against, the standards they have developed for lending may also provide a measure of value, and the asset tends to be more valuable than it would otherwise be. Examples of such high-quality assets have included oil and gas, maritime vessels and certain types of real estate.

Flexibility and scarcity are factors that tend also to make an asset more valuable. Thus, multipurpose assets tend to be more valuable than single-purpose assets. Flexibility is especially important in the case of real estate: a factory useful for only one type of assembly-line production tends to be less attractive than, say, a downtown hotel that can be converted economically into efficiency apartments. Assets that are scarce, at least on a long-term basis (such as copper mines or domestic oil), may have special values all their own.

Certain assets that appear to have these characteristics may, of course, not have them because of legal impediments. For example,

U.S. margin regulations make common stocks worse collateral than other assets that lack common stocks' characteristics of liquidity, marketability, flexibility and measurability. Other assets may have special value because they can be used to create tax shelter. Because tax savings allow these assets to throw off more cash, tax-sheltered assets tend to be most attractive in the eyes of creditors. Thus, assets such as real estate, timberlands, to some extent oil and gas as well as other natural resources, and until recently, motion pictures have been outstanding examples of this.

These three factors—the amount of encumbrances, the operations and the nature of the assets themselves—tend to be interrelated and may be offsetting. Thus, a company that is less encumbered tends to be freer to invest in assets lacking high quality. The property and casualty insurance industry provides a good example of this: where an insurer's capital and surplus are small relative to stated liabilities (and to premium income, which in turn tends to be related to the size of liabilities), that insurer will concentrate its investments in government and corporate debt instruments. Only as capital ratios improve relative to stated liabilities (and premium income) will insurers tend to invest a portion of their assets in such lower-quality instruments as equity securities, especially common stocks.

High-quality asset businesses tend to be far more attractive holdings at given prices—say, when the common stocks are selling at ten times earnings—than are comparable businesses with lower-quality asset values. This is so because such businesses have a tendency to be subject to certain dynamic developments. And frequently, the common stocks of businesses with high-quality assets may sell at lower price-earnings ratios than comparable businesses with lower-quality assets. This tends to happen when stock traders desire to pay premiums for aggressive managements, although companies with high-quality assets oftentimes are run by careful rather than aggressive managers.

High-quality assets are most commonly used to finance rapid growth, both in present product lines and into diversified areas—as in such large businesses as Philip Morris and W. R. Grace—or in emerging growth companies, such as Ups 'N Downs and Henry Pratt Company.

Surplus liquid assets not needed in a business (sometimes called surplus surplus*) may be extracted from these companies. This was, for example, the basis of the takeovers in 1968 and 1969 of strongly capitalized insurers, such as Reliance Insurance and Great American Holding Company. At the time of takeover, the workouts for shareholders were more than twice what the shares had been selling at one year earlier.

A company's high-quality assets may be used to finance the takeover of that company on a better price basis than would otherwise be available. An example of this—a case where a mouse swallowed an elephant—was the 1962 acquisition by Albermarle Paper Manufacturing Company, a small company, of the entire capital of the much larger and extremely well financed Ethyl Corporation. Albermarle not only swallowed the elephant, but also adopted its name.

When a company lacks encumbrances as measured against the amount of obligations it owes, the nature of its operations and/or its potential to sell or convert all or part of its assets to a more liquid or useful form, that company is deemed by us to have a strong financial position, one of the four main characteristics sought in an equity investment using the financial-integrity approach. Generally, it is our view that if a company has little or no outstanding obligations, it is in a strong financial position, unless operating losses seem to have some prospect of being so large that the company's strength will be impaired.

*"Surplus surplus" is a name we think, but are not sure, was invented by the New York State superintendent of insurance around 1969.

Chapter 13

Earnings

◈

*A hen is only an egg's way
of making another egg.*

SAMUEL BUTLER

INCOME ACCOUNTS are important. However, except in very special cases, there is no "primacy of earnings": that is myth, pure and simple. The one special case where there probably is a primacy of *current* earnings and earnings *estimates for the immediate future* is in the trading of common stocks. The long-term earnings record tends to be significant also in the analysis of a going concern, since unless it has a favorable long-term record of relatively consistent profitability, no equity issues of a company can qualify as high-quality.

In this chapter, we examine the reasons why, outside the limited sphere of day-to-day stock trading, there is no primacy of earnings. We also review appropriate roles for current reported earnings within the trading environment, and the long-term earnings record in the investment environment. In this chapter, too, earnings are "parsed" in order to gain insights into what earnings and income mean and do not mean, and how earnings ought to be used as one tool in corporate and security analysis.

WEALTH OR EARNINGS?

In the United States, as in all societies that are beyond the survival level, the goal of most businesses appears to be the creation of wealth rather than generation of reported net income. Of course, the generation of reported net income and the creation of wealth are related: the creation of reported net income is just one method of creating wealth. There are two additional methods of creating wealth—creating unrealized appreciation, and realizing the appreciation that has been created.

Where businessmen have choices, the generation of reported earnings from operations tends to be the least desirable method for creating wealth, simply because reported earnings from operations are less tax sheltered than are other methods of wealth creation. This is one of the reasons why asset-conversion activities by corporations seem to have grown in importance at the expense of ordinary going-concern activities.

It ought to be noted in passing that those investors most ready to analyze corporations based on a primacy-of-earnings concept tend to be the same investors who in the management of portfolios renounce primacy of earnings in favor of stock market performance and total return; the creation of reported net income in the form of dividends and interest net of ordinary expenses tends to be secondary to achieving unrealized and realized appreciation.

It is well known that privately held corporations, even those that are strict going-concern operations, usually attempt to report earnings in a manner that minimizes income taxes—an important consideration to these businessmen in realizing wealth-creation goals. Publicly held corporations, on the other hand, frequently attempt to report the best earnings possible. This is not because businessmen think that current earnings per se are so all-important, but, rather, because the ability to report favorable current earnings may have the most favorable impact on stock prices and in this instance provides the greatest potential for wealth creation. High common-stock prices provide insiders with opportunities to realize values by selling or borrowing. They also give a company opportunities to issue new equities in public underwritings for cash, or to acquire other companies either for cash or by the direct issuance of common stock or other equity securities.

A principal reason why others believe there should be a primacy of earnings is the tenet—which, as far as we can tell, is unproved for most companies—that the single best tool for predicting future earnings is past earnings. Even if this were so, it would not necessarily justify a primacy-of-earnings approach to fundamental evaluations. No responsible analyst would rely on just one tool of analysis, even if it is the single best tool. Thus, in predicting future earnings for a strict going concern—say, American Telephone and Telegraph Company or General Motors Corporation—the investor does not look only at past earnings to help him to gauge the future profits prospects. Rather, good analysts make use of the various tools available to them. They appreciate that at the minimum, present asset values help in appraising the reasonableness of earnings predictions. For example, during the 1962 new-issue boom, certain Maryland savings and loan common stocks were being touted as having burgeoning earnings, and one in particular was bid up to prices around 12 because 1963 earnings were being estimated at $1 per share, based on the acceleration of past growth trends. Net asset value in late 1962 was about $2 per share. Those who looked at net asset value and not just the past earnings record, and those who believed that it was unlikely that savings and loan associations could earn a 50 percent return on equity or anything even close to it, avoided investing in a stock promotion for a company that was adjudicated bankrupt in 1963, and where the value of the common stock was wiped out.

Moreover, it appears probable that past earnings are not the best predictor of future earnings. Indeed, a fundamental concept of asset-conversion analysis is that by and large the future will be different from the past for reasons such as the possibility of mergers or refinancings.

Frequently, the best tool for projecting future earnings is the structure and amount of asset value at a given moment. Society Corporation's position in the early 1960's is one example of this. Society Corporation was and is a bank holding company based in Cleveland, Ohio. At that time, banks in general were earning between 8 percent and 12 percent of net worth. Society, with a net worth of about $50 a share, was earning about $1.50 a share from operations when it converted from a mutual savings bank to a commercial bank holding company in 1962. This equaled a return on net worth of only 3 percent. An investor could reason with a fair degree of confidence that over time Society probably would be earning a return on its equity close to that which was being achieved in the commercial banking industry in general. At least, there did not appear to be any insurmountable problems preventing this. Furthermore, book value, too, would be steadily increasing. The anticipated results occurred; reported earnings increased year by year, and by 1966 operating earnings were $5 per share on a year-end book value of $62. The prediction of Society Corporation's future earnings could not have been based on the past earnings record. An examination of the asset values and the belief that such asset values would be used much the way other commercial bank holding companies used theirs were the basis for the earnings forecast. This approach is probably better described as asset conversion rather than strict going-concern. The key item in evaluating Society Corporation was the probability that it would convert its assets to more productive uses.

Although it is difficult to generalize about the role of current reported earnings as an influence on common-stock prices, in buoyant general markets the main influences on common-stock prices of companies that are strict going concerns seem to be current reported earnings, reported earnings estimated for the immediate future, sponsorship and industry identification. Greater weight tends to be given to earnings paid out as dividends than to earnings retained by the firm. There also tends to be an emphasis on trend, with great weight given to earnings that are going up.

To these earnings, a multiple—that is, a price–earnings ratio—that is dependent on the above earnings record plus industry identification is applied. Standard and Poor's, for example, publishes price–earnings ratios by industry in its *Analyst's Handbook* and *Trade Surveys.**

---

*The price-earnings ratio or multiple refers to the relationship between stock price and earnings per share. Thus, if a common stock sells at 22 and the earnings attributable to that common stock are $2.50 per share, the price–earnings ratio or multiplier is 8.8 times (22 divided by $2.50).

It is important in these trading situations that not only should the company have a growth record; for its stock to attain a high multiple, it should also be situated in an industry that has a favorable image. Thus, a company with a less-than-good earnings record may attain a very high multiple if it is situated in a growth industry, whereas a company with steadily increasing earnings may sell at a very low multiple if it has an inappropriate industry identification.

Sponsorship, as we have already noted in Chapter 10, also tends to contribute to the making of current stock market prices. "Sponsorship" means that a company is well regarded or is actually owned by interests with a history of Wall Street success. Sponsors can be all sorts of people and institutions, ranging from broker-dealers who have been imaginative and successful creators, such as Allen and Company, to people from outside the financial community who are deemed to have the "magic touch," as, for example, Harold Geneen, James Ling and H. Ross Perot. A company can attain a good industry identification through appropriate sponsorship, but sometimes such sponsorship can be substituted for industry identification.

A good example of how effective industry identification can be is provided by looking at the comparative earnings of Polaroid Corporation at the end of March 1974, when its common stock was selling at 41 times current earnings, whereas at the same time CIT Financial common stock was selling at 9 times earnings. Polaroid's earnings record had been very spotty, but CIT had shown annual earnings increases for the prior fifteen years. A comparison of their reported per-share earnings in the five years to December 31, 1973, is as follows:

	EARNINGS PER SHARE	
	Polaroid Corporation	*CIT Financial Corporation*
1969	$2.20	$3.15
1970	2.01	3.27
1971	1.86	3.77
1972	1.30	4.15
1973	1.58	4.28

Polaroid sold at over 40 times earnings because of its industry identification with instant photography. CIT Financial, on the other hand, was a diversified financial-services company.

THE LONG-TERM EARNINGS RECORD

In fundamental analysis, special attention should be given to the importance of a favorable long-term earnings record—that is, a company's ability to have enjoyed, at least for accounting purposes, annual profits from operations over a period of three years, five years and longer. Such a record or lack of it can be extremely important in many types of analysis, even though it lacks the universal significance attributed to it by some analysts for all corporate evaluations.

As we have commented in the previous chapter, there is an integral relationship between earnings records and asset values. The major component of net asset value for most publicly owned businesses is retained earnings—past profits that have not been paid out. There is a general tendency, therefore, for past records of profitability to be reflected in the book value reported in a company's relatively recent balance sheets.

Over and above this, there are two types of analysis in which a company's long-term earnings record becomes especially significant. In the first, the business to be analyzed is to be viewed as a strict going concern, likely to conduct its operations in the future as it has in the past, and financed about the same as in the past, with management and control groups essentially unchanged.

The second area of analysis where a long-term earnings record becomes especially significant is in gauging the quality of an issuer. Where an operating business lacks consistent profits—indeed, where an issuer lacks long-term profits that have been on a rising trend—it lacks a crucial attribute necessary to rank as high quality. Securities of an issuer lacking a good earnings record frequently are highly attractive—as are, for example, asset-conversion issues selling at depressed prices—but they are not high quality.

It should be reemphasized, furthermore, that many portfolios should be restricted in whole or in great part to high-quality issues (especially when the portfolio managers have neither know-how nor know-who) where a principal objective has to be the generation of regular cash income and where there are fiduciary obligations to the portfolio beneficiaries. In these instances, we suggest that suitable securities consist, at the minimum, of the issues of companies whose financial statements combine both favorable long-term profits records and strong present financial positions. We would not emphasize the long-term earnings record at the expense of the present financial position, or vice versa.

"PARSING" THE INCOME ACCOUNT

Earnings sometimes seem to mean all things to all investors. Yet earnings are likely to be most valuable as analytical material insofar as more appreciation is gained of the various meanings of earnings. It is important to distinguish between the static-equilibrium approach to earnings and the dynamic-disequilibrium approach to earnings.

The static-equilibrium approach to net income looks at current earnings and the earnings record as principal factors in the determination of what a current common-stock market price ought to be. It is generally agreed that there tend to be equilibrium prices at a given moment for certain common stocks with certain current earnings and industry identifications, though in every instance there are important exceptions. For example, at this writing most electric-utility common stocks are selling in a range between eight and twelve times latest twelve months' earnings; most commercial-bank stocks are selling in a range between nine and eleven times earnings; and most savings and loan stocks are priced at from five to seven times earnings. Say that an investor uncovers a savings and loan concern selling at two times latest twelve months' earnings. This fact could be the basis for investing in the common stock of the savings and loan company, assuming it is found after investigation that other things are roughly equal. This stock could have a reasonable appreciation potential if the tendency toward equilibrium prices took hold and if it were to sell in line with the price–earnings ratios at which other savings and loan stocks were selling.

The static-equilibrium concept is not only important to outside investors, but also has a significant role in investment banking. Considerable use is made of the static-equilibrium concept in the pricing of new-issue underwritings. Managing underwriters usually attempt to price a new issue at a price-earnings ratio moderately below that at which the seasoned issues of companies in the same or similar industries are selling. Then, typically, the new issue is merchandised by emphasizing, among other things, that its earnings multiple is below that of comparable issues. (See Appendix I for a discussion of the pricing of Schaefer Corporation common stock when that issue was marketed publicly.)

The dynamic-disequilibrium concept of earnings involves the use of the past and current record of reported earnings as a base for estimating future earnings. The projected increase in earnings is then used as a basis for predicting a future stock price. Thus, if a savings and loan common stock is selling at 7 and earnings are $1 per share (or just about in line with 7 times the industry price–earnings ratio), an analyst attuned to dynamic disequilibrium and estimating next year's earnings at $1.50 might conclude that the stock will appreciate from 7 to 10½, or 7 times $1.50 per-share earnings.

We have already discussed in this chapter the uses and limitations of this pure dynamic-disequilibrium approach. The analyst relying on earnings to evaluate a business or a common stock will be helped if he has some appreciation of the difference between the role of earnings in a static-equilibrium approach and the role of earnings in a dynamic-disequilibrium approach. It has been our experience that many analysts fail to distinguish between static equilibrium and dynamic disequilibrium.

It ought to be noted also that definitions of earnings, net income or periodic earnings are usually not precise. We give several of the definitions that are used by various practitioners and scholars in different contexts. In each of these, earnings can be defined as

- *What accountants computing results in accordance with Generally Accepted Accounting Principles report them to be.*
  This is the most common definition of earnings used by others,

and is most frequently but not always restricted by those with a stock market orientation to recurring earnings after income taxes from continuing operations.

* *What the accountants computing results in accordance with Generally Accepted Accounting Principles report them to be, as measured by overall performance, including extraordinary items and results of discontinued operations.*

* *The increase in value of a business (after adding back stockholder distributions) from one period to the next, with the increase measured by valuation tools that are not subject to GAAP assumptions and GAAP discipline.*

The best example of this is investment trusts, where "true" earnings results are measured by changes in net asset value, as measured by stock market prices adjusted for dividend distributions.

* *The increase in ability to make stockholder distributions over and above actual stockholder distributions which do not reduce actual invested capital.*

Such distributions to stockholders are usually in cash in the form of dividends, but they do not necessarily have to be so. For example, an alternative method of distributing corporate cash to stockholders could be to have a company repurchase its own shares for cash.

* *The increase in ability to make payments to all security holders, not just equity holders, during a period.*

Earnings can be measured by improvements in the overall financial position, or what is known in some scholarly circles as "better-offness." An example of this can be found in the case of DPF, which had been a computer leasing company. From fiscal 1972 through fiscal 1975, DPF reduced its senior secured debt from $28.3 million to $965,000. During that period, aggregate losses for accounting purposes were reported at over $4 million. For practical purposes, it was obvious that DPF was profitable in a meaningful economic sense, despite its reported loss for accounting purposes, because of its ability to achieve its prime objective of becoming better off by putting its financial house in order through reducing senior indebtedness.

- *The increase in ability to improve future sales, accounting profits and/or cash flow during a period.*

  Earnings might be measured for a period in this case not by any reference to accounting results, but rather, say, by the perfection or development of a new product that has gained trade acceptance during its initial marketing.

The achievement of earnings as defined by GAAP does not even necessarily contribute to solvency. For example, in the early 1950's a new cigarette called Parliament, the original filter cigarette, was introduced by Benson and Hedges, then a very small cigarette company. Parliaments were inordinately successful, and Benson and Hedges expanded by leaps and bounds. Unfortunately for Benson and Hedges, working capital requirements ballooned, since in its industry it was (and is) necessary that cigarette tobaccos be aged for an average of three years. The faster the Benson and Hedges business expanded, the more difficult it was to finance its requirements for larger inventories. The more Benson and Hedges expanded as a small independent, the greater its accounting earnings were and the closer the company came to insolvency. As a small independent operator, Benson and Hedges' earnings were not "real." They could be made real only by selling out to an entity that could finance Parliament's expansion. Eventually, Benson and Hedges merged into Philip Morris, for whom Parliament's earnings were, of course, completely real, because Philip Morris had sufficient financial resources to benefit fully from the expansion that was taking place.

Reported accounting results and stock prices obtain such tremendous weight in many market calculations because they are the measurements that are both precise and visible. In an investment trust, one knows the value of the portfolio with precision, based on what the closing prices are and/or what the mean between bid and asked is (where no stock sale has occurred). Equity real estate investment trusts, on the other hand, may have a portfolio that would be readily convertible into cash over a period of a month or two, but because there is no daily price quotation for the real estate portfolio, its asset value can only be roughly estimated on any given day.

Therefore, the value of the real estate asset portfolio is not given the same weight as the value of an investment-trust portfolio, even though in the case of large investment trusts blockage* would prevent liquidation of the portfolio in less than a few months' time at any prices other than those reflecting a large discount from market.

Precision and visibility, even if they do not reflect realization values, deserve a special significance, because they appear to (and in a sense do) reduce uncertainties. An absence of precision and measurability usually, and understandably, detracts from perceptions of value.

Given the varied economic definitions of earnings, it may be wise to distinguish between earnings and earning power. By "earnings" is meant only reported accounting earnings. On the other hand, in referring to "earning power" the stress is on wealth creation. There is no need to equate a past earnings record with earning power. There is no a priori reason to view accounting earnings as the best indicator of earning power. Among other things, the amount of resources in the business at a given moment may be as good or a better indicator of earning power.

---

*Blockage occurs when a holder of a large block of freely tradable securities is unable, because of "thin markets," to dispose of that block at any prices other than ones that are at a substantial discount from prevailing market prices.

Chapter 14

Roles of Cash Dividends
in Securities Analysis
and Portfolio Management

❧❦❧

Leave a little on the table for the dealer.

Cash dividends are money payments to corporate shareholders paid out of a company's accounting earned surplus, made in proportion to each shareholder's ownership interest in the class of stock receiving the dividend. Once the dividend is declared, the stockholder has no meaningful choice other than to take it. Control of the size and timing of the pay-out is usually with the company and not the outside stockholder.

We have already pointed out, perhaps ad nauseam, that it is impractical to view finance and investment problems as if there existed monolithic stockholders and monolithic corporations, or as if there was any necessary relationship between the value of a business and the price of its common stock. Yet, insofar as the three most widely accepted theories about the relationship of cash dividends to value and common-stock prices are concerned, the underlying assumptions appear to be based on just such perceptions. The three most widely accepted theories are those propounded by John Burr Williams, Modigliani and Miller, and Graham and Dodd.

It is important for investors relying on a financial-integrity approach to investing to understand the roles cash dividends play in securities analysis, portfolio management and corporate finance. We believe the real roles of cash dividends tend to be different from those postulated in traditional theories. For us, there are five principal roles of cash dividends. First, dividend levels and changes in dividends, up or down, seem likely to have impacts on stock market prices. Second, cash dividends are important placebos for noncontrol investors insofar as such investors lack confidence in the merits of the equity securities they hold. Third, dividends are crucial in portfolio management where prudent managers seek a positive cash-carry—that is, where they strive to have income from the holding of securities exceed interest expense (and possibly dividend costs too) incurred in connection with obligations or quasi-obligations assumed in connection with the portfolio being managed. Fourth, the receipt of dividend income may be a legal necessity for certain security holders, such as various fiduciaries. Finally, it is our view that for any investment to be attractive, the investor has to perceive a bailout sooner or later, as we point out in Chapter 3, "The Significance of Market Performance"—and dividends are one form of bailout.

In a rational world, no investment can be attractive unless there are prospects for a bailout. Bailouts can be of two types: in the first, control of a business can be obtained; in the second, there are prospects that the investment will become convertible into cash in whole or in part. Noncontrol investments can become convertible into cash because the securities are marketable; because the minority investor can hope to exercise certain rights, such as rights of appraisal under state law; and/or because the investor can look forward to the receipt of cash dividends.

We think it is important to distinguish between the significance of interest income to typical holders of senior securities and the significance of dividend income to common stockholders. The goals of common stockholders tend to be less well defined than are those of holders of credit instruments.

Two of the three theories—John Burr Williams's and Graham and Dodd's—appear to be compatible with our views, provided the underlying assumptions of each theory are modified to fit in with our ideas of economic and financial reality. The Modigliani and Miller theory, on the other hand, may be useful as a theoretical exercise; it does not appear to have any practical application.

THE THREE CONVENTIONAL THEORIES

The first theory, propounded by John Burr Williams in a book entitled *The Theory of Investment Value*,[40] states that a common stock is worth the sum of all the dividends expected to be paid out on it in the future, each discounted to its present worth. The second theory, propounded by F. Modigliani and M. H. Miller in 1958,[41] in an article entitled "The Cost of Capital, Corporation Finance and the Theory of Investment," states in effect that as long as management is presumed to be acting in the best interests of the stockholders, retained earnings should be regarded as equivalent to a fully subscribed, preemptive issue of common stock, and therefore that dividend pay-out is not material in the valuations of a common stock. The third theory is detailed in Chapter 35 of Graham and Dodd's *Security Analysis*,[42] and states that in the case of the vast majority of companies, higher common-stock prices will prevail when earnings are paid out as dividends rather than retained in a business. Graham and Dodd feel that the only exceptions to this rule are cases where a company's return on investments is unusually large, and where the company's stocks sell at high multiples of earnings and at huge premiums over book value.

The Williams theory might be of use in an ideal world, but it is of little help in a complex, wealth-creating economy such as ours. The Williams theory, undiluted, would only apply in a tax-free world where the universal raison d'être for owning common stocks was to

[40]John Burr Williams, *The Theory of Investment Value* (Cambridge, Mass.: Harvard University Press, 1938).

[41]F. Modigliani and M. H. Miller, "The Cost of Capital, Corporation Finance and the Theory of Investment," *American Economic Review*, Vol. 48, No. 3 (June 1958).

[42]Graham and Dodd *et al., op. cit.*

receive dividends and the raison d'être of all corporate activities was to pay dividends to common stockholders.

The Williams theory, to be realistic, could be restated to posit that a common stock held by noncontrol stockholders is worth the sum of all the net after-tax cash expected to be realizable in the future from ownership of the common stock, with such net cash being realizable either from cash disbursements by the company (whether in the form of dividends or otherwise, such as liquidating in whole or in part), and from sources outside the company (whether they are stock purchasers or lenders willing to treat the common stock as collateral for borrowings by the shareholder). Such cash realizations would be discounted to reflect time factors and the probabilities of realizations as well as tax considerations and trading costs. Purely and simply, such a theory equates with our bailout views of investment value.

If one wanted to make the realistic assumption that the ultimate goal of all noncontrol investment is cash realization, then the Williams theory as we have modified it would fit in well with our perceptions of the real world. However, even that has to be modified. It would still not apply universally, since the ultimate goal of *all* investment is not cash realization. For many investors (for example, a corporation that has no intention of ever paying cash to its equity holders) the goal of its investment may not be cash realization, but control over the growth of unrealized investment values. Other investing entities may combine goals of ultimate cash realization and continued reinvestment.

Unlike the Williams approach to evaluating common stock, the Modigliani and Miller assumptions seem utterly unrealistic. There does not appear to be any basis in fact for assuming either that managements act in the best interests of stockholders or that stockholders have an absolute community of interests among themselves. The simple fact is that relationships among managements and stockholders of public companies are always combinations of communities of interest and conflicts of interest.

Managements frequently, even traditionally, pay lip service to the proposition that they work in the best interests of all stockholders, especially outside stockholders. Increased management salaries and perquisites are justified on the basis that stockholders' best interests are served by using such compensation devices to attract and hold highly motivated personnel.

Companies go private by buying out their stockholders at discounts from realizable values (as did the George A. Fuller Company in 1965, the Marmon Group in 1970, Nardis of Dallas in 1974 and Bournes, Incorporated in 1976). This activity is justified on the basis that it is in the best interests of the stockholders to force them to take, in cash, a value that represents a premium over the prevailing stock market prices—even though the prices may reflect a thin market in which very few shares could be bought or sold without increasing or depressing stock market prices. This activity may in fact be working in the best interests of many of the outside stockholders, but certainly not all. The Modigliani and Miller view of the fiduciary management selflessly toiling for the ideal stockholder simply does not accurately describe how all managements of public companies think and operate. Nor does it accurately describe the objectives of the many different types of stockholders.

That managements do not tend to work primarily in the best interests of all stockholders has been pointed out by John K. Galbraith in his book *The New Industrial State.*[43] Management itself collectively and individually constitutes a group that always has some conflict of interest with at least some outside stockholders. Other groups of whose interests the management is keenly aware (and whose interests are at least partially adverse to the interests of some of the stockholders) are other securities holders, such as institutional creditors, labor unions, suppliers, customers and the staff of the company itself.

If there is any generalization to be made, it would be that management, in balancing the interests of the various groups they feel they have to serve, tends to work more in the best interests of those groups that bring the most benefits to the management. Activities in these directions, though, are tempered by the need and sometimes the desire to guard the interests of other groups, especially those whom

[43]John Kenneth Galbraith, *The New Industrial State* (Boston: Houghton Mifflin, 1967).

management has to constantly deal or negotiate with on a one-to-one basis. Conversely, there is a tendency to guard least the interests of those who are truly outsiders and passive, with whom management rarely, if ever, deals personally. The outside groups that managements of publicly owned corporations tend to view impersonally are the outside stockholders and the Internal Revenue Service, among other tax-collection agencies.

Since managements have virtually no community of interests with tax collectors, there is no tendency to guard the interests of this group, except as required by law and in reaction to threats of audit or other investigatory activity. True, over and above the law, outside stockholders tend to receive better treatment than tax collectors, even though they may be more passive. Most managements do not view outside stockholders either as allies or as adversaries. And there are times when managements want what most outside stockholders want—for example, a high price for the company's common stock. But this convergence of interests may occur less frequently than many people suppose.

Probably the best indications that managements do not, on the most practical level, work in the best interests of stockholders can be found in the need for an elaborate legal structure to protect outside stockholders from predatory practices by insiders. This legal structure is contained mostly within the securities laws as embodied in the Securities Act of 1933, the Securities and Exchange Act of 1934 and the Investment Company Act of 1940, all as amended. Enforcement of stockholder rights against insiders is undertaken by the regulatory authorities themselves and through the private bar, which brings representative and derivative class actions on behalf of stockholder groups. Left without these legal constraints, we have little doubt that many managements would be far less cognizant of the stockholder's best interests than is now the case.*

---

*The one group that might be viewed in the broadest perspective as dedicated almost solely to the interests of outside, passive investors is the Securities and Exchange Commission. On a practical level this is not wholly true, but it is our view that the Securities and Exchange Commission has been more dedicated to the interests of outside, passive investors than any other group in the economy.

The third general theory, that of Graham and Dodd, describes stock market behavior. In brief, it notes the tendency for earnings paid out as dividends to have a greater market value than earnings retained. Graham and Dodd note:

For the vast majority of common stocks, the dividend record and prospects have always been the most important factor controlling investment quality and value.

In the majority of cases, the price of the common stock has been influenced more markedly by dividend rate than by the reported earnings:

Because (1) dividends play a dominant role in the market price of a typical common stock and (2) the discounted value of near dividends is higher than the present worth of distant dividends, of two companies with the same earning power and in the same general position in an industry, the one paying the larger dividend will almost always sell at a higher price.[44]

While these statements are realistic, their thrust seems to us to be misdirected. A more appropriate emphasis would be not on where a stock would sell in the near future because of its dividend, but rather on which stock—the low dividend payer or the high dividend payer—is more attractive to which type of investor.

CASH DIVIDENDS AS A FACTOR IN MARKET PERFORMANCE

If we were to generalize about the subject, we would approach the stock market impact of dividend payments differently from the way Graham and Dodd do. Other things being equal, the common stock whose issuer is a low dividend payer would be the better buy for investors seeking market appreciation, rather than a cash-carry. As Graham and Dodd agree, of two companies with the same earning power and with the same general position in the industry, the lower dividend company should tend to sell at the lower price; this, by

[44]Graham and Dodd *et al., op. cit.,* pp. 480–81.

itself, should make the lower dividend payer a more attractive buy for many investors. Furthermore, the company whose common stock is available at the lower price will have more room to increase its dividend and eventually command the higher price. It appears likely that market price action may be more affected by the trend in dividend payments than by the amount of the dividends. The company paying the lower dividend will retain more earnings and in the future be in a better position to improve its industry status, its financial position and therefore its earnings. It is entirely possible that, assuming the companies are in the same position now, had the company paying the lower dividend paid a higher dividend, it could never have achieved the position it now has.

A reasonable countervailing argument can be made that high dividend payers tend to be the better buy because a high pay-out ratio may indicate a management more attuned to meeting the desires of most outside stockholders. We believe this argument has elements of validity. Its applicability, however, is limited, since dividend policy does not appear to us to be a particularly good measure of either management ability or management interests. Insofar as there is a tendency for there to be a strong relationship between the long-term economic interests of a company and the long-term prices of that company's common stock, stockholders are eventually benefited by small or no dividends, to the same extent as companies benefited from profitably reinvesting cash that would otherwise have been paid out as dividends.

Graham and Dodd also state:

Long experience has taught investors to be somewhat mistrustful of the benefits claimed to accrue to them from retained and reinvested earnings. In very many cases, a large accumulated surplus failed not only to produce a comparable increase in the earnings and dividends, but even to assure the continuance of the previously established rate of disbursement.[45]

This statement is, of course, true, but it is equally true that too high dividends can hurt companies and stockholders far more than

[45]*Ibid.*, p. 484.

conservative dividend policies. There are many cases where companies paid high dividends long after it was prudent for them to do so, and as a consequence the stockholders suffered mightily. Examples range from Automobile Banking and Chrysler Corporation to Middlesex Water, U.S. Pipe and Foundry and United Fruit. These companies and their long-term stockholders would have been better off had dividend rates been lower and had the companies retained earnings to finance necessary expenditures.

The Graham and Dodd approach has validity from a stockholder's short-run viewpoint, but does not appear to give much weight to the legitimate long-term needs of a corporation. The Graham and Dodd approach does recognize corporate and stockholder long-term needs if it is assumed that high dividends result in high stock prices that an issuer is able to take advantage of by issuing new stocks at prices based on market values. But this assumption is largely unrealistic. Except for public utilities, most corporations, as a practical matter, can issue new common stock only very occasionally, either in sales for cash or in merger and acquisition transactions.

We are in agreement with Graham and Dodd that corporate dividends and corporate dividend policies are likely to have a meaningful impact on common-stock prices. As we point out above, though, different assumptions bring different results. For the broad range of companies, we cannot conclude that high dividends are better than low dividends.

THE PLACEBO EFFECT OF CASH DIVIDENDS

Cash dividends increase in importance for securities holders insofar as the holder lacks confidence in the outlook or management or in the reliability of the disclosures used by him in his buy, hold or sell decisions. Put simply, for the uninformed or distrustful stockholder, cash dividends are a hedge against being wrong. Truly a bird in hand (cash return) for them is worth two, three or four times the bird in the bush (the appreciation potential arising out of a company's reinvesting retained earnings and its common stock's being available at a lower price because of the lower dividend).

CASH DIVIDENDS
AND PORTFOLIO MANAGEMENT

Dividends increase in importance with the shareholder's need for immediate cash income from his portfolio. Of course, when the prime lending rate exceeds 7 percent, and good-grade common stocks return no more than 6 percent, it may be asked, Should those in need of income invest in common stocks at all? Such a question misses several points. First, many shareholders desiring income are in locked-in positions, unwilling to sell common shares they own because of, say, an ultra-low cost basis for income-tax purposes. Second, many investors seek inflation hedges—securities that combine high cash returns with appreciation potential. Specific common stocks are likely to have substantially more appreciation potential than senior securities (either because their prices are unusually depressed or because equity holders can participate in the long-term growth of a business), whereas the holder of a senior security without equity privileges has a contractually defined limit on potential appreciation. Although it is true that the smaller appreciation potential of senior securities is made up for, at least in part, by the fact that they are easier to finance, this finance factor may be academic for the prudent outside investor who abhors borrowing on margin to invest in the securities of companies about which his knowledge is limited, over which his control is nil and where his costs of borrowing might exceed his return on his portfolio.

Dividends become a negative factor for shareholders who want tax shelter or who have no need for income and are confident that management will reinvest retained earnings on a highly productive basis. In a sense and except for the fact that it does not provide a cash return, unrealized appreciation is the ultimate in income-tax shelter. Dividend income tends to be unimportant, also, where a company is not essentially a going concern, but rather is an asset-conversion or a workout situation (that is, with prospects of being liquidated, acquired or reorganized), because of the expectation by shareholders that realization will be obtained on a more advantageous tax basis than if dividends were paid.

An attractive feature of securities with a high cash return is the positive cash-carry. A safe high cash return not only eases any investor's pain where performance is disappointing, but also makes a transaction eminently more affordable and easier to finance than would otherwise be the case. This is so because of the benefits a cash-carry brings to the financial position of a holder. For example, at the time of this writing, Source Capital Preferred sells at 24, and pays a $2.40 dividend; it is a margin eligible security. Assuming an investor can borrow 50 percent of the cost of 10,000 shares, incurring a 7½ percent interest cost, his cash-carry would be as follows:

10,000 shares Source Capital Preferred at 24 net	$240,000
50% of purchase price borrowed	120,000
Cash investment required	120,000
Annual dividend income on 10,000 shares	$24,000
Interest cost on borrowing of $120,000 at 7½%	9,000
Cash-carry	$15,000
Cash return on investment (Cash-carry as percent of cash investment	12.5%

We believe that the Source Capital Preferred $2.40 dividend is exceptionally safe and that the security is de facto an AAA issue. It is the senior security of a large, now conservatively managed, registered investment company, which is forbidden by law to incur any material amount of obligations that would be senior to this preferred stock issue. Against this background and assuming our analysis is absolutely correct, it may be instructive to review for the reader those factors that a portfolio manager ought to consider before determining that a cash-carry investment in Source Preferred is both attractive and suitable. First, the investor who believes the cost of borrowing will increase may forgo a Source Preferred investment. Since the investor may not be able to control the cost of his borrowing, there could be adverse cash-carry consequences if interest rates on the bank borrowings increase to over 10 percent and the investor is required to retire or pay down his bank loan at a time when he is unable to refinance. Second, there is a risk of depreciation in the market price of Source

Capital Preferred stock if long-term interest rates rise markedly or the market becomes irrational. Some indication of the depreciation possibilities inherent in Source Preferred can be gleaned from the price history of the issue: in 1974, Source Capital Preferred was quoted as low as 17⅜ bid. It ought to be noted, too, that Source Capital Preferred is not overly marketable; there are only about 1.6 million shares outstanding, and these are traded in the over-the-counter market in small volume. Any security holder who might have to sell at any particular moment might be able to dispose of his shares only at discount prices.

While the positive 12.5 percent cash-carry return appears attractive by itself, appreciation opportunities are limited for the issue. Commencing September 30, 1977, the issue became callable at the option of the company at $30 per share, and the call price will decline each year until it reaches $27.50 in 1982. The issue will not, in rational markets, sell at any appreciable premium over its call price.

Alternative opportunities could be more attractive. We do not know the entire universe of securities, but conceivably there could be other issues that offer a better combination of cash-carry safety of income and high return.

Unlike most other domestic preferred stocks, Source Capital Preferred has only limited special tax benefits for corporate holders, through the availability of an 85 percent tax exclusion. As an investment company electing to be taxed under Subchapter M of the Internal Revenue Code, Source Capital itself is not a taxable entity, but instead "flows through" its income to the shareholders. Unless and until the bulk of Source Capital's investments is in dividend-paying equities rather than interest-paying debt instruments, only a portion of Source Capital Preferred's dividend payments to its corporate stockholders will be tax-sheltered. At present, a corporate holder of Source Preferred is subject to full income taxes on about two thirds of the dividends, and only in connection with about one third can the corporate holder exclude 85 percent of the payments from its taxable income.

Finally, Source Capital Preferred lacks general recognition by others as a high-quality issue. This factor almost automatically excludes the stock from consideration for all sorts of institutional and quasi-institutional portfolios.

One of the pervasive elements of corporate finance is demonstrated by this cash-carry example. How attractive a security or situation is, is in part a function of how financially strong it is. With the prime lending rate of 7⅜ percent, Source Capital Preferred at 24 is in our view a very attractive cash-carry situation for many; were the prime 10½ percent, not only would there be no cash-carry for Source Capital Preferred at 24, but in the absence of the issue's being called or tendered at a price in excess of 24, the stock would be unattractive.

CASH DIVIDENDS AND LEGAL LISTS

Cash-dividend income is a legal or quasi-legal necessity for many securities holders. Legal lists in many states require fiduciaries' common-stock investments to be restricted to securities that are currently paying dividends and have paid dividends for a number of years in the past. The accounting practices for business-entity investors (such as insurance and investment companies) usually permit them to report as income on common-stock investments where they hold less than 20 percent of the issue only the dividends received. These stockholders cannot report as net income any equity in the undistributed earnings of companies whose common stocks they hold in their portfolios. The accounting rule governing this is contained in Opinion 18 of the Accounting Principles Board, which states that there is a presumption that undistributed equity in profits or losses of companies whose stocks are in the portfolio are to be included in the business entities' accounts if 20 percent or more of the stock of such a company is owned.

CASH DIVIDENDS AND BAILOUTS

The ability to convert assets to cash tends to be a key consideration for many buyers of securities for control purposes. It always is a key consideration for outside investors.

Companies with pools of unencumbered liquidity tend to be looked upon as attractive acquisitions for control buyers, in part because there is a lack of uncertainty about minimum values to anyone. Furthermore, large pools of cash may frequently be worth substantial stock market paper premiums to acquirers of corporate control when those acquirers pay in paper consisting of warrants, common stocks, preferred stocks and subordinated debentures, not cash. For example, Schenley Industries' cash was worth a substantial premium over stated value to Glen Alden in 1968 and again in 1971 when Glen Alden acquired Schenley securities mostly by the issuance of subordinated debentures. Roan Selection Trust's cash also was worth a premium to Amax in 1970.

Assuming that an investor can have no element of control over the company in whose common stock he has invested, that stockholder will want to have opportunities sooner or later to convert that investment into cash. There are but three ways that such a minority interest can be converted to cash: first, the security can be marketed; second, the issuer can become involved in asset-conversion activities, such as mergers and acquisitions, liquidations or going-private transactions; and third, cash dividends can be paid to stockholders. Frequently, the prospect of cash dividends is the only meaningful assurance a minority investor may have that a cash return will be received on an otherwise locked-up investment.

Without being exhaustive, there are a few simple rules about minority-interest investments of which an outside investor in public companies ought to be aware. Once a company has become public, it is required to remain a filing company with the Securities and Exchange Commission as long as there are three hundred or more stockholders of record of any class of equity securities.[46] For control

---

[46]Section 12(g)4 of the Securities Exchange Act of 1934 states:

Registration of any class of security pursuant to this subsection shall be terminated ninety days, or such shorter period as the Commission may determine, after the issuer files a certification with the Commission that the number of holders of record of such class of security is reduced to less than three hundred persons. The Commission shall after notice and opportunity for hearing deny termination of registration if it finds that the certification is untrue. Termination of registration shall be deferred pending final determination on the question of denial.

Companies filing with the Securities and Exchange Commission comply with either Section 12 or Section 15 of the Securities Exchange Act of 1934. Section 15d has language similar to Section 12(g)4, permitting deregistration when an issuer has fewer than three hundred shareholders of record.

stockholders, there usually are important advantages to having 100 percent control of a company, compared with less than 100 percent. Also, there are usually important advantages in being private rather than public. However, regardless of the state of incorporation, majorities having a "business purpose" do have the right to force out the minorities through a vote of the requisite number of shares, or where the majority owns enough shares, through a short-form merger, which does not require a vote. Whether compensation to the minority in the force-out has to be adequate depends in part on state law, including the adequacy of appraisal rights for dissenting stockholders, and on compliance with appropriate disclosure requirements under federal securities laws.

It is our experience that the acquisition of a portfolio of minority interests is attractive because of the likelihood that parents will eventually attempt to acquire, through mop-up mergers, 100 percent interests in subsidiaries at prices reflecting substantial premiums above stock market prices (which are depressed in part because such securities are liable to lack marketability). Such securities, which have been acquired in recent years by their parents at substantial premiums above market, include Indian Head, Marcor, and Otis Elevator Company.

In acquiring these types of minority-interest securities, however, it frequently is important to the investor that such securities pay dividends, in part because an investor may need income and in part because the receipt of dividends may be far more certain than cash tender offers or mop-up mergers that may never occur. When situations exist where the parent company finds it essential to receive cash from subsidiaries in the form of dividends on outstanding common stock, cash income may be virtually assured for the outside investor. Two such subsidiaries are Reliance Insurance Company, 97-percent-owned by the Reliance Group, and Mountain States Telephone and Telegraph, 88-percent-owned by American Telephone and Telegraph. Both Reliance Insurance and Mountain States Telephone have had relatively liberal dividend policies. It is a fair bet that such policies will continue.

THE GOALS OF SECURITIES HOLDERS

It is important within the financial-integrity approach to distinguish between the goals of virtually all holders of senior securities and many holders of equity securities. A problem arises because many commentators impute to equity owners the same ultimate goals that exist for debt owners.

Many owners of senior securities, especially financial institutions, are interested solely in cash return—interest payable in cash, plus a return of principal, also payable in cash. Most senior securities have limited lives, so that if repayment of principal in whole or in part cannot be obtained from sale in the market, in time repayment will be obtained from the issuer.

In contrast, equity holders may sometimes be interested in cash returns in the form of dividends and the ability to sell shares, not to the issuer, but to the market. However, some equity holders are also interested in an earnings return—in having a perpetual participation in an enterprise that through the plow-back of earnings increases in value over time. Such investors are under no illusion that increases in value will be, or are necessarily likely to be, reflected in stock market prices at any given moment.

It is probable that most long-term equity investors have a variety of goals, combining the pure cash-return goals characteristic of many senior-security holders, and the earnings-return goals characteristic of a person for whom dividends have significant tax disadvantages and who is not particularly aware of stock market price fluctuations. We think that many economic, accounting and stock market theorists fail to recognize the existence of this second type of investor.

Chapter 15

Shareholder Distributions, Primarily from the Company Point of View

❦

FIRST FELLOW: *"Did you know that Dave's a millionaire?"*
SECOND FELLOW: *"Dave's no millionaire. My goodness, you don't even know what a millionaire is."*
FIRST FELLOW: *"Oh, yeah, what is a millionaire?"*
SECOND FELLOW: *"A millionaire? Why, a millionaire is someone who has at least ten thousand dollars cash."*
FIRST FELLOW: *"You're right. That kind of money Dave ain't got."*

CASH DIVIDENDS OR RETAINED EARNINGS

A BASIC DIFFERENCE between us and other analysts, including Graham and Dodd, is that others believe an appropriate dividend policy is derived from looking at pay-out policies through the stockholder's, rather than the company's, point of view. It is our view that for most companies, the formulation of appropriate shareholder distribution policies requires that stockholder needs and desires be distinctly subservient to the needs of the corporation itself.

Others believe, at least by implication, that the price at which a stock sells, relative to a company's earnings and asset values, is some-how related to an appropriate pay-out policy. We, on the other hand, believe that dividend pay-outs have to be regarded as a residual use of corporate cash, and that company requirements for cash in other areas must have primacy. Dividend policy has to be dictated by company needs, both for funds for expansion and for maintaining a margin of safety. Furthermore, we think the price at which a common stock sells (except in special cases, of which public utilities are the prime example) should have little to do with a company's pay-out policy. The special-case exception is a going-concern company that knows it has to period-ically obtain capital from the sale of new issues of common stock, and uses dividends to support the price of its stock so that it will be able to market shares publicly at a more assured price than otherwise.

Graham and Dodd, in support of this other view, write in *Security Analysis:*

The higher the average multiplier of earnings in the stock list, the greater the proportion of issues which presumably should retain all or nearly all of their profits . . . For—presumably again—the rate of return on reinvestment will substantially exceed, in a typical case, what the stockholder could earn on the same money received in dividends. A good corporate-earnings picture and opportunities for capital expansion generally go together. Thus, the favorable business and stockmarket developments of the 1950's have greatly extended the field of companies for which, in theory at least, low dividends and high reinvestment would appear the best policy for stockholders. Carried to its logical conclusion, this analysis would suggest that nearly all really success-ful companies should follow a program of full reinvestment of profits, and that cash dividend should be paid only to the extent that opportunities for profitable expansion or diversification were not present.[47]

We question the Graham and Dodd analysis on two counts. First, the high price–earnings ratio or multiple seems wholly unrelated to the business's needs for cash. The underlying assumption Graham and Dodd appear to use here is that the market has been appraising the business's prospects accurately in the multiple it has assigned to the

---

[47]Graham and Dodd *et al., op. cit.,* p. 490.

shares. There is no empirical evidence supporting such a view. Indeed, the only logical conclusion to draw is that companies should retain earnings when they have opportunities for profitable investment, regardless of the price of their common stock. Whether or not they have opportunities for profitable investment of the funds is not something that is going to be told to companies or their managements by the stock market appraisal of how their earnings are capitalized.

The fire and casualty insurance industry serves as an example of the use of retained earnings as an engine of compound growth when stocks generally sell at low multiples and steep discounts from net asset value. As a rule of thumb, fire and casualty insurers pay out as dividends about one-half of their net investment income and reinvest the other half. These reinvested earnings, plus cash generated from increasing volume of insurance underwriting premiums (and when available, insurance underwriting profits), are used to purchase income-producing securities. Thus, though the underwriting performance of the industry from the mid-1950's on was poor (generally little better than break-even), net investment income increased steadily from 1960 through 1975. This steady increase in investment income—despite an erratic underwriting performance, with statutory losses in eight of the fifteen years—is shown in the following table, covering the years 1960 through 1975, prepared from data in *Best's Aggregates and Averages:*[48]

[48](Oldwich, N.J.: A. M. Best Co., 1976).

Year	Investment Income	Underwriting Profit (or Loss)
1975	$3,143	($2,880)
1974	2,891	(1,761)
1973	2,491	226
1972	2,068	915
1971	1,785	679
1970	1,439	(154)
1969	1,238	(395)
1968	1,101	(200)
1967	987	10

Year	Investment Income	Underwriting Profit (or Loss)
1966	895	103
1965	852	(425)
1964	782	(348)
1963	721	(218)
1962	673	3
1961	620	30
1960	592	66

Insofar as the company does not have profitable use for the reinvestment of the funds and is financially strong enough to have a margin of safety, funds should be distributed to shareholders. The cash should be distributed in a manner that is best suited for the various interests involved; frequently, such distributions will not be in dividends, but in the company's repurchasing its own shares.

From the corporation's point of view, it sometimes is important to have consistent, sound policies of (a) paying regular dividends and (b) increasing dividends periodically. This occurs when the market prices of the shares are determined primarily by the dividend return and when corporate capital requirements are far too huge to be financed either internally or by debt. Consequently, new equity has to be marketed every few years. Thus, liberal dividend policies become an integral part of corporate financial policy for such companies. These companies are characterized by great operational stability, so that the type of investor attracted can depend on a steady dividend income continually covered by earnings. However, these corporate characteristics do not describe the vast majority of publicly held companies, and there is no reason for supposing that what might be an appropriate dividend policy for these companies is also applicable to others.

This is not to say that many a corporation in its own interests and in its management and controlling stockholders' interests does not frequently find it desirable to maintain consistent and even liberal dividend policies. One reason an incumbent management might want to pay liberal dividends is that low dividend pay-outs may result in low stock market prices, with the consequence that the business becomes more susceptible to a raid. Higher dividends may protect a management's position. This may be especially true where corporate prudence would dictate that a dividend be reduced or eliminated, either of which action would tend to result in gross stockholder dissatisfaction.

Influential stockholders, including management, may infrequently have needs for the cash-return income that comes from dividends. Sometimes, too, an increased dividend will result in an increased stock price that could be important to insiders (or to the company itself) intending to sell all or part of their holdings.

Occasionally, companies have no practical internal use for cash, especially if diversification and acquisitions would result in antitrust problems for those operating in relatively mature industries, such as General Motors and Ford.

A long-run, consistent dividend policy is frequently essential if a company is to obtain general recognition in the financial community as a high-quality issuer. Such recognition tends to result in better prices for a company's common stock over the long term, and may attract outside stockholders who are stable investors interested in income (insurance companies for example) rather than in-and-out traders or go-go speculators.

STOCK DIVIDENDS

There is a school of thought that asserts that there would be benefits to corporations and stockholders if corporations paying cash dividends would, as a consistent annual policy, also pay stock dividends to shareholders, the market value of which would be in an amount about equal to retained earnings for the year. Thus, if XYZ stock sells at 20, earns $2 and pays a cash dividend of $1.20, it is recommended by many people that the $.80 of retained earnings be paid out in the form of a stock dividend—in this case 4 percent, or $.80 divided by $20. If the following year's retained earnings equal $1.10 and the stock price is 34, the suggested stock dividend would be 3 percent.

Proponents of this policy believe it benefits shareholders. Shareholders receive on a tax-free basis new stock that, if they desire to do so, they can convert to cash by selling the shares received, and they would be taxed at only capital-gains rates rather than at dividend-income rates. Because of the stock-dividend policy, the corporation would have less need to raise cash dividends and consequently less need to seek new equity financing from its existing shareholders. Viewed in this light, there is something to be said for a policy of periodic stock dividends and less frequent subscription rights to shareholders, compared with the policy most public utilities employ—of raising the common cash dividend periodically to support the price of the stock, and then selling new shares to stockholders, often via subscription rights.

Although this may be so in the special case of utilities, the advantages of regular stock dividends in most situations most of the time seem highly limited. Even in the case of public utilities, the advantage of periodic stock dividends over periodic increases in the cash-dividend rate may be limited. A utility's need for outside equity financing on a continuing basis tends to be so huge as to dwarf into insignificance the amount of cash that could be retained by paying stock dividends instead of periodically increasing the cash dividend. Stockholders and the utility are best served by the policy that results in the stock's selling at the most favorable price most consistently. Many commentators feel that periodic increases in the cash dividend have a more favorable market impact than regular stock dividends, but we do not know of any definitive studies on one or the other.

One small utility, Citizens Utilities, has a two-issue common-stock capitalization: an A stock, which pays a cash dividend; and a B stock, which pays only a stock dividend in a market-value amount equal to the cash dividend on the A. The B is convertible into the A, but has virtually always sold at a premium over the A. Duplication of the Citizens Utilities capitalization would be impossible now, because Internal Revenue has slammed the barn door shut, so that for any stock issued now with Citizens Utilities B features, IRS holds that the stock dividend is the equivalent of a cash dividend. And as we point out in Chapter 9, one of the three things that make a tax position unattractive is a taxable event—such as the distribution of a Citizens Utilities B stock dividend—where the event that gives rise to the tax does not also give rise to the cash with which to pay the tax.

It is rare to find U.S. companies paying regular stock dividends, especially among those that also pay cash dividends. Stock-dividend policies do make some sense for companies that do not pay cash dividends but that do plow back cash: stock dividends give shareholders evidence, in the form of a salable stock certificate, that corporate progress is being made. Stock dividends also make some sense, however limited, for companies with a public-utility type of dynamics, in which new equity will be publicly marketed on a regular, recurring, reasonably predictable basis. However, most companies pay, or intend to pay, regular cash dividends, and most do not have a public-utility type of dynamics. Most companies seek outside equity financing on an irregular and highly unpredictable basis, if at all. For such companies, payments of stock dividends result in regular increases in the aggregate amount of cash paid out, with possibly little or no benefit to shareholders. This would not have been the case had the company raised the cash-dividend rate, say, once every three years. A simple example shows how a company that desires to maintain a regular rate can be locked into increasing cash outlays on a compounding basis if it also wants to pay regular stock dividends. Assume Company XYZ's dividend rate is $1 cash plus 5 percent stock, and there are 1 million shares outstanding. If this dividend situation is maintained, XYZ's annual cash-dividend pay-out (in thousands) will be as follows:

Year	Dividend Cash Expenditure	Annual Increase in Cash Outlays for Cash Dividends Caused by Stock-Dividend Program
Present	$1,000	$0
1	1,050	50
2	1,103	103
3	1,158	158
4	1,216	216

Year	Dividend Cash Expenditure	Annual Increase in Cash Outlays for Cash Dividends Caused by Stock-Dividend Program
5	1,276	276
6	1,340	340
7	1,407	407
8	1,477	477
9	1,551	551
10	1,629	629

The payment of stock dividends gives rise to a number of administrative headaches too. There have to be adjustments of past per-share figures on earnings, dividends and book value, and of calculations in connection with antidilution provisions in convertibles and warrant instruments; stockholders have to be mailed new certificates, which they then have to safeguard; and there may be a tendency for XYZ's stockholder list to become burdened with large numbers of odd-lot shareholders, whom it is quite expensive to service with dividend and stockholder-report mailings, relative to the market value of their investment. If we were advising XYZ, we would suggest to them that both the company and their shareholders would be better off if XYZ gave up the 5 percent annual stock dividend and instead increased the regular dividend rate by, say, 5 percent once every three years.

Stock dividends, too, pose administrative problems for stockholders, many of whom seem to believe that retaining stock dividends only results in their having more paper and more paperwork. Those who sell the shares received find that their equity in the company is diluted.

DISTRIBUTION OF ASSETS
OTHER THAN CASH

A company may be in a position to distribute assets other than cash to stockholders. Sometimes those assets distributed can be dividends for tax purposes and can encompass such things as portfolio securities (distributed by Standard Oil of Indiana from 1948 to 1963); chocolate inventories (by Rockwood Chocolate in the 1950's); and even whiskey (by Schenley Distillers during World War II). Such distributions are rare because of possible disadvantages to shareholders, since the dividend event that gave rise to the tax does not provide the cash with which to pay it.

For tax reasons, most distributions to shareholders that are "in kind" rather than in cash are tax-sheltered distributions. The most famous of such recent distributions was that of DuPont's holdings in General Motors Company common stock during 1962, 1964 and 1965. By act of Congress, these distributions were exempted from tax as a dividend.

The income-tax code has numerous provisions that allow shareholders to receive distributions in kind and in cash on a tax-sheltered basis. Such provisions are in the tax-code sections dealing with spin-offs, split-offs, split-ups, redemptions, reorganizations and liquidations. Discussion of these is beyond the purview of this book.

LIQUIDATION

A word on liquidation seems appropriate, however. The common definition of corporate liquidation concerns the pay-out in cash and/or in kind of an amount greater than the company's accumulated retained earnings. In some circles, liquidation seems to bear a stigma as something that is nonproductive. Our view as to what liquidation is and what it means tends to be different. To us, any payment by a corporation to its shareholders—even quarterly dividends—is a form of liquidation. Whether or not permanent capital other than retained earnings is invaded is an accounting question, not an economic one. Certainly, no stigma of nonproductivity ought to attach to stockholder distributions of any sort, in any amount, as long as the company distributing can afford to do so and believes the distribution is a good enough use of cash. In fact, the vast majority of companies are unable to make any material-sized distribution now, not because they lack adequate retained earnings, but rather because they lack adequate liquidity. In most cases, the companies are prevented from distributing more than a portion of annual earnings to shareholders, both by common sense and by restrictions in their various loan agreements. In the broadest and most meaningful sense, we do not believe there is any such thing as liquidation. Rather, there is only asset conversion—a conversion of assets to different uses and/or ownership, where much of the time they will be more productive.

STOCK REPURCHASES

Both dividends and stock repurchases result in cash being distributed to the stockholder. Despite stigmas or hangups about liquidation, buying in common stocks in certain instances can be a viable alternative for companies with the requisite liquidity.

On an overall basis, buy-ins have relative advantages for stockholders: in the usual case, such receipts of cash are taxed only on a capital-gains basis; on the part of the stockholder, the receipt of the cash usually is optional, rather than mandatory (as is the case with dividend receipts); weak shareholders sell out, with possible favorable implications for future market prices; and if, as is frequently the case, buy-ins are at a price below the value based on corporate reality, the per-share corporate-reality value of the shares not bought in is enhanced.

There are advantages to corporations as well. Insofar as the common stock is dividend-paying and, as is usual, the company desires to maintain a dividend rate, cash requirements for future dividend payments are reduced; earnings per share, book value per share and corporate-reality value per share may be enhanced; and a program can result in the elimination of all, or virtually all, public shareholders. Furthermore, where the price of the stock can be a tool to be used by the company in, say, future acquisitions, buy-ins can result in a more favorable price for shares that remain outstanding than would otherwise be the case.*

*However, it should be noted that according to Opinion 16 of the Accounting Principles Board, companies buying in their own shares are prohibited for a two-year period thereafter from using pooling-of-interests accounting for financial-reporting purposes in connection with mergers and acquisitions.

Buy-ins, of course, bring certain relative disadvantages to public shareholders. First and foremost, if the buy-ins are of massive size, investors may be forced out of a company altogether, at a price that may be very low compared with corporate reality, even though such a price could be at a substantial premium over market. Even if not forced out, they would find that the shares remaining after a buy-in may have only very limited marketability, since buy-ins are usually only a sometime, irregular source of cash to stockholders, whereas dividends can be counted on as a regular, continuing source of cash receipts. Companies buying in common, other than in privately negotiated transactions, are inherently in a conflicted position with public shareholders: the companies are buyers and the public are sellers. And public stockholders understand dividends, but there is something remote and mysterious about buy-ins.

Buy-ins also bring certain other relative disadvantages to corporations, even to those that unquestionably have surplus cash and no better use of it than to repurchase shares selling at prices that are attractive relative to corporate reality. First, there are many legal strictures against buying in, whether by open-market purchase,* by tender or by use of the proxy machinery; there even can be difficulties when purchases are made in private transactions. Buy-ins give rise to accounting problems, especially in regard to acquisitions within the following two years. Besides inherent conflicts with public shareholders, there also may be conflicts with insiders who might want to purchase shares. And there may be appearances of pay-offs to inside shareholders who desire to sell.

We stress that buy-ins are a legitimate use of corporate cash. As a practical matter, buy-ins are likely to remain a limited activity simply because for most corporations, no matter how attractively priced their managements think their stock is, share repurchases are impractical—

---

*The principal stricture against open-market purchases is contained in the Proposed Securities and Exchange Act Regulation 13(e)2. Most would-be corporate open-market repurchases abide by 13(e)2 (though it is only a proposal, in existence since 1972) in order to avoid running into accusations of market manipulations that are violations of antifraud statutes, particularly Rule 10(b)5.

the company lacks either the liquidity or the legal authority to repurchase or retire shares. In many cases, the companies will have expansion opportunities—such as Xerox and Texas Instruments had—which make share repurchase relatively unattractive. In other cases, laws prevent repurchases, as in the cases of electric utilities or commercial banks. In most cases, though, companies will lack enough cash or borrowing power to undertake meaningful buy-in programs. However, the buy-in program conducted by IBM Corporation that commenced in 1977 may have given buy-ins a new cachet and respectability that was lacking previously. IBM sought to acquire as many as 5 million of its own shares via a cash tender offer at $280 per share; the corporation succeeded in acquiring 2,567,564 shares in that tender offer.

The repurchase of large amounts of publicly owned shares by companies, or the purchase of such shares by insiders, results in a company going private. It is difficult to define "going private" with precision. In November 1977 the SEC proposed certain regulations to control going-private transactions.* These regulations, embodied in Proposed Rule 13(e)3, have not been enacted. In the proposed rule, the SEC defines a going-private transaction as one which has either a reasonable likelihood or the purpose of producing directly or indirectly the delisting of a class of equity securities from a national securities exchange; the removal of a class of equity securities from any requirement to be registered with, or to report to, the SEC; or causing a class of equity securities that is authorized to be quoted in an interdealer quotation system of a registered national securities association (the NASD) to cease to be so authorized.

---

*Proposed Rule 13(e)3 is contained in Securities Exchange Act Release 14185, dated November 17, 1977.

Chapter 16

Losses and Loss Companies

❦

We lose on every sale,
but make it up on the volume.

QUALITY CONSIDERATIONS
AND TAX-LOSS COMPANIES

CONVENTIONAL WISDOM states that investments should be restricted to going-concern companies with records of continuously profitable operations. This is a valid approach insofar as investments should be restricted to the securities of high-quality issuers. Common sense states, though, that corporations that have been suffering economic (as distinct from purely tax) losses can be attractive asset-conversion acquisitions under the following conditions:

1. The resources employed in this business can be put to another use or somehow otherwise redeployed so that former losses are stemmed.
2. The business lacks overwhelming amounts of indebtedness or other encumbrances. An absence of obligations is a rarity among

loss corporations, because in effect most of them have financed their losses by incurring debt. Exceptions are most often found in former loss companies that are reorganized and recapitalized—especially under Chapters X and XI of the bankruptcy statutes—and in companies whose losses are created by the one- or two-time sale of assets in bulk.

3. A loss corporation may have available to it tax benefits growing out of the former losses. Such benefits can be, *inter alia,* in the form of ordinary loss carry-backs (a cash recovery obtained from the Internal Revenue Service equal to as much as the actual income taxes paid in the current year and the three immediately prior years); and ordinary tax-loss carry-forwards (unused tax credits that remain after the carry-back is utilized and that may be used to offset taxes on profits for a period of five years after the loss was incurred—see Chapter 12). Other tax benefits can take the form of capital-loss carry-backs and carry-forwards to offset capital-gains taxes.

Another area of tax benefits is the creatable ordinary loss and the creatable capital loss. Creatable losses are those that come into being through realized losses by the actual sale or write-down of assets. For example, in 1974 Source Capital was an investment company purchasing private placements, and had a portfolio that its directors claimed had a present market value of around $190 million, compared with an original cost of approximately $250 million. Of the $60 million loss (assuming the directors' valuations were close to correct), only about $15 million was realized losses and $45 million was unrealized losses. Source, therefore, theoretically could have created capital losses almost at will to offset capital gains, through the sale of portions of the securities in its portfolio on which it had realized losses.

A cautionary word about tax losses is in order for outside investors. In purchasing securities of loss corporations, the tax-loss aspect of those corporations is always of insignificant importance compared to the other considerations—the prospect that operating losses will be stemmed, or the presence or absence of encumbrances.

A good example of how effective the purchase of a loss corporation can be is shown in the 1968 purchase by Lady Rose of Masters, Incorporated, which was accomplished by merging Lady Rose into Masters. This was done by issuing new equity to Lady Rose, so that it ended up owning 89 percent of the combined capitalization.

Masters, a small hard-goods discount-store operation, had petitioned for an arrangement under Chapter XI of the bankruptcy statutes in 1963. Operated since then by a committee of creditors who had previously operated leased departments in Masters Stores, the company had been unprofitable from 1963. But because of capital contributions by new investors, massive property sales and an adjustment with general creditors (under which they accepted $.40 on the dollar on an installment basis), by 1968 Masters' total indebtedness, other than rental obligations, was less than $400,000. At the time of the merger with Lady Rose, Masters' stock could have been purchased in the market at $1; most stockholders had options to subscribe to new Masters shares at $1.25 per share. None of these options were exercised.

Lady Rose, which had run soft-goods concessions as a lessee in certain Masters Stores and whose principals, the Biblowitz brothers, were important members of the Masters creditors' committee, had been a well-financed, highly profitable operator of ladies' and children's wear departments for forty years. Although the Lady Rose management had little or no knowledge about hard-goods operations, they believed Masters afforded them a good opportunity on three grounds involving asset-conversion and tax-loss utilization. First, they would be able to expand the profitability of the Lady Rose soft-goods operations in Masters; second, they might be able to attract competent hard-goods management (and also establish some sort of reasonable credit-rating for Masters); and third, they might be able to utilize the $1.6 million of cash to be realized from tax savings out of the $3.2 million unutilized Masters tax-loss carry-forward as a basis for expanding the new company dramatically.

The Biblowitzes were right. The new Masters became highly profitable. By early 1970, the $3.2 million tax loss had been fully utilized. In 1969, there was a public offering of Masters common stock at $16 per share.

It should be noted, however, that if the Biblowitzes had been wrong, their exposure would have been very great. In order to utilize Masters' tax loss, Lady Rose had to merge in a tax-free transaction with Masters: that is, the tax-loss carry-forwards were usable on a company-only basis and not on a consolidated-return basis. Thus, the Biblowitzes put at risk, through merger with a company that had no profits and had been insolvent, a solid business built up over forty years. If Lady Rose had not merged with Masters, it could have insulated itself from all the risks in Masters, especially the financing of future losses in case Masters could not be turned around.

Other examples of where, in recent years, loss corporations have become valuable because assets could be redeployed, because there was a lack of encumbrances and because tax benefits were available, include Chicago Northwest Railway (now Northwest Industries), Minneapolis and St. Louis Railway (now MSL Industries), Studebaker Corporation (now Studebaker-Worthington), Textron, Interstate Stores (now Toys R Us) and Cletrac (whose tax-loss carry-forward was utilized by the company that is now Amerada-Hess). These businesses all became highly profitable for many reasons, a principal one in each case being the ability to use the huge sums of cash that in effect were generated because they didn't have to pay income taxes.

ON ACCOUNTING AND INCOME

For financial-accounting purposes, the utilization of tax benefits does not give rise to ordinary net income, but rather is treated as an extraordinary item. Whether accounted for as ordinary or extraordinary, however, the cash savings from nonpayment of taxes are real for companies. In fact, the cash savings were crucial to the financing of the Masters expansion program after the 1968 merger. Treating tax savings as an extraordinary item focuses on the fact that cash generated from operating earnings as reported are deemed to be a more significant figure by the accounting profession than is cash generated from tax-loss carry-forwards. This view is valid, but it does not detract from the obvious fact that cash generated from the utilization of tax benefits has a value all its own for companies. Masters' post-1968 reinvestment of its cash savings resulted in marked increases in Masters' future earnings; the reinvestment of these cash savings would have so resulted, for accounting reporting purposes, whether it had been labeled as recurring net income from operations or as an extraordinary item.

BE WARY OF ACQUIRING EQUITY SECURITIES OF THE ENCUMBERED FIRM

The principal and very real danger in investing in loss corporations is that financial reverses and/or mismanagement may have created so many encumbrances that there is no practical way to invest safely and profitably in the enterprise.

Realizing current losses on a one-time basis is a recognized method for making future earnings better than they otherwise would be. Many companies that took huge write-downs—largely on injudicious acquisitions and on expansion undertaken during the period of excesses that reached its heyday in 1968—serve as good examples. Taking those huge write-downs came to be known as "big-bath accounting," and those who took big baths include Boise-Cascade, United Brands, DPF, and LTV Corporation.

Are managements to be viewed as operators, investors, or both? Most companies that took big-bath write-downs accounted for them as nonrecurring, extraordinary events. This bothered many who felt that in reporting profits the big baths should be treated as a normal, recurring event. It seems to us, though, that much of security analysis and much of accounting is directed toward appraising businesses and their managements solely as operations. If so, the big baths were indeed nonrecurring. As a matter of fact, a feature that differentiates us from conventional security analysts is that convention seems to emphasize operations at the expense of financial factors, whereas we tend to de-emphasize operating factors, or rather, give financial factors, such as liquidity, greater importance for most companies most of the time.

Insofar as a company and a management are to be appraised as operations and as operators, it is logical to view the big bath as non-recurring. Insofar as a company and a management are to be appraised as investors responsible for obtaining a return from the resources entrusted to them by being operators, by being financiers, by being investors in new productive assets and by being specialists in mergers and acquisitions (that is, by viewing them as asset converters), there is nothing per se nonrecurring about the losses that are suffered. They reflect only one measure of the results of the managements' stewardship.

COMMERCIAL BANKS' PORTFOLIO LOSSES

Commercial banks should be singled out as a special case where the realization of certain types of current losses is likely to result in future earnings increases. The principal earnings assets of banks are investments in loans to customers (mostly short-term loans, but also mortgages and other longer-term instruments) and investments in securities, mostly U.S. Treasury notes and bills as well as municipal obligations that have maturities of five years or less. As loan demand increases and interest rates rise, the market value of commercial banks' securities portfolios goes down. At this time, banks realize losses by selling securities and reinvesting the proceeds in loans that bear higher interest. Thus, commercial banks realize losses on the sale of securities, but because of this, are able to reinvest in loans that in the following period yield increased interest income over what was previously being earned. The tax code encourages commercial banks to take such losses on the sale of securities, and the losses are treated as ordinary, not capital, losses, no matter how long the holding period. Until changed by the Revenue Act of 1969, commercial-bank profits on the sale of securities held more than six months were treated as capital gains, whereas losses on such sales were treated as ordinary losses. Now, both profits and losses are treated as conventional income or expense, taxable or deductible at ordinary rates.

THE "TURNED THE CORNER" THEORY

In the years of the new-issue bull markets, 1962 and 1968, there was a theory that the best small companies to invest in were those that were suffering losses, so that when they "turned the corner" their growth records would look so much the better. Because of the tremendous uncertainties involved with predicting outlooks for small companies with no records of profits, and because new issues are normally not priced on bargain bases relative to corporate reality, we think such an approach will not prove especially profitable for most outside investors. Such securities virtually never qualify as attractive as a result of any judgments made using the financial-integrity approach.

Chapter 17

A Short Primer on Asset-Conversion Investing: Prearbitrage and Postarbitrage

One good deal may be worth twenty years
of brilliant operations.

IF A DEAL MAKER were to think about theories of efficient markets, he would conclude that if there were efficient markets at all, there would be two efficient markets—one measuring the prices at which outsiders trade common stocks in the open market, and the other reflecting the value of businesses. Prices, or values, in one market usually would be unrelated to prices, or values, in the other. Put simply, the deal maker would conclude that prices paid for common stocks for investment purposes are different from prices paid for control of businesses. Frequently, the value of control of businesses would be below the market price of common stocks. In that instance, the activist would seek to sell common stock owned personally, and/or have the controlled company issue new common stock. New common stock would be issuable through the sale to the public, for cash, of new issues, or through issuing new securities in merger and acquisition transactions. These types of activities are described in Appendixes I and II, on Schaefer Corporation and Leasco Data

Processing. This was what most of the new-issue boom of the late 1960's was all about.

On the other hand, insiders frequently will conclude that the market prices of common stocks are materially below the values of the businesses these common stocks represent. In that event, insiders or companies themselves seek to acquire common stocks at prices that represent some differential between the values being ascribed to noncontrol shares in the stock market and the value of the enterprises.

These two disparate markets exist for the same commodity—common stocks. That valuations ordinarily should be different between these two markets seems obvious. After all, when valuing whole businesses the standards of analysis and the decision considerations tend to be different than when trying to predict open-market stock prices. Business buyers frequently use as an essential part of judging attractiveness the same four elements we described in Chapter 2 on the financial-integrity approach—strong financial position, reasonably honest people running the company, availability of reasonable amounts of information and a discount price relative to estimates of net asset value. In contrast, the conventional fundamentalist or stock trader usually emphasizes the near-term outlook, which in turn involves judgments about technical positions and earnings per share as well as price–earnings ratios, which are heavily influenced by the particular company's industry identification.

The market for companies and control of them appears to be, on its own terms, a highly active one, especially during periods when (a) funds are available for borrowing and/or (b) asset-conversion-conscious insiders control companies whose common stocks are selling at high-enough prices so that something is to be gained by issuing those shares in merger and acquisition activities. If a broker or finder believes he has a "do-able" deal in terms of control, he has no trouble finding potential buyers to look at the company he proposes to offer.

Thus, there is a long-term arbitrage that takes place because of the disparities between market prices and control values. But this arbitrage is far from a perfect one, in part because people in control

of companies whose stock market prices are depressed are sometimes not asset-conversion-conscious or in any event do not want to
take advantage of the low stock market prices by having the company
acquire publicly held shares, having the insiders acquire the shares or
having a third party acquire shares by direct purchase, merger or
acquisition. For example, at the time of this writing, Baker Fentress,
a registered closed-end investment trust, is selling at around 44; its
unencumbered asset value, easily measurable, is not less than $63
per share; and even after allowing for capital-gains taxes and liquidation expenses, minimum net asset value would be well in excess of
$50 per share. As a matter of fact, because certain controlled affili-
ates appear to have values substantially in excess of the market prices
used to determine Baker Fentress' net asset value, it is a fair guess
that a realistic liquidating value for the Baker Fentress common
stock should approach $80 per share.

Through stock ownership, the Baker Fentress management and
control group appear, at least to the outsider, to be firmly in control,
and there seems to be little to indicate that there is any significant
interest of management in taking those corporate actions that would
result in the market price of the Baker Fentress stock rising so that it
more nearly approaches Baker Fentress' value as determined under a
financial-integrity approach.

Baker Fentress appears to be an attractive investment using our
approach, because the stockholder benefits from having competent
investment management working to enhance, for the benefit of the
stockholder, a good-grade, unencumbered asset value that the stockholder acquired at a substantial discount from a reasonable measure
of net asset value. Yet, it is easy to understand why the Baker Fentress common stock may lack appeal for the activist and the aggressive outsider. Baker Fentress does not appear to be a do-able deal.
There is little, if any, evidence that any asset-conversion activities
will occur for the benefit of Baker Fentress security holders.

Many outsiders emphasizing the financial-integrity approach
ought to be able to achieve more than satisfactory long-term investment results, even if they do not consider the prospects for asset
conversion part of their investment approach. These results seem

attainable by acquiring Baker Fentress common stock and similar equity securities. Equity investments in sound businesses bought at what are perceived to be low prices based on long-term business standards of valuation can bring the investor not only comfort but above-average returns. Comfort is created because (a) the investor is in a conservative position and (b), by definition, the businesses in which he is investing have been run conservatively. Above-average return over the long term ought to be achievable, too, because if the purchase price for stock is low relative to the value of the net assets being acquired, prospects ought to be reasonably good for appreciation. After all, if on this basis, a company earns an average return on the value of assets employed in a business, investors whose stock purchase prices represent a substantial discount from that asset value will enjoy above-average returns, based on that investor's cost for his stock.

However, such an approach is unsatisfactory for activists and more aggressive outsiders. They need do-able deals in which the probabilities are that asset-conversion events will take place (so that someone will pay them substantial premiums above market for their stockholdings), or in which net assets in a business will be employed more aggressively in the future than in the past, either by the present control group or a new group.

Trying to spot do-able deals before they are announced is something we describe as prearbitrage activities, although we have heard others use the phrase "pre-deal investing." After deals are rumored or announced, market activity tends to be dominated by professional arbitragers, a small coterie of Wall Street people who, as a group, are extremely competent, well-financed traders, who enjoy low transaction costs and who also tend to be astute in judging when and how do-able deals that have been announced will be consummated. During periods when professional arbitrage activities are under way, it frequently is difficult for nonprofessional arbitragers to compete. The Wall Street firms best known as professional arbitrageurs include Goldman Sachs and Company, Salomon Brothers, Bear Stearns and Company, First Manhattan Company, L. F. Rothschild Unterberg Towbin, Ivan F. Boesky and Company, and Sheriff Securities Corporation, all of whom are member firms of the New York Stock Exchange.

In contrast, we believe there often are important, relatively non-competitive opportunities for outside investors in prearbitrage activities and in postarbitrage periods.

Uncovering prearbitrage do-able deals, insofar as those deals involve mergers and acquisitions or tender offers, not only creates investment opportunities, but also creates finders' and brokers' fee opportunities. As is detailed later in Appendix II on Leasco, in the vast majority of instances the ability to spot do-able deals entails using a combination of the financial-integrity approach and personal relationships, or know-who. It seems to us that very few deals are even contemplated that are not going to be negotiated transactions. And negotiations, by definition, always involve know-who.

However, even without any know-who, investors using financial-integrity standards may have opportunities for uncovering do-able deals merely by the study of publicly available documents describing situations in companies whose securities appear attractive, even though it has been our experience that without know-who, predicting just what situations will prove to be do-able entails as much luck as skill.

Do-able asset-conversion activities that might be spotted are of four types:

1. More aggressive employment of existing assets
2. Merger and acquisition activities
3. Corporate contests for control
4. Going private

Brief examples of situations where do-able deals could have been spotted on a prearbitrage basis are as follows:

More Aggressive Employment of Existing Assets

In 1974 and 1975, a group headed by Frederick Klingenstein of Wertheim and Company acquired control of Barber Oil Company, listed on the New York Stock Exchange. The Klingenstein group paid an average price of about $25 for their position in Barber Oil, an investment company registered under the Investment Company Act of 1940, whose net asset value was stated to be approximately $40 per share. As a business, Barber Oil was unencumbered, and it consisted essentially of a pool of capital amounting to approximately $100 million, part of which was invested in marketable securities of major oil and gas companies, part of which was in interests in oil and gas properties, and part of which was in oil tankers. After the Klingensteins acquired control, the price of Barber Oil declined for a protracted period. The shares were available at prices ranging from approximately 17 to 21. In 1976, Barber Oil announced that it would seek to be deregistered as an investment company and that henceforth it would employ its resources to aggressively expand in the energy business, using its unencumbered equity base of $100 million as the foundation for an acquisition program that would be financed by incurring debt. In short order, additional oil properties were acquired as well as a large coal company, Paramount Coal. At this writing, in early 1978, Barber Oil is trading around 27.

Merger and Acquisition Activity

Since its founding in the early 1920's, Amerada Petroleum, a debt-free company, had built up one of the largest reserves of oil and gas in the United States, and by 1968 Amerada also had important interests in Libya. The company engaged only in oil and gas exploration and production having no downstream capabilities (that is, it did not transport, refine or market petroleum products). Amerada also had a substantial cash surplus. In 1968, the Hess Oil and Chemical Company purchased from The Bank of England a 9 percent interest in Amerada at a price of 80. Up until that time, the Amerada stock had never sold as high as 80. Within a year of the Hess Oil and Chemical purchase of Amerada, the chairman of the board of Amerada, Mr. Jacobsen, died. Leon Hess, the head of Hess Oil and Chemical, obtained a seat on the Amerada board. Shortly thereafter a merger was proposed under which the Amerada stock worked out at a market value of not less than $125. After Hess had acquired its 9 percent interest and before Mr. Hess obtained board representation, the Amerada shares still could have been acquired for less than 80.

Corporate Contests for Control

In recent years, contests for control usually have taken the form of cash tender offers, a far less cumbersome takeover mechanism than engaging in proxy contests or offering to acquire target companies' common stocks in exchange for the acquiring companies' securities. Corporations that are candidates for contested takeovers are those with the following conditions: the companies are incorporated and domiciled in states where there are no strong anti-takeover statutes;* share ownership is widespread or there are blocks that may be tied up via private transactions;† there is a possible low will of the management to resist a takeover attempt; there is a general absence of impediments to the takeover, such as a company's being in a regulated industry (say, insurance, commercial banking, or aviation); there do not appear to be antitrust problems; and there do not appear to be important people or institutions, such as customers, employees or suppliers, who could harm the takeover target by terminating relationships with the company. One example of a contested tender offer is the November 1975 cash tender by Babcock International, a subsidiary of Babcock and Wilcox, for all the shares of the American Chain and Cable Company at 27 net per share, in cash. Prior to the tender offer, the shares had traded in 1975 in a range between 14 and 20. American Chain was a New York corporation, its management held little stock and it was not in a regulated industry. Initially,

---

*At this writing, thirty-two states, including such important corporate states as Delaware, New York and Ohio, have anti-takeover statutes. State anti-takeover statutes, however, have become a considerably less important deterrent to raiders because of recent court decisions holding that takeover regulations are essentially a federal concern and that state laws are preempted by federal laws, particularly the Williams Act, enacted in 1968 to regulate cash tender offers. (*Great Western United Corporation* v. *Kidwell,* 577 F 2d 1256, 1281–87 [5th Cir 1978].)

†See Appendix II.

American Chain and Cable resisted the offer, but when Babcock raised the price to 32 in December, the new offer was approved by the American Chain and Cable management, several members of which obtained employment contracts. There have been scores of contested cash takeovers in the period 1975–78, including those for the common stocks of Allied Thermal, Husky Oil, Apco, Otis Elevator, ESB, Aztec Oil and Gas, Sea World, Babcock and Wilcox, Marcor, Royal Industries and Carrier Corporation.

Going Private

Many companies that are attractive under the financial-integrity approach and that are nonregulated are also candidates for going private, as was Barbara Lynn Stores. In mid-1974, its stock was trading at 2 to 2½, although the company had a highly liquid book value of 8. The insiders proposed a merger at 4, which was voted on favorably. There was a stockholder suit opposing the merger, but the suit was settled when it was agreed that the cash merger price would be increased. In early 1975, all public shareholders received $4.40 per share, or virtually double the market value before the going-private transaction.

POSTARBITRAGE

Postarbitrage situations are created after an asset-conversion event has taken place and securities owned by public shareholders remain outstanding. Usually these holdings are minority interests in companies. Postarbitrage investment opportunities seem to be present on a reasonably regular basis for outside investors in postarbitrage periods. In order to understand why, it may be profitable to simulate the thinking processes of professional arbitrageurs, who are acutely conscious of the time value of money and who are inclined to acquire securities in concert for the same reason. Thus, when offers to acquire securities occur and less than all the shares tendered are accepted (a so-called partial offer, or partial), arbitragers tend to dispose of the masses of stock they have accumulated shortly after the conclusion of an offer. This, of course, depresses market prices.

In addition, conventional stockholders are frequently reluctant to hold the shares of common stocks in postarbitrage situations, because the shares at that point may not be marketable, are delisted and, occasionally, if there are less than three hundred shareholders of record for an over-the-counter issue, are even deregistered with the Securities and Exchange Commission. Thus, in post-arbitrage markets equity securities may sell at ultradepressed prices. As a group, these securities then become highly attractive holdings. For example, in November 1974 Loew's acquired control of CNA Financial Corporation by a partial tender offer for CNA common stock at 5. Immediately after the conclusion of the tender offer, in December 1974 and January 1975 CNA common traded in volume on the New York Stock Exchange between 2½ and 3. At this writing in early 1978, CNA common is selling around 11.

In August 1974, Mobil Oil sought through a cash tender offer at a price of 35 a majority of the outstanding common stock of Marcor Corporation. The cash tender was oversubscribed, with Mobil receiving far more stock than it had sought. Purchases were made on a pro-rata basis, and unpurchased shares were returned to share owners. Subsequent to the tender, the shares were available for a protracted period at prices ranging between 15 and 17 per share. Within a year after the tender offer expired, however, Mobil proposed a cash merger at a price of 35. Eventually all shareholders received 35. Similar profit opportunities for outsiders after control was acquired through partials occurred in, among others, the common stocks of American Medicorp, Signal Company, and Veeder Industries.

Another postarbitrage opportunity existed for Indian Head debentures. There had been a cash tender in 1974, which would have resulted in a value for the debentures of $70.12. After the tender offer, the debentures sold at prices well below 70.12—as low as 48. Eventually, there was a cash merger in 1976 at a price that resulted in debenture holders having the right to receive $84.14 in cash.

Postarbitrage positions do not, of course, always work out. An example of an unprofitable postarbitrage investment for outsiders is provided by Schenley Industries common stock. Control of Schenley was obtained in 1968, when there were both private purchases and an exchange offer that had a market value of around 54. After control had been obtained, the Schenley business prospered. Nonetheless, in 1971 a merger force-out at a price of about 29 occurred—in perspective, a very modest price, even though it represented the highest price at which Schenley common stock sold in the two years before the February 1971 vote on the merger.

In postarbitrage investing, it is very important to avoid managements that seem to have predatory predilections. Again, the public record, through proxy statements or Part II of the 10-K, gives indications of which managements might be predatory. Postarbitrage activities have significant disadvantages, especially where there is no know-who. It is usually impossible to determine when a so-called mop-up merger might occur; indeed, a mop-up merger might never happen (though it is our experience that the vast majority of controlling shareholders prefer 100 percent ownership rather than less). Finally, postarbitrage securities tend to be relatively unmarketable, and are sometimes not marketable at all.

One important rule of thumb we tend to follow in postarbitrage investing is to acquire positions in securities at prices two thirds or less than control shareholders paid in the recent past to obtain control. The postarbitrage world is such that equity securities often sell for 50 percent or less of the price paid for control.

In general, purchases based on this approach have worked out well in recent years, as witnessed by profits that were realizable, *inter alia,* on postarbitrage investments in CNA Financial, Marcor, Transocean Oil, Indian Head, American Medicorp, and Veeder Industries. However, this rule of thumb is far from a panacea and an investment technique that will always prove successful. In some instances, control buyers will be able to mop up public stock at prices well below those paid for control, even though the controlled business prospers in the interim between the acquisition of control and the buy-out of the public. For one thing, controlling stockholders may succeed in forcing out public stockholders at prices well below control prices (as per the Schenley situation discussed previously). After all, the timing and conditions for proposing a force-out merger are within the control of insiders. However, closing the transaction is not something wholly within the insiders' province, because of the probability of stockholder suits to improve prices paid in force-out mergers. Second, there are times when acquirers overpay to obtain control of basically sick businesses; in those instances, the minority stockholder is unlikely to fare well. One example is Commonwealth Refining, in which Tesoro Petroleum acquired a controlling interest in 1976 by paying $13.50 per share. In 1978, Commonwealth sought protection of the bankruptcy courts by filing a petition for an arrangement under Chapter XI of the bankruptcy statutes. At this writing, Commonwealth common stock is quoted at around $.50 bid.

In sum, though, we think an investment program based on acquiring issues in postarbitrage markets at prices well below those paid by controlling shareholders for the same security should work out well. Where this approach is further limited by applying financial-integrity standards, we think prospects are that such investments ought to work out exceptionally well.

SECTION SIX

APPENDIXES—
CASE STUDIES

Introduction
to Appendixes I and II

❦

The "strong-form theory" of the efficient market
"holds that present market prices reflect all information that
is knowable *about a company, including all relevant information that*
might be developed by exhaustive study, including interviews
with corporate managements, by numerous fully
competent institutional security analysts."

CHARLES D. KUEHNER,
"Efficient Markets and Random Walk,"
Financial Analysts Handbook

A PURPOSE OF THIS BOOK has been to recommend investment programs and techniques for unaffiliated stockholders in an environment where Mr. Kuehner's description of the strong-form theory of the efficient market becomes irrelevant. We approach the analysis of securities in the same manner that most control buyers approach the acquisition of corporations. There are, admittedly, marked differences between passive investors on the one hand and insiders and promoters on the other. For one thing, we recommend throughout the book that outsiders adopt a more conservative posture than insiders, partly because outsiders may lack knowledge, but more importantly because outsiders lack control.

In presenting our positions, considerable space is devoted to describing the real world faced by both outsiders and insiders. Appendixes I and II are case studies, showing how insiders, promoters and private-placement investors actually used the real-world environment we have described previously in this book to achieve—mostly profitably—certain asset-conversion goals. Appendix I, "The Use of Creative Finance to Benefit Controlling Stockholders," describes how F. & M. Schaefer Corporation, whose subsidiary brews Schaefer beer, went public. Appendix II, "Creative Finance Applied to a Corporate Takeover," describes how Leasco Data Processing Company was able to gain control of Reliance Insurance Company by obtaining the right to acquire key blocks of Reliance equity securities without committing any funds to the purchase of that stock unless Leasco in fact obtained control of Reliance.

The descriptions in Appendixes I and II essentially focus on the viewpoints of activists and insiders. Although this emphasis may seem misplaced in a book directed largely toward unaffiliated stockholders, we think the appendixes are quite appropriate, even for those readers who have no interest in ever investing on any other basis than as an intelligent outsider holding only readily marketable securities. The more passivists understand about the real world of finance, the more success they are likely to achieve, regardless of the investment approach followed.

Interestingly enough, the actual events described in Appendixes I and II occurred about ten years ago. Yet, Schaefer and Leasco seem more appropriate case studies than other more recent materials. The reason for this, pure and simple, is that the essential element in both cases was the market bailout—something relatively easy for promoters and insiders conscious of asset conversion to achieve in 1968, and something much harder to accomplish in the less buoyant stock market atmosphere of the 1970's.

How is "market bailout" defined? A market bailout occurs when insiders using sound, conservative approaches to valuation are able to take advantage of the prices at which common stocks sell in public stock markets when those prices are far in excess of what the equity of the corporation is worth.

Market bailouts for asset-conversion-conscious insiders can take several forms: the sale of new issues for cash; mergers and similar transactions that are paid for by the issuance of equity securities that are salable (or can be used as collateral for borrowings) at prices related to high stock market prices; mergers and similar transactions under which stockholders, in effect, swap publicly traded equity securities that are overpriced by corporate standards for securities, whether debt or equity, that are reasonably valued from a corporate point of view; and transactions in which a relatively overpriced common stock is used as a basic element for obtaining attractive senior financing.

Schaefer and Leasco are complex market bailout transactions. We choose them as case studies because they give more insight into techniques used and problems faced by promoters and insiders than any other transactions of which we are aware. Indeed, except for tax-loss considerations, the Schaefer transaction is so complex that it touches on most of the considerations that tend to arise in structuring market bailouts.

Schaefer and Leasco turned out to be complicated because the deals were structured to achieve complicated objectives. In the case of Schaefer, the goal seemed to be for the Schaefer family to extract as much cash as they could from the business and still remain in control of it. In the Leasco case, the objective was to tie up large blocks of shares of Reliance Insurance Company to enable Leasco to obtain control of Reliance without actually having to buy those blocks unless Leasco did in fact gain control. Also, Leasco used creative finance to enable it to account for its acquisition of Reliance on a pooling-of-interests basis.

To repeat, the key element in both Schaefer and Leasco that made the transactions feasible was that outside investors interested in market reality were willing to pay much higher prices for Schaefer and Leasco common stock than would be justified by corporate reality. Thus, in a very real sense the Schaefer and Leasco transactions resulted from the arbitrage mentioned before—insiders taking advantage of the gap between the high stock market valuation of the two businesses and their more theoretical corporate values. The arbitrage became meaningful insofar as there could be actual realizations—that is, insofar as common stock could actually be issued or sold at prices based on the value attributed to the companies in the stock market.

Appendixes I and II demonstrate that value is not a monolithic concept. Rather, whether something is attractive or not at a given price depends in part on the position of the people or entities involved and what they want out of a "deal." Efficient market theories (such as that postulated in the epigraph to this introduction), which state that stock market prices are the best evidence of (a unitary) value, do not appear to be particularly relevant to an understanding of the real-world materials discussed in Appendixes I and II.

The important lessons of Appendixes I and II may be that financial success is not easy to achieve and that even the most brilliant insiders come a cropper some of the time. Leasco's management was outstanding for 1968 conditions, but that did not seem to be true for 1969. The Schaefer transactions were magnificently constructed insofar as the Schaefer family objectives were concerned. Yet, given moderately different objectives, there might have been even more to gain by following other courses of action.

A second lesson illustrates the importance of know-who and know-how in the financial community. Know-who was important for all sorts of people, including the members of the public fortunate enough to know somebody who could obtain for them Schaefer stock at the initial offering when the company went public with a "hot issue." And of course, nothing could have been accomplished in either Schaefer or Leasco if a lot of very smart, very hard-working people had not brought a plethora of know-how to these complex transactions. The doers had to use flexibility and imagination, the limits of which were governed by the disciplines with which they were involved. These disciplines included knowledge of securities markets, knowledge of who buys what securities for what purposes, securities law, securities industry self-regulation, income taxation, accounting and the foibles of fellow human beings.

The Use of Creative Finance to Benefit Controlling Stockholders— Schaefer Corporation

What looks like a stone wall to a layman is frequently a triumphal arch to a lawyer.

MR. DOOLEY

I T IS LIKELY that more fortunes within the financial community are obtained through the discount purchase of securities in negotiated transactions than through brilliant analysis resulting in the purchase at market prices of securities that will appreciate dramatically. A discount purchase is one in which a stockholder obtains securities at a price below that which prevails or is to be created in a public market.

Only a small minority of the Wall Street success stories come out of an outside investor's acting on a feeling about the growth of a particular industry, such as feeling in 1955 that "copying is going to be a great business; ergo, I shall buy and hold Xerox." Rather, the more common method of amassing wealth in the financial community is to be involved in a deal that enables you to buy common stock at, say, $.42 or $1 per share, for which the public has paid or will pay, say, $26 per share. A large number of deals resulting in such discount purchases have been put together, including, to name a few, Eastman

Dillon promoting Westcoast Transmission, American Securities promoting Western Union International, Ladenburg Thalmann promoting Guerdon Industries, and Lehman Brothers promoting Monterrey Oil. Discount purchases are not confined to investment bankers and brokers; other deals have included Albermarle Paper purchasing Ethyl Corporation, Malcolm McLean acquiring certain shipping interests, and Northwest Industries acquiring Velsicol Chemical.

In this appendix, we describe one set of discount-purchase transactions in detail; these culminated in the November 1968 public offering of the F. & M. Schaefer Corporation, parent company of the producer and marketer of Schaefer beer.

The reason for picking Schaefer as a case study is that it is one of the more complex transactions, so that many of the key elements that go into a discount-purchase transaction are covered. It should be noted, however, that an important element not covered in the Schaefer transaction is the use of tax-loss carry-backs and tax-loss carry-forwards.

There are a number of valuable lessons to learn from the Schaefer case study. The first concerns the mechanics of such transactions. It is also important to have some appreciation of what goes into Schaefer-type transactions in order to understand Wall Street. Another equally important lesson has to do with understanding the problems and goals of the various parties to the transactions.

The transactions are examined from eight points of view: (1) the selling stockholders; (2) the company's operating executives; (3) the promoters of the transactions; (4) the commercial banks that provided short-term financing; (5) the institutional lenders (basically life insurance companies) that provided the bulk of the long-term financing; (6) the underwriters who marketed the initial issue to the public; (7) the public itself; and finally (8) the new business that emerged as a publicly owned, rather than a closely held, enterprise.

Like all things on Wall Street, everything in this transaction, including discount purchasing, had its problems, as this appendix shows. In some contexts, the public shareholder who was able to obtain stock at $26 in the initial offering had fewer problems and a more attractive holding than some of the other parties who purchased stock at $1 per share two months earlier.

THE PROBLEMS COVERED
IN THIS APPENDIX

The mechanical problems faced in this complex deal included the following:

1. Tax problems, especially for the sellers and the purchasers of discount securities
2. Accounting problems for the public company
3. Commercial-bank borrowings
4. Private-placement borrowings from institutional lenders, such as life insurance companies
5. Warrants
6. Convertible securities
7. Senior loans versus subordinated loans
8. Corporate tax shelter
9. Public underwriting
10. Rights of registration
11. Rule 144
12. Cash returns versus no cash returns
13. Qualified stock options
14. Significance of financial positions in deal making
15. Significance of reported earnings for a public company
16. NASD Rules of Fair Practice

All the information used here was obtained from publicly available documents, mostly from SEC files. There were no interviews or conversations with anyone associated with the transactions. There is no question that if "field work" had been done, the appendix would be more complete. It is also possible that with the personal explanation of those involved in the transactions, certain of our concepts would be changed. This goes with our thesis that in security analysis, studying documents is no substitute for field work and vice versa. However, the point of forgoing field work is to demonstrate that vast amounts of information frequently are available, so that quite meaningful results often can be obtained by trained analysts relying solely on publicly available documents.

THE BACKGROUND OF THE DEAL

On June 10, 1968, the F. & M. Schaefer Corporation (hereafter called Corporation) was incorporated in New York State. Corporation's purpose was twofold: to acquire all the capital stock of the F. & M. Schaefer Brewing Company (hereafter called Brewing), also a New York corporation; and to go public via an underwritten public offering. Both of these events did in fact occur less than six months after incorporation.

The market for new underwritings was favorable in June 1968. Market players were seeking a reprise of the 1961–1962 new-issue spree, in which they had bought issues at the initial offering price and realized a profit when the shares sold at immediate premiums. They were looking for securities of companies in growth industries, especially those that were outperforming their own industries in terms of steadily increasing sales, market penetration and profits. The brewing industry was viewed by many as poised for relatively rapid growth, because the progeny of the post–World War II "baby boom" were reaching beer-drinking age and because higher profit package sales, especially cans, were taking over from draft beer, which was generally a brewer's lowest-profit-margin product.

Brewing, which had been in the beer business since 1842, was a strong, prosperous, family-owned business in mid to late 1968. It had Schaefer beer plants in Albany, Brooklyn and Baltimore. Sales of Schaefer beer, marketed in the northeastern United States, had increased steadily from 2.8 million barrels in 1958 to 4.7 million barrels in 1967, and in 1968 barrel sales were running some 7 percent ahead of 1967. Market penetration, too, had been on the rise. Beer sales in barrels increased from an estimated 3.3 percent of the industry total in 1958 to about 4.4 percent in 1967. Brewing seemed bound to at least hold its market share in 1968, based on results for the first nine months of that year.

Brewing had been quite profitable and was growing rapidly. Net sales had increased steadily from $151 million in calendar 1963 to $181 million in 1967. Income before extraordinary credits was $2,546,000 in 1963 and had increased year by year to $5,127,000 in 1967, although operating profits had dipped modestly in 1964 because of a $1,349,000 pretax expense incurred in connection with promotions by the company at the New York World's Fair. As is true of many private companies, Brewing's profit figures seem to have been conservatively stated,* and were reported, after tax accruals, at the approximate maximum income-tax rates.

Moreover, the company was well financed. The Brewing balance sheet that would have been available before June 10, 1968, is not public information, but the July 31, 1968, audit statement shows that the company was quite comfortable. Cash and equivalent was $10,405,000, and current assets aggregated $40,468,000. Current liabilities were $19,970,000, leaving working capital of $20,498,000. The only other liabilities were $3,029,000 of employee benefits and $15,210,000 of long-term debt, $15 million of which was in the form of 5.17 percent notes held by the Prudential Insurance Company of America. These notes matured serially to 1983, but annual amortization during the next six years would be only a modest $500,000 for 1968 and 1969, and $825,000 for 1970, 1971, 1972 and 1973.

Tangible asset value was stated at $53,149,000, probably a conservative figure. Property, plant and equipment—which included a malting plant in Buffalo, New York, and six distributing centers, as well as the three breweries—was carried at a net value of $44,877,000, after deducting accumulated depreciation of $38,841,000. This $44,877,000 amounted to only $8.56 per barrel of capacity, based on Brewing's 1967 capacity of 5,240,000 barrels. In light of the fact that replacement costs were running about three times this per barrel of capacity,† Brewing's property, plant and equipment seem to have

---

*One indication that Brewing's accounting practices were conservative was that Brewing, which was charging over $4 million per year against the income accounts for depreciation, used the same depreciation methods (the 200 percent, double-declining-balance method) for book purposes as it did for tax purposes. Nor does the fact that Brewing "flowed through" investment credits, which amounted to $275,000 in 1967, indicate otherwise; the amount involved was small, particularly compared with depreciation charges. The company's five-year statements had been audited by Price Waterhouse and Company, and certified "clean."

†Brewing had plans to construct a new 1.7-million-barrel facility in eastern Pennsylvania. The initial phase of the Pennsylvania construction was to provide an

been worth at least the amounts for which they were carried on the books.

DISCOUNT PURCHASES OF RESTRICTED CORPORATE STOCK

A week after Corporation was organized, R. W. Pressprich and Company purchased 160,000 newly issued shares of Corporation common for $66,667, or $.42 per share. This was the first discount purchase.

Pressprich, located at 80 Pine Street in New York City, was a medium-sized New York Stock Exchange member firm, which for many years has been highly regarded in the financial community. Pressprich was a principal, if not the principal, architect of the Corporation-Brewing transaction and subsequent public offering, and also arranged the financing that gave Corporation the wherewithal to effect the purchase.

Pressprich agreed not to resell these 160,000 shares before March 15, 1971, without first offering them to Corporation at $.42 per share.

On September 20, 1968, the day Corporation signed a purchase agreement for the acquisition of all of Brewing's capital stock, an additional 170,000 shares of newly issued Corporation common stock were sold at $1 per share. The purchasers of these shares included members of the Schaefer family, members of the Brewing executive management committee, and a group of institutional

---

850,000-barrel annual capacity at an estimated cost of approximately $38 million, or $44.71 per barrel, some five times as much as the net book value of existing plant. Even assuming that the remainder of the proposed Pennsylvania plant could be built for a relatively small sum, the total cost was unlikely to be less than $25 per barrel, or some three times the net book carrying value of the existing plant. Notwithstanding any other factors, such as labor-saving innovations and other efficiencies in new plants, Brewing's property, plant and equipment do not seem to have been overvalued on the books.

investors who were to lend Corporation funds for the acquisition of Brewing. Thus, all of them were providing other benefits for Corporation, either at present or prospectively. The purchasers, their relationship to Corporation and the special terms of their purchases are shown in the table on the next page.

As noted, all of the shares issued in these two discount-purchase transactions, except the 150,000 purchased by the institutional investors, were sold subject to contractual restrictions on public resale. The shares could be sold privately to another sophisticated holder who would agree to be bound by the restrictions on resale agreed to by the discount purchasers. Such a resale would be unlikely, however, and even if accomplished, the price realized would be a substantial discount (probably 25 percent to 60 percent) from the current market price.

Apart from these contractual restrictions on resale, the 330,000 shares involved were restricted for Securities and Exchange Commission purposes. Accordingly, public resale was limited by law. Under the rules and regulations in effect in 1968, these shares could have been sold publicly only through a registered offering via a registration statement filed with the Securities and Exchange Commission, unless the Commission was to issue a "no action" letter or a holder was able to obtain a legal opinion that there had been a "change of circumstances." As a practical matter, the chances of any of these purchasers' getting a "no action" letter or change of circumstances opinion were slim at best.

Thus, at the time of the discount purchases, the only way for the purchasers to sell their Corporation equity securities publicly was by registration with the SEC for a new public offering in which their shares would be sold. As a result, registration rights—an agreement by Corporation to register with the SEC for the distribution of restricted shares—were crucial, at least to those discount purchasers who were not in a position of control in Corporation. Both the institutional investors and Pressprich negotiated fairly strong registration rights, which are discussed at some length later in this appendix.

PURCHASERS OF 170,000 CORPORATION COMMON
@ $1 PER SHARE

Purchaser	No. Shares Purchased	Relationship with Corporation	Contractual Non-SEC Restrictions on Resale
Five members of the Schaefer family	15,000	All were beneficial owners of Brewing's capital stock; two were officers and directors of Corporation; three were officers and directors of Brewing (including the two who were officers and directors of Corporation)	Two of five agree not to sell shares, except upon death and disability, until January 1, 1974, and then only 20% per year
Five members of the Brewing executive management committee	5,000	Three of five were also on the board of Corporation	For practical purposes, same restrictions as for the two Schaefer family members above
Seven institutional investors: Equitable Life New York Life John Hancock Mutual Life New England Mutual Life Investors Syndicate of America Investors Syndicate Life Insurance & Annuity Co.	150,000	Lend Corporation $65,000,000: $37,143,000 in 7¾% senior notes, due 1989; $27,857,000 in 5¾% subordinated notes with equity privileges De facto purchase of stock is conditioned on lending $65,000,000	No contractual restrictions on resale

Since April 1972, Rule 144 has provided holders of restricted stock purchased previously another mechanism for reselling their shares. Basically, under this rule such a holder who has held shares outright for two years may sell them in regular market transactions on the New York Stock Exchange. The sales can occur only once every three months, however, and the number of shares that may be sold is limited to the greater of 1 percent of the outstanding stock of the company, or the weekly average traded for the four weeks preceding the filing of a Form 144 with the SEC. In this case, 1 percent of Corporation's common stock at the time it went public would have been 18,000 shares.*

CORPORATION'S ACQUISITION OF BREWING

The Purchase Agreement

On September 20, 1968, Corporation signed an agreement under which it was to acquire all of Brewing's outstanding capital stock for $106 million in cash and notes. This stock consisted of two issues. The Class A participating second preferred stock was owned by Arjayess, a corporation wholly owned by Rudolph J. Schaefer. The Class B stock was held by four trusts set up in 1944 for the benefit of various members of the Schaefer family.

Under the terms of the purchase agreement, Corporation was to acquire the Class A stock for a cash payment of $6 million. The remaining $100 million of the purchase price, paid to the holders of the Class B stock, was in the form of a cash payment of $10 million and various notes, detailed on the next page.

The purchase was contingent upon Corporation's receiving net

---

*Parenthetically, restricted shares issued after the passage of Rule 144 in April 1972 can only be sold publicly pursuant to that rule or via registration. "No action" letters and "change of circumstances" opinions no longer exist in such cases. From 1972 until late 1978, when resale restrictions were liberalized, sales under Rule 144 could occur only once every six months, and the number of shares that could be sold was limited to the lesser of 1 percent of the outstanding stock of the company, or the weekly average traded for the four weeks preceding the filing of a Form 144.

proceeds of at least $35 million from a public offering of its common stock. The actual purchase was to take place simultaneously with Corporation's receipt of these proceeds, but not later than December 31, 1968. In fact, the closing took place during the first week of December.

Brewing's officers and employees were to remain in their positions after the acquisition, at the same or improved rates of compensation.

Financing the Acquisition

Corporation needed about $121.8 million to accomplish this acquisition; $106 million of this, of course, was the purchase price to be paid to Brewing's selling stockholders. In addition, Corporation needed $15 million to prepay the 5.17 percent Brewing notes that were held by Prudential Insurance, and $800,000 to pay expenses incurred in connection with arranging this deal.

Seller	Security Sold	Amount and Type of Payment
Arjayess	Class A participating second preferred	$6,000,000 cash
Four trusts	Class B stock minimum of minimum of	$10,000,000 cash $30,000,000 4% note, due 1/15/69[A] $40,000,000 4% note, due 7/15/69[A] $20,000,000 4% junior subordinated convertible notes, due 1/15/98[A]
		$106,000,000

[A]This 4 percent interest figure probably reflects the minimum interest that could be paid without the Internal Revenue Service assigning "imputed interest" to the indebtedness. This is a crucial consideration, since the consequence of such imputation is to tax the holder of the indebtedness as if he had received interest payments at the imputed rate. Thus, for example, if the IRS chose to impute an 8 percent interest rate to the $20 million junior subordinated notes, the trusts would be deemed to have received income for tax purposes of $1.6 million per year. This is precisely the kind of situation that Chapter 9 warns against, since the transaction that generates the taxable event does not generate the funds with which to pay the taxes thereby owing.

Two parties shared the bulk of the $800,000 expense item. The first was the eminent New York City law firm of White and Case, whose legal fees were around $350,000. White and Case had represented the Schaefers and Brewing for a long time. One partner, Glover Johnson, had been a consultant to Brewing, on a retainer, since 1955 and was a director of that company. He was also a successor trustee of the four Schaefer trusts, for which he was to receive an annual fee of 2 percent of trust income after 1968. The firm became counsel for Corporation, and Mr. Johnson and his partner, John C. Reed, became directors of Corporation.*

In addition to White and Case's legal fees, Pressprich received a fee of $425,000, primarily for its work in connection with the placement of Corporation's long-term notes. This $425,000 fee was separate from Pressprich's discount purchase of 160,000 shares of Corporation stock. The bulk of the fee, of course, was conditioned on going public.

After its organization, Corporation obtained $236,667 in cash from the proceeds of its sales of common stock at a discount. It had also conditioned the acquisition of Brewing on the receipt of $35 million from its public offering, which would be available to it. Under the terms of the purchase agreement, Corporation had arranged to borrow $20 million from the Schaefer family trusts, to whom $20 million of junior subordinated debentures were to be issued. These funds, aggregating a little over $55 million, together with the $6 million surplus cash that Brewing had, still left it considerably short of its $121.8 million goal, however. To fill the gap, Corporation arranged to borrow $65 million from the seven institutional investors that had participated in the second discount purchase. Thus, Corporation's sources of funds and securities issued or issuable would be as follows:

---

*The other members of Corporation's twelve-man board of directors were three Schaefer family members, three executives of Brewing, two executives of Pressprich, and two outside directors—the chief executive officer of United Aircraft and a vice-chairman of the board of the First National City Bank.

Source of Funds	Amount of Funds	Consideration to Be Issued
Pressprich, Schaefer family, five Brewing executives, and seven institutional investors providing $65,000,000 of long-term financing	$ 236,667	330,000 restricted common shares
Seven institutional investors	36,142,857	7¾% senior notes, due 1989
Seven institutional investors	27,857,143	5¾% convertible subordinated notes, due 1989 with warrants
Four Schaefer family trusts	20,000,000	4% junior subordinated notes, due 1998
Public, not less than	35,000,000[A]	1,500,000 freely tradable common shares
Use of surplus cash in Brewing	6,000,000	
	$125,236,667[B]	

[A]Public offering actually raised about $36,000,000 for Corporation.
[B]Excess over $121,800,000 becomes Corporation funds.

This was not the picture as of the time of the public offering, however. The institutional investors would not lend any funds before January 15, 1969, and their investment was to be phased in over eighteen months, according to the following schedule:

Date	Amount to Be Invested at This Date
1/15/69	$31,845,357
7/15/69	8,222,500
1/15/70	13,510,714
7/15/70	11,421,429
	$65,000,000

The reason for this phasing is not clear, especially since Corporation was obligated to pay the entire $106 million purchase price to the Brewing shareholders by July 15, 1969. It may have been due to the investment scheduling requirements of individual lenders, all of which have schedules of cash inflows and outflows, or it may have involved things peculiar to these transactions. In any event, the arrangement left Corporation with a temporary shortfall, which it covered by arranging a short-term loan from First National City Bank of New York at the prime rate.*

Corporation's Debt Securities Described

The financing scheme outlined above called for the issuance of $85 million worth of debt by Corporation. A little over $36 million of this was in the form of 7¾ percent, twenty-year senior notes. The balance was in subordinated notes of varying terms, all of which had equity privileges.

The $20 million of 4 percent, thirty-year notes issued to the Schaefer trusts carried conversion rights. Beginning January 15, 1971, they were convertible into Corporation common at a price of $40 per share. This conversion price could be reduced on January 15, 1972, to the average price of the stock on the New York Stock Exchange for the sixty trading days prior to January 15, 1972, but in no event could it fall below the initial offering price at which Corporation went public ($26). Thus, if for the sixty trading days before January 15, 1972, the average price for Corporation common stock was $40 or better, the 4 percent notes would be convertible into 500,000 common; if the average price was $35, the 4 percent notes would be convertible into 571,429 Corporation common; and if the average price was $26 or less, the 4 percent notes would be convertible into 769,231 common.

*Corporation also entered into an agreement with First National City on November 25, 1968, under which the bank would provide any interim funds that might be needed to meet the payments due the four Schaefer trusts by July 15, 1969. This was estimated at under $25 million.

The 5¾ percent, twenty-year subordinated notes issued to the institutional investors were structured somewhat differently. Approximately $1.2 million of the $27,857,143 issue was convertible into Corporation common at prices ranging from $10 to $6.50 per share (one quarter of the respective maximum and minimum conversion prices for the 4 percent notes), based on the same timetable and the same sixty-day average-price formula used for the 4 percent notes.

The remainder of the issue was not convertible. Instead, the seven institutions received warrants, exercisable beginning January 15, 1971, to purchase 84,866 Corporation common at $10 per share. Like the conversion rights, the warrants could be adjusted on January 15, 1972, depending on the sixty-day average New York Stock Exchange price of the stock, into warrants to purchase as much as 130,563 Corporation common at $6.50 per share. These warrants were detachable from the 5¾ percent notes, and were transferable upon compliance with SEC registration requirements. The institutional holders had registration rights in connection with both the warrants and the common stock, issuable upon conversion of the notes.

The equity privileges of all of these subordinated securities were protected by anti-dilution provisions similar to those usually found in publicly held convertible securities and warrants. For example, in the event of a two-for-one stock split, the conversion price would be reduced by 50 percent, so that the holder of the notes or warrants would receive the same proportionate equity share on conversion or exercise as it would have before the split. Assuming, as actually happened, that in 1972 the conversion and warrant prices were reduced to the minimum allowed, then in the event of such a split, the 4¾ percent notes would be convertible at $13, and the 5¾ percent notes or warrants at $3.25.

While the anti-dilution protections accorded these subordinated notes are fairly standard, other features of the subordinateds are quite different from those commonly associated with publicly held senior securities with equity privileges. Particularly noteworthy in this regard are the provisions for mandatory and voluntary redemption, and the various protective provisions granted the holders of these notes.

Mandatory Redemption Provisions

The conventional public issue of senior securities with equity privileges has only very small amortization, or sinking fund, provisions that operate in the early years after issuance. For example, a typical twenty-year publicly owned subordinated debenture might have a sinking fund provision that becomes operative after ten years and provides thereafter for annual redemptions of 3 percent of the issue at par.

A relatively small sinking fund provision does, of course, operate to the benefit of the public holder of a convertible note. Rapid pay-back of debt to such an investor would diminish the value of his conversion privilege by "forcing conversion" whenever the market price exceeds the conversion price at the time of redemption.

This phenomenon of forced conversion is best explained by a concrete example. Assume that Corporation calls for redemption $1 million of debentures convertible at $6.50 at a time when its stock is selling for $8 a share. The holder of the debentures can redeem them at par, realizing $1 million. But his conversion privilege entitles him to receive 153,846 shares of common stock. If he sells these shares short at $8 when the redemption is announced, converting the debentures to make delivery against the short sale, he will realize $1,230,769 before commissions and other trading costs of the short sale. The economic benefit of this latter strategy—in this case, $230,769—is what forces conversion. Such forced conversion will, of course, occur whether the redemption of the convertible notes is pursuant to a mandatory sinking fund provision or to a voluntary (by Corporation) call.

In the context of this deal, the interests of the Schaefer family trusts in terms of sinking fund provisions were essentially the same as that of a public holder of a convertible note. Accordingly, the mandatory redemption provisions governing the 4 percent notes were similar to those for a typical public issue: the sinking fund was not to become operative until January 15, 1979, about ten years after issuance; thereafter, annual redemptions at par would amount to $500,000, or 2½ percent of the original issue, until the debt held by the institutional investors was to be retired in 1989; annual redemptions would then double for the last ten years, leaving a $6 million unamortized balance, payable at maturity.

The interest of the institutional investors involved in this deal was somewhat different: a steady and relatively rapid pay-back of their loans, rather than a straight conversion privilege, was their primary goal. Accordingly, the 5¾ percent notes issued to them had sinking fund provisions requiring annual redemption at par of 6¼ percent of the debt outstanding, beginning January 15, 1974, five years or less after issuance. In dollar terms, this amounts to annual redemptions of $1.7 million for sixteen years. This redemption scheme does not diminish the value of the institutional investors' equity privileges, because of the way in which those privileges were structured. The great bulk of the 5¾ percent notes were accompanied by warrants that, as noted above, were detachable from the notes. As to the $1.2 million of debt that was in the form of convertibles, the institutional investors were protected by a provision that in the event of prepayment, warrants to purchase would be issued in lieu of, and on the same basis as, the conversion privileges. These warrants were to expire in 1989.

Voluntary Redemption Provisions

Typically, the issuer's right to voluntarily call a publicly held subordinated debenture with equity privileges is pervasive. The issue is callable in whole or in part anytime after issuance at par. Thus, the issuer is in a position to force conversion if the price at which the common stock is selling is above the price at which the senior security is convertible.* Corporation's voluntary call provisions were quite different from those typically found in connection with a public issue.

*In some instances, warrants can be exercised by the surrender of senior securities valued, for purposes of exercise, at par. If the senior security has a market value of less than par, then the senior-security-warrant package becomes the equivalent of a convertible security.

The 5¾ percent notes carried a five-year call protection, so that Corporation could not voluntarily redeem the notes until January 15, 1974. After that, Corporation could voluntarily redeem $1,740,884 of notes at par each year. No additional calls were permitted until January 15, 1979; thereafter, such calls were permitted, but only at a premium. The prepayment premium was 105.75 percent of par in 1979, declining gradually to par in 1988.

The 4 percent notes carried an eight-year call protection. Thus, there could be no voluntary call before January 15, 1977. After that date, the notes were callable at a premium—104 percent of par in 1977, gradually declining to par in 1998. In addition, Corporation was granted rights to voluntarily call $500,000 of notes per year at par beginning January 15, 1979, and $1 million of notes per year beginning January 15, 1988.

Protective Provisions

The usual public issue of subordinated debentures or notes, or even preferred stock, tends to have protective provisions that are few and generally not too meaningful. The protective provisions of the 4 percent notes issued to the Schaefer family trusts were similarly skimpy. Indeed, if anything, these notes were less well protected than the typical public issue, since they were fully subordinated not only to the senior notes, but also to the subordinated notes held by the institutional investors.

The notes held by the institutional investors, by contrast, contained protective provisions that were far stronger than those found in any publicly traded subordinated debenture of which we are aware. These included both negative covenants (things Corporation was prohibited from doing) and positive covenants (things Corporation was required to do). For example, the terms of the purchase agreement under which these notes were issued required Corporation to maintain a certain minimum working capital at all times, and limited amounts that could be borrowed by Corporation and by its subsidiaries, depending on certain earnings and net tangible assets tests.

It also imposed restrictions on rental charges incurred, dividend payments, the repurchase of shares and the voluntary redemption of senior securities. Further, the agreement contained prohibitions against sale and lease-back transactions and against investment in the securities of other companies or entities, other than subsidiaries and the U.S. government.

Other Distinguishing Features

Although, as noted, the 4 percent notes contained fairly insignificant protective provisions, they contained a very interesting and unusual control provision. The holder was given the right to accelerate payment of the entire amount in the event that one person acquired beneficially 30 percent or more of Corporation's voting securities, or two or more holders acquired voting stock of Corporation for the purpose of exercising control. This should have effectively discouraged anyone from seeking to oust the Schaefer family from control of Corporation.

One final difference between Corporation's subordinates and similar publicly held issues that is worthy of note is that they were private placements. Although this statement may seem to belabor the obvious, in fact the status of the notes as the product of purchase agreements between Corporation and the acquirers is significant in terms of the protection afforded the holders. A public debt issue is issued under a trust indenture, which is an agreement, conforming to the SEC-administered Trust Indenture Act of 1939, between the issuer and a large-bank-designated trustee for the debt securities holders. In the event of default or breach of the agreement, the individual holder of a public debt issue is not usually in a position to take action against the issuing company on his own unless he and others represent not less than 25 percent of the outstanding debt issue. Rather, the debt holder has to wait for the trustee to take action. The trustee will take action only in strict conformity with his interpretation of the indenture. Thus, the public debt security holder may be less protected than the public common stockholder, who tends to be free to take legal actions on behalf of all stockholders or the company itself. The institutional investors involved in this deal have an advantage not possessed by public investors, in that they can themselves move rapidly against Corporation in the event of default or breach of the purchase agreement.

Conversely, there may be situations in which the very fact that this issue is held by only a handful of owners places the institutional investors in a less favorable position than that enjoyed by a public investor. For example, if the issuer wants to modify the terms of a loan agreement without recourse to the bankruptcy statutes, it is in a position to negotiate changes with a few private lenders. The issuer cannot, as a practical matter, do so with a trustee for indebtedness or with individual public investors, however. Thus, the private investor may be forced to agree to changes adverse to his interests in order to avoid bankruptcy of the issuer, whereas full service may be continued on subordinated debentures because they are publicly held.*

ARRANGING THE PUBLIC OFFERING

On September 26, 1968, a little over three months after its incorporation, Corporation filed a preliminary registration statement with the SEC, showing an intent to offer 1 million shares of common stock at a maximum price of $26 per share. At the time of the filing, Pressprich was to manage the syndicate that would underwrite the offering, but that firm was soon replaced by White, Weld and Company, a leading New York City investment banking firm prior

---

*This phenomenon reached its peak in recent years with the debt restructuring of a number of troubled real estate investment trusts. In certain instances, such as Chase Manhattan Mortgage and Realty Trust, senior lenders even invested new funds in the real estate investment trusts, part of which were in fact used to continue to fully service the subordinated debentures. See additional discussion on page 92.

to its merger in 1978 into Merrill, Lynch, Pierce, Fenner and Smith. Although White, Weld did not actually execute a written agreement with Corporation or with any of the proposed members of the underwriting group until just before the registration statement became effective on November 27, 1968, it was busy putting together an underwriting group during the incubation period in which the SEC was reviewing and commenting on Corporation's filing. In all, the underwriting group included 128 firms—117 U.S. firms and 11 European businesses. White, Weld, as manager, underwrote 218,000 of the 1.5 million shares offered. The underwriting group also included Dillon Read; Halsey Stuart; Kidder, Peabody; Kuhn Loeb & Co.; Lazard Freres; Paine, Webber, Jackson and Curtis; and Paribas.

The issue was offered for sale at $26 per share on November 27, 1968, and was an immediate success. The warning in the prospectus that Corporation's large debt load and negative tangible net worth made the issue highly speculative certainly did not depress the price, and may even have been the reason the issue went to a premium. In any case, the stock closed at 31 bid on the date of the issue.*

Of the $39 million gross proceeds from the offering, 6 percent (amounting to $1.56 per share), was retained as underwriting discount;† $1,065,000 of this (amounting to $.71 per share) went to White, Weld for its management fee and for the legal, advertising and other expenses incurred in connection with the underwriting.

---

*At year-end, its price was 30 bid. Corporation's stock was listed for trading on the New York Stock Exchange on January 24, 1969. .

†This gross spread was about standard for a fairly large new-issue offering of an industrial issuer going public. Although there have been new issues of common stock marketed at a smaller gross spread when a company was going public (most notably Communications Satellite Corporation, or Comsat, whose gross spread was 4 percent when it went public in 1965), this is unusual.

Smaller, unseasoned issuers call for higher gross spreads, frequently as high as 18 percent, exclusive of other considerations—such as continued financial consulting fees, board representation and rights of first refusal on future company offerings—granted to the underwriter.

The balance was paid to certain dealers, including the underwriters, as a sales commission.*

Corporation incurred expenses of about $330,000 in connection with the underwriting, over and above the underwriting discount. These included such items as legal fees ($100,000), accounting fees ($75,000), printing costs ($75,000), SEC and blue sky (state security regulation) fees ($30,000), liability insurance ($35,000) and transfer agent fees ($15,000).

Contemporaneously with the public offering, Corporation granted options to its employees to purchase 98,134 Corporation common shares. These were granted pursuant to a qualified stock-option plan covering 200,000 shares of Corporation common, which had been approved on October 30, 1968. These options, which were granted at 100 percent of market value on the date of grant, were good for five years if the holder remained employed by Corporation or a subsidiary. Upon the exercise of the qualified option, Corporation would lend the employee 90 percent of the exercise price at 4 percent interest; 20 percent of the outstanding amount was to be repaid annually for the first four years, the balance in the fifth year. These options enabled the holder to profit on a tax-sheltered capital-gains basis from appreciation in the market value of Corporation's stock.

PROBLEMS AND WEALTH-CREATION
POTENTIALS FOR THE PARTIES
IN INTEREST

The Selling Stockholders

The selling stockholders were Arjayess, a corporation wholly owned by Rudolph J. Schaefer, and four trusts for members of the Schaefer family.

*This sales commission of $.85, or $85 per 100 shares, was considerably higher than $.32 per share, or $32 per 100 shares selling at 26, the standard commission prevailing in 1968 for round lots (usually 100 shares) of outstanding stock listed on the New York Stock Exchange.

There are a number of things that motivated the Schaefers to follow the course of action they did rather than the alternative opportunities that might be summarized as follows:

1. Brewing could have gone public by offering its stock via a Pressprich or White, Weld and Company or equivalent underwriting.
2. Brewing could have remained as it was—as a private company—and used its borrowing power to incur debt, the proceeds of which might then be distributed to the Schaefer family stockholders.
3. Brewing could have sold out to a larger company—say, been merged into or otherwise acquired by a mass merchandiser, following in a general way the acquisition of Miller Brewing by Philip Morris in 1969, or Hamm's Brewing by Heublein in 1965.
4. Brewing could have done nothing, in which event cash distributions to its shareholders would have been no larger than annual earnings of around $5 million per year.

The Schaefer family, through these transactions, obtained by July 15, 1969, some $86 million in cash on a tax-sheltered (capital-gains rather than dividend-income) basis, after which they were still left in control of the company. The company, too, was now public, with a huge stock market value in which the Schaefers expected to participate, at least to some extent. Unlike the other stockholders' holdings, though, the Schaefers' security holdings would provide the four trusts with an $800,000 annual cash return, because the four trusts held $20 million of 4 percent convertible debentures, rather than common stock on which it was likely that no dividends would be paid. Assuming that the average price for Corporation's common stock for the sixty trading days before January 15, 1972, was 40 or more, the Schaefer family interests would own 19.6 percent of Corporation's equity on an all-converted, all-exercised basis. Assuming, on the other hand, that the average price for Corporation's common stock for the sixty trading days before January 15, 1972, was 26 or less, the Schaefer family interests would own 26.1 percent of Corporation's equity on an all-converted, all-exercised basis. In either event, the Schaefer family would control Corporation. The Schaefer family ownership interests are computed as follows:

	At Price of 40 or More	At Price of 26 or Less
No. shares outstanding after public offering	1,830,000	1,830,000
No. shares owned by Schaefer family interests of outstanding	15,000	15,000
% owned by Schaefer family interests	0.8%	0.8%
No. shares issuable upon conversion of debt, exercise of warrants and exercise of qualified options	798,134	1,175,057
No. shares issuable to Schaefer upon conversion of 4% notes	500,000	769,231
No. shares to be outstanding on all-converted, all-exercised basis	2,628,134	3,005,057
No. shares to be held by Schaefers	515,000	784,231
% owned by Schaefer family interests	19.6%	26.1%

Each of the alternative opportunities had special disadvantages. The Schaefer family interests could have contemplated, and may well have studied, merely offering some of the Brewing stock held by Arjayess and the four trusts in a so-called underwritten secondary offering. Such an offering would have resulted in the sellers' realizing cash on a capital-gains basis and would also have left the Schaefer interests in control of a public company. Furthermore, this public company, unlike Corporation, would enjoy considerable financial strength. However, it would have been virtually impossible for a secondary underwriting to be arranged on such a basis that the Schaefer family interests would be able to realize $86 million in cash. Indeed, Corporation's $39 million gross proceeds from its underwriting was relatively large for an issue of this type. Not only were the Schaefer family interests able to realize $86 million of cash from doing what they did, but they may well have achieved a much better after-market for their remaining holdings in Brewing's parent than would have been the case on straight underwriting. Because certain influential Wall Street entities (Pressprich and the seven institutional investors) were important shareholders, Corporation may well have become a better-sponsored security in 1969 and 1970 than would otherwise have been the case. Corporation's stock price rose almost steadily after the initial offering in November 1969, reaching a peak in February 1970, when the shares sold at a price of $59, equal to 25 times 1969 earnings of $2.30 per share.

Had Brewing remained a private company, its ability to borrow from lending institutions would have been considerably poorer than as part of a public vehicle. One crucial factor that made the $65 million borrowing by Corporation attractive to the seven institutions was their obtaining discount purchases of equity interests—that is, 150,000 common at $1 per share, and rights to obtain between 200,000 and 307,692 common shares at between $10 and $6.50 per share, depending on where the stock (which was to go public at 26) would be selling three years later.

It is possible that the Schaefer family interests could have received maximum tax shelter by remaining private and by having borrowed funds flow into Brewing. Since the family owned 100 percent of Brewing, the funds might have been usable by them without any, or any appreciable, amounts being distributed to Arjayess or the four trusts. However, such a course of action could raise tax problems for Brewing, namely, a Section 531 problem on the unlawful retention of surplus, even though this probably would have been vitiated by Brewing's plans to spend at least $38 million to construct a new facility in eastern Pennsylvania. In any event, we have no information about the amount of tax shelter available to Arjayess on its receipt of $6 million. Also, it is probable that the four trusts have obtained more tax shelter from returns on their investments than would have been feasible if the same funds had been invested in Brewing. There is no question that with the considerable planning that went into the transactions, they were designed so that the combined tax impacts on Arjayess and the four trusts were minimized.

Had Brewing chosen to sell out to a larger company, it is

extremely unlikely that the Schaefer family interests could have retained the same type of control over Brewing that became available to them through the creation of Corporation, which alone may have discouraged this approach. In addition, it probably was difficult to find an acquirer with whom an agreement could be reached that would result in the Schaefer family interests' receiving $86 million in cash (either from the acquirer's treasury or from the sale of shares received), plus a meaningful equity interest in the common stock of the acquiring company. It is possible, but not probable, that an acquirer with a usable tax-loss carry-forward might pay out that much cash for Brewing (for example, see the Northwest Industries acquisition of Buckingham Corporation in 1971). If the Schaefer interests were to receive $86 million cash either directly from the acquirer or through the sale of common stock of the acquirer received, the acquiring company in all probability would have had to account for the Brewing acquisition on a purchase basis rather than a pooling-of-interests basis. In addition, the sale of Brewing to a larger company could easily have been stopped or made difficult because of antitrust proceedings of the U.S. Department of Justice or the Federal Trade Commission.

Had Brewing remained as it was, a private, relatively debt-free corporation, there would have been no large-scale cash distributions to Arjayess or the four trusts. In addition, assuming there was no intention to ever go public, Brewing's business might have suffered because of the difficulty of offering key personnel meaningful equity interests in the enterprise.

On balance, the transaction that did take place did have many advantages for the Schaefer family interests. This does not mean that there was not a considerable number of disadvantages that ensued. First, the Schaefers were now in control of a highly leveraged public company with new sets of obligations to important outside interest groups. The seven institutional investors placed restrictions on operations and financing in accordance with the terms of the various purchase agreements. Both Corporation and the Schaefers were now subject to SEC requirements as to reporting and corporate conduct.

Also, lawyers representing minority interests would be very

ready and able to seek redress for what they believed were wrongs to stockholders. If Brewing had remained closely held and if the Schaefer family interests desired to acquire for themselves, say, a beer distributor, there would have been no need to offer this distributor first to Brewing; however, as a public entity, Corporation would find that such a transaction would be extremely suspect, and quite possibly impossible to do as a practical matter.

Furthermore, as a result of going public, corporate objectives changed. As a private company, Brewing would strive to maximize economic profits, whereas, as a public entity, Corporation tends to strive to maximize immediate accounting profits. Frequently, the maximization of economic profits is in direct conflict with the maximization of immediate accounting profits. As a private company, Brewing would take as much depreciation as it could in order to reduce income taxes and accounting profits, and Brewing would be more willing to launch expensive programs—say, very large-scale advertising—the benefits of which may not be apparent for many years.

The Schaefer family interests were left with a large ownership interest in and control of a financially weakened company that was not as well prepared to meet competitive onslaughts as it might otherwise have been. As a matter of fact, in the early 1970's the principal national companies, Anheuser-Busch, Schlitz and Miller's, commenced raiding regional markets with programs consisting of price-cutting and other forms of aggressive merchandising. Such programs were relatively successful for the nationals. Corporation's accounting earnings per share peaked at $2.30 in 1970 and declined to $1.75 in 1971. Corporation suffered a deficit of in excess of $1 million in 1972, and deficit operations continued through 1973. The business was nominally profitable in 1974, 1976, and 1977, reported a massive deficit in 1975, and presumably will have suffered a large loss in 1978.

Although the Schaefer family interests did create a large market value for their holdings in Corporation, such value was not readily realizable. Unlike the outside stockholders' shares, shares in Corporation held by the Schaefers were "tainted"—that is, they were not freely salable. As a practical matter, sales of large amounts of stock by them probably could only be accomplished by having another registered secondary or by selling the shares privately at a very substantial discount from market. A registered secondary might be accomplishable only via an underwriting, the cost of which might run from 7 percent to 10 percent of the gross proceeds, and at that, might be accomplishable only during periods when both the new-issue market was doing well and Corporation itself was prospering.

Brewing's Executive Employees

Two principal changes occurred for Brewing's executive employees. First, they received a new financial incentive in the form of discount purchases of Corporation stock, which theoretically could be disposed of by public sale in whole or in part at some future date. Second, Brewing's executive employees were now managing a consolidated enterprise that was heavily in debt and publicly owned, rather than a private company with excess financial resources.

The discount purchases by these executives were of two types. The first was the aggregate of 5,000 shares of Corporation common purchased at $1 per share by five members of Brewing's executive management committee two months before Brewing went public at 26. On a gross valuation basis, this transaction resulted in a windfall of $25 per share, or $25,000 for each of the five individuals. Such a calculation, though, would be misleading. The reasons why the difference between a $1 purchase price and a $26 market price was something less than $25 can be summarized as follows:

1. The $1 price was a cash cost, whereas the $26 market value was not a value these executives could realize in cash, either by selling the stock or by using it as collateral for loans. In this sense—that is, as measured by ability to realize cash—the shares could be deemed to have a value of $26 only if they were registered with the SEC and if they were held beneficially by outsiders, not

insiders. These are strictures that could adversely affect value even in the absence of specific contractual restrictions.

2. At the time of purchase, there was no assurance that Corporation could go public at all, or if it could, at what price it would go public. Value should have been adjusted to provide an estimate for this uncertainty.

3. The $1 shares were acquired subject to specific contractual restrictions. Each executive agreed to resell the shares to Corporation at $1 per share in the event he left Brewing before January 1, 1974, except in the case of death, disability or approved retirement. After January 1, 1974, only 20 percent of the shares became free of their contractual restrictions per year cumulatively.

By having the opportunity to purchase Corporation shares at $1 per, the five executives did receive something of value, although for income-tax purposes this was not construed to be a discount or bargain purchase. The reasons why the purchase was not so construed was that based on what the tangibles were in Corporation's business on September 20, 1968 (the purchase date), the shares were not even worth $1. Also, others also paid the same price at that time. Had IRS considered the shares a bargain purchase, these executives would have had to treat the difference between the fair value of the shares received (26, for tax purposes?) and the $1 per-share cost as employment compensation to be taxed at ordinary income rates. If that had been the case, it is very probable some or all of the executives would have considered the right to buy shares at $1 per share on September 20, 1968, as something with a negative value.

Also, these five executives received, in the form of equity ownership incentive, qualified stock options as part of a program under which designated employees, including certain officers and directors of Brewing, received options to purchase 98,134 Corporation common at 26. The options were granted at fair market value (26 per share) on the date the underwriting agreement was signed. These options were to expire five years from the date of grant or earlier in the event of termination of employment, disability or death. In the case of some of the options, if they were not exercised during the first four years after grant, the exercise price could be payable by borrowing 90 percent of the required funds from Corporation. Such borrowings would bear interest at 4 percent, and the notes would be repayable at the rate of 20 percent per year. Put simply, these qualified options permitted the holders potential profit, on a tax-sheltered basis, from appreciation in Corporation's stock price, without any cash outlay at all for five years and with very attractive financing terms for the next five years.

The tax shelter existed because the options were, for IRS purposes, "qualified."* If the employees had received nonqualified or nonstatutory stock options, then the excess of the fair value of those options over their cost would, in the majority of cases and unless carefully structured, be taxable as employee compensation in the year of receipt. The worst tax posture a taxpayer can find himself in would result from such a nonstatutory stock option. (As has been noted in Chapter 9, the poorest tax position is that in which the taxpayer is subject to tax at maximum rates; in which the taxpayer has no control over the timing of the payment of the tax, and especially lacks the ability to defer it to future periods; and in which the event which gives rise to the taxable event does not give rise to the cash with which to pay the tax.)

However, to achieve the tax-sheltered status granted through the qualified options, employees had to abide by restrictions of the law that limited the economic attractiveness of such incentives. In a meaningful sense, the most important tax shelter that had existed for a qualified option was that it avoided the unusually onerous tax burdens that tended to be present for nonstatutory stock options. *Inter alia,* for an option to be qualified it had to consist of the following:

1. The option price could not be less than fair market value at the date of grant.
2. The option had to be granted within about ten years from the date an overall plan was approved by stockholders and adopted by the corporation.
3. Once an option was granted, it had to be exercised within five years.

*The Revenue Act of 1976 removes virtually all economic incentives for qualified stock options. As such, they are now rarely used for executive compensation.

4. The option could not be exercisable while any qualified option granted to the employee at a higher price was still outstanding.
5. The option was not transferable during the life of the employee.

Even when these qualified conditions were fulfilled, the usable tax shelter for the employee was limited for the following reasons:

1. Under the 1969 amendments to the Internal Revenue Code, at the time of exercise the bargain element of the option would become a tax preference—that is, the employee could, under certain conditions, become subject to a tax of 10 percent* of his bargain at the time the option was exercised.
2. To realize a capital gain on his profit, the employee would have to hold the stock for three years. If he held it less than three years, the difference between the option price and the fair value on the exercise date would be taxable at ordinary income rates.

For example, suppose an employee received an option on 1,000 shares at 30 on November 27, 1968; that he exercised the option on November 27, 1973, when the stock was priced at 50; and that he sold the stock on June 5, 1974, at 65. His tax picture would be as follows when filing his 1974 return:

Sell 1,000 shares at 65	$65,000
Purchase 1,000 shares at 30	30,000
Gain before income taxes	$35,000
Tax on gains:* At ordinary income-tax rates, difference between 30 and 50	$20,000
At capital-gains rates	$15,000

*Based on the CCH Master Tax Guide.

*The tax rate on tax preference items was raised to 15 percent from 10 percent in 1976.

As the operating heads of Brewing and its parent, Corporation, the officers and directors of the public company now found themselves influenced by a different discipline than when they were officers and directors of a private company with excess financial resources. The different discipline was not necessarily better or worse, but it was different.

1. In a public company, all other things being equal, there is a tendency toward more aggressiveness in striving for near-term results and less emphasis on long-range planning, especially if such long-range planning might adversely affect near-term profits. For example, there might be less institutional advertising.

2. In a public company, there is a tendency toward making reported results as good as possible, even though it would make actual economic results worse than they ought to be. For example, the Corporation-Brewing transaction could have been structured so that depreciation charges against income would have been based on Corporation's purchase price for Brewing, $106 million, rather than on Brewing's net asset value, $53 million. The tax savings would have been highly significant. However, if that had been done, Corporation's reported earnings from 1969 forward would have been substantially lower, with consequent possible adverse effects on stock market valuations. For public companies, stock market consciousness frequently takes precedence over tax consciousness and underlying business-value consciousness. In private companies, the question usually never arises; the private company will opt for maximum tax savings.

3. With the public as partners, Corporation's and Brewing's executives, as well as the corporation itself, became subject to a whole gamut of new disciplines in terms of what they were required to disclose in the way of information and the liabilities to which they became subject, both to government authorities and stockholders, because they were public.

4. Managements with public stock to use tend to be more conscious of values that can be created by using the stock, especially when it is selling at a liberal price. This, for example, manifests itself in

certain public companies having active merger, acquisition and refinancing programs.

The Commercial Bank Providing Bridge Financing

First National City Bank provided $24.9 million of loans to Corporation with interest at the prime rate. In addition, the bank received a commitment, or standby, fee equal to an annual rate of ⅛ percent of the unused balance (that is, the portion of the $24.9 million not borrowed) from September 26, 1968, to the closing or December 31, 1968, whichever was earlier. Subsequently, the commitment fee on the unused balance was increased to ¼ percent. These loans, in the form of short-term notes, were issued in July 1969 and were retired within one year as the seven institutions invested their funds into Corporation in the form of long-term senior notes and subordinated notes. Corporation did have the right to prepay the bank loan at any time, but would have incurred a ¼ percent prepayment penalty if it used funds obtained by borrowings at a lower interest cost than First National City's prime rate.

From the bank's point of view, the loan in the form of bridge financing seemed reasonably safe. First, there was the "take out" by the permanent lenders, the seven institutions who were committed to invest further sums on January 15, 1970, and July 15, 1970, the first proceeds of which were to be used to repay these short-term notes. Second, Corporation consolidated with Brewing was a profitable, growing business with operating earnings in excess of $1 million per month, a substantial balance-sheet cushion behind these notes in the form of about $12 million of subordinated notes, $20 million of junior subordinated notes and a stockholder's equity (including over $50 million of nonamortizing good will) of about $37 million. Also, Corporation was managed by a highly reputable and successful group.

Returns to the bank exceeded merely interest at the prime rate. The loan itself probably required compensating balances of 10 percent to 20 percent of the notes outstanding to be kept on deposit. First

National City may also have become the bank of deposit, as well as the lending bank, in connection with other Corporation activities, and the transactions may have resulted in creating trust business for the bank. As far as corporate trust activities are concerned, First National City did become the registrar for Corporation common. As far as personal trust is concerned, First National City could conceivably have obtained investment management and/or custodian business from the Schaefer family in connection with the handling of their portfolios.

Although the financing of acquisitions is attractive, banks view it as the least productive part of their lending activities. These are virtually the first loans to be cut out in periods when money is tight or generally unavailable, as in 1966, from 1969 to 1970, and again in 1973 and 1974.

The Wall Street Promoters

Pressprich, then a prestigious New York Stock Exchange member firm, appeared to have profited handsomely from the transaction under which Corporation purchased Brewing's equity securities simultaneously with Corporation's going public. Off the top, Pressprich received fees of $425,000 for arranging Corporation's financing; and for $.42 per share, or a total of about $67,000, Pressprich purchased 160,000 common five months before the public subscribed to freely tradable shares of the same issue at 26 per share (equal to $4,160,000 for 160,000 shares). The 160,000 common held by Pressprich were, for SEC purposes, unregistered, or restricted, shares; in any event, Pressprich had agreed with Corporation not to sell the shares to anyone before March 15, 1971, without first offering the shares to Corporation at $.42 per share. Even with these restrictions on resale, the 160,000 share acquisition seemed to have been quite a bargain for Pressprich from any point of view except that of the Internal Revenue Service.

Less visible and less tangible were other benefits to Pressprich. First, the firm gained two seats on Corporation's board of directors, which probably resulted in small fees and elements of control over important assets. "Control," a many-faceted concept, could extend, for example, to having Pressprich's directors influence the company in registering shares for distribution with the SEC, including the 160,000 shares held by Pressprich. In the normal situation, however, the Pressprich directors would be outside directors, and their de facto control over the affairs of Corporation would be manifestly less than would the inside directors' and management members', whether directors or not. The liabilities of the outside directors, however, could easily be just as large as anyone else's in the case of judicial or administrative findings of wrongdoing that harmed Corporation or its stockholders. (This is why many people are reluctant to serve on boards, especially since neither corporate indemnification provisions nor directors' liability insurance can give a director assured insulation from liabilities. Yet, on balance, most people probably feel there is a net benefit to them and to their organization from serving as outside directors on the boards of public corporations.)

Another benefit that may well have been available to Pressprich was future business from happy clients. The happy clients were of two types, both of whom had enormous amounts of investible funds (the sort of clients that investment bankers and stockbrokers like Pressprich like best). The first set of clients were the shareholders of Brewing who received $86 million in cash, namely, the corporation controlled by Rudolph Schaefer, Arjayess, and the four trusts for the benefit of various members of the Schaefer family. The second set of happy clients were the seven institutions that purchased corporation senior and subordinated notes with equity privileges, which by themselves seemed a reasonable investment. These institutions also split amongst themselves 150,000 shares of Corporation common purchased for $1 per share.

Finally, the successful completion of Corporation's public underwriting and subsequent favorable market action for Corporation stock unquestionably enhanced Pressprich's reputation, both within the financial community and with others of means who were seeking the creative finance that the Schaefer case had demonstrated. The success of the transactions, therefore, could easily result in

Pressprich's gaining access to much more new investment banking business unrelated to the Schaefer transactions than would have been the case had Pressprich not concluded successfully the Schaefer deal.

One footnote is that Pressprich was a member of the National Association of Securities Dealers, commonly known as the NASD. All New York Stock Exchange member firms are also NASD members. The new (since 1970) NASD Rules of Fair Practice that relate to corporate financing would have prevented Pressprich from doing what it did in 1968. First, Pressprich would have had to have held its $.42 stock for at least six months and in all probability one year before Corporation could have gone public. If it did not, the NASD probably would rule under current regulations that the $.42 purchase price was integrated with the $26 public offering and resulted in Pressprich receiving unreasonable compensation. Also, if the transactions were to be undertaken now, it is quite possible that the NASD would rule that Pressprich's purchase of stock would be limited to 10 percent of the public offering. The Corporation public offering was for 1.5 million shares, which would limit Pressprich's prior purchase to 150,000 shares.

In any event, Pressprich's discount purchase of 160,000 shares appears to have been perfectly legitimate in 1968 and was certainly not then an uncommon transaction within the investment community.

The Underwriters of the Public Issue and Their Securities Salesmen

When Pressprich became involved with the Corporation-Brewing transactions, it was contemplated that R. W. Pressprich and Company would manage the underwriting of 1 million Corporation common at around 26, which later increased to 1.5 million shares. In fact, when the preliminary registration statement was filed with the Securities and Exchange Commission on September 26, 1968, R. W. Pressprich and Company was listed as the managing underwriter.

We do not know the reasons why White, Weld and Company was substituted as managing underwriter for Pressprich, and why

Pressprich was not a member of the Corporation's underwriting group in any capacity when the 1.5 million shares were marketed on November 27, 1968. The probabilities are that the National Association of Securities Dealers, under its Rules of Fair Practice as they then existed, frowned on Pressprich or any Pressprich affiliate participating in the Corporation underwriting, because only a few months previously Pressprich had purchased 160,000 shares at $.42 per share. When the preliminary registration statement was filed with the SEC, the maximum filing price was 26.

The switch from Pressprich to White, Weld brings to light three important points. First, in putting together complex transactions, things rarely, if ever, go smoothly, and all sorts of changes are usually made in midstream. Second, it is likely that the part of the compensation to Pressprich consisting of financial fees and bargain purchases of Corporation stock were in economic fact payments for arranging the public underwriting.

Third, it would appear as if White, Weld, as managing underwriter, was undercompensated, compared with what was received by certain other insiders and quasi-insiders, namely the selling stockholders, Pressprich and the lending institutions. After all, the achievement of the public distribution and the raising of over $30 million was a *sine qua non*. Yet, White, Weld purchased no discount stock and received no special fees: it participated only in its share of the underwriting spread, or discount, of $1.56 per share, or $2,340,000.

Under the NASD Rules of Fair Practice, as well as in connection with certain blue sky laws, it may have been inappropriate for the underwriters to seek materially greater amounts of compensation. Even so, the transaction probably was a reasonably profitable one from White, Weld's point of view. White, Weld obtained by far the largest participation in the underwriting, 218,000 shares, or 14.5 percent of the 1.5-million-share issue. The next largest participation for a firm in the underwriting group was 33,000 shares, taken down by Dillon, Read and Kuhn, Loeb. The next lowest bracket was 22,000 shares, and firms participating at this level were Halsey, Stuart; Kidder, Peabody; Lazard Freres; Lehman Brothers; Paine, Webber, Jackson and Curtis; Paribas; Shields; Stone and Webster Securities; and G. H. Walker. Since the issue was in demand, these underwriters and their sales forces were able to realize their allotted compensation both for performing the underwriting function and as selected dealers.

Compensation to White, Weld, other underwriters and members of the selling group, most or all of whom were also underwriters, was spelled out in three agreements which had been prepared previously but which were executed on November 26, 1968, the day the offering was declared effective by the SEC and the day before the actual offering. The first agreement was the Underwriting Agreement (sometimes called the Purchase Agreement), entered into between White, Weld and Corporation. The second agreement was the Agreement Among Underwriters (sometimes simply called the Agreement Among) between White, Weld as representative of all the underwriters and each individual firm that became a party to the underwriting. The third agreement was the Selected Dealer Agreement between White, Weld as representative of the underwriter and each selected dealer.

The Underwriting Agreement spelled out in specifics the various terms between White, Weld and Corporation, including the representations and warranties each gave to the other, the conditions of closing, indemnifications and so on. Briefly, Corporation agreed to sell to each of the underwriters, and each of the underwriters agreed to purchase, the specified number of Corporation shares allotted to them (218,000 for White, Weld) at $24.44 per share. Payment was to be made to Corporation on December 4, 1968, one week after the offering, but in no event more than eight business days after December 4.

The Agreement Among as well as the Selected Dealer Agreement gave White, Weld strong control over how the issue would be marketed and by whom. One of the matters in the Agreement Among was that the underwriters were to act severally, not jointly, so that default by one member of the group would not make all other members liable. In economic terms, the Agreement Among and the Selected Dealer Agreement outlined how the $1.56 underwriting discount (the difference between the $26 public offering price and the

$24.44 to be paid to Corporation) was to be split. In tabular form, the split was to be as follows:

Payment for	To	Per Share	Total Amount
Management expenses (estimated)	White, Weld White, Weld[A]	$ .31 $ .05	$265,000 75,000
Selected dealers who market shares	Selected dealers, all or most of whom may be underwriters	$ .85	1,275,000
Underwriting or syndicate function	Underwriters	$ .35	525,000
		$1.56	$2,340,000
NASD members who market shares but are not selected dealers	NASD members who are not selected dealers (none will be underwriters)	Up to $.26[B]	?[B]

[A]Estimated to cover expenses of underwriting. Charges for White, Weld expenses to the underwriting group.

[B]Payable out of $.85 fee given to selected dealers.

The $.85 concession to selected dealers is basically sales compensation, equal to about a triple commission over the standard New York Stock Exchange commission rates. The extra promotional consideration available to salesmen, some of whom might obtain close to 50 percent of the $.85, goes a long away toward explaining why the financial community has such a vested interest in promoting new-issue booms. It also explains why the securities laws are so written that the SEC tries to make its rules and laws on conditioning markets so much stricter when underwritings are involved.

Handling a good-grade hot issue such as Schaefer brought other benefits to White, Weld. First, it unquestionably brought profit contributions and overhead coverage to its underwriting department. Second, it benefited White, Weld's sales force by giving them attractive merchandise to sell and at rates that allowed them high compensation for an easy sell. Third, it enhanced White, Weld's ability to participate in underwritings managed by others: the odds are that because Kuhn, Loeb and Lehman were invited by White, Weld into important positions in Corporation's underwriting, Kuhn, Loeb and Lehman would be more desirous of inviting White, Weld into their underwriting groups for attractive issues than would otherwise have been the case. Also, in the event White, Weld was to find itself in the type of promotional position that Pressprich was in, in these transactions, Pressprich or others might be more sympathetic to managing an underwriting of a White, Weld deal than it would otherwise.

The Institutional Lenders Providing Long-Term Financing

The seven financial institutions had two reasons for investing $65 million into Corporation's senior notes and subordinated notes. First and—at least in the case of the six insurance-company investors— foremost was the thesis that these were reasonably safe long-term loans affording a cash return in the form of interest income close to what good-grade bonds were then paying. Second, the seven institutions obtained very significant equity kickers in the form of the discount purchase of 150,000 common at $1 and of warrants to purchase between 84,866 and 130,563 common at a price that could be 75 percent below the market price three years later; they also gained the right to convert $1,151,340 of subordinated notes into common stock at a price that could be 75 percent below the market price three years later (or $6.50 a share).

It should be noted, however, that on conservative analysis the total $65 million investment could at best be called only fairly safe. It was far from risk-free, since $27,857,143 (or 42.9 percent) of the $65 million commitment was in the form of subordinates. Thus, in the event Corporation suffered serious financial reverses, the subordinates could be junior in payment not only to these senior notes, but also to other senior notes that might be issued in the future. On an overall basis, these issues failed four of the seven safety tests promulgated by Graham and Dodd in *Security Analysis*. (Graham and Dodd advise forgoing investing in any senior security that ever fails one test.) Corporation's senior securities seemed to have qualified under the following three tests:

1. Nature and location of the business
2. Size of the enterprise
3. Terms of the issue

Tests where these $65 million of securities were found wanting were

1. Record of solvency, at least insofar as Corporation was concerned, since it was a new entity operating under a new (that is, public) discipline
2. Relationship of earnings to interest requirements
3. Relationship of the value of the property to funded debt
4. Relationship of the stock capitalization to funded debt

Interestingly enough, Graham and Dodd do not have an eighth test, which may be the single most direct test of senior security safety—the relationship of cash flow to debt service, or the cash flow available to meet both interest and principal payments.

Although the institutional investors would hardly consider the $65 million loans top drawer from a safety angle, they were good enough. The important aspect was the equity kicker. In appraising the equity kicker, the institutions looked at three things:

1. The discount from market at which they could obtain shares
2. The appraisal of the outlook for the business, on the theory that the long-term price of the stock would tend to be related to the performance of the company (in this analysis, the institutions used many of the same variables that were used when appraising the safety of the loan)
3. The rights of registration that would permit the institutions to dispose of the shares

Rights of registration were more important to the seven institutions than they were to the other purchasers of discount stock, namely, the selling stockholders, Brewing executives and Pressprich.

These purchasers were all represented on the board and might be in a position to influence the company to register the shares they held with the SEC. The seven institutions, in contrast, could only be assured of registration rights in contractual provisions.

Registration rights are extremely valuable to purchasers of unregistered discount securities, especially those who acquire large amounts of restricted securities. For those acquiring small blocks of restricted securities, the use of the SEC's Rule 144, in effect since April 15, 1972, is practical.

Just how valuable registration rights are depends on the various contractual rights embodied in the agreements that relate to the stock market situation for the particular securities. The contractual provision can be quite diverse, ranging from very strong to almost meaningless. (Registration rights also encompass matters not discussed here but that are essentially legal, such as indemnification provisions and agreements to supply documentation.) We think the registration rights received by the seven institutional lenders were very strong. Briefly reviewed, the principal economic provisions of the registration rights to the institutional investors were as follows:

Effective date. The institutions' rights of registration became effective January 15, 1971, or about two years after the initial investment. Incidentally, Pressprich obtained registration rights which were different from the institutions' rights and which became effective March 15, 1971.

Expiration date. None.

Demand, or trigger, rights. This refers to the right of a security holder to require a company to file a registration statement enabling the beneficiaries of such registration rights to publicly offer their shares. The institution or institutions could make four such requests; Pressprich could make one.

Piggyback rights. This refers to rights to have holders' shares included in a registration statement filed by the company or by other selling stockholders. The institutions and Pressprich had unlimited rights in this regard. It is advantageous to be able to piggyback, but it frequently is disadvantageous to be piggybacked by others. For example, assume John Hancock and New York Life used a trigger right to register 75,000 shares for sale. Left alone, the 75,000 shares might be sold at or near the market price. However, the agreement would give all other holders of restricted securities the right to join in, or piggyback, any registration. The John Hancock and New York Life request to register 75,000 shares could easily result in, say, 530,000 shares being registered and sold. This could result in severely depressing the market price, or as a practical matter, making sale of John Hancock's and New York Life's 75,000 shares unachievable.

Number of times registration can be requested. In the institution's case, it was four for trigger (one for Pressprich), unlimited for piggyback.

Expenses. With minor exceptions, expenses were to be borne by Corporation.

Requirement that registration be underwritten. None.

Obligation of company to keep registration effective after nine months. Yes.

The Public Investors

Those of the investing public who were fortunate enough to get in on a new hot issue at the time of the initial offering paid 26 per share for Corporation common on November 27, 1968. Pressprich had paid $.42 per share five months before for Corporation common, and others had paid $1 per share just two months before. And the public stood in line for the privilege!

The Corporation common stock bought by the public was not, in economic fact, the same Corporation common purchased by insiders and quasi-insiders. For one thing, any public shareholder was free to dispose of his shares at any time. Indeed, any public purchaser who obtained his shares on the initial offering could have disposed of his stock at a profit at any time from the afternoon of the offering through April 1971, a period of almost thirty months. The purchasers of discount-priced securities, however, were prevented from selling any stock before January 1971 at the earliest. In each instance, the purchasers of discount securities were subject to a number of constraints or were required to perform special services; the public investors, though, were purely passive and assumed no obligations.

This is not to say that the public received a highly advantageous position compared with the Schaefer family, Brewing executives, Pressprich or the institutional lenders; that would be silly. It is to say that the public investors were marching, or do march, to the beat of a different drummer than the promoters' and insiders'. As a consequence, by the standards used by the public the $26 issue price was a bargain.

The public in 1968 tended to be uninterested in things that contributed to value if they did not also contribute to market performance. The public stockholders acquiring Corporation common stock sought, above all, immediate stock market performance. New issues such as Corporation's offering gave great promise in 1968 of immediate performance for the following reasons:

1. Underwriters consciously try to price new issues so that they will sell at premiums after the offering. Normally, the strongest determinant of a market price will be industry identification as it relates to earnings, especially earnings trends. In pricing Corporation common where the earnings trend was favorable, the underwriters appeared to have attached to Schaefer a price–earnings ratio moderately below that at which other brewing equities with favorable operating trends were selling.

2. Good market performance is more likely to occur when an issue is well sponsored. Corporation's bankers and promoters were well regarded; its underwriting group was top drawer; investors in the company's common stock included very astute names, such as John Hancock, Investors Syndicates and New York Life; and the issue was to be listed on the New York Stock Exchange.

3. Securities salesmen love to push new issues. A rule of thumb in 1968 was that salesmen's compensation for placing a new issue should be about three times the then standard New York Stock Exchange commission for an order of similar size. Sales forces tend to talk up new issues, if for no other reason than that they are very interested in them. This contributes to creating instant performance.

It would have been difficult, if not impossible, to have Brewing or Corporation go public via an offering if the business was not one with a favorable industry identification and a "growth story." In 1968, virtually all the companies in the new-issue boom had growth-industry identifications in areas such as computers, electronics, franchises and nursing homes. There were little or no sales of common stocks of companies going public for the first time in industries such as railroads, textiles or general-line fire and casualty insurance.

Yet there are things other than positive industry identification and growth prospects that contribute to value. For example, in Brewing itself one of the great elements of value to others than the public was the fact that Brewing had unused financial resources; this was one of the bases giving Corporation the ability to borrow $65 million from the seven institutions. Other elements of value that the public would not normally consider include usable tax-loss carry-forwards (or better yet, creatable tax losses) in companies unencumbered by other obligations, and large asset values, whether reflected in accounting figures or not.

In fact, the trick in underwriting is that if an equity security is discount-priced based on business standards, it probably cannot be underwritten. The public that buys new common-stock issues tends to want instant performance, which cannot be gotten out of an issue that is not susceptible to being made popular. If an issue is popular, it is unlikely to be discount-priced based on business standards. However, once an issue has an identification that makes it susceptible to popularization, the underwriter will (a) popularize it and (b) try to price it at a discount based solely on stock market standards—that is, it will be priced at a price–earnings ratio moderately below the PE ratio at which the stocks of similar companies that are already public sell.

In giving the public a discount in new issues based on stock market standards, the underwriter tends to be moderate, not gross in his relative underpricing. The public, after all, tends to buy new-issue sizzles, not steaks, in the form of ephemerals (sponsorship, PE ratios, growth, and so on) that they believe should contribute to immediate performance. Purchases are not based on any fundamental bedrock of real knowledge about the business. Thus, suspicions are easily aroused. Too low a price—say, offering Corporation stock at ten times earnings when Anheuser-Busch is selling at twenty times earnings—would detract from the salability of the Corporation common-stock issue, whereas an offering at sixteen times earnings probably would contribute to it.

The New Public Company

Things are seldom what they seem,
Skim milk masquerades as cream.

W. S. GILBERT

As mentioned previously, the Brewing operation has been transformed into a new one with a different discipline—not better or worse, but different. The differences are basically as follows:

New Corporation	*Old Brewing*
Heavy debt load	Excess financial resources
More attuned to immediate results	
Requirements for public obligations including filings	
A common stock usable for employee incentives	
A common stock usable for acquisitions	
Emphasizes AFF—accounting fudge factor—reported earnings. (Especially pronounced in failure to write up assets to reflect Corporation's $106 million purchase price for Brewing's equity securities)	Emphasis TS—tax shelter

SUMMARY

Deals are not like a chess game, where by definition if one side wins, the other loses; they are not zero sum. A well-structured deal has something in it for everyone. Few readers of or writers on finance will ever be involved in the design and architecture of a deal of the dimensions described here. But an understanding and appreciation of its structure should help to provide some insights into the realities of a world of finance rarely seen but always present.

Appendix II

Creative Finance Applied to a Corporate Takeover— Leasco Data Processing Company

Somebody always has to pay for lunch.

If you are involved in corporate takeovers or mergers and acquisitions, commonly your most important problems do not revolve around whether a proposed acquisition is attractive on its own financial merits. Rather, the more usual problems revolve around whether or not a deal is "do-able": Can you actually obtain control or consummate a merger or other corporate reorganization at a cost that keeps the bargain a bargain? From a control buyer's point of view, it always is much easier to ferret out corporations whose stocks are selling at bargain prices than it is to get control of these corporations.

THE STORY

The subject covered in this appendix is how Leasco Data Processing Company—better known as Leasco and now named The Reliance Group—in the summer and fall of 1968 financed the purchase for cash of the large-block holdings of common stock of the Reliance Insurance Company. The purchase of the Reliance blocks was the key to making the takeover of Reliance by Leasco do-able. And to make the Reliance deal do-able, Leasco was willing, even anxious, to give investors who would put up the $57.5 million needed an outstandingly attractive bargain.

There never was any serious question that Reliance would be a uniquely good acquisition for Leasco, provided Leasco could obtain control of Reliance by issuing Leasco equity securities in the form of Leasco subordinated debentures, preferred stocks, common stock or warrants, or combinations thereof.

In the late 1960's, old-line, conservatively managed fire and casualty insurance companies were genuinely attractive acquisitions for "conglomerateurs." Not only did Leasco acquire Reliance (after being moderately hindered by competition from Data Processing Financial and General Corporation), but *inter alia,* Home Insurance was acquired by City Investing, Great American Insurance by National General Corporation, and Hartford Fire by International Telephone. Insurance-company stocks tended to be depressed because the companies were suffering underwriting losses from their pure insurance operations, and the stock market emphasized earnings from operations rather than other elements that made insurance companies valuable, namely, the steadily increasing profits from dividends and interest on their investment portfolios, and the huge pools of liquidity built up through their holdings of marketable bonds and stocks. Most important, it seemed likely to the acquirers that a good portion of this liquidity (called redundant capital or "surplus surplus") could be removed from the insurance companies and used by their new parents.

Over and above the possible use of surplus surplus, insurers such as Reliance and Hartford Fire were attractive to acquisition-minded companies, such as Leasco and International Telephone, for two additional reasons. First, there was the opportunity to manage earnings to be reported to stockholders in the future, but only if the acquisition could be accounted for in reports to stockholders through the use of pooling-of-interests accounting rules as they then existed (prior to November 1, 1970) rather than through purchase accounting. The insurance companies had invested a portion of their assets in common-stock portfolios that by the late 1960's had enjoyed substantial market appreciation. If the insurance companies could be acquired under a pooling, the acquiring companies would carry the insurance companies' portfolios in their own books at the insurance companies' original costs. In a purchase-accounting situation, on the other hand, the acquirers would have to write the insurers' portfolios up to the portfolios' market values and, in addition, would probably have to reflect as an intangible asset the excess of the acquirer's purchase price over the market value of the insurers' assets. (The acquirers' purchase price would be measured by the market value of the securities issued by the acquirer to consummate the takeover.)

Of course, if pooling occurred, the acquirer could virtually assure itself of being able to create future earnings in reporting to stockholders, because in order to create such instant earnings, all that Leasco or ITT would have to do would be to sell off (or to induce their insurance subsidiaries to sell off) common stocks for which the cost basis was well below market. The difference between proceeds of securities sales and the cost basis for the securities would equal earnings that could be reported to stockholders.

At the time it was endeavoring to acquire Reliance, Leasco knew through Reliance's consolidated balance sheet that as of December 31, 1967, the insurer's common-stock portfolio had a carrying value of $110.8 million, compared with a market value of $215 million. By the summer of 1968, the market value of that portfolio had appreciated. If pooling were used, Leasco, in its consolidated statement to be issued after the Reliance takeover, would carry the Reliance portfolio at $110.8 million. Even assuming that all warrants were exercised (which would bring a lot of new cash into Leasco) and that all convertible securities were converted, Leasco would still have under 10 million common shares outstanding. So, at the worst, there was a maximum potential for the creation by Leasco of over $10 per share of instant pretax earnings, provided it could pool Reliance.

The ability to pool Reliance would give Leasco a reservoir of future earnings that it might be able to call upon and that, after 25 percent capital-gains taxes, would still be in excess of $7 per share. This was viewed as quite a potential windfall by Leasco, which up to that time had never in any one year earned as much as $1 a share since it started business in 1961 (although Leasco stock was, in July 1968, selling between 65 and 70).

Leasco, though, it should be noted, would not have complete influence over the creation of instant earnings, since by contract the assets that remained in Reliance were to be under the control of the old Reliance management; however, insofar as Leasco would be able to extract assets from Reliance, it would have full control over the creation of instant earnings by selling low-cost stock out of its portfolio.

An additional area of attraction in acquiring companies such as Reliance and Hartford Fire was that they gave the acquirers entrée into the financial services industry. In particular, Leasco thought that the acquisition of Reliance, with its huge resources and widespread sales force coupled with Leasco management, could provide the foundation for building a financial empire that might encompass not only leasing and insurance, but also areas such as mutual funds and commercial banking. As a matter of fact, within three months of its acquisition of Reliance, Leasco turned its attention to acquiring control of Chemical New York, the parent company of Chemical Bank and Trust Company, the nation's fifth largest commercial banking institution. The stab at Chemical by Leasco was not only abortive, but also ill advised. It apparently resulted in the withdrawal of Wall Street sponsorship from Leasco,[49] and at the minimum contributed to Leasco's inability to consummate a public underwriting in 1969 or 1970, which has much to do with the outcome of the story that is the subject of this appendix.

Early in 1968, Leasco became convinced that Reliance would be

---

[49] An excellent account of the Leasco attempt to take over Chemical appears in John Brooks's *The Go-Go Years* (New York: Doubleday, 1974).

a desirable acquisition. Leasco was a small computer-leasing company founded in 1961 and run by Saul Steinberg, who at that time had not yet reached age thirty. For the year ending September 30, 1967, Leasco's total income was reported at $14.4 million, and its net income was reported at $1.8 million before taxes and $1.4 million after taxes. Stated net worth was about $16 million. The Leasco equity in mid-1968, though, was valued in the stock market at around $120 million. Reliance, on the other hand, had net premiums earned of around $300 million in 1967; its net income was almost $20 million and its stated net worth was $230 million. Before Leasco became interested, the value the stock market placed on Reliance's equity rarely exceeded $190 million. By any reasonable non-stock-market statistical measure, Reliance was ten times the company Leasco was. But by the one most important stock market measure—stock price—Reliance was only about one and one-half times the company Leasco was; and in addition, Leasco was on the move up, whereas Reliance seemed to be going nowhere.

Leasco became interested in Reliance after it had been solicited by the New York Stock Exchange member firm of Carter, Berlind and Weill through a report written by a security analyst, Edward Netter, who specialized in insurance stocks. For their services, Carter, Berlind and Weill (now Shearson, Hayden Stone) received a fee of $750,000 after the takeover was concluded successfully. Initially, through early April 1968 Leasco purchased in the open market 132,000 of the 5.5 million Reliance shares outstanding, at about $33 per share.

In the spring of 1968, the Leasco management, together with partners of Leasco's investment banker, White, Weld, approached the Reliance management about Leasco's acquiring Reliance. Leasco was rebuffed, and Reliance management was probably prepared to continue to oppose Leasco no matter what proposals for a Leasco-Reliance combination Leasco might make. Reliance opposition would make a deal manifestly less do-able by Leasco, and less valuable even if it were do-able. If Leasco could obtain Reliance management cooperation (or failing that, an absence of Reliance management opposition), it would make a transaction more feasible and more valuable for Leasco for the following reasons:

1. Cooperation, or the absence of opposition, would likely short-circuit any others who might want to bid for Reliance, such as Data Processing Financial and General.
2. Stockholder solicitation would be made immensely easier, because Leasco otherwise probably could not obtain a stockholder list or have Reliance mail an exchange offer on its behalf. Without access to a stockholder list, Leasco would be able to solicit Reliance shareholders only through newspaper advertisements or through a proxy contest, which of itself would result in all sorts of new timing, legal and administrative problems.
3. Reliance obstruction in the courts and with regulatory agencies—the Securities and Exchange Commission and the Pennsylvania Insurance Commission—would be eliminated if management was at least neutral.
4. With friendly management, a smaller consideration could be offered to Reliance stockholders. When Leasco thought Reliance would oppose, it prepared to offer Reliance shareholders a package of securities consisting of subordinated debentures and warrants, which for tax purposes would be construed to be an installment sale, making it almost the equivalent of a tax-free transaction to Reliance shareholders. After Reliance management opposition was eliminated, preferred stock was substituted for the debentures. This not only resulted in the exchange offer's becoming fully taxable to the Reliance shareholders, but it also created the environment under which Leasco might be able to account for the Reliance acquisition as a pooling of interests.
5. The removal of uncertainty caused by management opposition made it manifestly easier to assure Leasco that enough Reliance shares would be tendered for control (50 percent) and/or for accounting purposes (95 percent), so that Leasco could account for the transaction as a pooling of interests. With management opposition, it would be difficult to get Wall Street's arbitrage community interested in the transaction; once interested, they

would purchase Reliance shares to tender, making a profit not only on the spread in price between Reliance securities purchased and Leasco securities sold short, but also on the soliciting dealer fee of $.90 per share, which would be paid them for each Reliance share tendered to Leasco. If arbitrageurs thought there were reasonable prospects that the exchange offer would not succeed, they would forgo purchasing Reliance. Contrariwise, confidence in its success would produce the purchasers of Reliance shares to be tendered, resulting in just the type of bandwagon effect that would be helpful in getting stock tendered to Leasco.

Leasco could see, however, that the active Reliance management might be vulnerable. Its shareholdings in its own company amounted to only about 43,000 shares. There were in existence blocks of Reliance stock, the equivalent of almost 800,000 shares (or 14 percent) of the outstanding stock, which were held by fourteen stockholders of record, who had exchanged shares in small insurance companies they owned for Reliance stock, principally in 1963 and 1965. The beneficial owners of these shares were Corroon & Black Corp., and in Chicago, the family of Alfred MacArthur, who was deceased. The Corroon interests and the MacArthur interests each had one representative out of the seventeen seats on the Reliance board. They were not part of the day-to-day management. Control of these shares by Leasco might be the lever that would avert active opposition by the Reliance management.

Leasco, though, could not be sure that even if it obtained control of this 14 percent block, it would be able to induce the Reliance management not to oppose a tender. First, virtually all these shares were in the form of Reliance Class A common, and the A stock had very limited rights of conversion into Reliance common; indeed, some of the A shares issued would not become convertible until 1979. Each share of Class A common was equivalent in all respects to ten shares of common, except that the A had only one vote per share rather than ten. Thus, although the A shares represented a 14 percent economic interest in the Reliance equity, they represented only a 1.4 percent voting interest; it might take years before that 1.4 percent voting interest could be changed into a percentage that would be of control use for Leasco. Furthermore, even if Leasco were to obtain a majority of Reliance's voting power, it could still take years to obtain a majority of the Reliance board of directors. Reliance had a system of class election under which directors were elected for staggered terms of four years; in addition, there was cumulative voting. Thus, assuming four of sixteen directors stood for election each year, if Leasco had a majority of Reliance's stock, it might be able to elect only three directors a year: it would take Leasco three years after it had a majority of Reliance's stock to elect a majority of the board of directors.

Against this background, Leasco's strategy was to attempt to tie down this 14 percent block, so that Leasco could call upon it in the event it obtained a majority interest in Reliance. If Leasco were armed with the potential ownership of a 14 percent equity interest in Reliance, it felt it might be able to bargain with the Reliance management, so that it would no longer oppose a tender, and indeed, with luck might even favor it.

The A holders made it known in July 1968 that they might be willing to commit to sell their shares to Leasco, but they wanted two things—cash, not Leasco paper, and a premium above the then market for Reliance common. Leasco accommodated them, entering into an agreement with the Corroon & Black and the MacArthur interests on July 23, 1968, at which time Reliance common was selling at 69. The essential elements of the July 23 agreement were as follows:

1. If Leasco accepted any Reliance shares under the tender offer it proposed to make, Leasco would be required to buy all these Corroon and MacArthur shareholdings for $72 per share in cash. If Leasco did not accept any Reliance shares under the tender offer, it would not be required to purchase any of these shares.

2. Payment of the $72 was to be made either by Leasco directly or by arranging that these selling shareholders tender their Reliance shares for Leasco securities, which would then be immediately sold to certain designated buyers to yield the sellers $72 per share in cash for their Reliance holdings. This latter provision became operative, and the $72 purchasers in September were a group of institutional investors.

By virtue of the July 23 agreement, Leasco had tied down this 14 percent interest without any cash outlay. It would only be committed to purchase them if Leasco obtained a majority of the Reliance shares, because of the terms of the tender offer that Leasco need not acquire any Reliance shares unless 50 percent of the outstanding stock was tendered. Furthermore, under the July agreement Leasco in effect obtained an option either to use its own cash and borrowings aggregating $57.5 million for the purchase of these shares or to substitute a third party or parties that would purchase Leasco securities from the Corroon and MacArthur interests for the same $57.5 million.

Under the terms of the exchange tender offer, the Leasco securities to be issued for a maximum of 5,582,540 Reliance shares were to be as follows: for each Reliance common share, Leasco was to exchange one share of Leasco $2.20 cumulative preferred stock, convertible into Leasco common at $90 per share (or into .6111 Leasco common), and one half of a Leasco warrant, two of which would entitle the holder, for a period of ten years, to buy one share of Leasco common at $87 per share.

With the July 23 agreement a *fait accompli,* Leasco now reentered negotiations with the Reliance management. These negotiations, unlike earlier efforts, were successful: Reliance management agreed to be neutral in connection with the forthcoming tender offer, and to (or in any event, did) mail the Leasco tender offer to all Reliance shareholders. The substance of the Leasco-Reliance pact was embodied in an August 1, 1968, agreement, the principal terms of which were as follows:

1. Reliance management would not oppose Leasco's removing the surplus surplus from Reliance, an amount that Leasco estimated was about $125 million.
2. For five years, Leasco was to elect only one third plus one of the Reliance board of directors.
3. Reliance was to take no action outside the ordinary course of business without the affirmative vote of at least two thirds of its directors.
4. A. Addison (Bill) Roberts was to continue as chief executive

officer and a director of Reliance. Parallel to this, Mr. Roberts also obtained a long-term employment contract at a substantial pay increase. The long-term contract for Bill Roberts probably protected Leasco at least as much as it did Roberts, because he was viewed as an exceptionally able operating insurance executive.

With management opposition removed, Leasco was ready to make its tender offer to exchange the package of Leasco preferred and warrants for Reliance common. The offer was made on Monday, August 19, 1968. The previous Friday, Leasco common had closed at 87⅝; thus, if the preferred stock to be issued on a share-for-share basis for Reliance common was valued at its conversion parity (.6111 common), it would have a market value of $53.55 per share. In addition, warrants exactly the same as Leasco was proposing to issue in the exchange were already trading over-the-counter at about $43 per warrant. The market value of the Leasco package, consisting of one preferred and one-half warrant, was therefore $75.05 (or $53.55 plus half of 43). Reliance closed on August 16 at 66½; Reliance shareholders were induced to tender for the Leasco package because of the almost nine-point spread between the market price of the Leasco package and the market price of Reliance common.

The Leasco exchange offer was a rip-roaring success, and by the second week of September it became obvious that Leasco not only would obtain control of Reliance, but also would obtain over 95 percent of the Reliance stock, in which event Leasco's independent auditors, Touche Ross and Co., would permit the Reliance acquisition to be accounted for as a full pooling of interests, provided other necessary conditions were met.

Now Leasco was faced with the problem of paying for the shares to be purchased at $72 cash from the Corroon and Black and the MacArthur interests in accordance with the terms of the July 23 agreement. Leasco believed it could pay for the shares from its own treasury, because it now had $46 million, most of which had been raised almost concurrently through the sale of Eurobonds by a new Leasco subsidiary, Leasco World Trade. However, Leasco clearly preferred to have the $57.5 million paid by third parties for two reasons.

First, Leasco believed that if it reinvested its own funds into productive activities rather than in the repurchase of its own securities, it would grow much faster. Second, insofar as Leasco itself repurchased this 14 percent interest, it would be unable to fully pool Reliance's accounting data, but would instead be stuck with a now-extinct accounting hybrid—part pooling, part purchase. Full pooling meant more benefits for future earnings than part pooling, part purchase.

Leasco turned to White, Weld to structure a package that third parties would buy. By the second week of September, the Leasco package had a stock market value of around 80 to 83 per unit. However, for the amount of units involved (799,050), it was too much to expect the third parties to pay the Corroon and MacArthur groups $72 per unit in cash virtually simultaneously with these groups' having exchanged their Reliance shares for the Leasco package. No third party buyer would be able to sell that amount of Leasco equity in the open market at 80 to 83 in the absence of a registration statement with the Securities and Exchange Commission. Offering about 800,000 of Leasco units at this time by what the market might interpret as being quasi-insiders might also depress the market from its 80–83 level.

Against this background, White, Weld and Lehman Brothers, which were now acting jointly as Leasco's main investment bankers, structured a deal that would be inordinately attractive to their institutional clients. In effect, Leasco would use its credit to guarantee that, at worst, a purchaser of the units for $72 could at the end of one year obtain his money back plus a return of 15.6 percent, most of which would be taxable as a capital gain. At best, the purchaser would obtain for his units $72, plus $.75 for each month the unit was held, plus a participation in the profits to be realized over $72, and plus $.75 per month in the event the units were sold pursuant to a planned public underwriting of these preferred shares and warrants. The investors were to obtain one half of the gain from the underwriting, as measured by the difference between 90 and 72, plus $.75 per month. Leasco was to pocket the other half. Insofar as the units were publicly sold at a price in excess of 90, the investors were to have one quarter of that gain and Leasco three quarters. With a buoyant market for Leasco, these investors might even be able to obtain a return of 55 percent or more on a no-risk or low-risk investment.*

This deal was embodied in a three-party contract, the Exchange and Purchase Agreement (or the E. & P.), which was dated September 17, 1968, and which was closed on September 19, the day the Leasco package attained a market value of 88⅝. The pertinent terms of the E. & P. were as follows:

1. There were three parties to the E. & P., namely, the selling stockholders, the purchasing investors and Leasco.
2. Sellers were to tender their Reliance shares in exchange for the Leasco package, and the purchasers were to acquire the Leasco package from the sellers at $72 cash per unit.
3. For the next year, the purchasers were to be guaranteed by Leasco proceeds of not less than $72 per share, plus $.75 for each month or portion thereof that the Leasco package was held by the purchasers. This $72 plus $.75 was known as "the guaranteed price."
4. The purchasers were to be given one half of the difference between $90 and the guaranteed price in the event that the units were sold, and also were to obtain one quarter of the guaranteed price in excess of $90.
5. Leasco was to arrange at its own expense (if it could) that these units would be registered with the Securities and Exchange Commission, so that they could be sold publicly, preferably through an underwritten public offering.

It is interesting to see who the institutional investors were who purchased this package, since they appear to be a more or less typical cross section of trusts, pension plans, mutual funds and insurance companies.

*Theoretically, the return on equity could have been infinite, assuming that the purchaser securing his purchase with Leasco's credit borrowed all of the purchase price. The purchaser would pay over the one year, say, 7 percent interest, which would compare with his guaranteed minimum return of 15.6 percent. However, the type of investors who bought the deal was institutions, which typically invest their own funds and for which the 15.6 percent to 50 percent return is more appropriate.

Institution	% of 799,050 Units Subscribed for
Continental Illinois National Bank, in various fiduciary capacities	28%
Chase Manhattan Bank, for various employee benefit trusts	26%
Commonwealth Capital Fund, Inc.	9%
Technology Fund, Inc.	5%
U.S. Trust Co., as trustee and/or agent	5%
Yale University	5%
Connecticut General Life Insurance Co.	3%
Bankhaus Burkhardt	2%
State Farm Mutual Automobile Insurance Co.	2%
Banque de Financement	2%
Banque Lambert S.C.S.	2%
N. M. Rothschild & Sons	2%
Employers Mutual Liability Insurance Co.	2%
Exchequer Associates	2%
Old Kent Bank, trustee	2%
L.D.P. Associates	2%
State Farm Life Insurance Co.	< 1%
State Farm Fire & Casualty	< 1%
General American Life	< 1%
First National Bank of Chicago, as agent	≤ 1%
	100%

First and foremost, the transaction provided the investors a very high return of 15.6 percent, at a time when Leasco was borrowing from banks at 6½ percent to 7½ percent. The investment, therefore, had considerable safety because of the Leasco guaranty. The return of 15.6 percent would be obtained as follows if the investors held the Leasco package for the full year:

Dividend on $2.20 convertible preferred	$2.20
$.75 per month for 12 months	9.00
Total return	$11.20
Return as % of $72 purchase price	15.6%

Most of the return had better tax-shelter characteristics than it would have had if it had been taxable to the investors as interest income. The $9 in particular was taxable at capital-gains rates. This tax-sheltered return to the investor would not per se result in diminished tax payments to Internal Revenue, because Leasco was not able to deduct from its tax return preferred dividends or any payments of the guaranteed price, as it would interest payments.

However, 15.6 percent was only the minimum return to the investors. Remember that at the time that the E. & P. closed, the Leasco package had a market value of 88⅝. Suppose that in about six months there could be a public offering of the units at 85 net; the investor would then receive a return at an annual rate of 27.4 percent, all with having undertaken only very minimal risk. The 27.4 percent return would be computed as follows:

6 months' dividend on $2.20 preferred	$1.10
$.75 per month for 6 months	4.50
½ of the difference between 85 and the guaranteed price of $72 plus $4.50	4.25
Total return	$9.85
6 months' return based on $72 purchase price	13.7%
6 months' return annualized	27.4%

Even the 27.4 percent return must have seemed modest during this period, because Leasco was a dynamic market performer; one could just as soon have postulated a public offering for the Leasco package at 95, 105 or 115, rather than at 85.

From Leasco's point of view, if the public offering had been consummated in, say, six months at then-prevailing market prices, Leasco would not only have purchased the key block necessary for it to obtain control of Reliance with virtually no cash outlay, it would also have made money on the deal. Depending on whether the price of a public offering six months later was 85, 95 or 105 net, cash inflows to Leasco per unit from the operation of the E. & P. would have been as follows:

	Public Offering Price per Unit		
	85	*95*	*105*
Cash outlays by Leasco: preferred dividend	$1.10	$1.10	$1.10
Cash inflow to Leasco: ½ of difference over $76.50 ($72 plus $4.50 to price of 90)	4.25	6.75	6.75
¾ of excess over 90	—	3.75	11.25
	4.25	10.50	18.00
Net cash benefit to Leasco per unit	$3.15	$9.40	$16.90
Aggregate cash benefit to Leasco	$2,517,000	$7,911,000	$13,504,000

If there had been a public offering as contemplated, both Leasco and the institutional investors would have profited enormously. It was not that both were going to get free lunches, but rather that the stock market public that was willing to pay extra premium prices for Leasco equities was supposed to treat both the institutional investors and Leasco to lunch.

Although the institutional investors had a highly attractive deal whether the shares they held were to be sold to the public at premium prices or whether the institutional investors were to receive only the guaranteed price, the transaction, like all transactions, had some risks and uncertainties. Many of these investors probably realized that Leasco was not the best credit risk in the world; all realized that under the securities laws, they would become statutory underwriters if there was to be a public offering of their units, in which case there would be some exposure to potential legal liabilities. As a matter of fact, a stockholder derivative action was brought by a Leasco shareholder against the institutional investors, claiming that Leasco was harmed because the E. & P. constituted a loan to Leasco at exorbitant rates and was in violation of margin regulations.* Nonetheless, the institutional investors did make a highly attractive deal, probably as close to a free lunch as anyone in the financial community ever gets.

Leasco would have done brilliantly had a public offering above the guaranteed price ever taken place. Not only would the July 23 agreement coupled with the E. & P. have enabled Leasco to create an environment under which it could get control of Reliance relatively easily, but it would also have enabled Leasco to share in the profits created by the sale of Leasco stock that had been issued for Reliance shares.

THE POSTSCRIPT

Unlike the institutional investors, Leasco had meaningful exposure; if a public underwriting was not accomplished by September 1969, Leasco would have had to pay the guaranteed price with its own funds. But subsequent events showed that this was not the worst fate that could befall Leasco; a fair argument could be made that had not Leasco acquired Reliance, Leasco today might be insolvent, or in any event, in quite serious trouble. All Leasco's operations other than Reliance proved to be operating disappointments and cash drains. In early 1974, Leasco was renamed The Reliance Group.

Leasco was unable to accomplish a public offering of the units in 1969. We are not certain of the reasons for this, but it seems a fair guess that Leasco's abortive attempt to acquire control of Chemical

---

*The suit did not result in any material liability to the institutional investors.

Bank in early 1969 was a contributing factor. It should be noted, too, that during early 1969 the market prices of virtually all computer-leasing stocks weakened. The Wall Street community rapidly withdrew support from Leasco, and its investment bankers produced various stated reasons for no longer underwriting Leasco securities.

By July 1969, Leasco was attempting to extend the terms of the E. & P. until October 1970. Many of the original institutional investors, holding about 25 percent of the units, refused to go along. Leasco found other institutional investors to take their place by paying the original investors the guaranteed price of $81 ($72, plus $.75 for each of twelve months). In order to induce the other original institutional investors and the new institutional investors to, in effect, extend the E. & P., Leasco offered the original E. & P. terms plus a bonus that was to depend on stock prices and was to be anywhere between $1 per unit and $3 per unit; it ended up being $1 per unit. However, the second E. & P. probably was not as attractive as the first year's E. & P.; unlike September 1968, September 1969 was not a time in which most people were caught up in euphoric optimism about how wonderful a stock market performer Leasco was likely to be in the next year. On October 1, 1970, Leasco had to make good on its guarantee, at which time it repurchased all 799,050 units at the guaranteed price for an aggregate cash outlay of over $72 million. By 1970, this put quite a crimp in Leasco's finances.

INVESTMENT LESSONS

In our view, the transactions described here are examples of the types of creative finance that can be used to accomplish corporate objectives, and of how astute investors can be prime beneficiaries of the product of someone else's creative finance. The essential ingredient that created the environment that permitted the institutional investors to come close to getting a free lunch was the stock market appraisal of Leasco. As long as the public might be willing to pay ultrahigh prices for Leasco equities, Leasco was more than willing to give the institutional investors the benefit of a bargain, just so long as it helped Leasco obtain its objectives. Leasco's objectives were to obtain control of Reliance by paper only, not cash; to account for the Reliance acquisition as a pooling; and to not commit to purchase a large block of Reliance stock unless that block was part of a control block. The institutional investors aided Leasco in those goals.*

It is probable that the type of opportunity that was offered here to the institutional investors would never be available to outside, passive investors who lacked know-who. Yet, we feel the appendix is instructive for all our readers because (1) it serves as a good example of the types of things many intelligent people are involved with in the finance industry, and (2) it gives the reader an insight into a financial instrument with which he may not be familiar, namely, the guaranty.

The Leasco-type guaranty is something commonly used in private transactions, in part because it results in capital-gains treatment for the buyers' profit and an off-balance-sheet liability for the issuer of the guaranty. In fact, the types of arrangement found in the E. & P. is known by many as a put-call agreement. "Put" means that the holder of a security can require someone else, under certain conditions, to repurchase that security: that is, the institutional investors could force Leasco or Leasco's nominee to pay them the guaranteed price at the end of a year. "Call" means that the holder can be required by someone else to sell the security he holds: that is, Leasco could, as a practical matter, have required the institutional investors to sell their holdings, as long as the institutional investors got at least the guaranteed price plus a market appreciation participation, if any.†

Whether or not a deal is potentially do-able is an important market consideration. Reliance stock was undoubtedly a very sound, fundamental value in late 1967 and early 1968 when it was selling in the mid-30's. If the company had been invulnerable to takeover and wholly uninterested in merger, it is fair to say there might have been moderate appreciation as earnings improved and as the market gave

---

*There is some question as to whether Leasco should ever have accounted for the Reliance acquisition on a pooling-of-interest basis, regardless of who paid cash for the 14 percent interest—but that subject is not part of this book.

†In fact, the lever in Leasco's call was that if the institutional investors chose not to heed the call, Leasco's guarantee, or put, would no longer be operative.

increased recognition to the business's exceptionally good quality. But it is very hard to postulate that without Leasco, or someone like Leasco, in the picture the market values attributable to Reliance common would have been in the 80's in the fall of 1968 and over 100 in late 1968 and early 1969. Leasco would not have been in the picture if it was obvious that Reliance was not a do-able deal.

The Leasco-Reliance transactions raise three very interesting questions, good answers to which are certainly a (if not the) royal road to investment riches.

1. How do you appraise managements such as Leasco's?
2. How do you spot do-able deals such as Reliance's before someone else does?
3. How do you get to be an institutional investor who is shown highly attractive private financings such as the E. & P.?

Unfortunately, we do not have magic answers.

THE APPRAISAL OF MANAGEMENT

The Leasco management showed a high, even rare, degree of ability in first recognizing the values of Reliance to Leasco, and in then engineering the takeover. Many conglomerate managements in 1968, on the other hand, demonstrated no abilities other than a knack for promoting the prices of the stocks of the companies they controlled. These others were just good at go-go. Not so with Leasco. The Reliance takeover represents strong evidence that Saul Steinberg and his associates were intelligent, resourceful businessmen who understood not only how to avoid the risks of committing cash to a deal that might not be do-able, but also what their company needed in the way of an acquisition and how to get it.

Yet, within a few months Leasco came a cropper, and the company was unable to close out the Reliance transaction by selling securities to the public rather than by using Leasco's corporate cash. It is possible that Leasco's inability to close the Reliance transaction via a public offering of the securities held by institutional investors was absolutely beyond its control: market prices did sag in 1969. It is possible, too, that the Leasco management itself was a major contributor to the company's inability to obtain a public offering: the abortive stab at acquiring Chemical Bank in February 1969 used up much of the good will and high regard Leasco had built up in the financial community. Whereas engineering the acquisition of Reliance was evidence of management brilliance, coveting Chemical was evidence of management insensitivity and stupidity, and yet both were the same management.

Which type of deal maker was the Leasco management? Brilliant, or insensitive and stupid? In our view, it was both. It accomplished a major financial tour de force in 1968, but came a cropper in 1969. Brilliant management in one context is not necessarily brilliant management in another; those who are good deal makers at one time may be bad in another period. A talent for obtaining operational efficiency, for example, may obscure a predilection for misunderstanding sophisticated finance. In 1968, there were good stock market reasons for equating good management with aggressive management; in 1975, there were good stock market reasons for equating good management with nonaggressive management (those whose policies keep their companies liquid). It is not necessarily contradictory that the same Leasco people who were such brilliant deal makers in 1968 were somewhat less than brilliant after 1969; it is possible that the same boldness that contributed to their company's positive accomplishments in 1968 also contributed to Leasco's failures after 1968.

Because it is so difficult to appraise managements, we do not believe that outside investors should, as a rule, pay premium prices to invest in the stocks of companies with superior managements. There usually are available many common stocks of good-grade companies where management is superior and where the price of the stock does not reflect that superiority.

On the other side of the coin, we think all investors should avoid the securities of companies deemed to have bad managements, regardless of the price of the equity security. This is an essential element of the financial-integrity approach. Bad managements are, in our view, easier to spot than good managements (see Chapter 6, "Following the Paper Trail"). Bad managements are marked by self-dealing and/or ineptness in virtually all areas except one—protecting their own positions. "Bad management," it should be noted, does not specifically refer to managements that do not contribute to their companies' having favorable stock market prices. Reliance had good management before the Leasco takeover, because they were skilled in operating a large insurance business as a going concern. As a matter of fact, one of the factors to look for in spotting do-able deals is companies that are well managed, at least in the custodial, going-concern sense. It is an untrue and misleading myth that companies seeking acquisitions—for example, Leasco—look for companies with bad managements. The opposite is true. Leasco would not have been interested in Reliance if they did not believe it was a well-run going concern. To have been interested otherwise when Leasco had no operating experience in the insurance industry really would have been stupid.

SPOTTING DO-ABLE DEALS

There is a school of thought that contends that the most do-able deals are those where shares are widely held and actively traded, and where directors and management own very little stock. This certainly was not the case for Leasco-Reliance, where there were blocks that accounted for 14 percent of the common stock issue; if those blocks could be tied up, Reliance would become (as it did) quite do-able, and if it could not, the prospects for obtaining control would be quite discouraging. Thus, there are no hard and fast rules by which an outsider without any inside contacts can tell whether a specific situation can or cannot be a do-able deal. Rather, frequently in a corporation there is a person or a few people who can deliver control, either by active cooperation or by a failure to oppose a takeover. Among potential acquirers, there are those who would try to accomplish an acquisition in a contested takeover and those who would never contest for control, regardless of how attractive the target company is or how much the acquirer needs to get control of the target. You usually cannot know who would do what without information from the people who will be active doers. In other words, you need know-who.

This inability of outsiders lacking know-who to spot do-able deals brings out another point for these investors. It probably pays to diversify such a portfolio of securities. Reliance was an excellent value in 1968, but without takeover activity it might have been a mediocre performer. We do not know of any a priori way for outsiders to spot such takeover interest where there is a lack of know-who, but it is our feeling that a portfolio of five Reliances bought at any time would probably work out well, not because all of them would be taken over, but because one or two might.

Although it may be wise to diversify where an investor lacks know-who, there is no logical course but to concentrate in areas where the investor has know-who. We do not mean this in the "hot tip" sense. Rather, as a hypothetical example, it is logical that Reliance, selling at around 40, would have been a good stock to concentrate in for an investor who was told by a member of the Corroon family that, while no transaction was pending and while he wasn't sure, he would be inclined to sell if someone would offer over $50 per common share for all their Reliance holdings.

HOW DO YOU GET TO BE SHOWN E. & P.-TYPE FINANCING?

We do not know. It is a matter of (a) having available resources and (b) having built up years of successful relationships with firms like White, Weld and Lehman Brothers who create E. & P. types of transactions. Needless to say, deals as attractive as the E. & P. are few and far between; each of the institutional investors involved had bought many deals that entailed considerably more exposure and considerably less promise of reward than the E. & P.

Appendix III

A Guide to SEC Corporate Filings—What They Are/ What They Tell You

(Reprinted Courtesy of Disclosure Incorporated)

◆◆◆◆

In our uncertain world, feelings about securities can be summarized in one way by a personal estimate of the likelihood of various changes in future earnings.

JAMES H. LORIE and MARY T. HAMILTON
The Stock Market—Theories and Evidence

IN THE UNCERTAIN world described in this book, feelings about securities probably ought *not* to be summarized, but if so, the summary would start with financial-integrity variables—variables that do not, at first blush, focus on estimates of changes in future earnings. A crucial emphasis of this book is that in terms of equity investing, the average investors ought to be familiar with public disclosure documents so that he can make judgments as to what his feelings about securities ought to be. And in order to develop feelings about a specific security, he may or may not find it important to estimate changes in future earnings. However, whether or not earnings estimates are important, disclosure documents clearly are.

The more the investor reads actual disclosure documents, the more meaningful and reliable they will become to him. These documents are readily available, and most of the reading is not too difficult, even for the neophyte. With practice, of course, the neophyte will become an old hand.

As a start toward becoming an old hand, it seems helpful to have a brief summary of the types of information that are contained in disclosure documents. Disclosure Incorporated has published just such a summary. With the kind permission of Disclosure Incorporated, that booklet* is reprinted in its entirety here.

FOREWORD

Full disclosure to the public of information filed with the Securities and Exchange Commission has been required of that agency by law since its formation over forty years ago. Today, more than 100,000 filings are made annually by over 11,000 companies, with page volume exceeding 2,000,000.

More and more individuals who require specific and detailed information about public corporations for investment analysis, accounting and legal research, and broad corporate intelligence have come to recognize SEC reports as the most comprehensive source available.

This booklet is designed to serve as a basic introduction to the content of major SEC reports so that you can consider how this invaluable information source can fit into your personal or professional research program.

The following pages present a brief synopsis of major SEC filings with details on what each contains, along with an explanation of the several DISCLOSURE Incorporated products designed to provide convenient access to this wealth of corporate data.

*Copyright © 1978 by Disclosure, Incorporated. All rights reserved. Free copies of the booklet are available from Disclosure Incorporated, 4827 Rugby Ave., Washington, D.C. 20014.

DISCLOSURE

A basic purpose of the Federal securities laws is to provide disclosure of material financial and other information on companies seeking to raise capital through the public offering of their securities, as well as companies whose securities are already publicly held. This aims at enabling investors to evaluate the securities of these companies on an informed and realistic basis.

The Securities Act of 1933 is a *disclosure* statute. It generally requires that, before securities may be offered to the public, a registration statement must be filed with the Commission disclosing prescribed categories of information. Before the sale of securities can begin, the registration statement must become "effective," and investors must be furnished a prospectus containing the most significant information in the registration statement.

The Securities Exchange Act of 1934 deals in large part with securities already outstanding and requires the registration of securities listed on a national securities exchange, as well as over-the-counter securities in which there is a substantial public interest. Issuers of registered securities must file annual and other periodic reports designed to provide a public file of current material information. The Exchange Act also requires disclosure of material information to holders of registered securities in solicitations of proxies for the election of directors or approval of corporate action at a stockholders' meeting, or in attempts to acquire control of a company through a tender offer or other planned stock acquisition. It provides that insiders of companies whose equity securities are registered must report their holdings and transactions in all equity securities of their companies.

I O - K

This is the official annual business and financial report which must be filed by most companies. The financial section (Part I) must be filed within 90 days of a company's fiscal year end. Supporting data

(Part II) of the 10-K contains the information normally required in a proxy statement. It must be filed within 120 days of fiscal year-end if a proxy is not filed separately in that period. Schedules to financial statements may be filed by amendment within the 120-day limit. No other source of corporate information provides more comprehensive or current information about a company than this report, with its schedules, exhibits and amendments.

ITEMS REPORTED IN FORM 10-K

Part I

1. *Business.* Identifies principal products and services of the company, principal markets and methods of distribution and, if "material," competitive factors, backlog and expectation of fulfillment, availability of raw materials, importance of patents, licenses, and franchises, estimated cost of research, number of employees, and effects of compliance with ecological laws; if there is more than one line of business, for each of the last five fiscal years a statement of total sales and net income for each line which, during either of the last two fiscal years, accounted for 10 percent or more of total sales or pre-tax income.

2. *Summary of Operations.* Summary of operations for each of the last five fiscal years and any additional years required to keep the summary from being misleading (per-share earnings and dividends are included). Includes explanatory material describing reasons for changes in revenues, earnings, etc.

3. *Properties.* Location and character of principal plants, mines, and other important properties and if held in fee or leased

4. *Parents and Subsidiaries.* List or diagram of all parents and subsidiaries and for each named, the percentage of voting securities owned, or other basis of control

5. *Legal Proceedings.* Brief description of material legal proceedings pending; when civil rights or ecological statutes are involved, proceedings must be disclosed

6. *Increases and Decreases in Outstanding Securities.* Information for each security including reacquired securities, new issues, securities issued in exchange for property, services or other securities, and new securities resulting from modification of outstanding securities

7. *Changes in Securities and Changes in Security for Registered Securities.* Material changes in rights of the holders of any class of registered security, or withdrawal or substitution of assets securing any class of registered securities of the registrant

8. *Defaults upon Senior Securities.* Material defaults in the payment of principal, interest, sinking fund or purchase fund installment, dividend, or other material default not cured within 30 days

9. *Approximate Number of Equity Security Holders.* Holders of record for each class of equity securities as of the end of the fiscal year

10. *Submission of Matters to a Vote of Security Holders.* Information relating to the convening of a meeting of shareholders, whether annual or special, and the matters voted upon, with particular emphasis on the election of directors

11. *Executive Officers of the Registrant.* List of all executive officers, nature of family relationship between them, positions and offices held

12. *Indemnification of Directors and Officers.* General effect under which any director or officer is insured or indemnified against any liability which he may incur in his capacity as such

13. *Financial Statements and Exhibits Filed.* Complete, audited annual financial information, and a list of exhibits filed

Part II

14. *Principal Security Holders and Security Holdings of Management.* Identification of owners of 10 percent or more of any class of securities and of securities held by directors and officers according to amount and percent of each class

15. *Directors of the Registrant.* Name, office, term of office, and specific background data on each
16. *Remuneration of Directors and Officers.* List of each director and 5 highest paid executive officers with aggregate annual remuneration exceeding $50,000—and total paid all officers and directors. (See footnote on page 83; requirements have been changed)
17. *Options Granted to Management to Purchase Securities.* Options granted to or exercised by directors and officers since the beginning of the fiscal year
18. *Interest of Management and Others in Certain Transactions.* Material changes in significant transactions of such things as assets, pension, retirement, savings or other similar plans, or unusual loans

Schedules

I. Marketable securities. Other security investments
II. Amounts due from directors, officers, and principal holders of equity securities other than affiliates
III. Investments in securities of affiliates
IV. Indebtedness of affiliates (not current)
V. Property, plant, and equipment
VI. Reserves for depreciation, depletion, and amortization of property, plant and equipment
VII. Intangible assets
VIII. Reserves for depreciation and amortization of intangible assets
IX. Bonds, mortgages, and similar debt
X. Indebtedness to affiliates (not current)
XI. Guarantees of securities of other issuers
XII. Reserves
XIII. Capital shares
XIV. Warrants or rights

XV. Other securities
XVI. Supplementary profit and loss information
XVII. Income from dividends (equity in net profit and loss of affiliates)

1 0 - Q

This is the quarterly financial report filed by most companies, which, although unaudited, provides a continuing view of a company's financial position during the year. It must be filed within 45 days of the close of a fiscal quarter.

ITEMS REPORTED IN FORM 1 0 - Q

Part I
Financial Statements

1. Income Statement
2. Balance Sheet
3. Statement of source and application of funds
4. A narrative analysis of material changes in the amount of revenue and expense items in relation to previous quarters, including the effect of any changes in accounting principles

Part II

1. Legal Proceedings. Brief description of material legal proceedings pending; when civil rights or ecological statutes are involved, proceedings must be disclosed
2. Changes in Securities. Material changes in the rights of holders of any class of registered security
3. Changes in Security for Registered Securities. Material withdrawal

or substitution of assets securing any class of registered securities of the registrant

4. Defaults upon Senior Securities. Material defaults in the payment if principal, interest, sinking fund or purchase fund installment, dividend, or other material default not cured within 30 days

5. Increase in Amount Outstanding of Securities or Indebtedness. Amounts of new issues, continuing issues or reissues of any class of security or indebtedness with a reasonable statement of the purposes for which the proceeds will be used

6. Decreases in Amount Outstanding of Securities or Indebtedness. Amounts of decreases, through one or more transactions, in any class of outstanding securities or indebtedness

7. Submission of Matters to a Vote of Security Holders. Information relating to the convening of a meeting of shareholders, whether annual or special, and the matters voted upon, with particular emphasis on the election of directors

8. Other materially Important Events. Information on any other item of interest to shareholders not already provided for in this form.

8 - K

This is a report of unscheduled material events or corporate changes deemed of importance to the shareholders or to the SEC—changes in the control of the registrant; acquisition or disposition of assets; institution of bankruptcy or receivership; change in auditor and other material events. The report is filed within 15 days of the occurrence of a reportable event.

7 - Q

This is the quarterly financial report filed by real estate companies in lieu of the 10-Q. Obsolete; see Form 10-Q.

I O - C

"Over-the-counter" companies use this form to report changes in name and amount of NASDAQ-listed securities. It is similar in purpose to the 8-K.

PROXY STATEMENT

A proxy statement provides official notification to designated classes of stockholders of matters to be brought to a vote at a shareholders' meeting. Proxy votes may be solicited for changing the company name, transferring large blocks of stock, electing new officers, or many other matters. Disclosures normally made via a proxy statement may in some cases be made using Form 10-K (Part II).

REGISTRATION STATEMENTS

Registration statements are of two principal types: (1) "offering" registrations filed under the 1933 Securities Act, and (2) "trading" registrations filed under the 1934 Securities Exchange Act.

"Offering" registrations are used to register securities before they may be offered to investors. Part I of the registration, a preliminary prospectus or "red herring," is promotional in tone; it carries all the sales features that will be contained in the final prospectus. Part II of the registration contains detailed information about marketing agreements, expenses of issuance and distribution, relationship of the company with experts named in the registration, sales to special parties, recent sales of unregistered securities, subsidiaries of registrant, franchises and concessions, indemnification of directors and officers, treatment of proceeds from stock being registered, and financial statements and exhibits.

"Offering" registration statements vary in purpose and content according to the type of organization issuing stock:

S-1   A generalized form which may be used for registration by an issuer when no other form is authorized or prescribed

S-2   Used by "development stage" companies other than insurance investment or mining companies

S-3   Used by operating or development stage companies which mine for minerals other than oil and natural gas

S-4   Used by closed-end investment companies registered under the Investment Company Act of 1940 on Form N-8-B-1

S-5   Used by open-end investment companies (mutual funds) registered under the Investment Act of 1940 on Form N-8B-1

S-6   Used by unit investment trusts registered under the Investment Act of 1940 on Form N-8B-2

S-7   A short form which may be used by companies which have a relatively healthy operating history and have filed under both the Securities Act of 1933 and 1934 in a timely manner

S-8   Used to register securities to be offered to employees under stock option and various other benefit plans

S-9   Rescinded in SEC Release No. 33-5791, December 20, 1976. Previously used as a short form similar to the S-7 for the registration of debt securities. The requirements are now incorporated in Form S-7.

S-10 Used for the registration of landowners' royalty interests, overriding royalty interests, participating interests, working interests, oil or gas payments, oil or gas fee interests, oil or gas leasehold interests and other producing and non-producing oil or gas interests or rights

S-11 Used by real estate companies, primarily limited partnerships and investment trusts

S-12 Used to register American Depository Receipts issued against securities of foreign issuers deposited with an American depository

S-13 Used for the registration of certificates, agreements, etc. relating to voting and voting-trust agreements

S-14 Used to register securities for the reorganization, merger, consolidation, transfer of assets or similar plan of acquisition s-15 No such form currently used

s-16 A short form which may be used for the registration of securities to be offered for sale by current or future security holders

"Trading" registrations are filed to permit trading among investors on a securities exchange or in the over-the-counter market. Registration statements which serve to register securities for trading fall into three categories:

1. Form 10 is used by companies during the first two years they are subject to the 1934 Act filing requirements. It is a combination registration statement and annual report with information content similar to that of SEC-required annual reports.
2. Form 8-A is used by 1934 Act registrants wishing to register *additional* securities for trading.
3. Form 8-B is used by "successor issuers" (usually companies which have changed their name or state of incorporation) as notification that previously registered securities are to be traded under a new corporate identification.

PROSPECTUS

When the sale of securities as proposed in an "offering" registration statement is approved by the SEC, any changes required by the SEC are incorporated into the prospectus. This document must be made available to investors before the sale of the security is initiated. It also contains the actual offering price, which may have been changed after the registration statement was approved.

ANNUAL REPORT TO SHAREHOLDERS (ARS)

The annual report to shareholders is the document that most major companies use to communicate directly with their shareholders.

Since it is not an official SEC filing, companies have considerable (but not complete) leeway in determining what types of information this report will contain, and how it is to be presented. It often provides nonfinancial details of the business which are not reported elsewhere, including forecasts of future programs and plans.

FORM 8

Form 8 is used to amend or supplement filings previously submitted. 1933 Act registration statements are amended by filing an amended registration statement (pre-effective amendment) or by the prospectus itself, as previously noted.

LISTING APPLICATION

Like the ARS, a listing application is not an official SEC filing. It is filed by the company with the NYSE, AMEX or other stock exchange to document proposed new listings. Usually a Form 8-A registration is filed with the SEC at about the same time.

N-IR

This report is the equivalent of the 10-K for registered management-investment firms. In addition to annual financial statements, this report shows diversification of assets, portfolio turnover activity, and capital gains experience.

N-IQ

This is the quarterly report of registered management-investment firms, which must be filed within one month after the quarter has ended. The N-IQ shows changes in portfolio securities, including the number of shares bought, sold and owned at the end of the quarter for each stock in the company's portfolio.

INFORMATION CONTENT OF SEC FILING FORMS

Columns F-10, 8-A, 8-B ('34 Act) and '33 Act "S" Type fall under the heading **Registration Statement.**

Information Attributes	10-K	N-1R	7-Q	10-Q	N-1Q	8-K	10-C	Proxy Statement	Prospectus	F-10	8-A	8-B	'33 Act "S" Type	ARS	Listing Application
Auditor															
Name	A	A	S					S	A	A			A	A	S
Opinion	A	A	S							A			A		
Changes						A		S							
Compensation Plans															
Equity	S	S	S					F	F	A			F		S
Monetary	S		S						F	A			F		S
Company Information															
Nature of Business	A								A	A			A	S	S
History	F								A				A	S	S
Organization and Change	F					A	S	S	A		F		A	S	
Debt Structure	A	A						S	A	A			A	A	
Depreciation and Other Schedules	A								A	A			A		
Dilution Factors	A					F			A	A			A	A	
Directors, Officers, Insiders															
Identification	F								A	A	A		A	F	
Background	S								F	A	S		A	S	
Holdings	S						S	A	A	A			A		
Compensation	S						S	A	A	A			A		

LEGEND

A *always included; included—if occurred or significant*
F *frequently included*
S *special circumstances only*

Registration Statement grouping: the '34 Act columns are **F-10** and **8-A 8-B**; together with **'33 Act "S" Type** they make up the Registration Statement.

Information Attributes	10-K	N-1R	7-Q	10-Q	N-1Q	8-K	10-C	Proxy Statement	Prospectus	F-10	8-A 8-B	'33 Act "S" Type	ARS	Listing Application
Earnings: Earnings Per Share	A	A	A							A			A	
Financial Information														
Annual Audited	A	A							F	A		F	A	
Interim Audited	S							S	S			S		
Interim Unaudited	F		A			S			S			S		
Foreign Operations	A							S	A	A		A	S	F
Labor Contracts								S	S	F	F			
Legal Agreements	F							S		F	F			
Legal Counsel								S		A		A		S
Loan Agreements	F	S	F					S	S	F	F			
Plants and Properties	A								S	F	A	F	S	
Portfolio Operations														
Content					A									
Management		A												
Product-Line Breakout	A									A		A	S	
Replacement Cost Data	S													
Securities Structure	A							S	A	A		A		
Subsidiaries	A							S	A	A		A	S	S
Underwriting								S	A	A		A		
Unregistered Securities	S							S	S	F		F		
Block Movements	S							F	S	A				S

LEGEND
A *always included; included—if occurred or significant*
F *frequently included*
S *special circumstances only*

DISCLOSURE PRODUCTS AND SERVICES

Each year the 11,000 publicly-held corporations file over 100,000 disclosure reports with the SEC. Replicas of the SEC corporate filings in full text form are the core of the DISCLOSURE system. DISCLOSURE makes these reports available to the public in the following ways:

SUBSCRIPTION SERVICES

Through DISCLOSURE'S subscription services you can automatically receive full text copies of SEC corporate filings in the most efficient and economical format—microfiche. A microfiche is a 4 × 6 inch film card containing up to 60 pages of information. Our microfiche subscriptions are available two convenient ways.

ExchangeList provides microfiche copies of SEC reports organized by stock exchange. As an ExchangeList customer, you will receive the current SEC reports which you have selected, filed by companies listed on the New York Stock Exchange, the American Stock Exchange or Over The Counter. In addition, your collection will be automatically updated as reports are filed with the Securities and Exchange Commission.

SelectList offers maximum flexibility in fulfilling your individual requirements for corporate information through SEC Reports.

As a SelectList customer, you will receive current SEC reports on microfiche that you have personally selected.

You can have reports in any combination of companies and report types, sent to you automatically as they are filed with the Securities and Exchange Commission.

If your informational requirements are for competitive surveillance, you can select SEC reports filed by your competitors. Other popular selections which might fulfill your needs are SEC reports filed by the Fortune 500 Industrial group, by investment portfolios, by regional groupings (all companies in a given state or local area) or by all companies in a specific industry. With SelectList you can have a collection of SEC reports that are of most value to you—your choice of companies and selection of reports.

REPORTLINE

ReportLine provides you with a fast convenient way to order paper and microfiche copies of Securities and Exchange Commission reports—by telephone—as you need them. These reports, filed by some 11,000 public corporations, include: 10-K, 18-K, 19-K, 20-K, 10-Q, 7-Q, 8-K, 19-C, Proxy, Annual Report to Shareholders, Registration Statements, Prospectus, N-1Q, N-1R, Listing Application and amendments to the listed reports.

Paper Service

An order received one day will be filled and shipped by the next working day. The price for priority paper copies is $.30 per page, $5 minimum, plus first class mail costs. Special arrangements can be made for air express deliveries of priority orders and will be charged at cost for the service.

Microfiche Service

All Reports on microfiche are priced at $7.50 per report and are sent to you the day after we receive your order. Shipping costs are included in the price.

THE COMPANY FILING INDEX

The Company Filing Index is a monthly publication, issued about the 20th of each month following our closing of the previous month's filings. It lists alphabetically, by company, all filings made with the SEC for which microfiche were produced by the end of the publication month. This date is usually the last business day of the month.

Under a company listing are recorded all reports on file for that company for that month. The type of report is identified as well as its effective date. The listing looks like this:

ABC Co.   A-82000000

Regst. S-1, Filed: 3/8/76
Prspect. Eff: 3/21/76

Thus the Company Filing Index is a current awareness publication listing all filings processed and kept on file by DISCLOSURE in any given month. It records, for ready reference, who filed and what was filed. The cost of a twelve month subscription is $90.00. When purchased with any other DISCLOSURE service the price is $67.50 (a 25% discount).

PRICE SCHEDULE

	Paper	Microfiche
ReportLine (*Billed with every order.*)	24-hour service: 30¢/page* $5.00 minimum 4-day service: 20¢/page* $5.00 minimum	$7.50/report*

For ReportLine call (301) 951-0106

	Paper	Microfiche
Demand Deposit Account (*Charges deducted from deposit. No invoices to process*)	$250 deposit 24-hour service: 30¢/page* $5.00 minimum 4-day service: 20¢/page* $5.00 minimum	$250 deposit $7.50/report*
Paper Copy Subscription	$250 minimum	
Microfiche Subscription		See your sales representative

*Plus first class postage. Next-day delivery via air courier available at additional charge.

Appendix IV

Examples of Variables Using the Financial-Integrity Approach—Pro and Con

❦

*In this book, we assume that the objective of the firm
is to maximize its value to its shareholders.
Value is represented by the market price of the company's common
stock which, in turn, is a reflection of the firm's
investment, financing, and dividend decisions.*

JAMES C. VAN HORNE
Financial Management and Policy

UNLIKE THE AUTHOR of the quotation above, users of the financial-integrity approach do not assume that a firm has any particular objective, or that if it did have one objective, it would be "to maximize its value to its shareholders," especially if "shareholders" means public investors. An assumption that a unitary and monolithic "value is represented by the market price of the company's common stock" is also rejected out of hand as unrealistic. Rather, financial integrity revolves around far less rigid assumptions than those postulated by Professor Van Horne.

As far as objectives of the firm are concerned, it is recognized that in the real world, most businesses will have a multiplicity of objectives, many of which will compete with one another. However, a central thesis for financial integrity is that an equity security probably should be avoided by unaffiliated investors if there is evidence that managements and control groups may intend to treat outside security holders unfairly. Fair treatment for outside security holders in no way implies maximizing for the benefit of common stockholders; rather, it means merely treating stockholders well enough within a milieu where insiders have to serve many constituencies.

Under the financial-integrity approach, value is not the first order of business. It is recognized that many securities that may be attractively priced are unsuitable for outside investors focusing on financial integrity. These investors insist, *inter alia*, that securities they hold be issued by firms whose financial positions are strong and are understandable to the investor, either because of the types of public disclosures that are made, or because of the investor's particular background, or both.

The purpose of this appendix is to cite specific evidence from public documents that indicates to us that a security may or may not be attractive using the financial-integrity approach described in Chapter 2. Under that approach, there has to be—besides managements or control groups who do not seem to take unfair advantage of stockholders—a lack of encumbrances, an availability of reasonable amounts of understandable information about the company and a belief by the investor that the common stock can be purchased at a price that represents a substantial discount from a conservative estimate of net asset value.

In early 1978, we thought that American Manufacturing Company common stock, inactively traded on the American Stock Exchange at prices around 50, was an attractive issue, based on the four standards essential to financial integrity. In this appendix, we cite those portions of SEC filings and stockholder mailings that caused us to favor American Manufacturing and its common stock. We also cite, from publications issued by other companies or about other companies, material on companies whose issues did not meet the four standards.

Two disclaimers should be made. First, and as we stated before, because we do not deem a security attractive based on financial-integrity standards does not mean that a security may not be attractively priced using other considerations. Second, the judgment as to whether or not a management or control group is treating shareholders fairly is something that is highly subjective; our citations from public records concerning management and control groups are meant only to show the basis for our investment judgments, and are in no way intended to reflect on the character or integrity of any individual or group.

LACK OF ENCUMBRANCES

Strong and weak financial positions are demonstrated by the respective financial statements of American Manufacturing Company, as of December 31, 1977, and AITS, as of March 31, 1977. Particular factors to focus on within the financial statements are the auditors' certificates, the balance sheet and footnotes to financial statements.*

The American Manufacturing auditors' certificate shows a clean audit, whereas AITS' certificate is, *as underlined by us,* qualified by the opinion that continuation of the business as a going concern is contingent upon the refinancing of indebtedness, which would have been in default had not lending institutions granted waivers.

---

*Accounting Trends and Techniques, an annual issued by the American Institute of Certified Public Accountants (New York), provides excellent surveys of how specific companies handle specific accounting items within financial accounting. *Accounting Trends and Techniques* is an annual compilation of the accounting practices of six hundred companies that are publicly owned.

HASKINS & SELLS

INTERNATIONALLY

DELOITTE, HASKINS & SELLS

100 GARDEN CITY PLAZA

GARDEN CITY, NEW YORK 11530

Auditors' Report

The Stockholders of
American Manufacturing Company, Inc.:

We have examined the consolidated balance sheet of American Manufacturing Company, Inc. and subsidiaries as of December 31, 1977 and 1976 and the related statements of consolidated income, capital and earned surplus and changes in consolidated financial position for the years then ended. Our examinations were made in accordance with generally accepted auditing standards and, accordingly, included such tests of the accounting records and such other auditing procedures as we considered necessary in the circumstances. We did not examine the financial statements of Eltra Corporation, a corporation in which American's interest is reported on the equity method of accounting. The financial statements of Eltra Corporation for the years ended September 30, 1977 and 1976 were examined by other auditors whose report thereon has been furnished to us, and our opinion expressed herein, insofar as it relates to the amounts shown for Eltra Corporation, is based solely upon the report of the other auditors.

In our report dated February 23, 1977, our opinion on the 1976 consolidated financial statements was qualified as being subject to the effects, if any, of the shareholder litigation relating to the merger of The Electric Auto-Lite Company and Mergenthaler Linotype Company. As explained in Note 8, the litigation has proceeded to the stage where there should be no material effect on the consolidated financial statements. Accordingly, our opinion on the 1976 consolidated financial statements, as presented herein, is different from that expressed in our previous report.

In our opinion, based upon our examinations and the report of other auditors, the abovementioned financial statements present fairly the financial position of the companies at December 31, 1977 and 1976 and the results of their operations and the changes in their financial position for the years ended, in conformity with generally accepted accounting principles applied on a consistent basis.

(signed)   *Haskins & Sells*

February 22, 1978

TOUCHE ROSS & CO.

Board of Directors and Stockholders
AITS, Inc.
Newton, Massachusetts

We have examined the balance sheet of AITS, Inc. and the consolidated balance sheet of AITS, Inc. and subsidiaries at March 31, 1977, and the related statements of operations and deficit, and changes in financial position for the year then ended, and the additional information listed in the accompanying index. Our examination was made in accordance with generally accepted auditing standards, and accordingly included such tests of the accounting records and such other auditing procedures as we considered necessary in the circumstances.

The accompanying financial statements have been prepared on the basis of the continuation of the Company as a going concern, which is dependent on the following:

a. *the completion of the renegotiation of the debt to the terms described in Note 5, and*

b. *generating sufficient earnings to meet the restructured debt repayment requirements as detailed in Note 5 to the consolidated financial statements or obtaining additional extensions for repayment of debt.*

In our opinion, subject to the effect, if any, of the resolution of the matters referred to in the preceding paragraph, the financial statements referred to above present fairly the financial position of AITS, Inc. and the consolidated financial position of the Company and its subsidiaries at March 31, 1977, and their results of operations and changes in financial position for the year then ended, in conformity with generally accepted accounting principles applied on a consistent basis. Further, it is our opinion that the additional information previously referred to presents fairly the information therein set forth.

The financial statements for the year ended March 31, 1976 were examined by other certified public accountants, whose report was qualified as to going concern.

(signed)   *Touche Ross & Co.*

Certified Public Accountants

May 3, 1977, except
Note 5, which is
as of July 6, 1977

The American Manufacturing balance sheet shows that that company was almost debt-free (long-term debt was only $2,861,031), with a strong working-capital position ($21,030,840 current assets, less $5,720,413 current liabilities, resulting in a working capital of $15,310,427), and a large net worth ($114,249,000).

In contrast, AITS was saddled with a huge debt load ($79,726,729, made up of $8,460,535 of current maturities of long-term debt, $35,441,385 of debt due to banks being renegotiated, and $35,824,809 long-term debt); and it suffered from an extreme net-worth deficit, whether measured by a tangible net-worth deficit ($29,213,834) or by a net worth deficit including $14,410,294 of intangibles ($14,803,540). In addition, $2 million of AITS' $5,900,519 of accounts payable was past due.

AMERICAN MANUFACTURING COMPANY, INC. AND SUBSIDIARIES
CONSOLIDATED BALANCE SHEET
DECEMBER 31, 1977 AND 1976

ASSETS	1977	1976
CURRENT ASSETS:		
Cash	$ 2,569,303	$ 1,642,797
Short-term investments—at cost, approximating market value:		
Held for dividends payable	1,768,044	1,705,600
Held for payment of income taxes	400,000	900,000
Other	100,058	13,405
Receivables:		
Trade, less allowance for doubtful accounts ($148,675 and $123,000)	5,378,716	4,352,593
Dividends from Eltra Corporation	932,567	932,567
Other	169,002	433,031
Inventories (Note 1)	9,208,275	8,324,709
Deferred Federal income taxes—current (Notes 1 and 3)	504,875	411,403
TOTAL CURRENT ASSETS	21,030,840	18,716,105
INTEREST IN ELTRA CORPORATION (Notes 1 and 2)	94,208,739	86,524,883
PLANT PROPERTY—At cost (Notes 1 and 4):		
Land	597,323	389,949
Buildings	5,601,614	5,364,459
Machinery and equipment	8,912,714	7,840,557
Leasehold improvements	64,982	110,753
TOTAL	15,176,633	13,705,718
Less accumulated depreciation and amortization	7,462,532	6,765,879
PLANT PROPERTY—NET	7,714,101	6,939,839
DEFERRED FEDERAL INCOME TAXES—relating to deferred pension credit (Note 1)	266,640	287,160
PREPAID EXPENSES, DEFERRED CHARGES, ETC.	336,270	226,943
TOTAL	$123,556,590	$112,694,930

See Notes to Financial Statements

*LIABILITIES AND
STOCKHOLDERS' EQUITY*

	1977	1976
CURRENT LIABILITIES:		
Accounts payable (principally trade)	$ 1,390,001	$ 1,306,946
Dividends payable	1,768,044	1,705,600
Accrued taxes on income	414,692	941,569
Other liabilities (including current portion of long-term debt)	2,147,676	1,903,668
TOTAL CURRENT LIABILITIES	5,720,413	5,857,783
LONG-TERM DEBT (Note 4)	2,861,031	833,443
DEFERRED CREDIT FROM ACQUISITION (Note 1)	170,559	255,838
DEFERRED PENSION CREDIT (Note 1)	555,654	598,398
STOCKHOLDERS' EQUITY (Notes 2 and 5)		
Common stock—Authorized 2,800,000 shares of $6.25 par value; 1,494,214 shares issued	9,338,838	9,338,838
Capital surplus	10,290,271	10,399,979
Earned surplus	99,185,947	89,994,293
Less cost of common stock in treasury (274,973 and 276,028 shares)	(4,566,123)	(4,583,642)
TOTAL STOCKHOLDERS' EQUITY	114,248,933	105,149,468
TOTAL	$123,556,590	$112,694,930

See Notes to Financial Statements

10-K
AITS, INC. AND SUBSIDIARIES
CONSOLIDATED BALANCE SHEET

	March 31,	
ASSETS (*Note 5*)	*1977*	*1976*
CURRENT ASSETS:		
Cash	$ 1,557,226	$ 2,579,567
Accounts and notes receivable, less allowance for possible losses of $4,966,592 and $4,659,704 (Note 2)	4,235,738	4,678,251
Inventories	327,268	316,506
Prepaid expenses	412,104	1,369,423
Certificates of deposit	1,527,778	3,125,347
TOTAL CURRENT ASSETS	8,060,114	12,069,094
PROPERTY AND EQUIPMENT, mortgaged—less accumulated depreciation (Notes 1, 3 and 5)	55,372,049	56,452,139
EXCESS OF COST OVER FAIR VALUE OF UNDERLYING NET ASSETS OF ACQUIRED BUSINESS, net of amortization (Notes 1, 6 and 7)	14,410,294	13,130,599
OTHER ASSETS (Note 7)	675,814	1,033,516
	$78,518,071	$82,685,348

See notes to consolidated financial statements

	March 31,	
LIABILITIES AND DEFICIENCY IN ASSETS	1977	1976
CURRENT LIABILITIES:		
Notes payable:		
Banks (Note 4)	$ 525,000	$11,642,642
Other	352,200	3,000,000
Current maturities of long-term debt (Note 5)	8,460,535	8,820,000
Accounts payable ($2,000,000 past due)	5,900,519	7,744,846
Customers' deposits	76,627	2,541,763
Accrued expenses:		
Interest	1,279,904	4,055,181
Professional services	1,365,949	1,014,731
Payroll, gaming and other taxes	1,100,332	1,178,030
Compensation and other	1,333,260	1,914,244
Federal income taxes (Note 6)	1,661,091	—
CURRENT LIABILITIES BEFORE DEBT DUE TO BANKS BEING RENEGOTIATED	22,055,417	41,911,437
Debt due to banks being renegotiated	35,441,385	—
TOTAL CURRENT LIABILITIES	57,496,802	41,911,437
LONG-TERM DEBT, less current maturities (Note 5)	35,824,809	54,320,000
COMMITMENTS AND CONTINGENCIES (Notes 5, 7 and 10)		
DEFICIENCY IN ASSETS (Notes 5 and 7):		
Preferred stock, $1.00 par—shares authorized, 500,000; outstanding, 2,000—		
Par value $ 2,000		
Additional paid-in capital 198,000	200,000	200,000
Common stock, $.10 par—shares authorized, 6,000,000; issued, 1,926,340	192,634	192,634
Additional paid-in capital	18,462,189	18,462,189
Deficit	(33,551,263)	(32,293,812)
	(14,696,440)	(13,438,989)
Treasury stock, at cost, 3,000 common shares	(107,100)	(107,100)
TOTAL DEFICIENCY IN ASSETS	(14,803,540)	(13,546,089)
	$78,518,071	$82,685,348

See notes to consolidated financial statements

The footnotes to the American Manufacturing financial statements did not point to any potential liabilities that seemed likely to seriously impact the business. The principal problems revolved around litigation described in footnote 8, but by year-end 1977, the risk of a large impact from unfavorable court decisions, though still in existence, seemed manageable. Footnotes to the AITS financial statements, on the other hand, indicated the possible existence of encumbrances over and above those appearing on the balance sheet—as, for example, the possibility discussed in AITS footnote 5 that North American Mortgage Investors (NAMI) might not honor a commitment to lend a needed $15 million to AITS.

AMERICAN MANUFACTURING COMPANY

8. Litigation

In connection with the merger of The Electric Auto-Lite Company ("Auto-Lite") and Mergenthaler Linotype Company ("Mergenthaler"), now Eltra Corporation, a derivative and class action was instituted by two Auto-Lite shareholders on June 26, 1963, against Auto-Lite, Mergenthaler and American Manufacturing Company, Inc., in the United States District Court for the Northern District of Illinois. The complaint asserted claims under both federal and state law. On January 20, 1970, the United States Supreme Court upheld a ruling of the District Court which had granted plaintiffs' motion for a summary judgment of liability on the ground that the merger proxy statement failed to bring out adequately the relationship between the Auto-Lite Board members and Mergenthaler. Following a trial on the issue of relief, the District Court, on April 11, 1975, awarded damages in the amount of $1,233,918 plus interest. On April 7, 1977, the Court of Appeals for the Seventh Circuit reversed this decision, holding that the terms of the merger were fair and that plaintiffs should recover no damages. The Court of Appeals further held that plaintiffs must pay their own attorneys' fees and expenses for their unsuccessful attempt to obtain damages. However, the Court held that Eltra Corporation should pay plaintiffs' fees and expenses through the Supreme Court's decision upholding the summary judgment of liability. On October 31, 1977, the United States Supreme Court declined to further review the case and on December 12, 1977, the Supreme Court denied a request for rehearing. Despite the ruling of the Seventh Circuit, plaintiffs took the position before the District Court that they were still entitled to recover damages under their state law claims. A judgment order has been entered by the District Court dismissing all damage claims, including plaintiffs' state law claims. Plaintiffs may attempt to secure appellate review of this order. It is the opinion of counsel in this matter that the amount ultimately awarded by the court for plaintiffs' fees and expenses will not be material to Eltra Corporation's financial position.

AITS FINANCIAL STATEMENTS IN 10-K

---

5. LONG-TERM DEBT
Long term debt consists of:

	March 31,	
	1977	1976
Notes payable to banks, with interest of $\frac{1}{2}$% above prime rate ($6\frac{1}{4}$% at March 31, 1977, payable $220,000 in 1978, $7,065,000 in 1979, $6,939,000 in 1980 and 1981 and $7,200,000 in 1982 and 1983 (a) (d)	$35,441,385	$25,000,000
Notes payable to bank, with interest of 4% above prime rate to a maximum of 10%, due November 15, 1978 (b) (d) (f)	15,000,000	17,500,000
Note payable to bank, with interest of $\frac{1}{2}$% above prime rate, payable $25,000 per week (b) (d) (f)	4,025,000	—
Notes payable to stockholders of an acquired company (c) (d) (f)	13,197,779	16,490,000
$9\frac{1}{2}$% note payable to bank, $150,000 including interest, due monthly commencing July 1, 1977 (f)	3,900,000	—
Notes payable to two principal stockholders, with interest of $\frac{1}{2}$% above prime rate, payments of $483,000 due quarterly commencing April 1, 1980 (e)	5,375,000	4,150,000
Other notes payable with interest at 5% to 8%	2,787,565	—
	79,726,729	63,140,000
Less:		
Current maturities	8,460,535	8,820,000
Debt due to banks being renegotiated	35,441,385	—
Long-term debt	$35,824,809	$54,320,000

The Company has been negotiating to restructure the various debt agreements covering the $35,441,385 notes and to revise payment schedules on such debt. As of July 6, 1977, the Company has not signed agreements with such major lenders but expects to have them signed shortly. During the fiscal year ended March 31, 1977, the Company did not make its required payments on prior agreements and obtained waivers on all defaults resulting therefrom. The Company has obtained deferrals of demands for payment through July 31, 1977. Such debt has been classified as "Debt due to banks being renegotiated," and are included as a current liability until the agreements are signed. The debt schedule in the next paragraph and the information in paragraph (a) below reflect the agreements in substantially the same format as they are presently in draft form.

Long-term debt (reflecting the debt agreements as now drafted) is payable as follows:

Year ending March 31,	Amount
1979	$19,378,362
1980	24,714,274
1981	9,056,394
1982	9,295,350
1983 and thereafter	8,821,814

The payments may be accelerated based upon earnings (see (a) below).

A. Principal payments are to be increased 90 days after each of the fiscal years ending March 31, 1978, 1979, and 1980 for all "cash flow" for each such year in excess of $20,000,000. The term "cash flow" is defined as net operating income before federal income tax, plus depreciation, amortization and interest. Additional payments may be required for the fiscal years ending March 31, 1981 and 1982 based upon the Company exceeding certain earnings levels.

Compensating balance requirements identical to those discussed under (b) are required on $25,000,000 of these notes.

B. The Company is expected to maintain compensating balances equal to 10% of the outstanding loan. Deficiencies in compensating balances require the payment of additional interest at the average Federal Fund rate plus ½ of 1%.

The Company's subsidiary has a mortgage loan commitment from North American Mortgage Investors (NAMI), a real estate investment trust, for $15,000,000 to close on October 15, 1978, and to mature on October 15, 1983, with no principal payments prior to maturity. This proposed borrowing is intended to partially repay the loans due on November 15, 1978. Interest will be payable at an annual rate of 4% above prime, but not more than 10%. This loan will be collateralized by a first mortgage on all real property and the personal guaranty of Meshulam Riklis in the amount of not more than commitment will terminate upon the bankruptcy or insolvency of Mr. Riklis. Fees of $862,500 were payable in connection with this commitment, of which $712,500 had been paid as of April 15, 1977. The remaining $150,000 is payable in equal installments of $75,000, payable on October 15, 1977 and April 15, 1978.

NAMI stated in its Form 10-K, filed with the Securities and Exchange Commission for the fiscal year ended December 31, 1976, that "since the unfunded commitments of the Trust and standby commitments outstanding exceed the Trust's available cash, it is conceivable that the Trust might not have sufficient funds to fulfill such commitments." The Company has obtained a commitment from its principal lender that if financing is not available prior to November 15, 1978, the note due to bank will be extended for one year.

C. These notes are comprised of a $4,583,332, 7% note due November 15, 1978, a $7,614,447 note, with interest of 2% over prime, not to exceed 9%, payable in monthly installments of $334,000, and a $1,000,000, 9½% note payable to an officer payable $200,000 quarterly.

D. The Hotel Riviera property and the stock of the Hotel Riviera, Inc. which represents substantially all of the assets of the Company, are pledged under the above agreements. Further, the agreements contain various restrictions substantially restricting the ability of the Company to borrow, declare dividends, reacquire shares, etc. The insolvency or death of Mr. Meshulam Riklis, the Chairman of the Board or Isidore Becker, President, is an event of default under several of these agreements. Mr. Riklis has personally guaranteed approximately $65,000,000 of the above notes.

E. These notes are due to Meshulam Riklis ($3,700,000) and Isidore Becker ($1,675,000).

F. Debt of Hotel Riviera, Inc.

MANAGEMENT AND CONTROL GROUP OBJECTIVES

An examination of Forms 10-K and proxy statements of American Manufacturing and its 28 percent owned affiliate, Eltra Corporation, indicates that management remuneration has been reasonable, that there have been no major transactions between the companies on the one hand and insiders on the other, and that since 1963 there has been no major litigation brought against the companies or insiders alleging wrongs that affect outside security holders. The American Manufacturing-Eltra disclosures in this regard should be contrasted with similar disclosures about remuneration, certain transactions and litigation made by Rapid American Corporation and Medallion Group.

Remuneration

Contrast the levels of compensation between American Manufacturing and Eltra, on the one hand, and Rapid American Corporation, on the other.

Eltra Proxy Statement Remuneration and Other Transactions with Management and Others

The following table sets forth (a) the direct remuneration accrued by the Corporation and its subsidiaries during the fiscal year ended

September 30, 1977 for the following persons for services in all capacities: (1) each director of the Corporation whose aggregate direct remuneration exceeded $40,000, (2) each of the three highest paid officers of the Corporation whose aggregate direct remuneration exceeded $40,000, and (3) all directors and officers of the Corporation as a group; (b) the estimated annual benefits proposed to be paid by the Corporation upon retirement to the persons named and to all directors and officers as a group, the amounts stated being based generally on assumed continuous employment until age 65 at the base salary for the fiscal year ended September 30, 1977; and (c) the aggregate deferred compensation for all years accrued as of September 30, 1977 for the persons named and for all directors and officers as a group:

Name of Individual or Identity of Group	Capacities in Which Remuneration Was Received	Aggregate Direct Remuneration*	Estimated Annual Benefits Upon Retirement	Aggregate Accrued Deferred Compensation as of September 30, 1977
J. A. KELLER	Director; Chairman of the Board of the Corporation; Director of subsidiaries of the Corporation	$ 247,267	$80,552	$133,333
RICHARD B. LOYND	Director; President of the Corporation	245,000	67,094	—
GLENN E. TAYLOR, JR.	Director; Executive Vice President for Finance of the Corporation; Director of a subsidiary of the Corporation	145,440	56,224	46,667
All directors and officers as a group which consists of 23 persons of whom 14 are eligible to receive retirement benefits.		1,248,327	453,569	324,667

*The Corporation provides for business purposes to certain directors and officers automobiles and club memberships which are not included in this table.

There was no deferred compensation accrued during the fiscal year ended September 30, 1977 for any officer or director.

Agreements between Mr. L. L. Garber and the Corporation provide, among other things, for payment of deferred annual compensation in the amount of $15,000 per year following his retirement on December 31, 1974 and ending at such time as his aggregate accrued deferred compensation ($144,667 accrued as of September 30, 1977) has been fully paid. Each payment of deferred compensation is subject to certain provisions prohibiting competition by Mr. Garber with the Corporation and its subsidiaries.

As of March 24, 1977, the Corporation entered into an agreement with Mr. J. A. Keller regarding his employment with the Corporation. The term of the agreement extends from that date until September 30, 1980 and, unless terminated effective as of that date, continues thereafter from year to year unless either party gives the other at least six months' notice of termination in advance of any subsequent September 30th. The agreement provides, among other things, for payment of a fixed salary in the amount of $155,000 per year and, pursuant to prior employment agreements between the parties, aggregate deferred compensation of $133,333 payable after termination of employment in 13 equal annual installments. Each payment of deferred compensation is contingent upon Mr. Keller during his lifetime making himself available to render advice and counsel to the Corporation and is subject to certain provisions prohibiting competition by Mr. Keller with the Corporation and its subsidiaries. The Corporation has accrued the $133,333 deferred compensation as indicated in the table on the previous page.

On March 24, 1976, the Corporation entered into an agreement with Mr. Richard B. Loynd regarding his employment with the Corporation. The term of the agreement extends from that date until September 30, 1981 unless Mr. Loynd gives notice to the Corporation on or before February 28, 1979 that he desires a new employment agreement with the Corporation in which event the agreement shall terminate on September 30, 1979. The agreement provides, among other things, for payment of a fixed salary in the amount of $155,000 per year.

As of November 30, 1977, the Corporation extended for one year a consulting agreement with Mr. Stephen A. Stone which provides, among other things, for payment of consulting fees of $2,000 per month. The consulting agreement prohibits competition by Mr. Stone with the Converse division of the Corporation for a period of five years from its termination. Mr. Stone has a one-third beneficial interest in a trust which leases property in Berlin, New Hampshire to the Corporation at an annual rental of about $80,000. Mr. Stone is one of many beneficiaries of a discretionary trust which leases property in Malden, Massachusetts to the Corporation at an annual rental of about $97,000. The Corporation or its subsidiaries became the lessee under each of these two leases in arms-length negotiations prior to the date Mr. Stone became a director of the Corporation. The Corporation has agreed to pay the cost of demolishing certain buildings on the Malden, Massachusetts property in order to reduce the Corporation's expenses.

As of January 1, 1977, the Corporation entered into an agreement with Mr. Glenn E. Taylor, Jr. regarding his employment with the Corporation which continues from year to year unless either party gives the other at least six months' notice of termination in advance of any subsequent September 30th. The agreement provides, among other things, for payment of a fixed salary in the amount of $98,675 per year and, pursuant to prior employment agreements between the parties, aggregate deferred compensation of $46,667 payable after termination of employment in ten equal annual installments. Each payment of deferred compensation is contingent upon Mr. Taylor during his lifetime making himself available to render advice and counsel to the Corporation and is subject to certain provisions prohibiting competition by Mr. Taylor with the Corporation and its subsidiaries. The Corporation has accrued the $46,667 deferred compensation as indicated in the above table.

During the fiscal year ended September 30, 1977, the Corporation paid American and its subsidiaries an aggregate of $81,589 for sales commissions and for purchases of products, and American made purchases from the Corporation in the amount of $44,003. Purchases from and sales to American were made at competitive prices. As stated under the heading "Principal Holders of Securities," American has a controlling interest in the Corporation.

Directors who are neither employees nor consultants of the

Corporation receive a fee of $200 for each meeting of the Board of Directors attended. Directors who are also employees of the Corporation (Messrs. Keller, Loynd, Taylor and Gurdon W. Wattles) and Mr. Stone, presently a consultant to the Corporation, receive no additional compensation for attendance at meetings of the Board of Directors. The Board of Directors met nine times during fiscal year 1977.

STOCK OPTIONS AND STOCK APPRECIATION RIGHTS

No stock options may be granted under the Corporation's 1959 Employee Stock Option Plan, as amended, after December 31, 1976. No stock options have been granted to any director or officer since March 24, 1976. The following tabulation shows as to certain directors and officers and as to all directors and officers as a group (i) the amount of shares of Common Stock acquired between October 1, 1976 and December 31, 1977 through the exercise of options granted prior to October 1, 1976, and (ii) the amount of shares of Common Stock subject to all unexercised options held as of December 31, 1977. All figures have been adjusted in accordance with the terms of the options to reflect the three-for-two stock split in March 1976.

Common Stock	J.A. Keller	Richard B. Loynd	Glenn E. Taylor, Jr.	All Directors and Officers as a Group
Exercised between October 1, 1976 and December 31, 1977:				
Number of shares	5,250	1,900	3,750	21,850
Aggregate option price of options exercised	$ 72,187	$26,125	$ 51,562	$390,468
Aggregate market value of shares on date options exercised	$142,737	$48,093	$105,821	$671,969
Unexercised at December 31, 1977:				
Number of shares	5,250	36,350	18,750	76,800
Average per share option price	$13.75	$17.31	$16.89	$17.58

Stock appreciation rights were granted under the Corporation's 1977 Employee Stock Appreciation Rights Plan on November 29, 1977 to five officers, other than Messrs. Keller, Loynd and Taylor. These unexercised stock appreciation rights are calculated on 4,250 shares of Common Stock having a per share price of $24.875.

AMERICAN MANUFACTURING ANNUAL
REPORT FOOTNOTE

5. Stock Option Plan

At December 31, 1977, there were unexercised options for 12,497 shares granted prior to 1975 under a stock option plan which expired April 5, 1975. The options are exercisable at various dates to November 20, 1982.

During 1975, the stockholders approved a new qualified Stock Option Plan dated April 6, 1975. Under the Plan, options to purchase common stock not exceeding an aggregate of 28,000 shares may be granted prior to April 6, 1980 to officers and employees at a price not less than market value at date of grant. The options granted expire five years after date of grant. No options are exercisable during the first year; during each of the second and third years options are exercisable for 15% of the shares, and thereafter options are exercisable in such amounts as are determined in each individual case by the option committee.

When options are exercised and common stock is issued, its cost is credited to the treasury stock account and the difference between option price and cost of treasury stock is charged or credited to capital surplus.

Changes in stock options during 1977 and 1976 were as follows:

	1977		1976	
	Number of Shares	*Aggregate Option Purchase Price*	*Number of Shares*	*Aggregate Option Purchase Price*
Unexercised options at beginning of year	22,322	$ 866,679	17,337	$593,871
Options granted	12,600	612,675	6,300	315,000
Options exercised	(1,055)	(31,711)	(450)	(13,444)
Options expired or canceled	(1,700)	(73,600)	(865)	(28,748)
Unexercised options at end of year	32,167	$1,374,043	22,322	$866,679

At December 31, 1977 a balance of 8,300 shares of common stock remained available for future option grants. Of the options unexercised at December 31, 1977, options for 8,677 shares were exercisable at that date.

The dilution in per-share earnings which could arise from exercise of options is less than one percent, therefore the earnings per share shown in the statement of consolidated income do not reflect such dilution.

AMERICAN MANUFACTURING
PROXY STATEMENT

Remuneration

The following table sets forth (a) the direct remuneration paid by the Company and its subsidiaries during the year ended December 31, 1976 to the following persons for services in all capacities: (1) each Director whose direct aggregate remuneration exceeded $40,000, (2) each of the three highest paid officers of the Company or its subsidiaries whose direct aggregate remuneration exceeded $40,000, and (3) all Directors and Officers of the Company and its subsidiaries as a group and (b) estimated annual benefits upon retirement at age 65 of persons indicated:

Name of Individual or Identity of Group and Capacity in Which Remuneration was Received	Direct Aggregate Remuneration for Fiscal Year	Estimated Annual Benefits Upon Retirement at Age 65*
Jack L. Gobble Director of the Company and President of Safety Railway Service Corp.	$ 55,200	$10,620
Harold V. Pate Director and Vice President of the Company	60,200	(See Note)
Robert B. Seidel Director and Vice President of the Company and President of Automatic Timing & Controls, a Division of the Company	56,224	25,989
Robert L. Stanton Director and Vice President of the Company	60,200	(See Note)
All directors and officers as a group: 18 persons 7 persons	515,956	87,895

*The amounts stated above are based on assumed continuous employment until age 65 under contributory pension plans.

The Company adopted in 1966 a profit-sharing savings plan effective January 1, 1966 for regular salaried employees in its Cordage Division. The Plan is of a contributory nature and provides for yearly contributions by the Company, based upon earnings of that division with a minimum contribution by the Company in each year of not less than $14,000 irrespective of earnings, credited to participants in proportion to their salaries and their contributions effected through payroll deduction. For the calendar year 1976 the contribution of the Company to the Plan was $87,572 of which $4,586 and $4,586 were allocated to Messrs. Pate and Stanton, respectively, and $7,212 were allocated to other officers of the Company employed in its Cordage Division.

Based upon the status of the Plan as at January 1, 1977 amounts allocated to Messrs. Pate and Stanton out of Company contributions made since the date of the Plan's inception (including earnings thereon and net increments in market values of securities purchased therewith) were $48,227 and $46,972, respectively. On that basis, amounts allocated to other officers of the Company employed in its Cordage Division amounted to approximately $64,391. There is no way to compute estimated annual benefits on retirement due to variability of earnings, forfeitures, withdrawals and other factors inherent in the nature of the Plan.

Neither Mr. Gurdon W. Wattles nor Mr. Robert Pulleyn are participants in the Plan.

STOCK OPTIONS

The following tabulation shows as to certain directors and officers and as to all directors and officers as a group the amount of shares subject to all unexercised options held as of February 9, 1977 and the changes, if any, since December 31, 1975:

Common Shares	*Jack L. Gobble*	*Harold V. Pate*	*Robert B. Seidel*	*Robert L. Stanton*	*All Directors and Officers as a Group*
Unexercised at December 31, 1975: Number of shares	1,050	1,900	2,000	1,200	8,975
Average per share option price	$34.12	$35.59	$35.50	$32.35	$34.55
Shares exercised since December 31, 1975	-0-	-0-	300	-0-	450
Shares expired or cancelled since December 31, 1975	-0-	-0-	-0-	-0-	-0-
Options granted since December 31, 1975	1,000	-0-	1,000	1,000	3,900
Unexercised at February 9, 1977: Number of shares	2,050	1,900	2,700	2,200	12,425
Average per share option price	$41.87	$35.59	$41.50	$40.38	$39.57

The following tabulation shows the high and low market prices of the Common Stock of the Company on the American Stock Exchange for each calendar quarter, commencing from January 1, 1976:

Calendar Quarter Ended	High	Low
March 31, 1976	51⅜	36
June 30, 1976	50¾	44
September 30, 1976	51½	46¼
December 31, 1976	51	44

The closing price on February 9, 1977 was $50.00.

RAPID AMERICAN CORPORATION
PROXY STATEMENT

Remuneration

The table on the following page sets forth certain information as to all direct remuneration paid, on an accrual basis, by Rapid and its subsidiaries during the fiscal year ended January 31, 1976 to (A) each person who was a director of Rapid during the fiscal year, and each of the three highest paid executive officers of Rapid during the fiscal year, whose aggregate direct remuneration exceeded $40,000, and (B) all persons who were either directors or executive officers of Rapid during that fiscal year, as a group. Information with respect to estimated annual retirement benefits at January 31, 1976 is also set forth for all named persons and all current directors and executive officers as a group.

The agreement between Rapid and McCrory, whereby Rapid agreed to render management assistance and services to McCrory and McCrory agreed to compensate Rapid for such assistance and services, was terminated as of January 31, 1976. During the year ended January 31, 1976, McCrory paid or accrued to Rapid approximately $900,000 pursuant to the management services agreement. It is intended by Rapid that all executives will be compensated by the particular subsidiary of Rapid to which they devote the principal portion of their business time. Accordingly, certain of these executives (including Meshulam

Riklis) who were not compensated by McCrory in its fiscal year ended January 31, 1976, are now receiving their salaries from McCrory.

Name of individual or number of persons in group	Capacities in which remuneration was received	Aggregate direct remuneration(1)	Estimated annual retirement benefits
Meshulam Riklis	Chairman of the Board and Chief Executive Officer of Rapid	$ 915,866(6)	$115,000(2)
Isidore A. Becker	President of Rapid and Chairman of the Board of Schenley	662,501(6)	115,000(2)
Lorence A. Silverberg	Executive Vice President of McCrory	350,978(4)	50,000(2)
Leonard C. Lane	Executive Vice President of Rapid	340,000(6)	60,000(2)
Haim Bernstein	Vice President of Rapid	137,500(3)	20,000(2)
All directors and executive officers as a group (11 in all as to aggregate direct remuneration, seven in all as to estimated annual retirement benefits)		2,700,101(5)	422,720

(1) Does not include accrued deferred compensation or payments made by Rapid pursuant to its medical expense reimbursement plan. Certain executive employees are eligible for reimbursement under this plan, which pays, within certain limits, all medical and dental expenses.

(2) Represents retirement benefits payable under employment contracts described below. Does not include deferred compensation payable under such employment contracts or amounts payable under any profit sharing plan.

(3) Does not include $12,500 paid to Mr. Bernstein by Meridan-York Corporation, a wholly-owned subsidiary of a retirement benefits plan maintained for certain employees of McCrory.

(4) Does not include deferred compensation of $12,000 paid to Mr. Silverberg.

(5) Includes $394,016 paid by McCrory to persons who were directors and/or executive officers of Rapid during the period. For information concerning deferred compensation and other contractual arrangements in respect of directors or executive officers, as well as accruals under profit-sharing plans see "Employment Agreements" below.

(6) Rapid used $1,000,000 of the proceeds from the sale of its Playtex operations in 1975 for bonuses to senior management of Rapid. Those bonuses, which are included in the above remuneration table, were as follows: Meshulam Riklis—$550,000; Isidore A. Becker—$350,000; and Leonard C. Lane—$100,000. See "Certain Litigation" below.

Employment Agreements

Effective November 20, 1972, Rapid entered into a five year employment contract with Meshulam Riklis, as chief executive officer, automatically renewable for an additional period of five years unless six months' prior notice of intention not to renew is given by either party, which provides for an annual salary of not less than $375,000, plus incentive compensation at the rate of 1% of Rapid's Consolidated After-Tax Operating Earnings (as defined) in each fiscal year beginning February 1, 1973, in excess of $20,000,000, up to a maximum of $100,000,000 per year. Such $375,000 annual salary is payable in any event, even if Mr. Riklis' employment is terminated by death, disability or discharge with or without cause. This contract superseded all previous contracts, with the exception of a contract with McCrory dated August 1, 1970, a contract with Rapid dated October 29, 1965 (both of which are described hereafter), and accruals under a contract with Rapid dated August 1, 1970. The contract provides for deferred compensation to be earned at the rate of not less than $50,000 per year, payable following the termination of Mr. Riklis' employment. The contract also provides for the payment of a retirement allowance for life following the termination of Mr. Riklis' employment at the rate of $100,000 per year, and upon Mr. Riklis' death, payments will continue to his surviving widow, if any, at the rate of $50,000 per year for her life; any pension plan benefits are deducted, and payments are subject to other limits and restrictions on competition with Rapid, are reduced by the receipt of disability payments and are subject to Mr. Riklis' availability to render certain advisory services to Rapid. In the event of the termination of his employment because of his incapacity, Mr. Riklis is to receive disability benefits at the rate of $100,000 per year for life, less any amounts earned from other employment; in the event of his death, his widow or his surviving children or his estate is to receive death benefits of $500,000, plus one year's incentive compensation (in addition to the incentive compensation earned by, but not yet paid to, Mr. Riklis prior to his death) payable over a ten year period. Mr. Riklis was also granted a non-qualified option to purchase 150,000 shares of Rapid Common Stock, at $25 per share, expiring at the earlier of

(1) 90 days after the termination of Mr. Riklis' employment for any reason other than his death, or (2) February 7, 1978, unless Mr. Riklis is in the employ of Rapid on November 21, 1977, in which event the expiration date is extended to February 7, 1983.

On October 29, 1965, Old Rapid entered into an agreement with Mr. Riklis whereunder Rapid is required to keep in force policies of key-man life insurance on Mr. Riklis' life having an aggregate face value of approximately $1,035,000 and, whether or not Mr. Riklis is still employed by Rapid at the time of his death, to offer to use the proceeds of such insurance policies to purchase, pro tanto, shares of Common Stock of Rapid at that time owned by him or his estate at its then market price (averaged over the 30 days prior to date of death.) Effective April 10, 1973, this agreement was amended so as to include an additional $2,500,000 of such insurance which had been carried by Glen Alden. The offer, which may be accepted in whole or in part by his legal representative, shall be enforceable only to the extent that, at the date of Mr. Riklis' death or within one year thereafter, Rapid shall be under no legal disability or restriction which would prevent such purchase. This agreement has not been superseded by any subsequent employment contract, and remains in effect.

On April 1, 1965, McCrory entered into an employment contract with Mr. Riklis, then its Chairman of the Board and President, which provided, *inter alia,* for the payment of a retirement allowance for life beginning with the later of (1) Mr. Riklis' 55th birthday, or (2) the termination of his employment. Such allowance is to be paid in equal monthly installments at the rate of $15,000 per year; any pension plan benefits shall be deducted, and payments are subject to other limits and restrictions on competition with McCrory, receipt of disability payments, etc. Effective August 1, 1970, Mr. Riklis' employment under such contract was terminated; only his retirement rights remain in effect. It is a condition to the payment of Mr. Riklis' retirement rights that he shall be available to render advisory services to McCrory if requested by the Board of Directors of McCrory, subject to certain limitations. In 1974, Mr. Riklis relinquished his right to receive any retirement allowance from McCrory, so long as he continues to be employed and paid by Rapid and Rapid continues to have a substantial interest in McCrory. During the year ended January 31, 1976, Mr. Riklis did not receive any compensation from McCrory or any of its subsidiaries. See "Remuneration" above.

Effective as of August 1, 1975, Isidore A. Becker entered into a five-year employment contract (the "Schenley Contract") with Schenley Industries, Inc., a subsidiary of Rapid ("Schenley"). The Schenley Contract is automatically renewable for an additional period of five years unless six months prior notice of intention not to renew is given by either party and supersedes all other employment contracts between Mr. Becker and Rapid or McCrory, including the contract which Mr. Becker entered into with Rapid on November 20, 1972 (the "Rapid Contract"). The Rapid Contract provided for an annual salary of not less than $275,000, plus incentive compensation at the rate of 1% of Rapid's Consolidated After Tax Operating Earnings (as defined) in each fiscal year beginning February 1, 1973, in excess of $20,000,000, up to a maximum of $100,000,000 per year and, among other things, provided for deferred compensation to be earned by Mr. Becker at the rate of not less than $50,000 per year, payable following the termination of Mr. Becker's employment. The Schenley Contract provides for an annual salary of not less than $350,000 per annum, has no provision for incentive or deferred compensation and it is Mr. Becker's intention to waive his previously accumulated deferred compensation (approximately $250,000). The Schenley Contract also provides for the payment of a retirement allowance for life following the termination of Mr. Becker's employment at the rate of $115,000 per year; upon Mr. Becker's death, the retirement payments will continue to his surviving widow, if any, at the rate of $57,500 per year for her life. Any pension plan benefits are deducted from these retirement payments. The payments to Mr. Becker are subject to his availability to render advisory services to Schenley and are reduced by receipt of disability payments. In the event of the termination of Mr. Becker's employment because of his incapacity, he is to receive disability benefits at the rate of $75,000 per annum for life. Additionally, his widow or his estate is to receive payments at the rate of $37,500 per year for 10 years after his death. Under the Rapid Contract, Mr. Becker was also granted a non-qualified option, which remains outstanding, to purchase 150,000 shares of Rapid Common Stock at $25 per share, expiring at the earlier of (1) 90 days after the termination of Mr. Becker's employment for any reason other than his death, or (2) February 7, 1978 unless Mr. Becker is in the employ of Rapid from November 21, 1977, in which event the expiration date is extended to February 7, 1983.

On April 1, 1965, McCrory entered into an employment contract with Mr. Becker, then its Financial Vice President and Treasurer, which provided, *inter alia,* for the payment of a retirement allowance for life beginning with the later of (1) Mr. Becker's 55th birthday, or (2) the termination of his employment. Such allowance is to be paid in equal monthly installments at the rate of $15,000 per year; any pension plan benefits are deducted and payments are subject to other limits and restrictions on compensation with McCrory, receipt of disability payments, etc. Effective August 1, 1970, Mr. Becker's employment under such contract was terminated; only his retirement rights remain in effect. It is a condition to the payment of Mr. Becker's retirement rights that he be available to render advisory services to McCrory if requested by the Board of Directors of McCrory, subject to certain limitations. In 1974, Mr. Becker relinquished his right to receive any retirement allowance from McCrory, so long as he continues to be employed and paid by Rapid and Rapid continues to have a substantial interest in McCrory. Pursuant to the Schenley Contract, Mr. Becker terminated his right to receive any retirement allowance from McCrory. Mr. Becker does not currently receive any compensation from McCrory or any of its subsidiaries.

On April 24, 1974, the Board of Directors of Rapid confirmed an opinion of counsel to Rapid that the determination of Rapid's Consolidated After-Tax Operating Earnings (as defined) under Mr. Riklis' and Mr. Becker's November 20, 1972 employment contracts should be made on the basis of generally accepted accounting principles existing at November 20, 1972. Thus, items (whether positive or negative) such as the $7,423,000 charge in the year ended January 31, 1974 for the write-off of excess of cost of investment over related equity, which would have been an extraordinary item on November 20, 1972 but which are no longer so treated, are not taken into account in determining Mr. Riklis' and Mr. Becker's incentive compensation.

Leonard C. Lane, Executive Vice President and a director of Rapid, is employed by Rapid as a senior executive officer under a five year employment contract effective February 1, 1974, automatically renewable for an additional period of five years unless six months' prior notice of intention not to renew is given by either party, which provides for an annual salary of not less than $240,000. The contract provides for deferred compensation to be earned at the rate of at least $45,000 per year, payable over a period of not more than 60 months following the termination of his employment. The contract also provides for the payment of a retirement allowance for life following the termination of his employment at the rate of $50,000 per year if he shall have been employed by Rapid and/or any of its subsidiaries or affiliates for less than five years from the date of the contract or $60,000 if he shall have been so employed for more than five years; certain pension plan benefits are deducted, and payments are subject to other limits and restrictions on competition with Rapid, and are reduced by receipt of disability payments, etc. As a condition to such retirement payments, Mr. Lane must be available for advisory services to the extent permitted by his health for a period of not more than 12 business days a year. Mr. Lane forfeits his retirement benefits if, within one year after termination of employment, he engages directly or indirectly in any activity competitive with the business of Rapid or any division or subsidiary thereof. In the event that Mr. Lane becomes incapacitated for twelve consecutive months, Mr. Lane's employment may be terminated, in which event, he is to receive disability benefits at the rate of $60,000 per year for life, less any amounts earned from other employment; in the event of his death, his widow or his surviving children, if any, or his estate is to receive death benefits of $335,000, payable over a ten year period. Mr. Lane is authorized to devote a reasonable amount of business time to his personal investments and to consultation in the public or private educational field. Mr. Lane has been receiving the sum of $15,182 semi-annually from McCrory since February 1, 1971, pursuant to the terms of a prior employment agreement; such payments terminated August 1, 1975.

Haim Bernstein, a Vice President and a director of Rapids, is employed by Rapid as a senior executive officer under a five year employment contract effective February 1, 1973, automatically renewable for an additional period of five years unless six months' prior notice of intention not to renew is given by either party, which provides for an annual salary of not less than $87,500 through January 31, 1974 and not less than $117,500 thereafter (to be reduced by any compensation in excess of $12,500 paid by any employee benefit trust of Rapid or any of its subsidiaries). The contract provides for accrual of deferred compensation at the rate of at least $30,000 per year accrued from August 1, 1970 through January 31, 1974, payable in no more than 42 monthly payments following the termination of his employment. The contract also provides for the payment of a retirement allowance for life following the termination of his employment at the rate of $12,000 per year if his employment with Rapid shall terminate prior to January 31, 1975 and at the rate of $13,000 per year if he shall be employed through January 31, 1975, which sum shall increase at the rate of $1,000 for each additional year he shall be employed by Rapid up to a maximum of $20,000 if he is employed through January 31, 1983; any pension plan benefits (other than pursuant to any profit sharing plan) are deducted, and payments are subject to other limits and restrictions on receipt of disability payments, etc. As a condition to such retirement payments, Mr. Bernstein must be available for advisory services to the extent permitted by his health for a period of not more than 12 business days a year. Mr. Bernstein forfeits his retirement benefits if, within one year after termination of employment, he engages directly or indirectly in any activity competitive with the business of Rapid or any division or subsidiary thereof. In the event that Mr. Bernstein becomes incapacitated for a period of twelve consecutive months, his employment may be terminated, in which event Mr. Bernstein is to receive disability benefits at the rate of $12,000 per year for life, less any amounts earned from other employment; in the event of his death, his widow or his estate is to receive death benefits of $100,000 payable at the rate of $2,000 per month. Mr. Bernstein is also Vice President—Administration of McCrory. Mr. Bernstein currently spends substantially all of his time on McCrory matters and, since February 1, 1976, McCrory has been paying Mr. Bernstein's salary. See "Remuneration" above and "Certain Transactions" below.

On June 7, 1974, Lorence A. Silverberg became Executive Vice President of McCrory and has entered into an employment contract with McCrory, to be employed as a senior executive through May 31, 1979. The contract, which is automatically renewable through May 31, 1984, unless six months' prior notice of intention not to renew is given by either party, provides for (1) an annual salary of not less than $200,000; (2) deferred compensation of $25,000 for each year or portion thereof in which Mr. Silverberg renders services under the contract, payable in 60 monthly installments commencing on termination of his employment thereunder; (3) incentive compensation equal to 1% of the Operating Earnings (as defined) in excess of $7,500,000 of the Variety Store Division of McCrory, commencing with the fiscal year beginning February 1, 1974; and (4) deferred compensation of $50,000 per year, payable monthly (the "Retirement Sum"), until Mr. Silverberg's death, commencing upon the termination of his employment. In the event that Mr. Silverberg becomes incapacitated for a period of twelve consecutive months, his employment may be terminated. In the event that Mr. Silverberg dies while he is entitled to receive the Retirement Sum, Mr. Silverberg's widow is to receive 50% of the Retirement Sum during her lifetime. Mr. Silverberg's right to receive the Retirement Sum is extinguished if Mr. Silverberg, within one year of termination of employment, without McCrory's consent, engages, directly or indirectly, in any activity competitive with the business of McCrory. In accordance with the terms of the contract, McCrory acquired, for $5,702, from Mr. Silverberg's previous employer, an insurance policy on Mr. Silverberg's life. McCrory is required to keep such policy and a further insurance policy, aggregating $300,000 of insurance, in effect until termination of Mr. Silverberg's employment and to pay, on Mr. Silverberg's behalf, all premiums on the policies. Mr. Silverberg has agreed to reimburse McCrory for its acquisition costs of, and the premiums paid on, the policies and has assigned the policies to McCrory to secure such obligation; in the event of Mr. Silverberg's death,

McCrory is entitled to receive, from the death benefits provided under the policies, an amount equal to Mr. Silverberg's unpaid obligation with respect thereto. Mr. Silverberg also has been receiving the sum of $3,000 quarterly from McCrory since July 1972, pursuant to the terms of a prior employment agreement and will continue to receive such payments until April 1, 1983.

The aggregate amounts of deferred compensation under the above-described employment contracts accrued, as at January 31, 1976, for the account of the following individuals, who are the only current directors or executive officers of Rapid who have deferred compensation arrangements with Rapid or any of its subsidiaries, were: Meshulam Riklis—$188,666; Haim Bernstein—$80,412; Leonard C. Lane—$238,750; and Lorence A. Silverberg—$127,569. (These accruals, except for Messrs. Silverberg and Lane, assume that the employee will retire at normal retirement age of 65 and are discounted to present value at interest rates of 6% to 8%.)

CERTAIN TRANSACTIONS

American Manufacturing and Eltra transactions with insiders have been insignificant, as is shown in the following American Manufacturing proxy statement:

Company Transactions with Eltra Corporation

During the year ended December 31, 1976, the Company and its subsidiaries made purchases from Eltra Corporation in the amount of $33,839 and Eltra paid the Company an aggregate of $55,795 for sales commissions and for purchases of products. Purchases from and sales to Eltra were made at competitive prices. The Company has a controlling interest in Eltra Corporation. Messrs. Lonegren, G. B. Wattles and G. W. Wattles were re-elected as Directors of Eltra Corporation at its annual meeting on February 8, 1977.

Contrast the above with "Item 18. Interest of Management and

Others in Certain Transactions" taken from Part II of the Medallion Group 10-K* for the year ended December 31, 1977, where it would appear that insiders may conceivably be entering into transactions with the company for a principal purpose of creating tax shelter for the insiders. However, it is difficult for us to understand the financial and economic implications of many of the transactions described in Item 18 of the Medallion 10-K.

MEDALLION GROUP 10-K

*Item 18. Interest of Management and Others
in Certain Transactions.*

Reference is made to Item 4 for information concerning transactions related to the acquisition of control of the Registrant by Messrs. Speiser, Hyman, and Baker and other transactions of the Registrant involving its management and principal stockholders.

As a result of several transactions, the real estate occupied by Capitol, which serves as its primary manufacturing and warehouse facility in Chicago, Illinois (the "Real Estate"), was transferred from Harris Trust and Savings Bank as Trustee ("Trust") (of which Eugene L. Young, president of Capitol and president and a director of Medallion, is a beneficial owner to the extent of approximately 11%) to Messrs. Speiser, Hyman and Baker, and Eugene L. Young as tenants-in-common (the "Transferees").

On April 6, 1966, Capitol and the Trust entered into a net-net lease ("Lease") pursuant to which the Trust leased the Real Estate to Capitol on a net-net basis at a rental of $5,500 per month for the period from June 1, 1966 until December 31, 1982. This Lease was assigned as additional security on an institutional loan secured by a first mortgage in the original amount of $300,000. The loan was for

---

*Medallion Group does not solicit proxies for its annual meetings. Accordingly, it makes the same disclosures in Part II of the 10-K that are made in proxy statements by companies that solicit proxies annually.

15 years at 6¼% interest and self-liquidating by the payment of $2,573 per month. Under the terms of this Lease, Capitol deposited $76,000 as a security for its performance under the Lease.

On June 2, 1975, Capitol entered into a contract to purchase the Real Estate from the Trust pursuant to a Real Estate Sale Contract ("Contract"). Pursuant to this Contract, Capitol agreed to pay $587,625.42 as the purchase price for the Real Estate payable as follows:

A. $155,765.70 by taking subject to the first mortgage
B. $355,856.72 by taking subject to the second mortgage and
C. assuming the obligation to repay the $76,000 security deposit under the Lease with interest at the rate of 4% per annum.

The Lease, pursuant to which Capitol occupies the premises, continues in all respects exactly as it did prior to any of the transactions described herein. Capitol's Lease rent of $5,500 per month is sufficient only to pay the second mortgage which Capitol is authorized to pay directly to the Trust which is now the mortgagee under the second mortgage. The Transferees have the obligation of paying $2,573 per month on the first mortgage until July 1, 1981. Since the Lease has been assigned to secure payment of the first mortgage in the event that the Transferees fail to make payment under the first mortgage, then the first mortgagee would have a prior lien on Capitol's rent of $5,500 per month to the extent of $2,573 per month leaving a potential obligation of $2,927 per month to be repaid on the second mortgage. However, should Capitol be called upon to make up this deficiency, it would have a right of offset and a claim against the Transferees and their equity in the Real Estate to that extent.

Upon the expiration of the Lease a potential conflict of interest may arise between Messrs. Young, Speiser, and Baker as the owners of the Real Estate and Capitol relating to future rent. It is the intention of the parties to have an independent appraisal made at the expiration of the Lease to determine a fair and equitable rental for the premises, if it is decided that it would be in the best interest of

Capitol to continue to occupy the premises rather than to incur the expense of relocating its very heavy equipment and machinery.

As part of the settlement agreement referred to in Item 5 hereof, on March 11, 1977, Mr. Hyman transferred his interest in the Land Trust to Messrs. Baker, Speiser and Young in consideration of their assuming his obligations with respect thereto.

Although no attempt was made to consummate the transactions described above with non-affiliated third parties, in the opinion of the management of the Registrant, such transactions were as fair to the Registrant as if such transactions had been consummated with non-affiliated third parties.

On June 27, 1975, Capitol sold substantially all of its machinery and equipment to a group of tenants-in-common consisting of Messrs. Speiser, Hyman, Baker, and Young and two persons not affiliated with the Registrant (the "Buyers") for $1,600,000, the market value as determined by independent appraisal. The purchase price was paid as follows:

A. $50,000 in cash
B. the delivery of two promissory notes each in the amount of $30,000 payable July 1, 1976 and July 1, 1977 and
C. the delivery of a non-recourse note ("Note") secured by a Security Agreement covering the machinery and equipment which was sold to the Buyers in the amount of $1,490,000 which bears interest at the rate of 12% per annum and is payable in 39 equal semi-annual installments of $15,700 each, and a final payment of $312,157 on January 1, 1995.

The Buyers also paid in cash to Capitol $43,000 as an advance payment of interest.

The Buyers leased the machinery and equipment on a net-net lease to Capitol for a term of 19 years and 6 months terminating December 31, 1994 at an annual rental of $297,600 for the year 1976 (the first rent not being due until 1976) and $203,400 per annum from 1977 through 1994 and a final rental payment of $7,500 in 1995 ("Equipment Lease").

Insofar as Messrs. Baker, Speiser and Young are associated with Capitol and Registrant, there is a possible conflict of interest in the event that the final payment under the Note is not made relating to whether Capitol should foreclose its lien on the machinery and equipment. If the final payment is made, a conflict might exist as to the terms and conditions of any further lease or the price of a sale of the machinery and equipment to Capitol.

Registrant has guaranteed the performance of Capitol under the Equipment Lease.

As a result of the sale of the machinery and equipment, Capitol and Medallion Leisure Corporation (which corporation was merged into the Registrant on November 6, 1975; "MLC") realized taxable income in the taxable year ending June 30, 1975; however, such income was deferred at June 30, 1975 in MLC's and the Registrant's affiliates' consolidated financial statements and recognized as income over the term of the Lease on a pro rata basis. The Registrant, Health Med, and Briarcliff Candy Corporation ("Briarcliff") are parties to a tax-sharing agreement (as described below) which provides for the Registrant to pay to Health Med an amount equal to the federal income taxes it would have paid had it filed a consolidated return with only its subsidiaries. In accordance with an understanding among MLC, Health Med, and Briarcliff, the amount of taxes resulting from the sale of the machinery and equipment will be payable over a period of three years commencing with the taxable year ending June 30, 1976.

On March 11, 1977, Mr. Hyman sold his interest in the above-described equipment and machinery to the Registrant effective as of January 1, 1978 for $24,000.

Although no attempt was made to consummate the transactions with non-affiliated third parties, the management of the Registrant is of the opinion that the transactions were as fair to the Registrant as if they had been consummated with non-affiliated third parties.

On June 27, 1975, Perfection sold substantially all of its production machinery and equipment to a group of tenants-in-common consisting of George W. Gable—½ interest, Leon C. Baker—⅙ interest, Seymour Hyman—⅙ interest, and Marvin M. Speiser—⅙ interest (the "Purchasers") for $293,500, the market value of the machinery and equipment as determined by an independent appraisal. The purchase price was paid as follows:

A. $8,500 in cash

B. the delivery of two promissory notes each in the amount of $5,000 payable January 2, 1976 and January 3, 1977, and

C. the delivery of a non-recourse note ("Note") secured by a Security Agreement covering the machinery and equipment which was sold to the Purchasers in the amount of $275,000. The Note bears interest at the rate of 12% per annum and is payable $20,160 on January 2, 1976, and in semi-annual installments of $17,675 commencing July 1, 1976, through January 1, 1995 and $55,000 on January 15, 1995.

The Purchasers also paid in cash to Perfection $8,000 as an advance payment of interest.

The Purchasers leased the machinery and equipment on a net-net lease to Perfection for a term of 19 years and 6 months terminating December 31, 1994 at an annual rental of $55,040 for the year 1976 (the first rent not being due until 1976) and $37,760 per annum for 1977 through 1994 and a final rental payment of $1,600 in 1995 ("Lease").

The relationship between the Purchasers (as officers or directors of Perfection, Health-Chem and Registrant) may constitute a possible conflict of interest in the event that the final payment under the Note is not made relating to whether Perfection should foreclose its lien on the machinery and equipment. If the final payment is made, a conflict might exist as to the terms and conditions of any further lease or the price of a sale of the machinery and equipment to Perfection.

Health-Chem and Registrant have guaranteed the performance of Perfection under its Lease.

As a result of the sale of the machinery and equipment, Perfection and Health-Chem realized taxable income in the taxable year ending June 30, 1975; however, such income was deferred at June 30, 1975 in Health-Chem's and the Registrant and affiliates' consolidated financial statements and recognized as income over the term of the Lease on a pro rata basis. Health-Chem, Health Med and Briarcliff are parties to a tax-sharing agreement as described below which provides for Health-Chem to pay to Health Med an amount equal to the federal income taxes it would have paid had it filed a consolidated return with only its subsidiaries. In accordance with an understanding among Health-Chem, Health Med and Briarcliff, the amount of taxes resulting from the sale of the machinery and equipment will be payable over a period of three years commencing with the taxable year ending June 30, 1976.

As of March 11, 1977, Mr. Hyman sold his interest in the above-described machinery and equipment to Health-Chem for $3,600.

Although no attempt was made to consummate the transactions with non-affiliated third parties, the management of the Registrant is of the opinion that the transactions were as fair to the Registrant as if they had been consummated with non-affiliated third parties.*

LITIGATION

American Manufacturing and Eltra have been almost free of the commencement of stockholder litigation since 1963, as is noted above. In contrast, various parties have felt aggrieved by Medallion Group or Medallion Group insiders. It ought to be noted that in our litigious society the filing of lawsuits is a commonplace occurrence, and the fact that Medallion and its principals have been involved in much litigation should in no way imply culpability or wrongdoing on the part of management, controlling stockholders or the company itself. Rather, as we stated before, we think the presence or absence of litigation should be an important factor for outside investors seeking to make investment decisions.

*[Descriptions of additional items under "Item 18. Interest of Management and Others in Certain Transactions" are described in the next 9 pages of the 1977 Medallion Group 10-K.]

MEDALLION GROUP IO-K

Item 5. Pending Legal Proceedings.

On June 9, 1969, two stockholders commenced a derivative lawsuit (*Mathes* v. *Ault*) in the Supreme Court of the State of New York against the Registrant and its directors seeking to rescind certain stock subscription agreements and Registrant's acquisition of Herculite on the grounds that the purchase price under the stock subscription agreements was inadequate, that the consideration paid by Registrant for HS Protective Fabrics Corporation was excessive and that both transactions were undertaken for an improper purpose. Registrant believes that the stock subscription agreements (which have been ratified by the stockholders) were a proper way of compensating the officers and directors involved. The stock subscriptions were terminated in connection with the extension of the maturity date of Registrant's 7% Convertible Notes held by Messrs. Baker and Speiser as described in Item 18. With regard to the acquisition of Herculite (the terms of which have also been ratified by the stockholders) management believes that, based upon the relative past and potential earnings of Herculite and Registrant, their relative balance sheet positions, and the market price of Registrant's Common Stock, the consideration to be paid for the Herculite operation was both fair and reasonable to Registrant. For these reasons, management regards the suit to be without merit. Counsel for Registrant believes, although it is not possible at this time to predict accurately the outcome of this action, that, on the basis of information presently available, Registrant is not subject to any substantial liability.

The Puerto Rican Treasury Department has asserted a claim of $92,000 plus interest against Registrant's former Puerto Rican subsidiary. A petition to reconsider is currently pending. Registrant's former Puerto Rican subsidiary has made a claim for a tax refund of $138,630 which is also currently pending.

On December 21, 1976, a judgment was entered in the United States District Court for the Eastern District of Michigan, Southern

Division, in favor of Harry Berman against the Registrant. The judgment requires Registrant to pay $36,463.50 plus interest at the rate of $4.81 per day from December 1, 1976 and upon payment Mr. Berman is required to deliver to the Registrant 6,154 shares of its Common Stock. Registrant is currently appealing this judgment.

On December 23, 1976, Seymour Hyman formerly Chairman of the Board and President of Health-Chem, commenced an action in the Supreme Court of the State of New York, County of New York, against the Registrant and its affiliated companies, Health Med, Herculite, HS Protective Fabrics Corporation, and Marvin M. Speiser, presently Chairman of the Board of the Registrant and Chairman of the Board of Health-Chem, and Leon C. Baker, Director and General Counsel of the Registrant and Health-Chem. The action alleged damages in the amount of $2,000,000 against the corporate defendants and $4,000,000 against each of the individual defendants.

On March 11, 1977 all of the parties agreed to a settlement of the action. The settlement involved (i) Mr. Hyman's cancellation of the balance on his employment contracts with Health-Chem and its wholly-owned subsidiary, Herculite (the employment agreement with Health-Chem was to continue until December 31, 1978 at a salary of $108,000 per annum and the agreement with Herculite was to continue until December 31, 1980 at a salary of $78,000 per annum plus a bonus based upon profits), (ii) the payment by Mr. Hyman of $25,000 in settlement of certain claims which Health-Chem had against Mr. Hyman, (iii) the issuance by Health-Chem of 1,565 shares of its newly-created Series "B" Convertible Preferred Stock ("Series B") to Mr. Hyman in exchange for 689,579 shares of the Registrant's Common Stock owned by Mr. Hyman (Series B is redeemable at $1,000 per share, has a cumulative annual dividend of $50.00 per share, has one vote per share, has a sinking fund requirement of $137,500 semi-annually less accumulated dividends for the prior six months, and is convertible into 125 shares of Health-Chem's Common Stock for each share of Series B), (iv) the purchase by Health-Chem from Mr. Hyman of his 7% Note in the amount of $168,750 (Health-Chem paid Mr. Hyman the face amount thereof, plus $8,220 of accrued interest), (v) the release by Mr. Hyman of the

Registrant and Health-Chem from any obligations to him under options to purchase shares from either company (Mr. Hyman held Non-Qualified Stock Options to purchase 75,000 shares of Health-Chem's Common Stock and 100,000 shares of the Registrant's Common Stock), and (vi) the release by the Registrant of Mr. Hyman of obligations under a subscription agreement to purchase an additional 22,000 shares of the Registrant's Common Stock. In addition, as further consideration for the settlement, Health-Chem transferred to Mr. Hyman the automobile it had previously provided to him for $5,000.

Various other insubstantial matters between the parties were also compromised and settled.

At Mr. Hyman's insistence, Marvin M. Speiser and Leon C. Baker granted Mr. Hyman a Put to expire on April 30, 1977 to sell the 1,565 shares of Series B to them for a purchase price of $1,150,000. On April 30, 1977, the Put was exercised and at a closing held on May 4, 1977, the 1,565 shares of Series B were purchased by Mr. Baker, Mr. Baker's brother, Mr. Speiser and Mr. Speiser's wife.

On June 2, 1977 an action entitled Marcel Goldberger and Robert S. Krauser on behalf of Health-Chem, Perfection Paint and Color Company, Inc., Time and Custom Spray, plaintiffs, v. Leon C. Baker, Marvin M. Speiser, Marvin S. Caligor, Sy Baskin, George W. Gable, Gerald Chige, Roy Marcus, Melvin Shore, Walter C. Drost, Eugene L. Young, John J. Blumers, Health-Chem, Health Med, the Registrant, Perfection Paint and Color Company, Inc., Time, and Custom Spray, defendants, was commenced in the United States District Court for the Southern District of New York. In their complaint, plaintiffs alleged that, commencing in December 1973, the individual and corporate defendants (except Health-Chem, Perfection, Time and Custom Spray) embarked upon an overall fraudulent and secret scheme to use their control of Health-Chem and its subsidiaries for their own ends and private gains to the detriment of Health-Chem. Specifically, plaintiffs alleged wrongdoing in connection with loans by Health-Chem to Health Med and the Registrant, the issuance and redemption by Health-Chem of its junior preferred stock held by Health Med, sale-leaseback transactions involving Health-Chem, Perfection, Time and

Custom Spray and certain of the individual defendants and unrelated third parties and the failure to make proper disclosure of these and certain other matters to Health-Chem's shareholders. Plaintiffs claimed that the defendants' conduct represented a violation of Sections 10b and 14 (a) of the Securities Exchange Act of 1934 and Rules 10b-5 and 14a-9 promulgated thereunder. In the action, plaintiffs asked the court to (a) set aside all actions taken at the Annual Meetings of Shareholders of Health-Chem held in 1973, 1974, 1975, 1976, and 1977, (b) require all of the defendants except Health-Chem and its subsidiaries to make restitution to Health-Chem and its shareholders of all salaries, bonuses, stock options and all other compensation, benefits, contract benefits and perquisites conferred upon the individual defendants, in their roles as officers of Health-Chem, since January 1, 1973 and (c) award damages in an unspecified amount for the alleged wrongs set forth in the complaint. On August 12, 1977, all of the defendants moved to dismiss the complaint on the ground that it failed to state a claim under the applicable Federal Securities Statutes. On October 20, 1977, the defendants' motion was granted and the plaintiff's complaint was dismissed with leave to file an amended complaint. On February 14, 1978 the court dismissed the complaint.

On November 4, 1977, an action entitled Health-Chem Corporation, Herculite Protective Fabrics Corp., Leon C. Baker, and Marvin M. Speiser v. Seymour Hyman, a/k/a Sy Hyman, was commenced in the United States District Court for the Southern District of New York. The complaint alleges that the defendant Hyman violated the Securities Exchange Act of 1934, and Rule 10b-5 promulgated thereunder, by failing to disclose that at the time the defendant, the plaintiffs and others entered into the settlement of the action described above (a) he knew that the stockholders derivative suit described above would be brought, and (b) he intended to violate the terms of the settlement by causing the same stockholders derivative suit to be brought; for each of which violations Health-Chem is alleged to be entitled to recover damages of $1,117,000. The complaint also alleges that, while an officer and director of Health-Chem and of Herculite, the defendant charged improper expenses to them for which he was reimbursed, and for which Health-Chem and Herculite should recover more than $200,000; and, in addition, that had the defendant disclosed these improper charges and reimbursements, Health-Chem's Board of Directors would not have ratified certain employment agreements between the defendant, Health-Chem, and Herculite, with resulting damage to Health-Chem and Herculite of $300,000. The complaint also asks recovery on behalf of Health-Chem of $10,000, representing the difference between the amount Mr. Hyman paid Health-Chem for and the fair market value of an automobile transferred by Health-Chem to Mr. Hyman as further consideration for the settlement described above, alleged to have been fraudulently entered into by the defendant. Finally, on behalf of the individual plaintiffs, Messrs. Baker and Speiser, the complaint alleges that the defendant's failures to disclose the material facts outlined above, in violation of the Securities Exchange Act of 1934, and Rule 10b-5 promulgated thereunder, injured them in the amounts of (a) $195,625, the value of the Put granted by Messrs. Speiser and Baker to the defendant which is described above and (b) $500,000, the damage caused them by the defendant's exercise of the Put. The complaint demands that Baker and Speiser be entitled to offset their recovery above against amounts they owe to the defendant as payment for the Health-Chem Series B purchased by them when the defendant exercised the Put, and to cancel certain letters of credit which they delivered to secure payment therefor.

In January 1977, Noel Hyman started a lawsuit in the Supreme Court of the State of New York, County of New York, against the Registrant and Marvin M. Speiser, its Chairman of the Board. The complaint alleges that Noel Hyman, brother of Seymour Hyman, former president of Health-Chem, received 40,000 shares of the Registrant's Common Stock as a finder's fee in connection with the acquisition of Union Broach. The complaint further alleges an oral arrangement between the defendants and the plaintiff pursuant to which he was allegedly guaranteed a price of $5.00 per share. The complaint seeks to recover the difference between the fair market price of the stock and $5.00 per share, or in the alternative to return the shares and receive payment in cash. Registrant's management believes the claim to be without merit.

On or about January 6, 1977, an Involuntary Petition in Bankruptcy was filed against Registrant's subsidiary, Medallion Pool Corporation ("Pool"). The action entitled, "In Re Medallion Pool Corporation", is pending in the United States District Court for the Eastern District of New York. On or about September 15, 1976, Registrant, through its attorneys, proposed to all of Pool's trade creditors a guarantee of payment in full of their proven claims against Pool on the basis of 36 equal monthly payments commencing September 1, 1978 and provided that 90% of the eligible creditors accepted the proposal. At the time of the filing of the Involuntary Petition in Bankruptcy, less than 90% of the creditors had accepted the proposal. Registrant on February 1, 1977, through its attorneys, proposed to purchase the claims against Medallion Pool Corporation by those trade creditors who had accepted the prior proposal before the filing of the Involuntary Petition in Bankruptcy, provided that this proposal was accepted before February 28, 1977. The purchase price to be paid was the same as in the prior proposal which was payment of 100% of the claim in 36 equal monthly installments commencing September 1, 1978. As a result of this proposal, through December 31, 1977 Registrant has purchased claims in the approximate amount of $272,631.00 (including $81,524 from affiliated companies).

On March 6, 1978, an action entitled Albert Sacklow, Trustee in Bankruptcy of Medallion Pool Corporation, v. Medallion Group, Inc., Health Med Corporation, Health-Chem Corporation, Herculite Protective Fabrics Corp., Factory Lease Co. Division of Capitol Hardware Mfg. Co., Inc., Marvin M. Speiser, Eugene L. Young, Leon C. Baker, Melvin Shore, Manufacturers Hanover Trust Company and Long Island Trust Company was commenced in the United States District Court for the Eastern District of New York. The Complaint alleges three causes of action. The first cause of action alleges that a certain secured loan to Pool from its corporate parent, Registrant, was in actuality a capital contribution and that transactions undertaken to satisfy the loan constituted a fraudulent transfer designed to defraud creditors in favor of Registrant. It is further alleged that all the corporate and individual defendants knew of the plan and agreed to it. The first cause of action seeks recovery against all defendants in the sum of $1,036,560 which was allegedly paid out of Pool's assets to satisfy the loan.

The second cause of action alleges that on or about September 6, 1976, Registrant caused Pool to discontinue operations and thereafter "dissipated" Pool's inventory which had a value of $804,000. It seeks recovery of that amount from Registrant and the individual defendants.

The third cause of action alleges that on or about September 30, 1976, Registrant caused inventory of Pool valued at approximately $86,000 to be transferred to Herculite and Factory Leasing Co. Division of Capitol. The complaint alleges that this was a preference and demands recovery against Herculite and Capitol in the sum of $86,000.

Defendants have not as yet answered the complaint.

In the opinion of management of the Registrant the action is without merit.

On or about March 21, 1978 an action entitled Ralph Limmer v. Medallion Group, Inc., Marvin M. Speiser, Leon C. Baker, Eugene L. Young, John J. Blumers, Melvin Shore, Seymour Baskin, Walter C. Drost, George W. Gable, George H. Cohen, Walter Kutler, William P. Willey, Seymour Hyman, J. K. Lasser & Co., Touche Ross & Co., Health Med Corp. and Health-Chem Corp. was commenced in the Supreme Court of the State of New York for the County of New York. The complaint alleges, among other things, that the individual defendants caused Registrant, its subsidiaries and affiliates to enter into certain sale-leaseback transactions which served no corporate purpose and were designed only to benefit the individual defendants. The complaint alleges that these transactions were a waste of the assets of Registrant, its subsidiaries and affiliates, and that the individuals' conduct represents a breach of their fiduciary duty as officers and directors.

The complaint also alleges that the individual defendants breached their fiduciary duties by causing Registrant and its subsidiaries to pay to the individual defendants excessive salaries, expenses and stock option benefits. The complaint further alleges that all defendants conspired to conceal this information from Registrant's stockholders.

For his relief, plaintiff seeks damages for the breaches of fiduciary duty described above as well as a judgment cancelling the sale-leaseback transactions; removing the individuals from corporate office; appointing a receiver to operate Registrant, Health-Chem Corporation and Health Med Corporation; cancelling certain stock options awarded to the individual defendants; requiring the individual defendants to dispose of their shares of Registrant and its subsidiaries and affiliates; enjoining the individual defendants from entering into certain transactions with or on behalf of Registrant and its subsidiaries and affiliates; and rescinding an earlier settlement agreement between Registrant and its subsidiaries and Seymour Hyman, and other relief, as well as the costs and disbursements of the action.

Defendants have not as yet answered the complaint.

In the opinion of management of Registrant the action is without merit.

As a result of a fire which occurred in the Maury County Jail located in Columbia, Tennessee on or about June 26, 1977, it is reported that approximately 42 persons died and many were injured.

Allegations have been made that Herculite manufactured a product which was present in the jail at the time of the fire.

Litigation has been commenced and claims made by numerous parties seeking to recover damages from Herculite and various other defendants. The damages sought include both compensatory and punitive damages. The pending litigation, claims made and anticipated claims and litigation including the very large claims for punitive damages, exceed Herculite's insurance coverage.

At this time Registrant's management is unable to ascertain whether or not its product was present in the jail or involved in the fire. In any event, Registrant, based upon advice of special counsel handling these matters, believes Herculite has a meritorious defense against any and all claims that may be made and that there is adequate insurance to cover any liability that may ultimately result from these claims.

On April 7, 1978 an action entitled B. W. Drennan Ltd. v. Vincent Lippe Incorporated, Medallion Leisure Corporation and Medallion

Group, Inc. was commenced in the Supreme Court of the State of New York for the County of New York. The complaint alleges that plaintiff had a sales representation agreement with the defendants and that defendants failed to live up to the terms of the sales representation agreement. Plaintiff requests damages in the amount of $500,000. Defendants have not as yet answered the complaint. Registrant's management is of the opinion that the action is without merit.

Except for litigation arising in the normal course of business against which Registrant or its operating affiliates are insured, there are no other legal proceedings pending which might subject Registrant to any substantial liability.

Reasonably Understandable Information

Both American Manufacturing and Eltra are relatively straighforward going-concern manufacturers' operations. The businesses are described in considerable detail in SEC filings and stockholder mailings. In the interests of brevity, these materials are not duplicated here.

Chemex Corporation, in sharp contrast, was, in May 1978, a business that would be extremely difficult to understand unless one were a cancer researcher with access to various scientific studies. As such, Chemex common stock would not be viewed by us as an attractive security for an outside investor under the financial-integrity approach, regardless of the price at which it was selling. The situation at Chemex was described in the "Inside Wall Street" column of the May 8, 1978, issue of *Business Week:*

CHEMEX RIDES HIGH ON ITS CANCER DRUG *

Since it was issued about three years ago, the stock of Chemex Corp.— a Riverton (Wyo.) company with no earnings, virtually no revenues, and a troubled past with the Securities & Exchange Commission—has multiplied

*Reprinted from the May 8, 1978 issue of *Business Week* by special permission. Copyright © 1976 by McGraw-Hill, Inc.

100-fold: from 10¢ to $10 a share. Chemex, traded over the counter, is valued at roughly $60 million because the company is working with an investigative drug, one that it claims has produced encouraging results in the treatment of cancer.

Chemex's drug is derived from the Larrea divaricata (creosote bush), an evergreen that grows in the Western U.S. Indians prized the bush for its medical qualities, and early settlers used it to brew "Mormon tea." Chemex's research with the compound includes the prevention of plaque formation on teeth, control of acne, and the treatment of ulcers and osteomyelitis. The major emphasis, however, is on control of cancer in humans and animals. *Success story.* Since December 1976, Chemex has treated 55 human cancer patients in Italy and Costa Rica with its creosote drug. It is applied topically on patients with skin cancer or taken orally by patients with other kinds of cancer. Dr. Russell T. Jordon, director of research for Chemex, cites the case of a 34-year-old man with a rapidly growing brain tumor that had failed to respond to conventional treatment. The compound, according to Jordon, caused the grapefruit-size tumor to wall itself off from the brain and become operable. He says the patient was operated on a year ago and that there has been no evidence of new tumor growth.

Jordon also claims that 24 patients treated for skin cancer have had no recurrence of the cancer. "In every instance where we could get the drug to the tumor, we have had a favorable long-term response," Jordon says. He notes that the drug does not cause the side effects of chemotherapy, but he says most patients complain of pain in the area that is treated.

Chemex is negotiating with a group of Costa Rican businessmen and doctors who expect to establish a Central American marketing operation. Chemex President Charles E. Hamilton says that the company will take a 10% cut of the gross receipts. Hamilton says Chemex hopes to apply to the Federal Food and Drug Administration for approval to test the drug on humans here within a year.

Curiously, Chemex is better known among investors than among scientists. One source at a major cancer research institute in New York, who is unfamiliar with Chemex, says: "If something interesting is developing, a scientist usually rushes to present it in a paper or publish an article about it. Major developments just don't sit around." Jordon says he has not written any articles for medical journals because he wants to secure patents first.

To be sure, Chemex's stock is being actively promoted by several brokers. "I like its potential," says Michael D. Hayes, a broker at Denver's First

Colorado Investment & Securities Inc., a firm whose partners have been to Europe, Costa Rica, and Nevada to check on Chemex's research. "It is a very emotional stock," Hayes says, "but I do not see any risk." Adds Stuart Kobrovsky of Fairmeadow Securities Inc. of Allentown, Pa., "The prospects are phenomenal."

Closed offering. Neither broker seems bothered by SEC charges stemming from a 1975 stock issue. The commission charged Chemex with failing to make a bona fide public offering, with the shares sold to friends and relatives of the founders rather than to the public. Chemex did not fight the charges, Hamilton says, because it did not want to waste the company's resources. Thus the company cannot make a Regulation A offering (using an abbreviated registration) for five years, and it must make a full registration if it makes another public offering.

Down the road, Hamilton says his plans call for Chemex to be acquired by a pharmaceutical firm. For now, though, Hamilton and two other officers and directors have each sold 60,000 Chemex shares since January. The three, however, still own 2.7 million of the 6.4 million shares outstanding.

COMMON-STOCK PRICE REPRESENTS A SUBSTANTIAL DISCOUNT FROM ESTIMATES OF NET ASSET VALUE

A reconstruction of the American Manufacturing balance sheet as of December 31, 1977, satisfies us that when the common stock was selling around 50 in early 1978, that price represented a substantial discount from our estimate of net asset value.

Our usual reconstruction is to first determine working capital, and then deduct from working capital all indebtedness in order to determine "net net working capital." After this figure is determined, other assets are added to net net working capital in order to determine an estimated net asset value before deferred income credits. Deferred income credits are then deducted to determine a net asset value. In estimating net asset value, we give free rein to our judgments, valuing assets (and sometimes liabilities) at book values, at market values, or at discounts to present value, with or without allowance for potential tax liabilities or tax benefits. Our reconstruction of the American Manufacturing balance sheet was as follows:

	(000)	*Per Common Share* *1,219,241 Shares*
Cash and equivalent	$ 4,837	
Receivables	6,481	
Inventories	9,208	
Other current	505	
Current assets	$ 21,031	
Current liabilities	5,720	
Working capital	$ 15,310	$12.56
Long-term debt	$2,861	
Net net working capital	$ 12,449	$10.21
Property, plant, net	$7,714	
Other assets	603	
Subtotal	$ 20,766	17.03
Investment in 3,215,748 shares of Eltra common (at market)	$ 83,609[A]	
Subtotal	$104,375	85.61
Less deferred income items	727	
Net asset value	$103,648	$85.01

[A]At carrying value, Eltra investment would be $94,209,000, or $8.70 per American Manufacturing share in excess of stock market value.

ABOUT THE AUTHORS

MARTIN J. WHITMAN is president of M. J. Whitman & Co., Inc., a member firm of the National Association of Securities Dealers, Inc., whose activities revolve around financial consulting, money mangement, and general brokerage. Since 1972, he has been a member of the faculty at Yale University. Mr. Whitman currently conducts two seminars at Yale's Graduate School of Organization and Management, "Finance and Investments" and "Investment Banking." He has also lectured in various forums, including the American Management Association, New York University, and the Wharton School of the University of Pennsylvania.

MARTIN SHUBIK, Seymour H. Knox Professor of Mathematical Institutional Economics at Yale University since 1975, has a joint appointment at Yale in the Department of Economics and at the Graduate School of Organization and Management. Mr. Shubik is known world-wide through the publication during the last twenty-five years of numerous articles on economics and game theory. He has published six books, including *Strategy and Market Structure* (1959) and *Game Theory and Related Approaches to Social Behavior* (1964). He has served as consultant to various corporations and governmental agencies.

INDEX

Printed in the United States of America
ED-03-13-13